D0204237

Beyond the Revolution

BEYOND THE

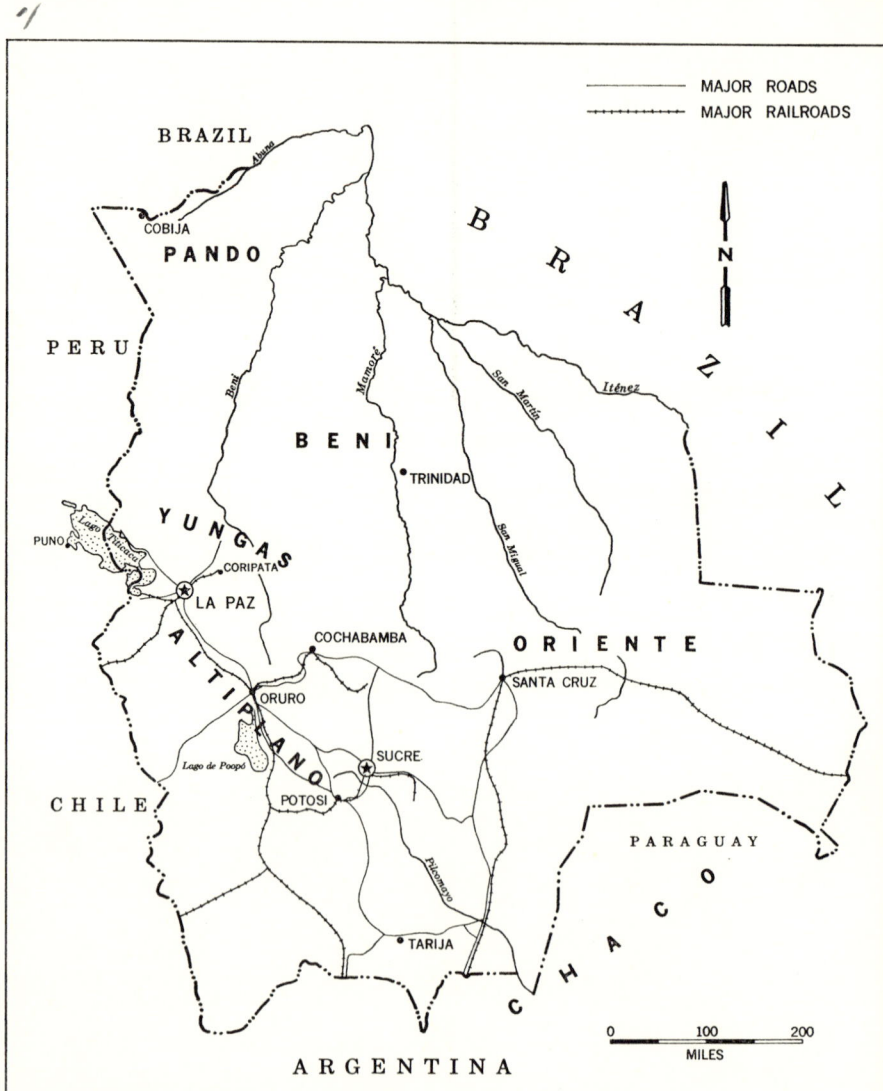

MAJOR ROADS
MAJOR RAILROADS

BRAZIL

COBIJA

PANDO

PERU

Abuna

B R A Z I L

Beni

Mamoré

San Martín

Iténez

BENI

• TRINIDAD

Lago Titicaca

PUNO

Y U N G A S

CORIPATAS

LA PAZ

COCHABAMBA

A L T I P L A N O

San Miguel

O R I E N T E

SANTA CRUZ

ORURO

Lago de Poopó

SUCRE

CHILE

POTOSI

• TARIJA

Pilcomayo

PARAGUAY

C H A C O

0   100   200
MILES

ARGENTINA

BOLIVIA

REVOLUTION

Bolivia
Since 1952

JAMES M. MALLOY
and
RICHARD S. THORN
Editors

University of Pittsburgh Press

Library of Congress Catalog Card Number 77–135848
ISBN 0–8229–3220–2
Copyright © 1971, University of Pittsburgh Press
All rights reserved
Henry M. Snyder & Co., Inc., London
Manufactured in the United States of America

Grateful acknowledgment is made to the Latin American Center, University of California, Los Angeles, for permission to reprint with adaptations Appendices H, N, and Q from *The Bolivian Revolution and U.S. Aid Since 1952* by James W. Wilkie, copyright 1969 by the Latin American Center; and to the University of Chicago Press for permission to reprint with adaptations the article by Melvin Burke, "Land Reform and Its Effect Upon Production and Productivity in the Lake Titicaca Region," first published in *Economic Development and Cultural Change,* © 1970 by the University of Chicago.

Dedicated to the memory
of our esteemed colleague
CARTER GOODRICH
1897–1971
Distinguished economist, historian,
diplomat, and teacher

His concern and affection
for Bolivia and its people
provided the inspiration for this book.

Contents

Illustrations

Tables

Preface

The Bolivian National Revolution of 1952 stands alongside the Mexican and Cuban revolutions as one of the most significant events in Latin American history. The national revolution was the beginning of a radical social and political experiment unique in Latin America. But the Bolivian revolutionary experience has gone largely unnoticed while the Mexican and Cuban revolutions have attracted the interest of the entire world. This is regrettable since the Bolivian experience is relevant for the rest of Latin America. In order to understand Bolivia today, we must understand the revolutionary process which was set in motion in April 1952. This book is an attempt to give some insight into the unfolding of this revolutionary process and to contribute to the understanding of what has happened and what is happening in Bolivia today. It also sheds some further light on the nature of the revolutionary ferment pervading Latin America.

This book is the outgrowth of an interdisciplinary seminar on Bolivia initiated at the University of Pittsburgh in 1966. The seminar was sponsored by the University's Center for International Studies and the Center for Latin American Studies. To achieve the goal of a comprehensive assessment of the revolution, it was necessary to supplement Pittsburgh's corps of Bolivian specialists with four distinguished Bolivian scholars from other universities. Over the next two years the group met frequently to plan the book and discuss the manuscripts. Although all the authors had access to the comments and criticisms of their colleagues, a uniformity of views was neither sought nor achieved; each author assumes responsibility for the views set forth in his chapter.

All the contributors to the volume have had the opportunity to observe some phase of the revolution at firsthand, and all maintain a continuing interest in Bolivia. They have joined together to construct a full-length, interdisciplinary portrait of the revolution. It is our intention that the volume will not only make a scholarly contribution to the various specialty fields it embraces but also prove of interest to those individuals concerned with modern revolution and the process of development.

We would like to acknowledge the generous support of the University of Pittsburgh's Center for International Studies and the unfailing cooperation of the center's director, Carl Beck. We owe a special thanks to Cole Blasier, director of the Latin American Studies Center, who, besides contributing his excellent essay, aided the project in numerous administrative ways. We would also like to thank Richard Patch, who did some of the early pathfinding work on the Bolivian Revolution, for his assistance in planning the project in its early stages. Finally, all the contributors to the volume wish to express their gratitude to the many Bolivians who cooperated with various aspects of their research.

This is a book without an ending. After eighteen years the revolution has yet to be consolidated in a new viable socio-political order. The recent emergence of the national leftist military government represents the latest development in this continuing drama. Our volume concentrates mainly on the period from 1952 to 1964, although several contributors have sought to take into account more recent developments. It is hoped that this book will contribute to a greater understanding of the Bolivian Revolution and provide a foundation for its further study.

J.M.M. AND R.S.T.

Abbreviations

CBF	Corporación de Fomento de Bolivia
CEPAL	Comisión Económica para América Latina
COB	Confederación Obrera Boliviana
COMIBOL	Corporación Minera de Bolivia
CSB	Confederación Socialista Boliviana
CSR	Célula Socialista Revolucionaria
CSTB	Confederación Sindical de Trabajadores de Bolivia
CTB	Confederación de Trabajadores de Bolivia
ENDE	Ministerio de Económica, Nacional Dirección de Electricidad
FDA	Frente Democrático Antifascista
FIB	Frente de Izquierda Boliviana
FOL	Federación Obrera Local
FOT	Federación Obrera del Trabajo
FSB	Falange Socialista Boliviana
FSTMB	Federación Sindical de Trabajadores Mineros de Bolivia
FUB	Federación Universitaria Boliviana
IBRD	International Bank for Reconstruction and Development
IDB	Inter-American Development Bank
MNR	Movimiento Nacionalista Revolucionario
MNRA	Movimiento Nacionalista Revolucionario Auténtico
PCB	Partido Comunista de Bolivia
PIR	Partido de la Izquierda Revolucionaria
PMNRA	Partido Movimiento Nacionalista Revolucionario Auténtico
POR	Partido Obrero Revolucionario
POS	Partido Obrero Socialista
PRIN	Partido Revolucionario de la Izquierda Nacional
PSOB	Partido Socialista Obrero Boliviano
PSR	Partido Socialista Revolucionario
PSU	Partido Socialista Unificado
PURS	Partido de la Unión Republicana Socialista
RADEPA	Razón de Patria
YPFB	Yacimientos Petrolíferos Fiscales Bolivianos

Beyond the Revolution

There is a bitter root
and a world of a thousand terraces.

Nor can the smallest hand
break the door of water.

Where are you going, where, where?
There are a thousand windows in
the sky—a battle of angry bees—
and there is a bitter root.

from FEDERICO GARCÍA LORCA,
"The Gazelle of the Bitter Root,"
translated by PAUL ZIMMER

CARTER GOODRICH

University of Pittsburgh

Bolivia in Time of Revolution

The Bolivian Revolution of 1952 opened with a burst of rifle and machine-gun fire at daybreak on the Wednesday of Easter Week. The firing ceased on the afternoon of Good Friday, and a new government was in possession of the capital city of La Paz.

The Hotel Sucre Palace, in which my wife and I were living, was not touched in the three days of street fighting. The manager refused to let the revolutionary forces plant a machine gun on the roof, and he took the precaution of flying the flags of Paraguay and the United Nations, since both the Paraguyan ambassador and the UN mission of technical assistance had offices in the building. The iron gates of the hotel were kept locked except during the brief informal truce on Good Friday morning, called so that the religious could go to mass and housewives could replenish their supplies. As the fighting went on, we could see from the hotel roof ambulances and trucks carrying wounded to a Red Cross station in the next street and returning for more, their stretchers still soaked with blood. On the third day we watched the firing approach us as troops loyal to the old government fought their way uphill to a point less than a quarter of a mile away.

Two families from our mission who had already found lodgings outside the hotel were less well protected but had more to see. From a park in Sopocachi, one couple watched a battery of *carabineros* ("military police") lobbing mortar shells into the lines of army cadets in the valley below. The boardinghouse in which they and their baby daughter were living became for a time the hiding place for five government soldiers, and my colleague was present when the local rebel leader collected a "cut" from the owner for sparing his guests by not attacking the building. The second couple found themselves between the lines of fire, and bullets entered their apartment.

Inside the hotel we soon learned that every waiter and chambermaid was a partisan of the revolutionary party, the *Movimiento Nationalista Revolucionario* (MNR). Some messages and many rumors reached us from the outside. An emissary of the MNR advised us against going to the office of the Bolivian coordinator of our program in the Congress building but assured us that the office itself would be protected. The taxi owner, whose cab we were renting, managed to let us know on the first morning that he had hidden the car so that it could not be requisitioned. On the third morning he reported that he himself had been pressed into service on the rebel side but, after an hour of street fighting, had persuaded the leaders that he could be of more use driving a truck.

The electric cables were cut in the course of the fighting, so candles were distributed to the guests and meals were cooked in an areaway and carried on the backs of Indians to the dining room on the top floor. As long as the telephone remained in use, the Paraguayan ambassador received reports in Guaraní (his country's Indian language) from his assistant in the town. One report was that the Papal Nuncio had brought the leaders of the two sides together in an unsuccessful attempt to arrange a truce. We knew that the uprising was being carried on by the combined forces of armed civilians of the MNR under the leadership of Hernán Siles and the carabineros under the command of Gen. Antonio Seleme, the minister of the interior, who had turned against his colleagues in the ruling military junta. It was not clear how power was to be divided between them in case of victory, but the general, believing that the rebel forces would be defeated for lack of ammunition, solved the problem on the second day by taking asylum in the Chilean Embassy. Still later we learned that the miners under Juan Lechín, in what was apparently the decisive action, had captured on the heights above the city a train bringing fresh munitions intended for the troops of the old government.

On the afternoon of Good Friday, the victorious revolutionary army streamed up the Prado past the hotel on the way to the Plaza Murillo and the Presidential Palace. The men, both civilians and military police, had broken ranks and carried their weapons casually, occasionally firing a few shots into the side streets and alleys. The various embassies sent word to their nationals to stay off the streets that night, a particularly appropriate warning, since the majority of the victors were ununiformed civilians. But the MNR leader, Hernán Siles, asked the churches to open and the bars to close, exhorting his followers to exercise restraint. To the surprise and admiration of the foreign community, there was no looting, even of such obvious targets as the handsome town house of the mineowner Carlos Víctor Aramayo, and the night passed without reprisals or disorder.

The firing which broke out at dawn on April 9 had provided a rude awakening for the young Canadian couple and the English electrical engineer who had joined our mission the night before after the long train ride over the Andes from Chile. Only the precise date, however, and the bizarre coincidence of the MNR's revolt with General Seleme's attempt at an old style personal coup could have provided much of a surprise to anyone who had been in close touch with Bolivian developments. There had been many signs of the growing strength of the MNR, The Movimiento had formed part of an earlier government, that of President Villarroel, which itself had been ousted by revolution in 1946. Five years later, although its principal leaders were in exile, the party made an extraordinary showing in the elections of May 1951. It came out far ahead of its closest rival but fell just short of the clear majority needed for automatic election. Before the Congress could act on the issue, President Mamerto Urriolagoitia resigned and turned his power over to a military junta of generals and colonels, organized for the express purpose of keeping the MNR out of office. This was the junta that fell in April 1952 when the MNR's 1951 candidates, Dr. Víctor Paz Estenssoro and Dr. Hernán Siles Zuazo, became president and vice-president under the new regime.

By the double test of votes and arms, the MNR demonstrated that it had a considerable basis of public support. The former test affected only the small upper- and middle-class group to which the franchise was limited because of the literacy test. The latter showed the support of the miners and urban workers as well as a wide spectrum of white-collar and middle-class backers. It remained to be seen whether the party could win the allegiance of the still almost completely apolitical Indians, thus justifying its claim to represent what it called *las clases mayoritarias* ("the majority classes").

Since I had been sent on missions to Bolivia during the governments of President Urriolagoitia and of the military junta and since I was stationed in La Paz from February 1952 until September 1953, certain of my impressions may assist in the interpretation of the revolution. I cannot relate them, however, without a somewhat extended discussion of the work of the United Nations technical assistance mission which gave me the opportunity to observe and participate in the life of the country.[1]

1949 UN MISSION TO BOLIVIA

My first visit to Bolivia and my first contact with the tensions in the mining industry took place in November 1949. The United Nations sent me, together with Gustavo Durán of the New York headquarters and Louis Swenson of the Economic Commission for Latin America at Santiago, Chile, to discuss several requests that the Bolivian government had made for technical assistance. We were received in La Paz by President Urriolagoitia, a member of an old Basque family (who had taken office the preceding month on the resignation of President Hertzog) and by officials of his administration. We found the minister of economics committed to the policy of developing the largely unused resources of the Oriente, which had formed the central element of advice and assistance from the United States since the days of the State Department's Bohan report,[2] and to the building of the Cochabama–Santa Cruz Road which was to make such development possible. He was, however, much concerned over the delay in construction and its unexpectedly high cost which, he feared, would use up the funds needed for complementary investment in the region.

At the suggestion of the Foreign Ministry, we called on leaders of the various political parties and on spokesmen for the mining industry. The list of parties included the Communist but not the MNR, which was under proscription for having attempted an armed revolt a few months earlier. Our first contact with the mineowners was with Carlos Víctor Aramayo, the only resident Bolivian head of one of the "Big Three" tin companies. He talked vigorously of the problems of tin production and told us in flawless Oxford English that government intervention was "disastrous." He added, however, that he intended to contribute to the diversification of the Bolivian economy by investing in the sugar industry of the Oriente. On the other hand, the local representative of the Patiño mines declared that his company would not make investments of this sort, explaining that to do so would lay it open to the charge of monopoly.

We were also urged to take a trip into the interior, where we spent a day visiting the world's greatest tin mine at Catavi. With an official from the Foreign Office, we rode in and out over the barren hills by *autocarril* —a Buick adapted to run on the single track railroad. At lunch we were entertained by a group of high executives, all from the United States except one Englishman. They talked informatively of the economics and technology of the industry and told us that within two years they would reach the critical point at which they would be down to mining ore that contained only 0.8 percent of tin. Afterward we were shown the surface works and some workers' housing by a manager who, after many years in the country, still needed help in Spanish to give orders to his chauffeur. We did not discuss the death of the two North American engineers who had been murdered earlier that year in the Union Hall at Siglo Veinte or the mass killing at Catavi in which miners and their women and children had been shot down by the military police. Yet it was not difficult for us to believe the driver of the autocarril, himself a member of the railroad union, who took the risk of telling us of the miners' hatred for the great company.

The negotiations in La Paz, as we came to realize, took place in the shadow of this controversy. There was some initial misunderstanding to clear away, since technical assistance was a new idea to Bolivia, and indeed, at that time, a very new thing anywhere in the world. What emerged was an agreement on a list of fields in which the United Nations should be asked to send experts to the country. The subjects themselves were conventional enough, but, in some cases, the reasons for their selection were directly related to the dissensions and disorders at the mines. Thus, one of the main tasks of the experts on public finance and mining would be to determine how much taxation the tin companies should bear. The companies were sure that competent experts would recommend lower export taxes, while the government was hopeful that ways could be found to draw still greater revenue from such apparently opulent corporations. At the same time, the expert on the standard of living, so the Bolivians hoped, might help settle the bitter controversy over the miners' wages. The tension between the government and the companies, plus the greater tension between the companies and the workers, formed the backdrop of the discussion. The more thoughtful of the Bolivian negotiators acted in the hope that these differences, which seemed beyond the nation's power to resolve, might somehow be settled by an appeal to an outside agency, an agency which must be, as they kept repeating, *altamente autorizada* ("highly authoritative").

THE KEENLEYSIDE REPORT

The response of the United Nations was to organize a highly qualified mission, in which I had no part, to spend much of the year 1950 in Bolivia. It was headed by Hugh L. Keenleyside, then a high official of the Canadian government and later director of technical assistance for the United Nations. It included fourteen experts from a number of nations. President Urriolagoitia, whose first act on assuming office was said to have been to order a private investigation of the social and economic conditions of the country, gave full cooperation to the mission and approved the publication of its findings.

The report, issued in 1951, is a notable document.[3] The technical studies are sober and detailed, containing analyses and recommendations for improvements in monetary and fiscal policy, in the various fields of production, and in social development. Some of these passages are still very useful for an understanding of Bolivian resources and development.

On the issues of greatest interest to the leaders of the MNR, the report could not have satisfied the leaders of the party. The authors recognized that in considerable parts of the country "the land tenure system almost completely blocked the development of a progressive agriculture," but they offered no drastic proposals for change. In addition, the report criticized the mining companies for their labor policies and the government for some of its policies toward the industry. Figures presented in one of the tables, which compared the president of the republic's salary of 360,000 bolivianos with the 1,800,000 of the general manager of a large mining corporation and a cabinet minister's 144,000 with the 510,000 of a mine superintendent, might have formed part of a nationalist argument for freeing the country from the dominance of such powerful foreign influence. Yet, the report declared that nationalization of the mining industry, "even if . . . theoretically desirable . . . would be wholly impossible in Bolivia in present conditions. The government has neither the financial resources nor the technical and administrative competence to undertake any such task."

It should not be surprising that the report of an international agency did not recommend drastic shifts of internal power such as were represented by the MNR's proposals of land reform and nationalization. What *was* surprising, and much commented on, was that an international document should speak so frankly and forcibly of the shortcomings of a member nation and that it should propose so novel a solution. The mission's first duty, said the report, was to explain "the paradoxical contrast between the potential wealth of Bolivia and the failure of the people to translate that wealth into the concrete evidence of a prosperous national economy." The report set its explanation in italics:

It is now the belief of the members of the mission—and in this belief they are supported by the opinion of every Bolivian with whom the matter was discussed —that the explanation of the paradox is to be found in the governmental and administrative instability that has constantly marked the history of that nation.

For this, the evidence was not merely that in 125 years of independence Bolivia had had some sixty presidents but that recent trends were in the wrong direction:

No legally elected Bolivian President has served out his term in the last quarter century . . . there have been seven presidents and eight revolutions in the last ten years, eight Ministers of Finance within 18 months.

The nation has failed to establish, or indeed to make possible, the development of an official administrative service of competence and stability. Bolivia simply does not possess enough senior (or indeed junior) civil servants with ability and experience to handle the problems with which the administrative machine must contend.

If the difficulty was diagnosed as "governmental and administrative," the principal remedy proposed was administrative. Nowhere did the report call attention to the difference between the two characterizations. It might perhaps have said that an international body could offer assistance in administration but could hardly offer a fully "governmental" solution if that meant determination of the internal balance of power and political policy. In any case, the mission put forward its first and most important recommendation, again in italics, in the following terms:

It is proposed that the United Nations assist the Bolivian government in obtaining the services of a number of experienced and competent administrative officials of unquestioned integrity drawn from a variety of countries, and that the Bolivian government appoint these officials on a temporary basis to positions of influence and authority as integral members of the Bolivian civil service.

These administrative assistants should "be given authority adequate to enable them to assist effectively in the establishment of a firm, orderly and enlightened public service. . . . An official of special competence and outstanding character" was to be "similarly appointed to act as special assistant in the office of the president as Coordinator of International Personnel in Bolivia." The proposal, said the mission, represented a new experiment, but Bolivia need fear no undue outside interference because "the aid is offered by the United Nations as a whole, and because the personnel involved—as in the case of the present mission itself—will be drawn from a variety of national sources."

THE AGREEMENT OF 1951

In the first half of 1951, Bolivia did more to confirm the truth of the Keenleyside findings than to observe the Keenleyside precepts. The bitterly contested presidential campaign was followed by the abdication of President Urriolagoitia and his call on the armed forces to take over the country. After some initial hesitation they agreed and formed a ministry of generals and colonels under the presidency of Gen. Hugo Ballivián.

By the end of July 1951, the junta had found time to consider the Keenleyside report, accept it in principle, and ask the United Nations to negotiate an agreement to put it into effect. The negotiating committee,[4] of which I was chairman, arrived in La Paz in mid-September. We were greeted by General Ballivián and by the foreign minister, Colonel Suárez, but for the real business of negotiation they turned us over to an able committee of civilians. Casto Rojas, a former head of the Central Bank, was chairman, and Alberto Crespo, whom I had met in 1949 as one of the leaders of the small Social Democratic party, was one of its most active members.

An agreement was signed on October 1, 1951, and proclaimed to the nation in an enthusiastic broadcast by President Ballivián. Its first clause announced acceptance of "the essential principles" of the Keenleyside report "as forming the basis for a comprehensive program for the economic and social development of Bolivia." An annex, embodied in a presidential decree, stated in great detail the rights and duties of the *asesores administrativos* ("administrative assistants"). They were, among other things,

to have direct access at all times to the minister or chief of the unit in which they serve,

to participate in all recommendations and determinations concerning appointments, transfers, promotions, demotions, and retirement of all senior personnel within the unit in which they serve, and

to direct the administrative and technical training of the personnel of the unit to which they have been assigned.

On this basis administrative assistants were to be provided for the Ministries of Finance, Mines, Agriculture, Public Works, and Labor, for the Budget Bureau, the office of the Controller General, and the Social Security Administration, with an additional assistant for public administration in general. In addition, the United Nations agreed to furnish ten technical experts appointed in the ordinary way, besides those to be recruited from the International Labor Organization and the Food and Agriculture Organization, and also to provide some thirty fellowships for study in other countries.

The Bolivian committee was anxious that technical assistance should lead promptly to economic aid, and at its suggestion an article was included indicating that one of the duties of the administrative assistants and experts would be to aid in drawing up projects for submission to international or national lending agencies. At one important point the agreement made a definite departure from the Keenleyside recommendations: the Bolivian negotiators insisted—we thought rightly—that the coordinator of the program should be a Bolivian rather than a foreigner. Otherwise, they said, Bolivia would become a laughingstock to its Latin American neighbors. Once this point was conceded, the remaining problem was to make sure that the head of the UN mission, the special representative of the secretary-general, should have assured access to the president, the coordinator, and the administrative assistants.

THE UN MISSION IN BOLIVIA

Alberto Crespo was named coordinator for the Bolivian side, and I was named special representative. He came to UN headquarters in January 1952 to assist in the planning, and I went to Bolivia briefly in February to set up a UN office and returned in March for a more permanent stay. The coordinator's office began to function smoothly with the young lawyer, Luís Adolfo Siles, as Crespo's second-in-command. The three administrative assistants and the one expert who arrived in March were well received by their opposite numbers in the administration. Three more members of the mission arrived in Holy Week, and another had already set out from Holland.

Events outside the office were of a different sort. On our first Sunday afternoon in Bolivia, my assistants and I took a stroll in the Indian district above the old church of San Francisco where we found signs scrawled on the adobe walls reading, *"Fuera* Goodrich," meaning "get out." These were the work of the extreme left, and, later, we found one in the workers' district of Villa Victoria written in Aymara and signed with the hammer and sickle. What was more important was the attitude of the MNR, since every foreign observer now told us that the outbreak of its revolution was a certainty and only the date was in doubt. The party's leader, Paz Estenssoro, speaking from exile in Argentina, had denounced the UN agreement on the ground that it represented an infringement of Bolivian sovereignty. No free nation, he declared, could properly concede to foreigners the authority assigned to the administrative assistants.

Late in February, I was given the entirely unexpected opportunity to meet in secret with Hernán Siles, who was leading the revolt from inside the country and, it was said, sleeping each night in a different house. His party, he declared, disagreed profoundly with the Keenleyside report and believed that Bolivians were fully capable of producing an efficient government. Questions of efficiency, however, were secondary to the liberation of the Bolivian people from domination by the mineowners and large landholders. Siles regarded the agreement as unconstitutional since it had been adopted by an unrepresentative government and without discussion in a freely elected Congress. On the other hand, he expressed his faith in the good intentions of the United Nations and in the integrity of the mission and its members. At the close of the interview, he offered his advice as to where the members of the mission should settle in the city so as not to be caught in the revolutionary fighting.

At the end of March, the junta performed what appears in retrospect to be almost a textbook example of diversionary propaganda. It brought back from Chile the remains of a hero of the War of the Pacific named Abaroa who had refused, in unprintable terms, a demand to surrender the bridge he was defending. After services in the cathedral, the casket was borne through the streets of La Paz to a new grave in the Parque Abaroa. Bystanders waved banners inscribed "To the Sea," claiming return of the nation's long-lost seacoast. After many speeches the president reviewed the great procession, which included thousands of schoolchildren, some groups of miners in oilskins wearing headlamps, and a number of goose-stepping units of the Bolivian army.

Just ten days later, the fighting began, and in this test the army appeared less impressive, in spite of the conspicuous gallantry of the cadets from the military academy. On Good Friday, as has been indicated, the junta was overthrown, and Siles took possession of the Presidential Palace. When I called on him on the afternoon of Easter Sunday, he greeted me as a friend because of our earlier encounter but added that, in any case, he would have received me without malice. Moreover, since the authorities at headquarters in New York had, on the holiday weekend, taken extraordinarily rapid action on a cable sent the preceding morning, I was able to convey to the new government an offer of emergency assistance on behalf of the United Nations and the related international organizations.

Mortar fire had destroyed some workers' homes in Villa Victoria, providing the occasion for bringing in a Canadian expert in low-cost housing, whose advice was appreciated; and an official of the World Health Organization came up from Lima to appraise the need for medical equipment. Such modest gestures, however, could hardly compete with the action of the Argentine government which sent over a bevy of nurses in powder blue uniforms to tend the wounded and a truck full of medical supplies that drove up and down the streets displaying the names of Juan and Evita Perón with the message that "Misery Knows No Frontiers."

As to the future of technical assistance, the same points in the same order were made by the principal spokesmen of the new government, President Paz Estenssoro after his triumphant return from exile, Vice-President Siles, and Foreign Minister Wálter Guevara Arze:

1. The agreement is intolerable and must be drastically altered.
2. The new government very much desires technical assistance from the United Nations.
3. You will find that we shall make much more serious use of such assistance than those generals and colonels would ever have done.

There was no doubt of the United Nations's desire to continue the program as long as there was hope of making it effective. At a time when the United States had not recognized the new government and bilateral aid was suspended, I happened to meet the Papal Nuncio in an anteroom of the Foreign Ministry. We could be there, he remarked, because the organizations we represented were universal. Moreover, the final decision to encourage our multinational mission to remain reflected, in part, the desire of the new regime to present itself in a favorable light among the member states of the United Nations.

Alberto Crespo found it necessary to resign as coordinator of the program. Luís Adolfo Siles,[5] though refusing to join the MNR, was able to remain in charge of the office because of his friendly relations with his half brother, the vice-president. From this time on, however, the principal negotiations on matters of substance were with the foreign minister. Members of the mission who had made contact with their Bolivian opposite numbers now, of course, had new officials with whom to deal. All the former ministers and many other leading citizens were either already in exile or awaiting safe-conduct in the various embassies or in the crowded Papal Nunciatura, which also had the right to grant asylum. Typists and chauffeurs, as well as officials, were included in the turnover. One of the administrative assistants told the story of a party member who applied for a job in the ministry of finance. When he was asked to state his qualifications, he protested, "Nobody asked me if I knew how to shoot when they gave me a gun last week."

The nature and tone of the new contacts differed from case to case. At one extreme, in defiance of all protocol, the ebullient Italian who was administrative assistant for social security was promptly sent off as head of a government mission to study social conditions in the mining camps. At the other extreme the controller general refused for six months to use the services of the able and correct Frenchman assigned to his office. As a party member the controller general believed that the original hostility of the MNR to the agreement was still the correct policy, but there was also a more personal explanation. He had learned the lessons of fiscal administration in the 1920s as a very young official from the mission of Prof. Edwin F. Kemmerer of Princeton University. Thus, the controller general had already had his technical assistance and felt no need for any more!

Though the leaders of the MNR remarked again and again that they, unlike the army officers of the junta, "knew how to govern," their administration exhibited the same defects described in the Keenleyside report. With personnel less experienced than the officials who had been replaced, though often more strongly motivated, the new regime could hardly be expected to produce overnight a corps of well-trained and self-confident civil servants. As a result, the members of the mission soon discovered that the important decisions within a ministry could rarely be made by anybody but the minister himself and, further, that many of these issues remained unresolved until they could be brought to the personal attention of the president.

Revision of the agreement for technical assistance was not given the priority suggested by the early declarations. Greater emphasis was placed on the development of the day-to-day work and on the active recruitment of additional experts. The revised agreement was not signed until nearly thirteen months after the revolution, on May 2, 1953. The new accord got rid of the most objectionable adjective by changing the title of the administrative assistants to *consultores técnicos* ("technical consultants"), and it dropped the elaborate catalogue of their functions. It retained, however, the technical consultants' position as members of the Bolivian civil service. The preamble to the document acknowledged the usefulness of the services already rendered but said that the program should be improved "to obtain technical assistance of greater effectiveness, always in conformity with the principles of sovereignty which rule and guide the actions of the government." On its part the government wished to consolidate its recovery measures "with absolute technical and administrative efficiency." Members of the mission were to collaborate in the planning efforts of a proposed National Commission of Coordination and Planning:

The technical consultants and the experts will furnish their technical collaboration to the minister or chief of the agency to which they are permanently assigned and will cooperate under his immediate direction in the execution of those projects which are . . . approved by the government, as well as in the improvement or the reorganization of their respective ministries or administrative agencies.

Except for the reference to the National Commission, which was never set up, the terms of the revised agreement reflected the arrangements that had already been worked out in practice. Certainly the work of the consultants and experts had on the whole more to do with execution than with administrative reorganization. This could hardly have been otherwise at a time presenting so many emergency problems. In some cases an important part of their function was that provided for in the clause proposed by the junta's committee, the drawing up of projects and justifications for aid from agencies of the United States government. One unusual service, rendered at the request of the Bolivian Development Corporation, was to provide outside experts to ensure impartial consideration of foreign contractors' bids for building a sugar mill in the Oriente. The mining engineers examined not only the tin mines but also the iron deposits of Mutún in southeastern Bolivia and the great unworked body of zinc ore at Mina Matilda near Lake Titicaca. The smelting expert investigated the applicability of certain modern techniques to an economy lacking in coal. Other projects were examined in oil production, road building, and electrical power. The last included a spectacular, if economically premature, proposal to drop water from Lake Titicaca through a tunnel into the depths of a nearby valley of an Amazon tributary. In the courageous and temporarily successful 1953 program of monetary stabilization, the difficult political decisions were made by the president and the government, but the substantive preparation of the reform was almost entirely the work of the UN *asesores-consultores* ("advisers-consultants") in the Central Bank and the ministry of finance. In this and other cases, it seemed to me that the more successful members of the mission exercised fully as much authority and influence within the government as any outsiders could properly do in an era of intense national feelings.[6]

THE GOVERNMENT'S PROBLEMS

The most urgent preoccupations of the government were usually with matters not included in the program of technical assistance. At the beginning, indeed, the problems were to assure the survival of the regime and sometimes to determine the balance of power within it. Civil servants from the orderly countries of Western Europe found it strange to work in offices with rifles or machine guns stacked in the closets, and the experts in the ministry of mines learned that the Dodge power wagon, given to the government by the United Nations to facilitate their travels to the mines, was doing double duty at night tracking down enemies of the regime. In one very minor conflict between supporters in the army and the military police, a stray bullet knocked a tile off the roof of our house and the cook rushed in shouting that it was "the Rosca revolution." Her fear was not merely that the bloodshed would begin again but that the aristocracy would come back into power.

On January 6, 1953, an attempt by part of the right wing of the MNR to secure the exclusion of Juan Lechín, the miners' leader, from the cabinet was quickly put down. The next day the trade unions celebrated in the Plaza Murillo and a number of left-wing speeches were made. But the president took the occasion to remind his supporters that Bolivia could live only by the sale of its tin to the capitalist countries:

The people must realize that Bolivia is not an island. It is in America. It is a backward country economically and from this it follows that it cannot speak in the language employed by others who talk of tunnels towards far-off countries for the export of our minerals.[7]

NATIONALIZATION OF THE TIN MINES

The government's first major decision was to nationalize the mines of the great tin companies. The mission had two experts in mining and, later, a third on the problem of smelting; Lechín was quicker than some of his fellow ministers in seeing how to make use of the UN personnel on technical questions. These experts were not, however, consulted by the committee which drafted the nationalization decree. The mission also had no part in the negotiations that led to the early reopening of the British and American markets for Bolivian tin to which the president's speech referred. The nationalization decree of October 31, 1952, affirmed the principle of compensation for the expropriated companies, but it also made counterclaims against them which left the final balance in doubt. The government itself, however, realized that compensation could not be avoided. Professor Blasier's chapter describes the agreement reached with the Patiño interests in June 1953, later extended to the two other large companies, by which a part of the gross proceeds was to be set aside for this purpose.[8] It seems clear, however, that informal understandings must have been arrived at still earlier, since the United States government had already made several purchases for its Texas City smelter and the private English firm of Williams-Harvey, in which the Patiño company held a large interest, had contracted in January 1953 to purchase more than 50 percent of the Bolivian output for the next three years. Within less than four months of expropriation, a Patiño smelter thus became once more the purchaser of the product of the ex-Patiño mines.

With characteristic MNR stage management, the nationalization decree was signed by the members of the government in the presence of a great throng of miners at the mining camp of María Barzola, in Catavi, where some of their fellows had been shot down by the military police. At sunrise the next Sunday a mass was celebrated at the top of the Cerro Rico at Potosí, the hill which in colonial times had been the world's richest source of silver and was still being mined for tin. The miners present took a vow that they would work their hardest for the good of the industry, now that it belonged to the people, and even give up the practice of "highgrading" or stealing particularly rich chunks of ore for backyard refining. On its part the government made particular efforts to retain the services of the foreigners who provided most of the operating and technical management of the industry. The miners' union and, apparently, the miners themselves had come to believe that these officials were an asset to their industry that should not be lost. At one camp, indeed, the miners held the departing manager captive until they received word from La Paz to release him. One who did decide to stay, the North American who became general manager of the Unificada mine at Potosí, was rewarded by what must have been one of the world's noisiest birthday celebrations. Wakened at 12:01 A.M. by a great blast of dynamite, he rushed to the door and found his miners and their womenfolk with two bands ready to begin a twenty-four hour fiesta. On the other hand, most managers and engineers refused to stay, either because they distrusted the new regime or because they feared possible blackballing for future employment by private companies. Perhaps a hundred remained but more than two hundred—North Americans, British, Dutch, Germans, and others—left the country. Those who left included almost every man who had been either a manager or a chief engineer of a major operation.

If the vows of Potosí had any lasting effect on labor productivity in the mines, it was more than offset by a decision that reflected the struggles of the preceding years. "All miners who had been dismissed for political reasons between 1946 and 1952 were reinstated in their jobs after the April 9 revolution, while no workers then employed were dismissed." [9] Because of their part in the revolution and the importance of their product to the economy, the miners could claim high priority for their demands; a later chapter will discuss the effect on the national economy of overstaffing and increased labor costs.[10]

THE INDIAN IN THE NATIONAL LIFE

The MNR's second major concern was to "incorporate the Indian in the national life." The barriers separating the three groups of white, *cholo* ("mixed Indian and white blood"), and Indian were supposedly distinct and impenetrable, yet the census taker would almost certainly record as *blanco* ("white") the exceptional full-blooded Indian who had acquired wealth and a comfortable home. Though the distinctions were always stated in racial terms, in practice they sometimes reflected differences in life style and economic status rather than descent. At any rate, the Indians to whom the MNR slogan primarily referred were neither those who had moved to the mining camps nor the members of the small jungle tribes in the eastern lowlands but rather the mass of the Quechua and Aymara population living and working on the land for the *haciendas* or in the remaining independent indigenous communities. For these Indians, known as *campesinos* ("country dwellers"), the degree of isolation from organized Bolivian society can hardly be exaggerated. It was to them that a municipal official in Cochabamba referred when he told me that the only solution for the problems of the country was to exterminate the Indians and replace them with European immigrants. Even when far more liberal members of the upper class discussed the need to improve the condition of the campesinos, the conversation was likely to betray traces of the traditional vague fear of Indian revolt.

The cholo occupied a different position. He was typically a town dweller performing a variety of functions in the lower reaches of the urban economy. He was obviously at home in La Paz, and so, even more obviously, was the chola with her brown derby and layers of bright skirts, sitting beside a pile of oranges on the street corner or on a mound of vegetables in the central market, or perhaps keeping shop in a hole in the adobe wall surrounding the gardens of a fashionable mansion. On the other hand, whenever Indians appeared in La Paz before the revolution, they kept mainly to the back streets, dressed in extremely ragged clothing, or drove llama trains loaded with llama dung to serve as fuel in their masters' town houses. Some of them served as bearers of burdens. One of these appeared at our office in the hotel staggering under a wooden box of supplies which, according to the stenciled label, weighed well over two hundred pounds. This he had carried upstairs on his back since Indians were not allowed to use the elevator. Though the campesinos could be independent enough in their own setting, as I learned from the hilarity which greeted my efforts to buy a digging stick in the village market at Tiahuanaco, they appeared in the city as members of an alien and inferior class.

Against this background, even city-based foreigners could see something of the changes brought about by the acts of the revolutionary government. A new Ministry of Countrymen's Affairs, *Asuntos Campesinos,* was established, proclaiming its policies in posters with inscriptions like the following:

> The Indian has served us for four centuries.
> Let us devote the next fifty years to serving him.

Its offices were on the Prado a few blocks from the Hotel Sucre Palace, and before long the broad sidewalks were crowded with Indian families waiting for conferences with its officials or signing up for the campaign against illiteracy.

More spectacular were the processions of tens of thousands of campesinos from all over the country that were brought in to La Paz by truckloads to celebrate various official holidays such as the Anniversary of the Revolution on April 9. Each group carried banners bearing the slogans of the revolution and, in some cases, of the attack on *analfabetismo* ("illiteracy"), and it was usually preceded by its own band playing panpipes or native drums or other instruments. Some of the men, and even a few women, carried guns. In each unit the first rank or two of the marchers typically included the village leaders with their staffs of office and others in the native costume of their region. The procession, which formed an ethnologist's or at least a photographer's review of the indigenous population of the country, moved for hours through the main streets of the city and ended in either the Plaza Murillo or the stadium where the president rendered an account of his stewardship.

In the meanwhile the campesinos of the Cochabamba region had formed strong agrarian syndicates, and agents of the ministry had been encouraging the development of similar organizations in other regions. A campesino militia had been organized and supplied with guns, putting it on the same footing with the miners' and workers' groups, both of whom had retained their rifles since the revolution. Efforts were made to spread educational facilities to the mass of the Indian population, the literacy requirement for voting was abolished, and suffrage was made universal.

THE LAND REFORM

The MNR began its second year in power by appointing a commission under the chairmanship of Vice-President Siles, instructed to make, within ninety days, proposals for carrying out the party's commitment to real agrarian reform. On this occasion my colleagues and I found the atmosphere quite different from that which had surrounded the earlier period of decision regarding the mines. Either because we had won more confidence or because land reform was a less sensitive issue (since this time the property to be expropriated was almost entirely Bolivian), the mission was given the opportunity to provide an expert on land reform and its administration. The man chosen was the well-known Mexican agricultural economist, Edmundo Flores. The government could be confident that, as a Mexican, he would be in sympathy with the general policy of agrarian reform; indeed, Foreign Minister Guevara had once told me that the purpose of the Bolivian revolution was to achieve the results of the Mexican revolution "without ten years of Pancho Villa." On our part, we knew that Flores was concerned that more should be done than had been done in Mexico to make the reform economically viable.[11]

All members of the commission were agreed on abolition of the prevailing system under which the Indian typically gave three or four days of labor a week to the *patrón* ("landlord") without wages, receiving in return the right to cultivate for his own use a small parcel of land on the estate. All were further agreed that the Indian should receive land of his own. There were disagreements as to whether the expropriated landlords should be compensated, and, if so, how—and whether the new owners should pay for the land they were to receive. The main motives for reform were moral and political, to redress injustice and to redistribute power. The preamble of the decree, however, described the old system as "irrational" as well as "unjust" and listed as one of the objectives "the liberation of the forces of agricultural production." Actually, several provisions of the decree were intended to promote economic efficiency. The *latifundio,* defined as a large rural property farmed by traditional techniques with servile labor, was abolished as serving no social purpose. On the other hand, there was an attempt to preserve what was called the *empresa agrícola* ("agricultural enterprise") which invested capital, used modern techniques, and paid wages—a provision which was, as Flores pointed out, quite unique in land reform legislation.[12] Other articles were intended to encourage reinvestment by landlords and settlement by campesinos in the underdeveloped areas of the Oriente. Elaborate attempts were made to adjust the provisions to the varying geographical conditions of the country, and in the end the decree contained no less than 176 articles. The full details are not worth recalling since many of them, as later chapters will show, were made inoperative either by subsequent inflation or by the actions of the campesinos themselves. From the beginning, it was clear that the Indians' small plots of land were now their own property and that unpaid labor was abolished. But how much land, if any, was to be kept by the patrón and how his former holdings were to be divided and worked were not, in practice, wholly determined by the text of the law.

Promulgation of the decree was again an exercise in MNR showmanship. The date chosen, August 2, was declared to be "The Day of the Indian." The place was in the Cochabamba valley whose campesinos, more strongly organized than those of other parts of Bolivia, had since the revolution already accomplished by force a land reform more drastic than that provided for by the decree. The ceremony, which I attended as one of my last official duties in the country,[13] took place in a field outside the village of Ucureña in the presence of a throng of one hundred thousand Indians. The members of the cabinet affixed their signatures. One of them, it was said, signed away several hundred thousand acres of family property.[14] Wálter Guevara, who, like many other educated Bolivians, had learned one of the Indian languages in childhood from the servants, made the address in Quechua. President Paz closed the proceedings with the traditional offering of chicha and coca leaf to *Pachamama* ("mother earth").

Within its first sixteen months in office, the new regime had nationalized the great tin mines, which were the nation's main source of foreign exchange, and overturned the organization of agriculture, which was the occupation of the great mass of the people. In the one case the government risked the opposition of powerful foreign and expatriate interests, and in the other it took away the basis of power from the class which had provided the principal leadership within the country. A formerly servile population, whose new prestige was symbolized by the processions in La Paz, had been given guns and the vote and, now, a right to the land and responsibility for its use. Why these risks were taken, what ends were sought, and how the country fared under these programs will be discussed in the chapters which follow.

NOTES

1. See Carter Goodrich, "Bolivia: Test of Technical Assistance," *Foreign Affairs,* 22 (April 1954), pp. 473–81; and *The Economic Transformation of Bolivia,* New York School of Industrial and Labor Relations, Cornell University Bulletin no. 34 (Ithaca, N.Y., 1955). I have drawn on parts of this bulletin in writing the present chapter. My colleagues in the mission, Mario C. J. Harrington and John Carman, have been good enough to check and supplement these recollections.

2. See p. 165.

3. *Report of the United Nations Mission of Technical Assistance to Bolivia* (New York, 1951). The quotations or specific references which follow are from pp. 53, 9 (table IV), 49–50, 2–4.

4. Two of the members had served on the Keenleyside mission, the English labor expert, David Blelloch, and the American professor of public administration, Albert Lepawsky. A third member, William Cox of headquarters' Legal Division, was appointed because the agreement would authorize the spending of UN funds under novel arrangements.

Dr. Keenleyside gives credit to Mr. Blelloch for the original suggestion that led to the principal proposal made in the report. See Hugh L. Keenleyside, *International Aid: A Summary* (New York, 1966), p. 62.

5. Both men returned to public life after periods of exile during the MNR regime. Alberto Crespo G. served for brief periods as foreign minister and as minister of defense in the cabinets of President René Barrientos Ortuño.

During his exile Luís Adolfo Siles Salinas spent an academic year in the United States as an Eisenhower Fellow, much of it at the New York School of Industrial and Labor Relations at Cornell University. In the elections of 1966 Siles was chosen as vice-president, running on the ticket headed by General Barrientos. After the latter's death on April 27, 1969, Siles succeeded to the presidency, a post that had been occupied by his father, Hernando Siles Reyes, and his half brother, Hernán Siles Zuazo. On September 26, 1969, Siles was deposed in the coup led by Gen. Alfredo Ovando Candia. He again went into exile, this time in Chile as his father had done forty years earlier.

6. One of the original group of asesores administrativos expressed the opinion in a confidential report that no foreign expert could have obtained more influence than the members of the mission had done. "The government," he said, "calls on us continuously for advice in the solution of all the problems, even the most delicate, which present themselves. Our counsels are followed and applied as far as the situation of the country permits." On the other hand, the adviser to the Banco Central, Arthur Karasz, has stated that at certain times his work suffered for lack of the additional authority that would have been given by the earlier Keenleyside provisions. See Karasz, "Experiment in Development: Bolivia Since 1952," in *Freedom and Reform in Latin America,* ed. Frederick B. Pike (South Bend, Ind., 1959).

In 1958, the UN General Assembly extended to other countries the principle of the Keenleyside report by inaugurating the so-called OPEX program "to provide governments with senior personnel to perform operational and executive functions within, and as members of, the public service of the countries concerned." The representative of the Bolivian government supported the proposal. Keenleyside, *International Aid,* pp. 259–60.

7. From the notes taken at the time by the secretary of the mission, Miss Cora Wyman. The passage appears in the original Spanish in Víctor Paz Estenssoro, *Discursos parlamentarios* (La Paz, 1955), p. 35.

8. See p. 64.

9. Robert J. Alexander, *The Bolivian National Revolution* (New Brunswick, N.J., 1958), p. 104.

10. See pp. 171–76.

11. Edmundo Flores, "Land Reform in Bolivia," *Land Economics* (May 1954), pp. 112–24; and his "Un año de reforma agraria en Bolivia," *El Trimestre Economico,* Mexico (April–June, 1955). See also his *Tratado de economia agricola* (Mexico, 1961). Dr. Flores was first brought to Bolivia on a joint appointment of the United Nations and the Food and Agriculture Organization.

12. Flores, "Land Reform in Bolivia," p. 120.

13. As of September 1, 1953, the international staff of the mission in Bolivia consisted—in addition to the special representative, the administrative assistant, and two bilingual secretaries—of technical consultants to the Ministries of Finance, Agriculture, and Labor, the Central Bank, the controller general, and the Social Security Administration, as well as experts in mining costs, tin smelting, hydroelectric power, petroleum production, land reform, and vocational education (provided by the International Labor Organization) and two experts in teacher training (provided by UNESCO).

Of these eighteen persons, one was stateless and the others were from eleven nations —Belgium, Canada, Chile, Cuba, France, Italy, Mexico, Netherlands, Switzerland, the United Kingdom, and the United States. The Communist member states and their nationals were not taking part in the technical assistance program at that time.

Arthur Karasz, in "Experiment in Development," cited in note 6, provides a thoughtful comment on the work of the mission on the basis of longer service in it. Since his work in particular and the work of the UN mission in general have received unfavorable comment from George Jackson Eder, the American lawyer and public official who served in 1956–1957 as executive director of Bolivia's National Monetary Stabilization Council, the Karasz essay is particularly in point. See George Jackson

Eder, *Inflation and Development in Latin America: A Case History of Inflation and Stabilization in Bolivia* (Ann Arbor, Mich., 1968), esp. pp. 476–82.

14. Fernando Iturralde. In spite of his Basque surname, he had written a book celebrating the Indian origins of the Bolivian people, *Los descendientes del imperio incaico* (Naples, Italy, 1951).

HERBERT S. KLEIN
Columbia University

Prelude to the Revolution

PRE-COLUMBIAN AND COLONIAL BOLIVIA

Bolivian society traces its origins to the advanced pre-Columbian civilizations of South America. The high Bolivian plateau known as the Altiplano was already densely populated several centuries before the Spanish Conquest. The Tiahuanaco empire, the first of the great Andean empires to extend over both the Peruvian coast and highlands, had its center in this region beginning in the seventh century A.D. After it reached its climax in the eleventh century, the Tiahuanaco empire was gradually replaced by simpler regional states.[1]

In the centuries that followed the collapse of the Tiahuanaco empire, the Bolivian highlands maintained both their dense populations and high technical civilizations through irrigational agriculture. By the fifteenth century this region was controlled mostly by some twelve nations of Aymara-speaking Indians. Competitors with the Quechua-speaking nation at Cuzco, these Aymara tribes fought with the latter for control of the new imperial structure forming in the highland region. Though the Aymara nations were eventually dominated by the Cuzco civilization, they, nevertheless, remained the most important non-Quechua group within the expanding Incan empire. Because of their influence they were the only conquered coastal or highland peoples to retain their language and cultural identity. But they were forced to accept a very large body of Quechua-speaking immigrants within their midst as a deliberate Incan policy of colonization.[2] It was this pattern of colonization and nonassimilation which gives Bolivia its current linguistic and cultural identity. Today the two major Indian languages in Bolivia are Quechua, spoken by 36 percent of the national population, and Aymara, spoken by another 24 percent.[3]

Under both Aymara and Quechua rule the basic unit of pre-Columbian society was the *ayllu* ("communal village"). These villages were corporate entities which ultimately controlled all land worked by the villagers and probably had some type of clan organization as well. Banded together in the Inca empire through a hierarchy of civil and church officials, these communities were ruled by local chiefs and nobility. It was this superstructure of native overlords and imperial bureaucracy which the Spaniards deliberately destroyed in the sixteenth century by their conquest of what is now Peru and Bolivia. They adopted a policy of protection toward the vital peasant village base of this empire, however, and left the governing of the ayllus to the village elders. The Spaniards recognized that the peasant village was a vital source of both revenue and free labor which they hoped to exploit on the scale of the sophisticated Incan imperial organization.[4]

The importance of the Bolivian highlands within Peruvian society was recognized almost immediately after the Spanish Conquest. Like the rest of the highland Peruvian region it had a dense, settled population of village agriculturalists who could easily be exploited. But even more importantly, it proved to be the center of the silver mining regions of Spanish South America and thus was to become one of the two most important centers of the New World colonial empire. When Potosí was discovered in 1545, the rich deposits of silver in the famous *Cerro Rico* ("rich hill") of Potosí represented the largest concentration of silver then available in the Western world. Almost immediately Spanish capital poured into the Bolivian highlands to develop this enormous resource, and the silver zones around Oruro and, above all, Potosí began to be fully exploited. Dependent on these arid, high altitude mining centers were such cities as Sucre, Cochabamba, and La Paz, which supplied them with food and other basic necessities.[5]

Thus the emphasis of Spanish colonial rule in Bolivia, or Upper Peru as it was then called, was exploitation of the rich mineral deposits through the use of forced Indian labor, wage and contract labor, and even some slaves. Both the highlands and the surrounding valleys of Peru and Bolivia became labor pools and supply centers for the mines. Silver mining was of such importance that, by the middle of the seventeenth century, the arid plateau city of Potosí had the largest population of any city in the entire hemisphere, something like one hundred fifty thousand persons.[6]

By the eighteenth century, however, the surface veins of silver had largely been exhausted and the Bolivian miners were forced into the exploitation of subsurface deposits,[7] requiring an enormous input of capital. Although such capital had been readily available in the sixteenth and seventeenth centuries, by the eighteenth century this was not the case. The general growth of commercial agriculture and New World trade was now absorbing large amounts of capital and the rising costs in silver mining resulted in less profits than were available from alternative sources of investment. Through special royal inducements there was some eighteenth century revival of mining prosperity, but the Wars of Independence and the collapse of the crucial mercury supplies from the mines of Huancavelica in lower Peru finally brought the mining industry to the point of almost total collapse.[8] Whereas there were forty refineries smelting ore in Potosí in 1803, by 1825 there were only fifteen, and production had declined by over 80 percent.[9] By the time of the first Bolivian national census, it was estimated that there were some ten thousand abandoned mines in the republic.[10]

EARLY NINETEENTH-CENTURY BOLIVIA

Incapable of exporting its silver at the levels of colonial production, Bolivia rapidly lost its advanced economic standing within Spanish America. Already by the end of the colonial period such marginal areas as the Río de la Plata and Chile were forging ahead on the basis of meat and cereal production; however, Bolivia was a net importer of basic foods, even those which were exclusively consumed by its Indian population.[11] In addition, none of its other mineral resources were of sufficient value to overcome the high transportation costs involved in simply getting the minerals to the coast.[12] Therefore, the Bolivian republic, with little taxable trade and few exportable resources beyond its very modest precious metals production, was forced to rely on the direct taxation of its Indian peasant masses.

Making up over two-thirds of the national population in the early days of the republic, these Indians by and large produced only a small surplus above subsistence level. Heavily taxed with corvée labor obligations, all Indians who were members of the free peasant communities (a majority until the middle of the nineteenth century) were also required to pay a head tax, and finally there was a consumption tax on the uniquely Indian-consumed product of coca. In short the poorest elements in the society were regressively taxed in the heaviest manner possible, and until well into the last quarter of the nineteenth century, this Indian taxation was the largest source of the national government's revenues.[13] With the more progressive states relying almost exclusively on the import and export taxes of a constantly expanding international commerce, it is easy to see why the Bolivian state rapidly lost its prominent position within the continent and began to be classified as one of the most backward of the new republics.

This economic decline was also reflected by political stagnation. Bolivia emerged with a series of *caudillos,* among whom was Marshal Andrés de Santa Cruz. Temporarily reorganizing the wartorn Bolivian economy and state finances, Santa Cruz, in the 1820s and 1830s, was able to unify Bolivia with Peru into a government known as the Confederation. But Chilean opposition destroyed the Confederation attempt, and Bolivia quickly turned in upon itself and, thenceforth, abandoned all attempts at international expansion. Rather, its efforts for the next half century would be primarily to integrate its far-flung borders into a coherent relationship with the core of the republic, the Altiplano, and the eastern Andean valleys. But this attempt was doomed to failure as Bolivia lacked the population and resources to exploit either its Amazon or Pacific frontiers. Despite the enormous wealth in nitrates and guano available on the Bolivian Pacific coast, the nation was incapable of exploiting them even on a joint basis with foreign capital. What little capital was available within Bolivia's upper class was totally committed to Altiplano mining. Rather, it was the Peruvians, the Chileans, the North Americans, and the English who exploited these resources, and soon the flag was following trade. Between the Chilean War with the Confederation in 1838–1839 and the outbreak of the War of the Pacific in 1879, Chile constantly and successfully expanded its claims against Bolivian sovereignty in the Pacific, and, finally, in the War of the Pacific it took everything.[14]

THE CONSERVATIVE OLIGARCHY AND THE SILVER REVIVAL, 1880–1899

The fall of the Pacific *litoral* ("coast") to Chile during the War of the Pacific was in many ways a blessing in disguise for Bolivia, for it marked a major turning point in national history. From the fall of the Confederation to the War of the Pacific, Bolivia had gone through one of the worst periods of caudillo rule experienced by any country in Latin America during the nineteenth century. However, silver mining had revived in the decades of the 1860s and 1870s under the impact of new capital inputs from Chile and England. By the time of the War of the Pacific international market conditions for silver and the introduction of new technology and capital had greatly revived the national mining industry.[15] It was the War of the Pacific which enabled the new mining entrepreneurs to capture political control of the nation and to definitively break the hold of the now discredited military officers on national political life.

Starting in 1880 Bolivia moved into an era of a limited-participation civilian government, with the national upper class dividing into Liberal and Conservative parties which then proceeded to share power. This intraclass political party system finally brought Bolivia the stability needed for economic development. Though the parties were split on personality and anticlerical issues, they were identical in their desire to promote economic growth. From 1880 to 1899 the nation was ruled by the Conservatives, whose principal function was to encourage the mining industry through the development of an international rail network. It was the transportation to the coast which had traditionally been the heaviest cost item in Bolivian mining. Railroad construction to the Pacific ports of Antofagasta and Arica finally reduced that cost to a reasonable level and permitted much larger bulk shipments of other previously unexploited ores as well.[16]

It was this renaissance in silver mining which also brought about major changes in the Bolivian social structure. With the revival of the mining centers and the steady growth of one or two major urban centers, the demand for food grew. The creation of a railroad and highway network connecting the urban and mining centers with previously isolated areas was the impetus for an important expansion in commercial agriculture. Though no reliable statistics are available for the nineteenth century on the production of foodstuffs, the rapid expansion of the *latifundia* ("large landholdings") system attests to the growth of this sector.

Whereas in 1846 over 63 percent of the Indians were still members of free landowning communities, by 1900 this percentage had declined to only 27 percent, reflecting a major growth in latifundias.[17] At the same time the development of mining and the general increase in commerce finally saw the Indian head tax, which from 1825 to 1860 had been the primary source of government revenues, become an insignificant item in government finance.

Simultaneously, there was a percentage decline of the Indian population and an increase of the mestizo, or *cholo* ("half-breed"), population, which by 1900 represented 27 percent of the national total. Forming a crucial middle cultural and economic layer between the whites and the Indians, the cholos greatly modified the bipolarity of traditional Bolivian society. They also formed the basic elements in the growth of the urban populations. By 1900 La Paz was finally emerging as a major metropolitan area, with a population of 60,000 persons, and its growth was to continue to be impressive in the years to come.[18]

THE LIBERAL OLIGARCHY AND THE CENTURY OF TIN

It was thus an economically expanding and socially developing nation which the Liberals inherited when they seized power from the Conservatives in the so-called Federal Revolution of 1899. Supposedly fought over the permanent placing of national institutions in the cities of Sucre or La Paz, the federal revolt was primarily a power struggle between the two parties themselves. Unfortunately for the Conservatives, their strength was too closely tied to the traditional Chuquisaca elite much of which was conterminous with the silver mining class. The Liberals, however, had the bulk of their strength in La Paz, which by this period was three times the size of Sucre and the largest urban center in the nation.[19]

The Liberal victory was also closely associated with a basic shift in the mining economy. As the world silver market began to collapse in the 1880s and early 1890s, there began a major shift to tin mining on the Bolivian Altiplano. Long found in association with silver, tin did not become an important product until the end of the nineteenth century, when the demand suddenly soared in all the major industralized countries. Thus, by 1900 tin had completely superceded silver as Bolivia's primary export, accounting for over 50 percent of its national exports.[20]

The shift to tin mining not only occurred at the same time as the Liberal revolt and was closely associated with the new party, but it also brought about a basic change within the capitalist class in Bolivia. Whereas the silver mining elite had been almost exclusively Bolivian, the new tin miners were far more cosmopolitan, including in the early years foreigners, as well as some new Bolivian entrepreneurs. Tin mining itself now absorbed far more capital and produced far more wealth than the old silver mining industry, and the new companies which emerged became complex international ventures directed by professional managers.

Given this new economic complexity and the political stability already achieved by the Conservatives and perpetuated by the Liberals, the tin mining elite found it profitable to withdraw from direct involvement in national political life. Whereas almost all the Bolivian presidents under the Conservative rule had been either silver magnates or partners in silver mining ventures, the Liberal leaders and subsequent presidents of the twentieth century were largely outside the mining elite. No tin magnate actively participated in leadership positions within the political system. Rather, they were now to rely on a far more effective system of pressure group politics, which in Bolivian terms came to be known vulgarly as the *Rosca* (literally, a padded head ring for carrying weights), a term used to designate the oligarchy and the groups of lawyers and others supporting them.[21]

The primary task of the Liberal politicians who ruled Bolivia from 1899–1920 was to settle Bolivia's chronic border problems and to continue and expand the communications network initiated under the Conservatives. Paid large sums from Chile for the Pacific coast territory and a large indemnity from Brazil for the loss of Amazon territory, Bolivia was able to finance a great railroad construction era. By 1920 most of the major cities were tied together by rails, La Paz was connected to two international Pacific ports, a new line was started to Lake Titicaca and the Peruvian border, and one had been built to Tarija and the Argentine frontier. The Liberals also concentrated on school construction and modern urban development, primarily in La Paz. The result of all their efforts was a major expansion of the vital communications infrastructure initiated under the Conservatives.

The period of Liberal rule was also the most quiescent in Bolivian political history. Dominated by the figure of Ismael Montes, the Liberal party easily destroyed the federalists who had supported the party during the revolution, and their success led to the total collapse of the Conservative party. It was not until 1914 that an effective two-party system was again established, when many of the politcal "outs" along with a large number of new and younger elements finally organized the Republican party. Like its two predecessors the Republican party was composed of the white upper and middle classes with a fundamental belief in the liberal and positivist ideologies held by their predecessors.[22]

THE REPUBLICAN PARTIES AND THE GREAT DEPRESSION

The abrasive quality of the strong-willed Montes and the disintegration of the ruling Liberal party finally permitted the Republicans, in 1920, to stage a successful coup on the model of the Liberal overthrow of 1899 and to become the ruling party. The new party, upon achieving political power, however, immediately split into two warring sections based on a conflict of personalities. The new parties were led by two Montes-style politicians, Bautista Saavedra, a La Paz lawyer who captured control of the Republican party, and Daniel Salamanca, a Cochabamba landowner who took his following into a separate party, the so-called *Partido Republicano Genuino* or Genuine Republican party (PRG). The rivalry between these two men would be the dominant theme in Bolivian politics for the next decade, until the Salamanca forces would in their turn capture the presidency.[23]

Below the surface of this political battle for personalities, the national economy in the decade of the 1920s was undergoing serious change. The early years of this decade had witnessed a brilliant postwar recovery of the Bolivian tin mining industry and the achievement by 1929 of its highest production figures. But this enormous output was already occurring in a period of steady price decline, a trend which would continue long after the Great Depression. By 1930 the international tin market was in a serious crisis and Bolivian production suffered. By that time the outlines of the industry had been formed, with the Big Three producers, Simón I. Patiño, the Aramayo family, and the German Mauricio Hochschild controlling over two-thirds of national production. The year 1930 would also mark the end not only of the period of company consolidation but also of major new capital investments, and, thereafter, the industry would become an ever higher-cost producer of lower-grade ore for the international market.[24]

The arrival of Salamanca to the presidency after the overthrow of the Saavedra-Siles Republicans in 1930 seemingly involved little change in traditional Bolivian government. But the Great Depression was brutally cutting into national income and forcing the closing of a large part of the vital mining industry. Salamanca was forced to take new measures. Attempting a policy of inflation and money manipulation, he ran into bitter hostility from the Liberal party, his key partner in the 1930 overthrow of the regular Republican party. The opposition of these two forces in the central government led to a tense political climate. The result of this conflict was to force Salamanca to accept the Liberals' veto over internal economic decisions though he refused to permit the party to join his cabinet. Rather, he sought to overcome the Liberal congressional control and to destroy the growing strike movements by turning national attention to other themes. The traditional recourse in such a situation was toward patriotism and foreign war, and Salamanca had these possibilities open to him through a long-standing border conflict with Paraguay.

THE CHACO WAR AND THE EXPERIMENT IN "MILITARY SOCIALISM"

Already in the mid-1920s Bolivia and Paraguay had begun a major program of fort construction in the largely uninhabited and poorly demarcated Chaco Boreal territory on the southeastern Bolivian frontier. In the height of the depression Salamanca had advocated an even heavier armaments and fortification program and had contracted for major European loans. Thus, when a border incident developed between the two states in June 1932, Salamanca deliberately provoked a full-scale Bolivian reprisal which inevitably led into open war between the two nations.[25]

The Chaco War was a long and costly disaster for Bolivia. The three years of bitter fighting on the southeastern frontiers left 100,000 Bolivian men dead, wounded, deserted, or captured. It also lost far more territory than Paraguay had claimed even in its most extreme demands. The fact that Bolivia entered the war with a better-equipped and supposedly far better-trained army only aggravated the sense of frustration at the disaster among the literate elite of the nation.[26]

Previously wedded to the traditional elite and party system, the young veterans of the middle- and upper-class families now refused to support their rule. Suddenly the Bolivian political spectrum was filled with a host of small parties and groups that had not existed in the prewar period. Although some socialist and Communist groups had been formed in Bolivia in the late 1920s, they had been destroyed by Salamanca during the war. Virtually no contract had existed between these extremely marginal groups (which were even poorly represented in the labor movement) and the traditional prewar parties. From 1935 on, however, this vacuum was filled by a host of competing groups all of which sapped the strength of the traditional parties on the right and encouraged the expansion of the extreme parties on the left.

The result of this new postwar political growth among the literate white and cholo elements in Bolivian society initially led to the inability of any one leader or party to gain control of the government. Thus in early 1936 the army seized power in a coup supported by a large number of the new moderate socialist groups. This was the army's first return to a governing situation since 1880.[27]

But this new politization of the army reflected the new currents of what everyone was beginning to call the *generación del Chaco*. It was the junior officers who overthrew the immediate postwar Liberal party regime—frontline officers with a great bond of sympathy to the new civilian parties. The two key leaders of these radical veteran officer groups were Col. David Toro and Maj. Germán Busch. Toro had been a prominent staff officer before the war and was known as a brilliant leader. He thus tended to bridge the prewar and postwar officer's positions, though he quickly identified himself with the latter, especially as he had been a leading frontline officer. Germán Busch, on the other hand, represented the new and younger men. On the eve of the conflict he had been a lieutenant and had risen rapidly in the ranks through skill and bravery, features commonly lacking in the badly discredited Bolivian officer corps.

Feeling themselves incapable of taking command, the groups around Busch supported Toro for the presidency, while they themselves cemented their hold over the key posts within the army. Indebted to these younger officers and sensing the national mood for change, Toro outlined a major program of reform or what he called "military socialism." This program consisted of a general expansion of Bolivia's skimpy welfare and labor legislation and an attempt to set up a corporate style political system to replace the representative democratic system established since the founding of the republic.[28]

The Toro government lasted almost two years. During that time the government produced a large number of changes in national social legislation. It also confiscated the holdings of the Standard Oil Company of New Jersey in a major test of strength to gain support from the discontented Busch faction.[29] Finally, it called into session a unique constitutional convention and congress which represented all the traditional parties as well as all the new political groups and the labor and veterans' movements.

Before this important 1938 congress actually met, however, the Toro regime was overthrown by Busch. Promising to continue the reform programs of Toro in a more effective manner, Busch permitted the 1938 convention and congress to meet and to write Bolivia's first constitution since 1880. Taking the limited parliamentary form of government of the old charter, the convention added an equal mass of provisions on the primacy of society over private property and the government's role in the positive defense of the welfare of all citizens. The convention debated these provisions from all political points of view, and for the first time in the history of the national legislature, radical and revolutionary programs were finally championed. The 1938 convention also finally crystallized the thought of the Chaco generation and became the arena in which new and larger political alliances were developed.[30]

Before the convention and congress could begin to implement its new charter, the Busch regime decided that this taste of democratic government was too disruptive. In April 1939 Busch announced the formation of a dictatorial regime, and, although he decreed the 1938 constitution to be in force, he abolished the congress which wrote it. He then attempted to rule by decree, only to find that he was incapable of effecting basic social change, largely because of his own political naïvete. All attempts to form a civilian-government coalition were destroyed by Busch. Even his famous June 1939 decree, imposing government control over mining income, was never put into effect. Frustrated by his inability to effect change, Busch grew despondent and in November 1939 committed suicide.[31]

THE RISE OF THE NATIONAL REVOLUTIONARY PARTIES

The suddenness of Busch's death allowed the upper officers to quickly reestablish their control over the army, and under the Busch-appointed chief of the general staff, Gen. Carlos Quintanilla, the younger officers were temporarily removed from power. The Quintanilla takeover of the presidency then permitted the traditional parties to reassert their ties to the army, and in March 1940 the three parties of the old elite, the Liberals, Republican Socialists,[32] and Genuine Republicans, had formed a coalition to back the Chaco War hero Gen. Enrique Peñaranda. Politically neutral, Peñaranda had supported the military socialist experiment of Toro and Busch. But he then supported Quintanilla's purging of the army and was effective in suppressing the attempt of Bernardo Bilbao Rioja to take over the army leadership and continue the reform government of Toro and Busch.

Though the traditional elite was now formed into an important political coalition (usually called the *Concordancia*) supporting common presidential slates, its victory was only temporary. While the Peñaranda candidacy for the 1940 elections gained the support of the moderate postwar reform groups, the radicals supported the candidacy of an unknown sociology professor from Cochabamba, the Marxist José Antonio Arze. In a supposedly airtight election with a limited suffrage based on literacy, the last-minute candidacy of Arze managed to gain 10,000 out of the 58,000 votes cast.[33] And immediately following the election the local radical groups these votes represented finally coalesced into a national political party, the *Partido de la Izquierda Revolucionaria* (PIR).[34] This was the first of the major new postwar parties to emerge in Bolivia. The PIR, together with the still very small Trotskyite *Partido Obrero Revolucionario* (POR), which had been established in 1934, now formed a major left wing in national politics.[35] These two parties were deeply tied to the now politicized labor movement and clearly had revolutionary overtones in their programs, although they were still willing to work within the political system.

Another defeat for the traditional parties occurred in the congressional elections of the same year. Though Peñaranda won the presidency, the moderate and radical reform parties gained a majority in the Chamber of Deputies and a heavy representation in the Senate. The result was a Congress even more radical than the 1938 convention.[36] Almost immediately Peñaranda and the Congress began to oppose each other, and the end result was the collapse of the upper-officer and traditional party alliance. And with it came the end of the traditional political system which had been created in 1880.

The source of the conflict between the president and Congress was the labor movement. Although the majority of the railroad and urban skilled workers had been organized by 1940, the mining industry, the key industry within the nation, was still not unionized. But under the encouragement of the reform governments of the late 1930s, the radicals finally organized the mine leaders, and by the early 1940s strikes over wages and working conditions developed at all the major mines in Bolivia.[37] One of these important strike efforts was an attempt to increase wages at the Patiño mines of Catavi in late 1942. Although successful in halting work at the mines, the local union was unable to gain either recognition for itself or any wage increases from the company. The Patiño company was able to use World War II antisabotage laws to get the government to send troops into the mines, and the result was a massacre of workers in December of 1942. The so-called Catavi massacre brought about an open rupture between Peñaranda and Congress. The result was a censure motion against the regime that failed by only one vote but was still a symbolic victory for the left.[38] The Catavi massacre finally destroyed the moderate reformist middle ground between the radical left and the traditional forces. The majority of the moderates formed themselves into the *Movimiento Nacionalista Revolucionario* (MNR) which took a strong prolabor and antigovernment position, while the remainder returned to the parties of the Concordancia.[39]

Though the PIR, POR, and MNR all were prolabor, their respective international sympathies prevented their initial coalition into a revolutionary force. The MNR contained both fascist and moderate socialist wings, and, while the war lasted in Europe, it was deeply committed to the German effort. The PIR also contained moderate and radical wings, but it, too, was wedded to European developments by its strong support of Russia and tended to view the MNR as a simple Berlin puppet. Although important in organizing the mines, the POR for its part had little impact on the literate whites and cholos of the nation and tended to be a strictly labor party with a strong anti-PIR position. The result of these divisions was the preservation of the traditional government for another decade, despite the basic weakness of the traditional parties and despite the continued divisions within the army between the radical and conservative elements. But the general weakness of the traditional system was also causing havoc in the pattern of the industrialist-party alliance. As early as the Toro regime Aramayo had challenged the old parties by trying to organize his own political party. Though he eventually agreed to withdraw from this attempt, this active and immediate intervention of one of the tin barons was enough to force the parties to drop their historical differences and form a rough coalition. Even so, the Big Three tin miners began to rely more heavily on the army instead of its old system of pressure-group politics and civilian politicians. This dissatisfaction and intervention of the previously passive mining elite, and their inability to co-opt the new radical elements, were major forces in the collapse of the traditional system.

Within the army itself the balance between the new and older officer alliances was again broken in late 1943 when a hitherto secret military lodge of ex–prisoner of war officers suddenly emerged in a leadership position. The so-called *Logia Mariscal Andrés de Santa Cruz* had been formed in the Paraguayan prisoner of war camps and brought back to Bolivia with the returning veterans. Quiescent during the late 1930s, the lodge reemerged with the defeat of the Busch and Bilbao Rioja forces in the early 1940s and from its base in the staff schools in Cochabamba captured the leadership of the army. Strongly fascist-oriented and sympathetic to moderate social reforms, these men organized a political arm of their lodge known as *Razón de Patria* (RADEPA), which in turn worked closely with the MNR. The result was a coalition between the two and their overthrow of the Peñaranda government in December 1943.[40]

The new government was led by the unknown Col. Gualberto Villarroel. Claiming direct ancestry from the regimes of military socialism, the new government promised major reforms and appointed the leader of the MNR, Víctor Paz Estenssoro, to be minister of finance. But the regime was too much of a replica of the last Busch years, without Busch's saving ingredient of toleration. In addition, Paz Estenssoro decided on a conservative fiscal policy to stem the inflation affecting the nation and, therefore, had no funds available for social reform. The army, for its part, engaged in physical violence against the traditional political leaders which had counterproductive results. Though the regime did organize Bolivia's first peasant congress, did promise to investigate land reform, and did strongly support the national miners federation (FSTMB),[41] it accomplished little in the way of concrete reforms. Even its writing of a new constitution in 1945 was illusory since the new constitution was almost an exact replica of the 1938 charter. Facing increasing hostility to their senseless violence, the officers of the RADEPA could think of little else but more violence, ending in the popular revolt of June 1946.[42]

In the resulting euphoria of the popular revolt, the PIR—which had been the leader of the revolt—joined forces with the traditional parties in an antifascist front. The result of this strange alliance was the destruction of the PIR. Although this new government was supposed to be a reformist, liberal, and antifascist regime, it soon turned into a strongly conservative force. The traditional parties were bent on destroying the power of the miners' union, and they succeeded in getting the PIR to endorse repressive action as the price for continuation in government. Thereupon several worker massacres followed, and by the late 1940s the previously powerful PIR found itself deprived of all its traditional sources of power. The miners had largely gone over to the POR, which wrote their revolutionary Pulacayo program,[43] and the middle-class Marxists had now joined the purged MNR.

In the so-called *sexenio* ("six-year period") between 1946 and 1952, the MNR went through a basic transformation. It rid itself of the more fascist of its followers and eliminated the profascist elements in its program. First working closely with the student- and church-dominated group, the *Falange Socialista Boliviana* (FSB), the MNR had attempted to reestablish its contact with the officer corps allied to the FSB. Because of several key betrayals, every one of its revolt attempts was destroyed. It then rejected the officer alliances and support from the largely middle-class FSB and moved to incorporate the working-class movement. It already had the sympathy of the miners' union from its Villarroel days, and it now attempted to gain an important foothold in the industrial workers' unions of La Paz. Finding the POR already in control of the miners' FSTMB, it simply co-opted these leaders into the party and accepted the revolutionary logic of the Pulacayo thesis as well. The result was an unusual amalgam of the middle class and radical labor into a decidedly leftist position. The FSTMB, under the leadership of its secretary-general, Juan Lechín, provided the party with an important mass base as well as a revolutionary ideology. This was clearly revealed in the civil war of August and September 1949 when the MNR led an almost totally civilian and workers' revolt against the central regime, a revolt which would prove a model for the 1952 overthrow. In this revolt the army held firm to the government, but it still took almost two months to put down the revolution. In the ensuing action the mines were bombed and key workers' suburbs in La Paz were attacked.[44]

Though the MNR had by this time adopted an openly revolutionary and prolabor stand, it still retained its middle-class support, which grew with each passing year. Economic nationalism and inflation were two issues which had potent appeal, and the MNR fully exploited them. That the inflation issue was now an important one can be seen in the cost of living crisis which was developing in the last years of the 1940s (see table 1).

Though the civilian governments of Hertzog and Urriolagoitia (1947–

1951) attempted to meet this crisis and at the same time to destroy the labor movement, they were unable to generate middle-class support. By the time of the 1951 elections, the MNR was able to obtain over fifty-four thousand votes, a plurality victory, despite the continued exile of the MNR presidential candidate, Víctor Paz Estenssoro.[45] Thus by May of 1951 when the politicians of the Unified Republican parties, the

TABLE 1
Cost of Living Index and Exchange Rates

Year	Cost of Living	Exchange Rate of Bolivianos to U.S. Dollar
1938	100.0	30.14
1939	140.7	42.97
1940	164.3	49.30
1941	221.8	61.60
1942	287.1	71.16
1943	311.3	70.76
1944	335.1	74.65
1945	361.2	77.94
1946	418.2	82.28
1947	493.7	87.40
1948	510.6	85.36
1949	561.3	93.52
1950	762.1	125.05
1951	967.2	147.90
1952	1,170.3	176.11

Source: Comision Económica para América Latina, *El desarrollo económico de Bolivia* (Mexico, 1958), p. 298.

Partido de la Unión Republicana Socialista (PURS),[46] literally abandoned the presidency to the army generals, even the most conservative of the political leaders finally admitted the total bankruptcy of the traditional political system.

BOLIVIAN SOCIETY AND ECONOMY ON THE EVE OF THE NATIONAL REVOLUTION

As this political system was disintegrating, social and economic tensions were also mounting in Bolivia to the point where basic reforms were finally accepted as necessary evils by leading elements in society. Though growth of population and urbanization had been slow in the nineteenth century, the twentieth century had seen a major expansion of both trends in Bolivia. People living in towns of five thousand or over rose from 14 percent of the national population in 1900 to 23 percent of the population in 1950.[47] The growth of individual urban centers was even more dramatic, as can be seen in table 2.

This urban expansion was set against a background of declining agriculture. Even though 72 percent of the economically active population

TABLE 2
POPULATION INCREASES

Department and Capital City	1900	1950	% of Increase
La Paz	446,500	948,446	112.4%
La Paz	71,860 (est.)	267,000 (est.)	271.5
Cochabamba	328,200	490,455	49.5
Cochabamba	21,900	80,795	268.9
Oruro	86,100	210,260	144.2
Oruro	15,900	62,975	296.0
Potosí	320,500	534,399	66.7
Potosí	20,900	43,579	108.5
Chuquisaca	187,800	282,980	50.6
Sucre	20,900	40,128	92.0
Santa Cruz	202,700	286,145	41.1
Santa Cruz	18,300	42,746	133.5
Approx. total population	1,766,451	3,019,031	70.9%

Source: Averanga Mollinedo, *Aspectos generales de la población boliviana.*
Note: The populations of departments with unimportant cities have been excluded. Also the total populations given are the corrected totals for both census figures.

was still engaged in agriculture in 1950, it produced only 33 percent of the gross national product. At the same time agricultural production was actually falling behind national needs. Whereas food imports in the period from 1925 to 1929 represented only 10 percent of the total national imports, by 1950 the figure had risen to 19 percent.[48]

These figures reflect the stagnation and lack of capital investment which were due to the large pool of free Indian labor available to the rural landowners who were basically unwilling to invest in increased production, since their free labor source and a minimum production provided them with an adequate income without the need to invest capital. Thus the greater the size of the property, the smaller the area of land under cultivation, until the extreme of 0.5 percent utility on ten thousand or more hectares was reached (see table 3). This situation strongly supports the thesis that the Bolivian latifundia was primarily a labor control device rather than a land utilization system.[49]

Bolivia, of course, also suffered from what many persons consider one of the worst distortions in the pattern of land ownership in Latin America. Whereas only 2 percent of the national land area was in cultivation, 92 percent of this cultivated area was held in estates of one thousand hectares or more, and these estates were owned by only 6 percent of

TABLE 3
AGRICULTURAL OWNERSHIP OF CULTIVATED LANDS
1950

Size of Property (in Hectares)	Number of Proprietors	Total Owned (in Hectares)	Total Exploited (in Hectares)	% of Exploited to Owned
Less than 5	51,198	73,877	40,028	54.2%
5 to 49	19,503	278,459	86,378	31.0
50 to 199	5,014	478,291	76,090	15.9
200 to 999	4,033	1,805,405	134,790	7.4
1,000 to 4,999	4,000	8,724,776	167,006	1.9
5,000 to 9,999	797	5,146,334	55,365	1.0
10,000 or over	615	16,233,954	85,850	0.5
Total	85,160 [a]	32,741,096	645,506	1.9%

Source: Oficina Nacional de Estadística y Census, Seccion Agropecuario, *Censo national agropecuario de 1950*, mimeographed (La Paz, 1950).
  a. Total number of proprietors was actually 86,377 with 1,217 unknown.

the total number of landowners. The converse relationship of *minifundia* ("subsistence land plots") was also apparent in the fact that 94 percent of the landowners owned only 8 percent of the total cultivated land.

The exporting sector of the economy presented an equally depressing picture. The vital tin industry had seriously stagnated since the Great Depression despite short cycles of prosperity. From the late 1930s onward there was little capital investment in mining, and the major mines began to run into lower quality ore veins, having exhausted their richer and more easily accessible sources. Aging plants and the declining quality of the product forced the costs of production up to levels that were rapidly becoming noncompetitive except in a time of wartime shortages.[50] In fact, neither in terms of tonnage nor of the value of the product has

Bolivian mining ever achieved the peak reached in 1929 (see appendix table 5).

The only major advance in the economy since 1930 was in the small sector of manufacturing and then almost exclusively in light industry. During the 1930s and early 1940s there had been an important expansion in this sector, though by 1950 it still employed only 4 percent of the economically active population and accounted for only 9 percent of the GNP. Not only was the importance of manufacturing to the internal economy still minor in 1950, but it appears from almost all indicators that from the mid-1940s on there was a steady decline in productivity even in this sector, a decline that accelerated at an even greater pace after 1950. Thus, for example, six major industries (cotton, wool, flour, beer, cigarettes, and cement), whose employees increased from 2,727 to 4,981 between 1935 and 1950, saw an actual decline in productivity from 3,179 bolivianos per worker (at adjusted 1955 prices) to 2,705 bolivianos over the same period.[51]

This stagnation in the industrial sector of the economy is largely explained by the very low investment of capital which resulted in aging and largely unreplaced machinery. As a UN study concluded after an extensive analysis of this sector, capital input had been extremely low in the period from 1930 to 1935, "and a good part of it has been used to create productive capacity in new areas, without, at the same time, being sufficient to avoid an effective decapitalization of certain older enterprises." It noted that "the maintenance of machinery and equipment [in Bolivia] for periods which are much longer than those judged normal in other economies demands a permanent input of important amounts of capital in parts and replacements, in order to avoid a severe decline in productive capacity." But the study found that the capital invested during this period was insufficient to perform all these functions and concluded that "as a consequence of this lack of capital investment, [there is] an observable decline in the condition of maintenance of the machines and equipment." [52]

To this stagnation in mining, agriculture, and industry must be added the impact of inflation. Although inflation and the decline in the value of the boliviano had become constant features of Bolivian society from the late 1930s on, the pace of this change increased dramatically in the last three years before the revolution (see table 1 on page 40).

There is little question that economic stagnation and increasingly severe inflation were taking their political toll on the previously submissive middle-class elements who had continued to support the traditional elite until almost the very end. The stagnation of mining and manufacturing may also have had its impact by the 1950s on a tightening of economic opportunity even in the previously expanding positions open to middle-rank white-collar and upper-rank blue-collar employees, though there is little direct evidence on this. It does seem evident, however, that the very rapid rise in the cost of living after 1949 and the concomitant severe decline in the value of the national currency certainly persuaded large numbers of uncommitted elements of the middle class to support openly the increasingly revolutionary MNR or, at the least, to adopt a position of benevolent neutrality toward the party.

THE COMING OF THE REVOLUTION

With this sympathy of the middle-class elements the MNR was able to gain enormous strength, despite the lossees of the 1949 civil war, and to capture the leadership of the entire revolutionary movement. This is clearly seen in the total collapse of the last possible intermediary force between outright revolution and the traditional oligarchy, the much-tamed PIR. In the last months of 1949 and the early days of 1950, this once powerful party was finally destroyed. Frustrated by the constant involvement of the PIR with the oligarchy, with its deliberate attempts to destroy the FSTMB, and with the total collapse of its revolutionary position and leadership, the youth of the party decided irrevocably to destroy the party and form a new revolutionary group. Although succeeding by late 1949 in forcing the PIR into official opposition, rebels within the party, especially after the disasterous 1949 elections, failed in their attempt to change the party into an official *Partido Comunista de Bolivia* (PCB). Under the leadership of Ricardo Anaya and Miguel Bonifaz, the radicals were defeated in the central committee and the party retained its traditional name and program.[53] But the youth finally decided to strike out on their own, and on January 17, 1950, they created Bolivia's first publicly avowed Communist party.[54] At a meeting of the PIR in the following March, fifty-one militants of the youth branch of the party accused the leadership of being tools of the oligarchy and Yankee imperialism and threw their support to the PCB. Thereafter the PIR rapidly declined and was temporarily dissolved in July 1952.[55]

Meanwhile, by late 1950 the MNR tried one last major attempt at peacefully overthrowing the government and made preparations to run in the presidential elections of 1951. At their fifth national convention in February 1951 they selected Víctor Paz Estenssoro and Hernán Siles Zuazo as their candidates for president and vice-president.[56] The unity of the old antifascist alliance had finally been destroyed and even the PURS was being rocked by internal dissensions, so the MNR was able to make great headway. Instead of joining forces, the PURS, the Liberals, the PIR, the POR, and even an Aramayo-sponsored party all ran their own separate presidential lists. The result was an electoral landslide for the MNR. Paz Estenssoro, still in exile, received some 54,000 votes in the presidential elections of May 6 in comparison with 39,000 for the PURS candidate, 13,000 for the FSB, 6,500 for the Aramayo-sponsored slate, 6,400 for the Liberals, and only 5,100 votes for José Antonio Arze and the completely discredited PIR.[57] Since no candidate had obtained an absolute majority, the election was to be decided in Congress. But it was clear from the large margins of victory achieved by Paz, and also by Hernán Siles Zuazo in the separate vice-presidential elections, that the party would ultimately triumph.

But the army decided to intervene with the consent of the then president, Mamerto Urriolagoitia. On May 16 he renounced the presidency, and Gen. Ovidio Quiroga, chief of staff and one of the key military leaders in destroying the civil war of 1949, announced that a military junta was being established under the leadership of Gen. Hugo Ballivián. Justifying its moves on the grounds that the MNR was in league with the Communists, the all-military regime annulled the elections and declared an end to civilian government. Only the PURS and the FSB gave their support to the Ballivián military regime, and the government could do little to stop a revolution that everyone now believed to be inevitable. The MNR had never been loath to take by force what it could not achieve by ballot, and, now that it had been deprived of a legitimate electoral victory, it was only a matter of time before a revolutionary attempt would occur.

At the same time the army leadership began to disintegrate. Key generals like Terrazas and Quiroga went abroad, and within the government conservative and liberal military elements were alternately attempting to appease the workers or suppress their activity.[58] Thus important conciliatory gestures made by the junta throughout the rest of 1951 and early 1952 could find little support.

To this crisis in leadership and popular support was added a miners' boycott of a purchasing agreement with the U.S. Reconstruction Finance

Corporation for Korean War tin purchases. This strike seriously weakened the government's economic position despite the undoubtedly beneficial economic effect which that war was having on the Bolivian economy. With negotiations between the United States and the miners at a standstill, workers were thrown out of jobs and a short-lived but severe depression hit the country. In February 1952 there was a hunger march in La Paz in protest against the policies of the government, and by the end of the month internal dissension within the regime had reached such proportions that the minister of government, General Seleme, who was then head of the *carabineros* ("national police"), openly pledged his entire force to the coming MNR revolt. On April 9, 1952, when Seleme was suddenly dismissed from the junta on charges of plotting a revolt, the revolution finally began.

The MNR acted quickly. Profiting from its experiences in the 1949 civil war, it distributed arms to civilians and workers. With the support of the carabineros the city was quickly taken. But an initially united military stand against the revolution created deep-seated fear, and Seleme and many of his military followers sought asylum in foreign embassies late on April 9. The army's initial show of unity, however, was only temporary, for it no longer could offer any unified leadership. The majority of key officers left their troops and went into exile before the fighting had ended, and after some fierce but localized fighting, the army surrendered on April 11 to the Siles regime. Thus, after three days of fighting and at the cost of some six hundred lives, the MNR returned to power. [59]

But unlike the party during the period from 1943 to 1946, the MNR of 1952 was a newly amalgamated party of middle-class and worker elements and represented a new type of radical populist movement. Its years of revolutionary activity and skilled political maneuvering had led it to accept the revolutionary programs of the radical, Marxist POR. Abandoning its traditional fascism and economic orthodoxy, it rapidly moved in the months following the revolution to a totally revolutionary position. Giving up all pretense of working within the system, the MNR began its famous revolutionary restructuring of society under the first Paz Estenssoro presidency from 1952 to 1956.

Thus began the Bolivian National Revolution. Having created a powerful civilian revolutionary movement which had been bitterly opposed by the oligarchy and the army throughout the 1940s and early 1950s, the MNR leaders felt under no obligation to offer a moderate program or compromise with any traditional institution, either political or military. Soon not only the urban white and cholo classes but also the rural Indian masses were in possession of arms, and the army and the national police force were completely disorganized. The aims of the party were known to all, arms were in the hands of a militant populace, and the exiled leaders returning from abroad were not to be restrained. Thus began Latin America's most dynamic social revolution since the Mexican holocaust of 1910.

NOTES

1. For the latest analysis of the still poorly understood Tiahuanacan empire, see Edward P. Lanning, *Peru Before the Incas* (Englewood Cliffs, N.J., 1967), pp. 127 ff. Also see the classic summary by Wendell C. Bennett, "The Archeology of the Central Andes," *Handbook of South American Indians,* ed. Julian H. Steward, Smithsonian Institution, Bureau of American Ethnology Bulletin no. 143 (Washington, D.C., 1946), pp. 109–18.

2. For a survey of Aymara culture, see Harry Tschopik, Jr., "The Aymara," in *Handbook of South American Indians,* II, pp. 501–74; Weston La Barre, *The Aymara Indians of the Lake Titicaca Plateau, Bolivia,* American Anthropological Association Memoir no. 68 (Menasha, Wis., 1948); José Fellman Velarde, *Los imperios andinos* (La Paz, 1961); and the detailed study of the Lupaqa kingdom by John V. Murra, "An Aymara Kingdom in 1567," *Ethnohistory,* 15, no. 2 (Spring 1968), pp. 115–51. For material on the pre-Columbian eastern lowland tribes, see William M. Denevan, *The Aboriginal Cultural Geography of the Llanos de Mojos of Bolivia,* Ibero-Americana no. 48 (Berkeley, Calif., 1966).

3. Dirección General de Estadistica y Censos, *Censo demografico 1950* (La Paz, 1955), p. 108.

4. For the standard survey of Incan society, see John H. Rowe, "Inca Culture at the Time of the Spanish Conquest," in *Handbook of South American Indians,* pp. 183–330.

5. For information on the early years of Potosí mineral production, see the pioneer study by Alvaro Jara, "Dans le Pérou du XVIᵉ siècle: La coubre de production des métaux monnayables," *Annales, E.S.C.,* 23, no. 3 (Mai–Juin 1967), pp. 590–603. For a summary history of the city, see Lewis Hanke, *The Imperial City of Potosí* (Hague, 1956), and the detailed articles accompanying the Lewis Hanke and Gunnar Mendoza edition of Bartolomé Arzáns de Orsúa y Vela, *Historia de la villa imperial de Potosí,* 3 vols. (Providence, R.I., 1965).

6. In the late seventeenth and early eighteenth centuries Potosí was still the most important center for government revenue, producing for the crown between 35 percent and 44 percent of the total government income in the viceroyalty. See Michel Colin, *Le Cuzco a la fin du XVIIᵉ et au début du XVIIIᵉ siècle* (Caen, 1966), pp. 208–19, and tables 10–12.

7. According to the admittedly crude calculations made in 1879 by Adolfo Soetbeer, Bolivian silver production reached its peak by the end of the first two decades of

the seventeenth century. Production thereafter slowly declined until 1700 when it suddenly took a sharp downward plunge only recovering moderately in the middle decades of the eighteenth century. A new downward plunge occurred after 1800, with the worst years being the period from 1811 to 1830, after which a moderate increase took place in the period from 1831 to 1850 followed by a new severe depression in the period from 1851 to 1865. By the latter years of the 1860s the modern mining era had begun and production began to climb dramatically. Adolfo Soetbeer, *Edelmetall-Produktion und werthverhaltniss zwischen gold und silber seit der entdeckung Amerika's bis zur gegenwart* (Gotha, 1879), pp. 78–79.

8. Guillermo Céspedes del Castillo, *Lima y Buenos Aires, repercusiones económicas y políticas de la creación del virreinato del Plata* (Sevilla, 1947), pp. 10–11, 77, 80, 165. Also see Arthur P. Whitaker, *The Huancavelica Mercury Mine* (Cambridge, Mass., 1941), pp. 74 ff.

9. Edmond Temple, *Travels in Various Parts of Peru Including a Year's Residence in Potosí*, vol. 1 (London, 1830), pp. 308–10.

10. José Maria Dalence, *Bosquejo estadístico de Bolivia* (Chuquisaca, 1851), p. 295.

11. Ibid., pp. 278–79, 309–31, 315–16.

12. Adam Dunin Iundzill, *Du commerce bolivien, considérations sur l'avenir des relations entre l'Europe et la Bolivie* (Paris, 1856), pp. 10–14. Iundzill estimated that 68 percent of the final price of European goods in Sucre, the chief highland city served by Bolivia's only port of Cobija, was accounted for by mule transport from the coast.

13. Dalence, *Bosquejo estadístico*, pp. 361–62. Even as late as 1868 a contemporary noted that the discriminatory head tax on Indians provided "the best and most secure source for government income" (Ramón Sotomayor Valdés, *Estudio histórico de Bolivia bajo la administración del General D. José María de Achá* . . . [Santiago de Chile, 1874], p. 572). In the budgets published by Rojas (i.e., 1845, 1847, 1860, and 1864) the income from the Indian head tax never fell below 37 percent of the budget and was always the largest single source of income. Casto Rojas, *Historia financiera de Bolivia* (La Paz, 1916), pp. 182–83, 222–23, 246–47. As Rojas concluded after a survey of the first fifty years of republican financial history: "From 1825 to 1879 the development of government income was insignificant. The country, given over to continuous revolts which sterilized the most important fiscal reforms, did not advance much either in its financial organization or in the development of public or private wealth" (Ibid., p. 412).

14. For general surveys of this period, see the following standard works: Sotomayor Valdes, *Estudio histórico;* Jorge Basadre, *Chile, Perú y Bolivia independientes* (Barcelona, 1948); Alcides Arguedas, *Historia general de Bolivia (el proceso de la nacionalidad), 1809–1921* (La Paz, 1922); Enrique Finot, *Nueva historia de Bolivia (ensayo de interpretación sociológica)*, 2d ed. (La Paz, 1954); and Robert N. Burr, *By Reason or Force, Chile and the Balancing of Power in South America, 1830–1905* (Berkeley, Calif., 1965).

15. Soetbeer, *Edelmetall-Produktion*, pp. 78–79, and Bureau of the American Republics, *Bolivia*, Bulletin no. 55 (Washington, D.C., 1892), p. 60. This sudden burgeoning of the silver industry had an immediate impact on the entire Bolivian economy as well as on government income. Overnight Bolivia's trade deficit was turned into a trade surplus, and, by 1886, Bolivia was exporting more than twice as much as she imported in total value of goods. Ibid., pp. 87, 91.

16. On the conservative era and its accomplishments, see Herbert S. Klein, *Origenes de la revolución nacional boliviana* (La Paz, 1968), pp. 22 ff.

17. Dalence, *Bosquejo estadístico*, pp. 234–36; George McCutcheon McBride,

The Agrarian Indian Communities of Highland Bolivia (New York, 1921), pp. 20, 24–25; and Oficina Nacional de Inmigración, *Censo nacional de la población de la República, 1 de setembre de 1900,* 2 vols. (La Paz, 1902–1904).

18. Ibid., I, p. 132.

19. Rodolfo Soria Galvamo, *Ultimas dias del gobierno Alonso,* 2d ed. (Potosí, 1920).

20. Eduardo Lopez Rivas, *Esquema de la historia económica de Bolivia* (Oruro, 1955), pp. 13 ff.

21. For a detailed study of the early career of the leading tin magnate, see Herbert S. Klein, "The Creation of the Patiño Tin Empire," *Inter-American Economic Affairs,* 19, no. 2 (Autumn 1965), pp. 3–23.

22. The Liberal era is analyzed in great detail in Herbert S. Klein, *Parties and Political Change in Bolivia, 1880–1952* (Cambridge, 1969), chap. 2. For biographies of the key leading Liberals and Republicans of the period see David Alvéstegui, *Salamanca, su gravitación sobre el destino de Bolivia,* 3 vols. (La Paz, 1957–1962); and Benigno Carrasco, *Hernando Siles* (La Paz, 1961).

23. Aside from the works of Klein, Alvéstegui, and Carrasco on the period of the 1920s, consult Porfirio Diaz Machicao, *Historia de Bolivia, Saavedra, 1920–1925* (La Paz, 1945), and his *Historia de Bolivia, Guzman, Siles, Blanco Galindo, 1925–1931* (La Paz, 1955).

24. On the tin crisis, see K. E. Knorr, *Tin Under Control* (Stanford, Calif., 1945).

25. Crucial documents on the background to the war are contained in Eduardo Arze Quiroga, ed., *Documentos para una historia de la guerra del Chaco, seleccionados del archivo de Daniel Salamanca,* 3 vols. (La Paz, 1951–1960). The popular thesis propounded by both Bolivians and Paraguayans was that the Chaco War was caused by a conflict over the oil rich Chaco borderlands of Bolivia. The thesis holds that Royal Dutch Shell sided with and provoked Paraguay and that Standard Oil supported Bolivian intransigence. But this popular interpretation ignores some fundamental facts. To begin with, the oil lands of the Chaco were never claimed by Paraguay even in their most extreme demands before 1932. Secondly, the Standard Oil Company seriously hampered the Bolivian war effort and actually sold Bolivian oil to Paraguay (through Argentine intermediaries) during the conflict. Oil, in fact, only became an issue after the total collapse of the Bolivian armies enabled Paraguay to get within striking distance of the Bolivian oil fields. For a more complete exposition of my own interpretation of the origins of the Chaco conflict, see Klein, *Parties and Political Change in Bolivia,* chap. 5.

26. The best study of the war in any language is David H. Zook, Jr., *The Conduct of the Chaco War* (New York, 1960); also see Porfirio Diaz Machicao, *Historia de Bolivia, Salamanca, la guerra del Chaco, Tejado Sorzano, 1931–1936* (La Paz, 1955).

27. In 1930 the army had set up a temporary junta after the overthrow of the Siles government by civilian forces. But this was only a caretaker regime under General Blanco-Galindo created simply to oversee the presidential elections of that same year.

28. Herbert S. Klein, "David Toro and the Establishment of 'Military Socialism' in Bolivia," *Hispanic American Historical Review,* 45, no. 1 (February 1965), pp. 25–52; Augusto Céspedes, *El dictador suicida, 40 años de historia de Bolivia* (Santiago de Chile, 1956); and Porfirio Diaz Machicao, *Historia de Bolivia, Toro, Busch, Quintanilla, 1936–1940* (La Paz, 1957).

29. A detailed discussion of the confiscation conflict is contained in Herbert S. Klein, "American Oil Companies in Latin America: The Bolivian Experience," *Inter-American Economic Affairs,* 18, no. 2 (Autumn 1964), pp. 47–72.

30. The debates of the convention are analyzed in Herbert S. Klein, "Social Constitutionalism in Latin America; the Bolivian Experience," *The Americas*, 22, no. 3 (January 1966), pp. 258–76.

31. Aside from the previously cited works of Céspedes and Diaz Machicao, see Herbert S. Klein, "Germán Busch and the Era of 'Military Socialism' in Bolivia," *Hispanic American Historical Review*, 47, no. 2 (May 1967), pp. 166–84.

32. The *Partido Republicano Socialista* was the old Saavedra wing of the Republican party. It was given the socialist title in 1935 by Saavedra in an effort to win postwar radical and moderate reformist support. But the socialist tag was meaningless, and the party, by the time of Saavedra's death in 1939, was totally identified with the traditional prewar political parties.

33. Céspedes, *El dictador suicida,* p. 231.

34. The background of the founding congress and its first programs are presented in Frente de Izquierda Boliviano, *¡Hacia la unidad de las izquierdas bolivianas!* (Santiago de Chile, 1939), and Partido de la Izquierda Revolucionaria, *Programa y estatutos del Partido de la Izquierda Revolucionaria* (La Paz, 1941).

35. For information on the early history of the POR, see Guillermo Lora, *José Aguirre Gainsborg, fundador del P.O.R.* (La Paz, 1960). For the changing programs of the POR, PIR, MNR, and all the other leading Bolivian political parties in the twentieth century, see the two excellent source books of documents, Alberto Cornejo S., *Programas políticos de Bolivia* (Cochabamba, 1949); and Mario Rolón Anaya, *Política y partidos en Bolivia* (La Paz, 1966).

36. *El Diario* (La Paz), March 13, 1940.

37. The history of the labor movement in this period is best analyzed in Augustin Barcelli S., *Medio siglo de luchas sindicales revolucionarias en Bolivia, 1905–1955* (La Paz, 1955).

38. Ibid., pp. 161–64. For the government's version of the Catavi massacre see Juan Manuel Balcazar, *Los problemas sociales en Bolivia, una mistificación demagogica: La 'massacre' de Catavi* (La Paz, 1947).

39. On the founding of the MNR see Augusto Céspedes, *El presidente colgado (historia boliviana)* (Buenos Aires, 1966); and Luis Peñaloza, *Historia del movimiento nacionalista revolucionario, 1941–1952* (La Paz, 1963).

40. Porfirio Diaz Machicao, *Historia de Bolivia, Peñaranda, 1940–1943* (La Paz, 1958), pp. 102–03.

41. The *Federación Sindical de Trabajadores Mineros de Bolivia* (FSTMB) was founded at Huanuni in June 1944 by some thirty delegates meeting at the first successful national mine workers' congress. Claiming some sixty thousand members, the FSTMB elected Juan Lechín as its first secretary-general. Barcelli, *Medio siglo de luchas sindicales,* pp. 165–66.

42. The best account of the Villarroel period is contained in Céspedes, *El presidente colgado.*

43. The *Tesis de Pulacayo,* a Trotskyite document proposing a permanent revolution led by the miners, was approved as official FSTMB ideology at the third national miners' congress meeting at the mining town of Pulacayo in November 1946. The thesis is reprinted in Guillero Lora, ed., *Programa obrero* (La Paz, 1963).

44. The best study of this period is Peñaloza, *Historia del MNR.* For information on the POR rationalization for its alliance with the MNR, see Guillermo Lora, "Revolution and Counter-Revolution in Bolivia, the Great Decade of Class Struggles," *Fourth International* (New York), 13, no. 3 (May–June 1952).

45. Peñaloza, *Historia del MNR,* p. 248.

46. The PURS, officially founded in 1946, was an amalgam of the old Salamanca and Saavedra wings of the 1914 Republican party. After the death of Saavedra in 1939, these two groups found themselves in almost constant cooperation. They joined with the Liberals in signing the Concordancia of that year and even temporarily united into a unified party with the PURS title. However, during the early 1940s the parties operated somewhat independently, and, after the Villarroel overthrow, they finally resolved to terminate their separate existences. From 1946 to 1952 the PURS controlled the presidency, enjoying the support of the PIR and the Liberal party.

47. Olen E. Leonard, *Bolivia, Land, People and Institutions* (Washington, D.C., 1952), p. 41; and Isidoro Alonso et al., *La iglesia en Peru y Bolivia, estructuras sociales* (Friburg and Bogota, 1962), p. 159.

48. Comisión Económica para América Latina, *El desarrollo económico de Bolivia* (also known as *Análisis y proyecciónes del desarrollo económico*), no. 4 (Mexico, 1958), p. 41 (hereafter cited as CEPAL).

49. This is the thesis proposed by William F. Carter in *Aymara Communities and the Bolivian Agrarian Reform,* University of Florida Monographs in the Social Sciences no. 24 (Gainesville, Fla., 1964).

50. CEPAL, p. 44.

51. Ibid., p. 128, cuadro 82.

52. Ibid., p. 123.

53. Miguel Bonifaz, *Bolivia, frustración y destino* (Sucre, 1965), pp. 176–77.

54. Partido Comunista de Bolivia, *Primer congreso nacional del P.C.B.,* documentos (La Paz, 1959), p. 92.

55. Bonifaz, *Bolivia,* pp. 177–80. In June of 1956 the PIR was refounded under the leadership of Ricardo Anaya as an essentially moderate reformist party. For the refounding declarations see Partido de la Izquierda Revolucionaria, *P.I.R. y desarrollo nacional, soluciones para los problemas nacionales* (La Paz, 1961), pp. 51 ff.

56. Peñaloza, *Historia del MNR,* p. 241.

57. Ibid., p. 248.

58. Ibid., pp. 250 ff.

59. Ibid., chaps. 21–22.

COLE BLASIER

University of Pittsburgh

The United States
and the Revolution

The Bolivian Revolution is the only genuine social revolution to which the United States provided early and sustained support. From 1952 to 1964 the United States provided more per capita economic assistance to Bolivia than to any other Latin American country.[1] In 1957 the United States provided a direct subsidy constituting more than 30 percent of the Bolivian government's central budget, and such payments were continued in lesser amounts for years. In at least one sense, the United States was deeply involved for a dozen years in making the Bolivian Revolution "work."

The U.S. government's response to the Bolivian Revolution contrasts sharply with its behavior toward almost all other important revolutionary movements. The United States sent armed forces against revolutionary movements in Mexico, Russia, and the borders of China. The Central Intelligence Agency (CIA) sponsored exile groups in their armed attacks against the revolutionary governments in Guatemala and Cuba. The Yugoslav Communists considered the United States one of their bitterest enemies until their break with Stalin, after which the United States began to provide important economic assistance to the revolutionary regime.

The author is indebted to the works and comments of Carter Goodrich, James Malloy, and Richard Thorn, and to William D. Broderick for his careful reading of the manuscript. My appreciation is expressed to the many Bolivians and U.S. officials who took valuable time to talk to me. Acknowledgment should also be made of the pioneering scholarship of Robert J. Alexander, Dwight B. Heath, and Richard Patch.

The exceptional nature of the U.S. involvement in Bolivia and the social significance of the revolution itself are sometimes minimized by those who claim that the Bolivian experience was not really very revolutionary. It is true that governmental control was retained by relatively moderate elements and the revolution has been accurately characterized as restrained, yet it would be a mistake to underestimate the sweeping social changes that took place in Bolivia, particularly in view of the nature of the Bolivian economy and polity before 1952.

If one is prepared to risk gross comparisons, it is reasonable to maintain that the Bolivian Revolution was almost as radical in its first dozen years as most contemporary social revolutions, with the clear exceptions of those in China and Cuba. The criteria here are the comprehensiveness and velocity of social change. Land reform went further in fourteen years in Bolivia than in twenty in Mexico. The nationalization of the large tin mines was relatively more significant in Bolivia than the nationalization of oil and other industrial properties in Mexico. And remember that even in Russia the genuine radicalization of the revolution did not occur until the introduction of forced collectivization and industrialization some dozen years after the 1917 Bolshevik coup.

Deeply influenced by Marxism, the Bolivian revolutionary program contained most of the elements of other revolutionary programs that have alarmed conservative circles in the United States:

1. Destruction of the economic and political power of the large landowning class by distribution of land to the peasants
2. Destruction of the economic and political power of the mining and financial elite through the nationalization of the large tin mines
3. Government ownership or regulation in other important sectors of the economy
4. Assumption of control of the central government by an alliance of organized labor, progressive members of the middle class, and the peasantry
5. An antiimperialist position in foreign relations, including a highly critical attitude toward the United States

There would, then, be sufficient cause for comment even if the United States had only maintained normal diplomatic and commercial relations with Bolivia. Such a bilateral relationship would have seemed mild as contrasted with the violent and embittered conflict that has characterized U.S. relationships with most revolutionary regimes. But U.S.-Bolivian relations became so intimate that their collaboration may have been closer than that between any other two countries in the hemisphere.

Let us, then, examine how the United States and Bolivia came to reconcile what appear to be traditionally conflicting interests. We shall also see the form their collaboration took and the impact of U.S. policies on the Bolivian Revolution.

THE MNR VERSUS IMPERIALISM

Attitudes critical of imperialism in the less developed countries, that is, opposition to economic and political domination by advanced industrial countries, are formed in many ways. Such attitudes often emerge early in university or other intellectual circles in the search for theories to explain social phenomena, or they may be precipitated by professional agitators, such as members of the international Communist movement, who have long sought to heighten and capitalize on these attitudes politically.

Both of these influences were at work in Bolivia long before the 1952 insurrection, with the Marxists among the first to voice these attitudes. The Bolivian Trotskyites nurtured their antiimperialism in an academic, debating society milieu. Other Marxists of a Stalinist persuasion used these attitudes to support the Soviet line, but their case was vitiated by public uncertainty as to whether their allegiance was primarily to Bolivia or to the Soviet Union.

One of the strongest of the antiimperialist parties by the early 1940s was the *Movimiento Nacionalista Revolucionario* (MNR), whose antiimperialist position seems to stem from deeper local roots. The leaders of the MNR had relatively little interest in the balance of power in the world, the forces of imperialism, or the Soviet Union. Their antiimperialism grew out of their personal experiences in and concern for Bolivia and was, therefore, the external face of the MNR's nationalism.

The brunt of the MNR's nationalist, antiimperialist attack was against the "tin barons" who controlled Bolivia's major industry and source of foreign exchange. Yet, its concern was not narrowly industrial. It held the tin barons responsible for the malaise of the whole society: the declining output of tin, stagnation in agricultural and industrial development, poverty, and social injustice. The tin barons, together with their allies, the "feudal oligarchy" who controlled the Bolivian countryside, composed the ruling elite, the *Rosca,* a term used to emphasize this group's exploitation of the people. Because the Rosca controlled the cities and the government as well, the MNR charged that it flaunted the formal machinery of government and constituted a superstate. Thus, the MNR's objectives were to bring it down by gaining control of the government and the tin mines, ending the exploitation of Bolivia by the Rosca and the international interests with which it was allied.

The linkage between the tin barons and imperialism requires an explanation. Control of the large tin mines was not vested in huge European or North American corporations that were operating branches in Bolivia in the fashion of oil companies in Venezuela or copper companies in Chile. Two of the three largest tin magnates, Simón Patiño and Carlos Víctor Aramayo, were Bolivians, and the third, Mauricio Hochschild, immigrated to Bolivia from Germany in 1911. But the three groups were incorporated abroad: the Patiño group in the United States, the Aramayo group in Switzerland, and the Hochschild group in Chile and Argentina. In addition, ownership was considered foreign because

the Bolivian majority stockholders of the enterprises in question generally resided abroad, and dividend payments due them were paid abroad. Thus, the enterprises were nominally considered foreign-owned and were treated as such under the Bolivian exchange control regulations.[2]

Moreover, Bolivia was desperately dependent on foreign markets to sell tin, and so prices were often controlled by foreign governments. In fact, since the ores were worthless unless they could be smelted and Bolivia did not have a major tin smelter under the MNR governments, the country was dependent on European or U.S. refineries. As a result, the MNR linked tin mining with international interests and imperialism.

The MNR's antiimperialism was more diffuse than that of revolutionary movements in many other countries. Revolutionaries in Mexico and later in Cuba could easily identify specific North American companies as well as the U.S. government as the major antagonists. In Bolivia, however, the MNR did not direct its attack at indigenous U.S. or European corporations or, in any important way, at the original tin barons as personalities. Most of the latter were either dead, too old, or too remote for that sort of attention. Instead, the MNR leveled its attack against an exploitive, corrupt, and outdated social system. Finally, it was difficult to single out a specific foreign country for criticism since the ore was refined in Great Britain, Western Europe, or the United States and sold in widely scattered markets.

Antiimperalism rapidly gathered momentum in Bolivia in the late 1930's just as the future leaders of the MNR were entering politics. Surprisingly, the imperialist issue was raised not so much because of a direct clash with an imperialist government but, rather, as a result of Bolivia's defeat in the Chaco War by its small neighbor Paraguay. The latent strength of antiimperialist sentiment during the tragic years of the war was evident in the widely held but unsubstantiated belief that rivalry between two U.S. and British petroleum companies, Standard Oil and Royal Dutch Shell, caused the conflict.[3]

National resentment against the ruling groups in Bolivia, who were held responsible for the Chaco War disaster, ran high as the public sought scapegoats. The first was the incumbent government, which was overthrown in 1936 by a group of young Chaco War veterans. Among the veterans' collaborators were the future leaders of the MNR. The new president, Colonel David Toro, who gave his administration the label of "military socialism," was in favor of controls over the tin mines, but Standard Oil of New Jersey provided a more convenient and less hazardous target. On March 13, 1937, President Toro annulled the petroleum concession of the Standard Oil Company and seized its properties. This action was partly the result of a national charge that the company was guilty of tax evasion and illegally exporting oil to Argentina, and partly due to the government's feeling that the company had not provided needed assistance during the war. It appeared that the government's antiimperialist stand tempered national frustrations and disappointments over the Bolivian defeat in the war.[4]

Many of the men who later founded and led the MNR were among the sponsors and supporters of the Standard Oil seizure. The socialist group with which Carlos Montenegro was associated influenced Toro's confiscation decree.[5] Víctor Paz Estenssoro, himself a veteran of the Chaco War, was undersecretary of the treasury in the Toro government. Elected deputy to Congress in 1938 and 1940, Paz spoke out strongly in defense of the nation's resources (linking oil with the tin question) and supported the efforts of the subsequent Busch regime to control the large tin companies and enforce the decree against Standard Oil.[6] The future leaders of the MNR charged that Standard Oil's demand for compensation of its losses was actually an attempt to recover possession of its oil rights and properties, and they signed a manifesto in July 1941 opposing as inadmissable and intolerable any change in the disposition of the case.[7] The MNR leaders stuck firmly to their guns partly because the oil dispute was related to their antiimperialist position on tin, which was to them a more important matter. They held that Bolivia should control its own natural resources, not suffer exploitation by foreign countries.

This fierce and open opposition to Standard Oil's claims brought the MNR group into direct conflict with the U.S. government. The United States was not concerned simply with securing compensation for a private U.S. company, the Bolivian oil controversy had far wider political and strategic implications. As war clouds gathered in Europe, the United States was concerned about access to oil in the Western Hemisphere, and the Bolivian confiscation set a disturbing precedent for negotiations in Venezuela and elsewhere. Moreover, the United States needed a good working relationship with the Bolivian government in order to insure easy access to tin, since the Asian sources of supply were first threatened and later cut off during the war. After hostilities broke out in Europe, the United States became increasingly preoccupied with the control of Axis nationals in Latin America. To encourage cooperation in continental defense, Washington was prepared to provide extensive economic assistance to Bolivia, a gesture which proved awkward in the face of the latter's refusal to cooperate in the matter of the confiscated Standard Oil property.

Tempted by the prospects of economic assistance and less committed to the move against Standard Oil than its predecessor governments, the Peñaranda administration, which took office in 1940, sought a compromise with the United States. But, unable to command a majority in the Congress, Peñaranda feared flying in the face of political opposition, including the MNR group, especially in view of public sentiments against giving in to Standard Oil.

THE UNITED STATES VERSUS THE MNR

Thus, as the world conflict deepened by the early summer of 1941, the United States appeared to have reached an impasse in its efforts to come to an agreement with the Bolivian government. Both governments were seeking a pretext for resolving the dispute over the Standard Oil properties in order for Bolivia to participate in hemispheric defense and the accompanying economic benefits. The so-called "Nazi putsch" episode of July 1941 set the stage for the realization of these objectives.

The origin of the episode was an alleged plot to overthrow the Bolivian government. The conspirators were supposed to have been Maj. Elías Belmonte, then Bolivian military attaché in Berlin, and the German minister in La Paz, Ernst Wendler. The charge was based on a photocopy of an alleged letter from Belmonte to Wendler in which the former described the plans for the coup. Douglas Jenkins, the U.S. minister in La Paz, turned the photocopy over to the minister of foreign relations, Alberto Ostria Gutiérrez, on July 18, 1941.[8] The letter declared that "the time is approaching to carry out our coup to liberate my poor country from a weak government of completely capitalist inclinations." The letter also recommended that the coup take place in the middle of July and proposed the concentration of "our forces" in Cochabamba.[9]

Belmonte was an army major who had opposed the pre–Chaco War leadership and exercised considerable influence as minister of government in the administration of President Germán Busch. He called for an authoritarian state for Bolivia in view of the low cultural and political level of the people. He was a long-standing critic of Standard Oil and saw the hand of the company behind attempts to discredit him with President Busch.[10]

On the basis of the document supplied by Jenkins and taking into account political and security considerations, the Peñaranda government declared the German minister *persona non grata* and expelled him from the country. The government declared a state of siege throughout Bolivia to cope with the supposed insurrectionary threat and, under its new emergency powers, closed three periodicals, including the daily *La Calle,* published by three of the leaders of the MNR. Armando Arze, Carlos Montenegro, and Augusto Céspedes were arrested, and the government used the opportunity to accuse the MNR group of fascism. The suppression of the publications and the arrests of their editors temporarily silenced some of the government's (and Standard Oil's) most vocal critics, thereby establishing a more propitious climate for settling the Standard Oil problem and collaboration with the United States against the Axis.

Two weeks after the alleged letter was released, on August 1, 1941, the United States proposed a long-term plan of collaboration to develop the Bolivian economy and natural resources, including highway development, agricultural diversification, and the expansion of tin output.[11] The La Paz press interpreted the proposal as an indication of favorable prospects for a large loan from the United States. Thus, the U.S. announcement appeared to be a means of rewarding a country which had taken a firm public stand against German influence in the Americas.

An examination of the historical record now suggests that the alleged Belmonte-Wendler letter was not authentic, that there was no Nazi plot to take over Bolivia, and that the charges of Nazism against the MNR were exaggerated, if not completely false.[12] But even if the U.S. revelation of the alleged letter was not expressly directed against the MNR group, the latter proved to be its victims, since the charge of Nazi-fascism against the MNR leaders stuck for more than a decade afterward.

Some five months later, on December 7, 1941, the Japanese attack on Pearl Harbor established a climate of sympathy for the United States in La Paz which facilitated a final resolution of the Standard Oil dispute and Bolivian collaboration in the joint defense effort. At an inter-American meeting in Rio de Janeiro on January 27, 1942, the Bolivian government and the Standard Oil Companies of Bolivia and of New Jersey reached an agreement providing for the payment of $1.5 million, plus accummulated interest, to the New Jersey company for its rights, interests, and property in Bolivia. On the very next day, January 28, a $25 million economic development program for Bolivia, to be financed by the United States, was also announced in Rio. That program was based on a report by Merwin L. Bohan, an official of the Department of State. Ironically, many of his group's recommendations were incorporated into the developmental strategy of the MNR government after 1952.[13] In spite of continuing criticism from such MNR leaders as Víctor Paz Estenssoro, the Bolivian government ultimately carried out its part of the agreement for compensating Standard Oil.

The lingering repercussions of the Nazi putsch episode were felt once again in December 1943 when a group of young military officers assisted the MNR leadership in the overthrow of President Peñaranda and the installation of Gualberto Villarroel as head of the Bolivian government. The new government desperately needed U.S. recognition so that negotiations for the sale of tin could continue, but the United States was deeply suspicious of the Villarroel administration and particularly of the participation in the cabinet of three MNR leaders. Despite the new government's efforts to dispel U.S. fears of Nazi influence, the State Department announced that considerations of hemispheric security were relevant to the recognition of the new regime and a determination would be made "whether outside influence unfriendly to the allied cause played any part [in the coup]." [14]

These fears proved so great that the United States refused to recognize the new government and succeeded in persuading all other American governments, except Argentina, not to do so until Villarroel had purged his cabinet of its MNR members. In a confidential document to other governments, the United States charged the MNR with anti-Semitism, hostility to democracy, fascist-oriented programs, connections with Nazi groups in Germany and Argentina, and Axis financial support.[15] Although Nazi ideas had influenced some MNR leaders and their military associates,[16] an examination of the historical record indicates that many of these charges were misleading, exaggerated, or false.[17] The MNR program, for example, charged the Jews who had immigrated to Bolivia from Europe with bribery, speculation, fraud, etc., but there appears to be no evidence that the MNR group, many of whose members themselves were mestizos, shared Hitler's views about the inferiority of the non-Aryan races.[18]

The effect of the U.S. charges on the Villarroel administration was as profound as it was on the political fortunes of the young MNR group. Thus it was not until June 23, 1944, some two months after the MNR cabinet members had resigned, that the United States extended formal recognition to the Villarroel government. The political impact of the U.S. charges against the MNR deepened in February 1946 when Washington made public its Blue Book on the Argentine situation. Although the book was directed primarily against the Perón regime in Argentina, the MNR party (once again a part of the Villarroel cabinet) was charged publicly with anti-Semitism and fascism.[19] Already beset by numerous domestic and international problems, the Villarroel administration was rapidly losing its grip on the country, and the charges in the U.S. Blue Book merely strengthened the hand of the opposition which overthrew Villarroel on July 21, 1946.

The anti-Nazi and antifascist policies of the United States resulted in the imprisonment of MNR leaders in July 1941, forced their withdrawal from the Villarroel administration's cabinet in 1944, and caused them to be charged with Nazi involvement as late as February 1946 while the MNR was still a part of the incumbent Villarroel administration. Clearly, U.S. policies had enormous repercussions on the fortunes of the MNR years before it assumed leadership in 1952. During the next six years, 1946–1952, the MNR leadership, often in exile, intensified its political and conspiratorial activities, immensely increasing its popular support which ultimately allowed the party to sieze control of the machinery of government.

U.S. RECOGNITION OF THE 1952 MNR GOVERNMENT

The causes of the 1952 revolutionary upheaval were domestic. The pre-1952 social structure and the power relationships that sustained it were based on the mining and export of tin ore. This was originally a fairly viable system since the profits were sufficient to support the managerial and service groups in the urban centers and the miners lacked the strength to change the system. Later, as the tin content of the ore gradually dropped lower and lower and Bolivia lost its position in the world tin market, the economic base of the old social system crumbled.

The rapid succession of presidents and cabinet ministers during the sexenio was a symptom of the weakness of the traditional political parties and their growing lack of popularity in the cities, to which was added the ferment of the increasingly powerful and recalcitrant labor unions. The decline of the ruling groups, growing discontent in the cities, and revolutionary turmoil in the mines all combined in the overthrow of the traditional parties in 1952.

While domestic causes were the source of the social upheaval in Bolivia, they were still intimately linked in the public mind with foreign relations. Not only did Bolivia depend on foreign markets, often controlled by foreign governments, for the sale of its principal exports, but the large tin magnates lived abroad as well, and profits flowed from the country to them. An aroused and frustrated nationalistic leadership found it convenient, if not always accurate, to attribute many of Bolivia's ills to foreign causes.

In the months preceding the April 1952 insurrection, Bolivia was once again faced with a chronic economic crisis, for the foreign demand for tin and the resultant high prices generated by the Korean War fell off. In 1951 negotiations between the Bolivian mining companies and Stuart Symington of the Reconstruction Finance Corporation (RFC) had reached an impasse as Symington sought to drive prices down from the Korean War highs by offering only $1.12 a pound. The Bolivians initially held out for $1.50 on the ground that they could not afford to sell below production costs, but by October Bolivian ore had begun to pile up in Chilean and Peruvian ports. The U.S. State Department, concerned about the political repercussions of the impasse, was reportedly hopeful that the RFC, which came under new leadership in early 1952, would soon reach an agreement with the Bolivians. The crisis, however, continued and the economic impact on Bolivia by the following March was described as disastrous, further depressing the already low standards of living. Especially critical was the effect on the national diet since Bolivia used its tin revenues to buy agricultural products abroad. No agreement had yet been reached on April 9, 1952, when the insurrection occurred.

The breakdown in negotiations with the United States on tin exports and the resulting popular discontent generated by the crisis facilitated the MNR's siezure of government, but the MNR was not inclined to have the revolution explained solely in terms of U.S. intransigence on tin sales. Paz Estenssoro said that to assert that the revolution succeeded simply because negotiations with the United States had broken down reflected a "shallow and superficial understanding of Bolivian problems." [20] The impasse over tin sales, however, did pose an extremely serious problem for the new MNR government since negotiations could not be resumed, even if agreement were possible, until the United States recognized the new regime.

Prospects for a cordial relationship between Washington and the new men in La Paz were not good in April 1952. The MNR leaders were the very same men whom Washington had tagged as Nazis during World War II and whom it had forced out of the Villarroel government in 1944. Party leaders, who made no secret of the Marxist influence on their party program, were strongly critical of U.S. imperialism and had enjoyed the support of the Communist party in the 1951 elections. Also, their vaguely leftist program, including proposals for the nationalization of the tin mines, disturbed conservative circles in Washington aroused by the anti-Communist campaigns of Senator Joseph McCarthy.

The MNR, however, did have some things in its favor. First and foremost, Paz Estenssoro had won a plurality in the 1951 elections; thus he had a constitutional claim to the office. While strong on revolutionary rhetoric, the MNR, with its right, left, and center factions, was not committed to a specific and detailed revolutionary program. The overthrow of the old regime in April 1952 was primarily an urban insurrection lasting only a few days and with relatively little loss of life; revolutionary transformations took place many months later.

As a result the United States was not faced with the question of whether to recognize a revolutionary regime in Bolivia since that revolution had not yet taken place. The major question seemed to be whether the MNR was in firm control and would respect Bolivia's international obligations. For example, the U.S. State Department was described as pondering whether the Paz-Siles administration would be able to control Juan Lechín and other labor radicals. Would Bolivia's neighbors, Chile, Peru, and Brazil, recognize the new government? (Argentina recognized it promptly.) Would the MNR respect civil liberties, especially in view of what appeared to be de facto suppression of the La Paz daily, *La Razón,* controlled by the Aramayo mining interests?

All of these considerations may have been secondary, since the major concern of the United States appears to have been whether the MNR government would nationalize the large tin mines and if so, whether it would provide prompt and fair compensation to stockholders. Also, the delay in U.S. recognition may have been caused by "concern over possible Argentine influence in Bolivia." [21] Obviously, the refusal to negotiate further tin purchases, which the withholding of recognition implied, gave the United States immense leverage.

Having suffered through the ordeal of nonrecognition in 1944, the MNR leadership made a great effort from the very first moments after the insurrection succeeded on April 12, 1952, to calm U.S. fears and pave the way for early recognition and, most important, continued U.S. purchases of tin. Within hours of becoming provisional president, Siles Zuazo promised a peaceful government that would respect international agreements and private property.[22] On April 16 the new foreign minister, Wálter Guevara Arze, formally requested U.S. recognition in a note to the American Embassy.[23] On his triumphant return from abroad, Paz Estenssoro reaffirmed the MNR's plans to nationalize the large tin mines, but he was careful to point out that this goal would not be done hurriedly, expressing a desire to reach an agreement about nationalization with the mineowners.[24] Siles was quoted early in May that the MNR was the last bulwark against communism and was independent of Moscow, Buenos Aires, and Washington.[25] He went on to distinguish nationalization from confiscation and to express his desire for the friendship and understanding of the American government and people. At the same time he gave formal assurances that his government proposed to meet the international obligations contracted by Bolivia "in the fullest sense." [26]

Meanwhile, the MNR government was building its bridges abroad with the help of the United Nations technical assistance mission headed by Dr. Carter Goodrich, then of Columbia University, who had arrived the year before the April revolution, when the mission was invited to Bolivia under an agreement negotiated with the pre-1952 government. Dr. Goodrich met secretly with Hernán Siles the February before the insurrection,[27] and the relationship established then facilitated the renegotiation of the UN mission's subsequent arrangements in Bolivia. Dr. Goodrich's willingness to work with the new government, his continued support of the mission's program at UN headquarters, and his persuasiveness with the new administration speeded the establishment of normal relations with the outside world. The fact that he was an American citizen as well may also have had some bearing on Washington's ultimate acceptance of the new government.

The United States formally recognized the MNR government on June 2, 1952, some seven weeks after the MNR siezed power, noting that the new government was in control of its national territory and had agreed to live up to its international obligations. Washington was quick to point out, however, that its recognition did not imply any judgment of Bolivian domestic problems,[28] but, in fact, the State Department agreed to recognize the MNR government only after it had been assured that compensation would be paid for the expropriated mining properties. Paz and Siles had already publicly expressed their intention to provide this compensation; moreover, it is likely that they privately made firm commitments to Washington in this regard. The sensitivity of the whole tin question is shown by Paz's announcement, only some twenty-four hours after the U.S. recognition, establishing a monopoly of all mineral exports. The government thereby took control of all foreign receipts for mineral exports.

The United States' grudging recognition of the Paz government eliminated a grave liability to the MNR regime and gave it a new lease on life. Formal communications between Bolivia and the United States were resumed, and, most important, the Bolivians were able to reopen their direct appeals for a long-term contract to sell tin at favorable prices. Ambassador Edward Sparks, a career foreign service officer, arrived in La Paz on June 3, 1952, the day after recognition was granted, and, thereafter, played an important role in strengthening U.S. ties with the new government. In September the United States bought up all available Bolivian tin not yet contracted for sale.

THE COMMUNIST ISSUE

During World War II the MNR was forced to defend itself against charges of Nazism. In the postwar period its critics sought to label it Communist, and Alfredo Cándia actually wrote a book on the subject entitled, *Bolivia, un experimento comunista en América.*[29] The MNR was forced to deal with this charge not only because of its profound implications for U.S.-Bolivian relations but also because of the widespread suspicion of the international Communist movement among nationalistic groups in Bolivia. Some friends of the MNR may have wished to dismiss the charge of communism as just another wild and irresponsible attack which some political leaders in Latin America continue to make against almost anybody. But there were good reasons for the MNR to deal seriously with these attacks because Marxist influence was apparent in the MNR's political platform and the Communists supported the MNR at several critical junctures.

The MNR program of 1942 reflects vaguely and imperfectly Marx's ideas about the class struggle, socialist uses of the state, and Lenin's ideas on imperialism. When Paz Estenssoro was a member of Congress in the early 1940s, he said, "I believe that Marxism is the best instrument for interpreting national realities," and expressed his agreement with the Marxist thesis that capitalism would eventually disappear.[30] In his view capitalism no longer served its original creative purposes in Bolivia and had been converted into an "instrument of international exploitation." Imperialism, its later form, would lead to "economic penetration, political action, and military invasion." [31]

Despite the Marxist influence on the MNR, there were several political parties in Bolivia oriented toward or associated with the various international Communist movements long before as well as after the MNR was founded. The first of these was the Trotskyite *Partido Obrero Revolucionario* (POR) founded abroad during the Chaco War. In late 1938 the POR issued its program and party statutes, affirming that the party was subject to the "democratic centralism" of the Fourth International.[32] Although not qualifying initially as a national section, by 1953 it was identified as the Bolivian Section of the Fourth International. The POR supported the MNR slate in the 1951 presidential elections, and after the April 1952 insurrection, the POR gave "critical support" to the MNR government, that is, it supported the government's efforts against "imperialism" and "reaction" while retaining the right of independent "constructive" criticism.[33] From 1952 on, some Trotskyites joined the MNR.

Politically more important was the *Partido de la Izquierda Revolucionaria* (PIR) originally led by the well-known and colorful José Antonio Arze and founded as an "independent Marxist party" in 1940. The date was too late for the PIR to play a role in the Third Communist International. The Comintern's last World Congress was in 1935, Soviet attention was totally absorbed by the German attack in 1941, and the Comintern was dissolved in 1943. Moreover the PIR did not consider it expedient to affiliate formally with the international Communist movement.[34] However, during World War II and thereafter the PIR followed the Soviet line, first supporting the Nazi-Soviet pact and later supporting the close collaboration between socialists and capitalists in Bolivia. In 1944, for example, Paz Estenssoro took Ricardo Anaya, a leader of the PIR, to task for his "collaborationist position" as being in conflict with the PIR's professed Marxist position.[35] After the war the PIR placed the United States at the head of the war camp and the USSR as the leader of the peaceful forces.[36]

During the 1940s the MNR and the PIR became bitter enemies competing for popular support among working- and middle-class elements. When the PIR leader, José Antonio Arze, sought admission to the Villarroel government in January 1944, his overture to the new administration, in the form of an open letter published in the press, was rejected. It is of interest, in this connection, that the Villarroel government's first special representative in Washington, Enrique Sanchez de Lozada, sought Arze's inclusion in the Villarroel cabinet. His proposal in this respect appears to be related to his strenuous efforts to secure U.S. recognition. Apparently he and others believed that José Antonio Arze's inclusion in the new cabinet, especially because of the latter's known pro-Soviet position, would quiet U.S. fears of the Nazi threat in Bolivia and improve the prospects of the new regime for recognition. Several weeks later Sanchez de Lozada, under suspicion for his maneuvers with regard to Arze, was replaced in Washington by Fernando Iturralde.[37]

Thereafter, the PIR joined the opposition against the Villarroel government and was active in the political movements which led to the overthrow of the Villarroel regime in July 1946.[38] The PIR associated closely with the traditional parties who controlled the succeeding government and was briefly represented in the Hertzog cabinet. Association with the right and, thus, with the repressions of the sexenio period (1946–1952) largely destroyed the popular following of the PIR and by 1950 the once strong popular party was in a shambles. The PIR leader, José Antonio Arze, received scarcely more than five thousand votes in the 1951 presidential elections.

During the 1940s the PIR was considered the Stalinist vehicle in Bolivia; but its persistence in pursuing the antifascist alliance after 1946, apart from being a serious strategic error in terms of its own following, may have alienated the leaders of the international Communist movement. The latter, it may be recalled, repudiated Earl Browder and other Communists who looked to a long-term reconciliation with capitalism. In any case, Soviet scholars have passed a harsh judgment on the PIR as a "petit bourgeois party" whose leadership was dominated by "opportunistic elements." [39]

Some fifty-one young members of the disintegrating PIR founded the Communist party of Bolivia in January 1950.[40] In July 1952, after the successful MNR insurrection, the PIR was formally dissolved and many of the remnant members formed a second Communist party. These two groups merged to form a single Communist party in December 1952.[41]

The first Communist group had supported Paz Estenssoro in the 1951 elections, and a pact signed by leading figures from the Communist party, the Miners' Union, and the MNR was published in the La Paz press.[42] Even if this pact was a falsification, there appears to have been an agreement, perhaps only tacit, that the Communists would support Paz Estenssoro in the elections, with the understanding that the MNR government, if successful, would allow the Communists full freedom to publish newspapers and magazines and cary on other political activities. Initially the Communists had wanted Juan Lechín to run for vice-president on the MNR ticket, but at Lechín's own request, they agreed to support the MNR vice-presidential candidate, Hernán Siles Zuazo.

The Communists also claimed credit for having participated in the April 1952 insurrection. According to a Soviet scholar, "the Communists took an active part in the April 1952 insurrection, distinguishing themselves by the seizure of the La Paz arsenal and by distributing captured arms to the insurrectionists. At the time of the April struggles a series of important leaders of the party, including Manuel Miranda, perished." [43]

The political importance of the Communists at this time should not, however, be exaggerated. The U.S. Department of State estimates the number of Communists in all Bolivia at less than two thousand.[44] The Communists were not represented in the MNR command which led the uprising; nor did they, while still party members, hold any ministerial or comparable posts in the subsequent MNR governments. The party's candidate received only twelve thousand votes in the 1956 presidential election as compared with more than three quarters of a million by MNR candidate Siles Zuazo. The Communist party did not have their first National Congress in Bolivia until 1959.[45]

In interpreting the MNR-Communist relationship, Wálter Guevara, the MNR foreign minister in the 1952 government, explained: "When the people of Bolivia were engaged in their final battle against the oligarchy of great mine owners and the feudal land holders, the Communists raised their voices with ours. They did us greater harm than good, but in a life and death struggle every one who helps is good, as the Western powers proved during the Second World War when they enthusiastically welcomed Soviet Russia as an ally." [46] He maintained that international communism "has no true interest in stating and solving the problems of the country in which it operates . . . local organizations are like pawns in . . . world politics." [47]

In a surprisingly prophetic statement Paz Estenssoro made his position on the Soviet-American conflict clear as early as 1944 when he said:

Especially in the case of nations like Bolivia international policy has to be formulated considering geographic and economic factors. In the event of a conflict of interest between the Anglo-American group and Russia, I believe that Bolivia will have to gravitate, necessarily, to the Anglo-American orbit, in which economically and ideologically opposed elements contend.[48]

In his history of the MNR, Luis Peñaloza gives an authoritative summing up of his party's position on this issue. After criticizing the PIR for zigzagging with the Soviet line, Peñaloza writes:

In contrast to [the PIR's] subordination to foreigners [*lo extranjero*], the Movimiento Nacionalista Revolucionario began its partisan activities claiming for the Bolivian people the right to direct their destiny . . . capturing attention not by being *for* or *against* the Reds or the Whites . . . but above all by claiming what seemed best for Bolivia.[49]

UNITED STATES EMERGENCY ASSISTANCE

After the issue of U.S. recognition was resolved, the next major crisis in U.S.-Bolivian relations was initiated by the nationalization of the three major tin mines in October 1952. The domestic situation was already gravely disturbed by the political upheaval following the April 1952 insurrection and by peasant uprisings in the Cochabamba valley and elsewhere. The nationalization decree created an atmosphere of uncertainty that jeopardized Bolivia's ability to sell tin abroad and, thus, to acquire foreign exchange for food imports, comprising one-fourth of the national diet. (And foreign exchange was needed for purposes other than food.) The crisis was further aggravated by a precipitous drop in the price of tin three months later, early in 1953. In little more than six months the price of tin dropped from about $1.20 a pound to below $.80. Despite concern over nationalization, the Reconstruction Finance

Corporation made a small spot purchase, five thousand tons at $1.17 a pound in January, but made no further purchases for several months.

The MNR leadership appears to have anticipated the negative reaction that nationalization would have on Bolivia's foreign customers. The nationalization decree itself fixed minimum compensation for the three tin groups at nearly $20 million and established a procedure for making this compensation effective. Moreover, Bolivian spokesmen promptly sought to provide reassurance about the new government's respect for private property. Ambassador Andrade in Washington and President Paz from La Paz stressed time and again that the nationlization of the tin mines was not directed against private property in general but only against the three giants of mining which had usurped the nation's right to rule itself. MNR spokesmen were quick to point out that small- and medium-sized mining companies remained independent and even received help from the government. Moreover they noted that the properties of other foreign companies, like W. R. Grace and Co., were not disturbed. In fact, Ambassador Andrade stressed:

There is genuine regret that nationalization became necessary. It is our feeling that private enterprise, under ordinary circumstance, can more quickly and effectively develop resources than can government. Bolivia's poverty is a further handicap to government exploitation of mineral resources. Nor does my government relish the bad reaction which nationalization has caused in some quarters of the United States.

We badly need and want the help of outside capital. The billions of dollars in the United States that seek profitable outlets, and the unparalleled technical skills which are a formidable part of your strength, will be welcome in Bolivia. . . . I repeat, my government will try to create an atmosphere which attracts private capital.[50]

The MNR government committed itself to no further nationalizations and, perhaps as a gesture of its faith in private foreign investment, entered into an agreement with U.S. financier Glen McCarthy for the investment of three million dollars in the development of sulphur deposits. Subsequent agreements with McCarthy, Gulf Oil, and other U.S. and foreign interests became the touchstone of the MNR government's willingness to collaborate with foreign capital in the development of the country.

Apart from the nationalization question, Bolivia presented the United States with another problem. On the one hand, the strategic U.S. stockpile of tin had grown large and the United States sought both to economize on the price and to lower the volume of minerals purchased.

Moreover, U.S. officials were disinclined to keep open indefinitely the government-owned tin smelter built in Texas during World War II, which was especially equipped to refine Bolivia's low-grade ores. Yet on the other hand, Bolivia had cooperated with the United States during World War II when tin was in such short supply, and it continued to be the only reliable, although costly, source of tin in the Western Hemisphere. Moreover, Bolivia was desperately dependent on the United States to buy a large part of its product, particularly those low-grade ores which could not be easily processed in European smelters. Low prices on the world market, added to U.S. reluctance to continue purchasing ore at earlier levels, were having a disastrous impact on the Bolivian economy. It appeared unlikely that the existing government could survive if relief were not forthcoming. In May 1953 Assistant Secretary John Moors Cabot told a congressional committee, "Bolivia is in a very serious economic state, and at the same time, we have stockpiled so much tin, we do not want any more, and I am trying to figure that one out." [51] Moreover, how could the United States provide economic assistance to a government which had not yet kept its promise to compensate the owners of the nationalized mines, including U.S. stockholders?

The uncertainty about the new regime's political orientation was another complicating factor. Concern about its alleged former Nazi connections had largely subsided, but the party's rumored ties with international communism, plus the latter's support for Paz Estenssoro in the 1951 elections, added a disturbing element to U.S.-Bolivian relations in the tense political climate of the Korean War and Senator Joseph McCarthy's anti-Communist crusades. The MNR's ambassador to the United States undertook from the outset of his assignment in Washington in 1952 to dispel fears about communism: "We state that [our government] is not Communist. We give assurances that it is not dominated by a foreign government." [52]

All of these various developments placed immense pressure on the MNR government to reach an agreement with the owners of the Big Three mines, especially with the Patiño group, the only group believed to have U.S. stockholders. President Paz estimated that U.S. citizens controlled from 20 percent to 25 percent of the Patiño companies.[53] Early in June, Paz was able to announce that a provisional agreement had been reached to pay off the Patiño interests according to a schedule depending on the amount and price of tin sold, but any obligation to make payment would cease if the price of tin fell below $.80 a pound. Similar agreements were reached later with the Aramayo and Hochschild interests. Pending the completion of negotiations for complete settlement, the three groups were to receive the following under the provisional agreement in millions of U.S. dollars:

Patiño	$2.28
Hochschild	2.16
Aramayo	1.32
	$5.77

As soon as the agreement with the Patiño interests was completed, President Paz gave an interview to the magazine, *U.S. News and World Report*. Bolivia still did not have a long-term contract to sell tin to the United States; however, when asked whether the United States should pay Bolivia more than the world market price for tin, Paz Estenssoro replied: "A tin contract with better prices should be reached. . . . Or, if that were not possible, the United States should seek a means of offsetting these price differences through our program of diversifying our economy." [54] Paz's reply proved prophetic.

About two weeks later, in reporting on the provisional agreements on compensation the *New York Times* editorialized that it was "only fair to record the gratifying fact that the right thing is being done." [55] Since the United States did not need tin, it continued, the argument for a new tin contract was largely "political." The article went on to praise the "moderate reform government" of the MNR for having resisted the blandishments of Perón and having kept "the Reds in check." In the view of the *Times* the United States could not afford to let the MNR government collapse, and the paper urged the signing of a long-term tin contract immediately, before the crisis made help too late.

Help was not long in coming. In a press release on July 6 the Department of State offered the Bolivians a one-year contract to buy tin at the world market price at the time of delivery.[56] In addition, the department committed itself to double the amount of technical assistance and to initiate studies of possible joint efforts to solve the country's economic problems, a broad hint of economic assistance to come. The announcement came at a crucial time, on the eve of the arrival in La Paz of the President's brother, Milton Eisenhower, on his first official fact-finding trip to Latin America.

In the July 6 press release the Department of State made its confidence in the MNR regime clear and set the stage for the close and friendly relations which characterize the succeeding decade. At this point, however, the department had indicated friendly intent, hinted that substantial economic assistance might be forthcoming, but had committed itself to relatively little in the way of material aid. Thus, the significance of Milton Eisenhower's visit was not that he set a new policy, but that he provided authoritative and influential confirmation of the Department's earlier judgments and initiated action to implement them.

In the highly charged anti-Communist atmosphere of 1953 and in the early months of the first Republican administration since Herbert Hoover, there were at least two important prerequisites to U.S. collaboration with the new nationalistic and revolutionary Bolivian government. First, the MNR leaders had to convince Washington that they were neither Communists nor pro-Soviet. In his book, *The Wine Is Bitter,* Milton Eisenhower dealt with this question directly. In fact, he used the Bolivian example to show how politicians, the mass media, and business leaders sometimes tag governments or political parties with communism "in good faith but without essential knowledge." He added: "Sometimes men with selfish interests knowingly make false statements which poison the American mind and enrage Latin Americans. . . . It is harmful in our own country and devastating hurtful throughout Latin America for us to carelessly or maliciously label as 'Communist' any internal efforts to achieve changes for the benefit of the masses of the people. . . . We should not confuse each move in Latin America toward socialization with Marxism, land reform with communists, or even anti-Yankeeism with pro-Sovietism." [57]

Dr. Eisenhower explained that Paz Estenssoro's government "may have been inexperienced, sometimes critical of us, and more inclined towards socialism than Americans generally prefer. . . . But they were not Communists." And he stoutly denied that the Bolivian land reform was Communist-inspired: "Feudalism is far closer to Communism than the system of owner operated farms installed by the Paz Estenssoro government. Why we should call land reform under such circumstances Communism is beyond me." In fact, he went on to argue that "rapid peaceful social change is the only way to avert violent revolution in Bolivia; physical strife would be the surest way of giving the Communists control."

The second prerequisite to U.S.-Bolivian collaboration was to convince Washington that the MNR government respected private property and would provide compensation for expropriated property, especially that of Americans. Dr. Eisenhower described how he "listened for hours to explanations of the Bolivian tin mine expropriation in conversations with President Paz Estenssoro, his Foreign Minister, and his able Ambassador in Washington. I recall distinctly spending most of one day at a small military school down a mountain." Dr. Eisenhower also talked with the former mineowners and other bitter critics of the expropriation so that he admitted to not having learned where the "full truth lies." But he did express his firm conviction that the MNR's "officials were honestly convinced that the expropriation with compensation was in the long-time interest of the nation." [58]

What Dr. Eisenhower saw and learned in Bolivia disposed him favorably toward the MNR government, and his personal assessment of the situation and his influence in the U.S. administration appear to have played a vital role in implementing a large, long-term program of U.S. economic assistance to Bolivia:

Bolivia was in real trouble when I arrived. The price of tin had fallen sharply and people were starving. President Paz Estenssoro urged me to have the United States send emergency food supplies. In response, I made my first call home and spoke to Secretary Dulles, asked him to ship surplus food to Bolivia if possible. We did.[59]

One of the top leaders of the MNR who dealt personally with Dr. Eisenhower has stated that the United States came to the aid of Bolivia at this time because Milton Eisenhower, an agriculturist by training, fell in love (*se apasionó*) with the agrarian reform.[60]

United States emergency assistance to Bolivia was formalized in an exchange of letters between Presidents Paz Estenssoro and Eisenhower on October 1 and October 14, 1953, respectively.[61] President Eisenhower authorized the following measures for emergency assistance:

1. To make available $5 million in agricultural products from Commodity Credit Corporation Stocks under the Famine Relief Act
2. To provide $4 million from Mutual Security Act funds for other essential commodities
3. To more than double the technical assistance program

President Eisenhower also referred to an earlier decision to purchase tin "at a time when this country has no immediate need for additional tin," because of traditional U.S. friendship with Bolivia and an awareness of the security threat to the free world when free men suffer from hunger or other severe misfortunes. Both presidents emphasized the emergency and humanitarian nature of the assistance but linked it to the development of Bolivian agriculture and the diversification of the economy, heretofore excessively dependent on tin exports. Counterpart funds generated by the sale of agricultural and other commodities were to be used in implementing Bolivia's diversification program.

John Moors Cabot, then assistant secretary for inter-American affairs, elaborated further on U.S. reasoning and motives in undertaking large-scale assistance to Bolivia. First, he was explicit, "We do not necessarily approve of all that the present Bolivian government has done." In fact, he said, "We have had to make strong representations to it regarding its attitude towards American interests." While declining to discuss the "bitter charges" in the nationalization controversy, Cabot explained, "What is important is to note that preliminary agreements have been reached between the Bolivian government and the former owners of the tin mines regarding compensation." [62] On another occasion Cabot said, "If we brought any pressure, it was on the Bolivian government, which we strongly urged to compensate American stockholders for their expropriated property." [63] These statements show that the United States insisted, as a condition of receiving economic assistance, that the MNR government reach an agreement with the former owners of the tin mines regarding compensation. Former Ambassador Andrade has confirmed this interpretation. [64]

Cabot was also more explicit than the president about the security factors bearing on the U.S. decision. Not only did he express his belief in the sincerity of the MNR government's opposition to "Communist imperialism," but he went on to describe the "implacable challenge of Communism" in the hemisphere:

The true test of hemispheric solidarity, upon which our security so importantly depends, is our willingness to sink our differences and to cooperate with regimes pursuing a different course from ours to achieve common goals. . . . We are therefore cooperating with it, for history has often described the fate of those who have quarreled over nonessentials in the face of mortal peril. [65]

No clearer statement than this is needed to show that the United States did not extend assistance to Bolivia solely as a humanitarian gesture toward a people faced with famine, but it felt that such assistance was also justified as a means of contributing to the security of the United States.

The crucial decision to come to the assistance of the new revolutionary government was much facilitated by the work of the Bolivian ambassador in Washington, Víctor Andrade. Andrade had been trained in an American school in La Paz and, therefore, did not have the German associations of some of his colleagues. As ambassador to the United States for Villarroel, he became well acquainted with Nelson Rockefeller and learned his way around Washington. In the early 1950s Andrade worked for the Rockefellers' International Basic Economy Corporation in Guayaquil, Ecuador.

Also, he had developed a personal relationship with Milton Eisenhower and the president. Andrade had had two long interviews with Milton Eisenhower before the latter went to Bolivia on his first official visit, briefing him thoroughly on the MNR as well as the oppositions' positions. Andrade played golf with President Eisenhower from time to time at the Burning Tree Club and had informal access to the president denied most ambassadors. In fact, during the consideration of the stabilization program the president called him aside one day on the first tee to obtain information relative to the proposed direct U.S. subsidy to the Bolivian budget. Andrade presented the Bolivian case as best he could but was visibly upset by the experience. The president, he recalls, indicated his favorable disposition toward the subsidy so as not to spoil Andrade's game. Andrade said that his most effective argument with the president was that aid to Bolivia would show the world that Eisenhower was not a reactionary, inflexible Republican but that he could support a revolution.[66]

An interesting sequel to the decision on emergency assistance was the visit of a congressional committee to Bolivia just a few weeks later on November 8 to 11, 1953. The leader of the congressional delegation was Senator Homer Capehart of Indiana and one of its other members was Senator John Bricker of Ohio, both of the conservative wing of the Republican party. Their published report of their visit was a technical, notably unpolemical account of economic conditions in Bolivia; and their conclusions, though restrained, were not unfavorable to the MNR government. For example, the report noted that the "committee was impressed with the fact that the Bolivians have a full realization of the problems confronting them and a desire to overcome them—the many obstacles confronting them notwithstanding." [67]

The United States continued to provide emergency economic and other assistance to Bolivia within the framework of the policies established in July 1953 and continued to buy Bolivian tin at world market prices until 1957, when the U.S. government divested itself of its uneconomic tin smelter in Texas City. Meanwhile, the United States increased economic assistance from the $11 million authorized in 1953 to about $20 million in each of the following two years, making Bolivia one of only three Latin American countries to receive outright grants, as opposed to loans (see figure 1). These three countries, Bolivia, Guatemala, and Haiti,

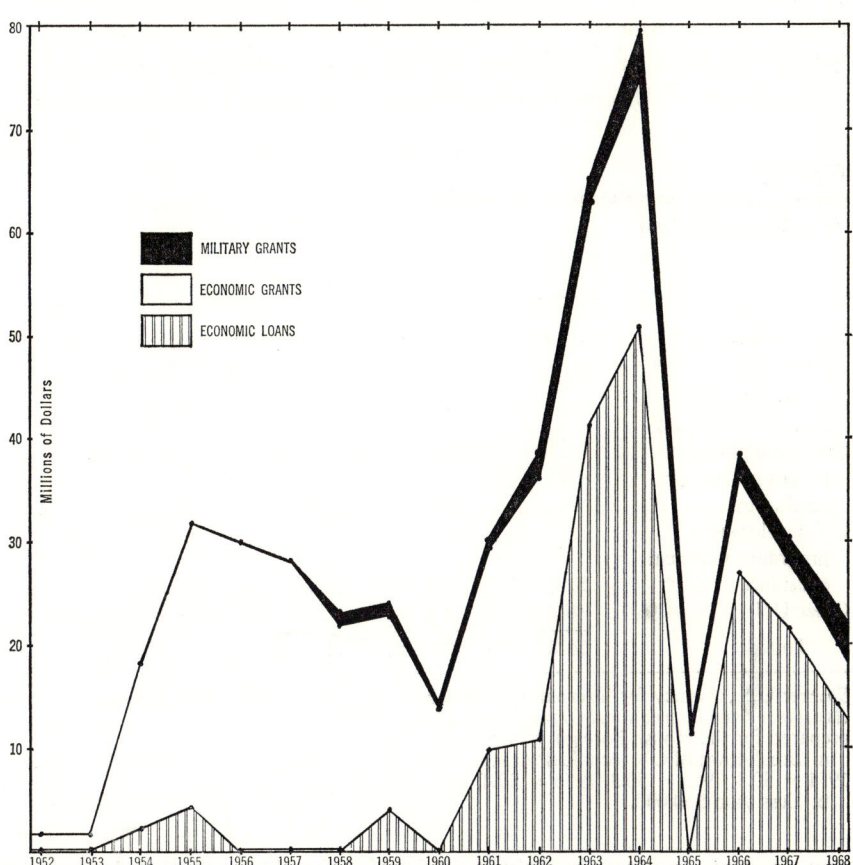

FIG. 1. U.S. ECONOMIC AND MILITARY ASSISTANCE TO BOLIVIA, 1952–1968

Source: U.S., Overseas Loans and Grants and Assistance from International Organizations, *Obligations and Loan Authorization, July 1, 1945–June 30, 1969* (Washington, D.C., 1969).
Note: For further details see appendix table 9.

received this special treatment because each faced emergency economic and political problems. The post-Arbenz regime in Guatemala received assistance to offset the alleged setbacks the country had suffered under Arbenz and to provide U.S. support for the new anti-Communist government. Grant aid was rushed to Haiti and Bolivia to prevent famine and chaos.

The tendency to justify U.S. emergency assistance in Bolivia as support of a government "showing courage and resourcefulness in combating the Communist problem" was intensified. Henry Holland, then assistant secretary for inter-American affairs, defended the expenditure as a way of helping the Bolivian government "to counteract Communist pressure." [68]

One result of U.S.-Bolivian collaboration was that it encouraged for-

TABLE 1
ASSISTANCE FROM INTERNATIONAL ORGANIZATIONS
(*In Millions of Dollars*)

Program	U.S. Fiscal Years								Total
	1953–1957	1958	1959	1960	1961	1962	1963	1964	
Inter-American Development Bank	—	—	—	—	$10.1	$4.5	$7.5	$1.1	$23.1
UN development program—special fund sector	—	—	—	$0.4	0.9	—	0.8	—	2.1
UN development program—technical assistance	$1.6 [a]	$0.5	$0.4	0.4	0.5	0.5	0.6	0.6	5.1
Other UN	0.2	0.1	0.1	— [b]	0.3	0.5	0.4	0.3	1.9
Total	$1.8	$0.6	$0.5	$0.8	$11.7	$5.5	$9.3	$2.0	$32.2

Source: U.S., Agency for International Development, *U.S. Overseas Loans and Grants and Assistance from International Organizations* (Washington, D.C., 1968), p. 161. Special report prepared for the House Foreign Affairs Committee.
    a. Breakdown of UN technical assistance for years 1953–1957 is as follows: 1953 = $0.2, 1954 = $0.3, 1955 = $0.3, 1956 = $0.4, 1957 = $0.4.
    b. Less than $50,000.

eign interests to invest in Bolivia. Of special significance is the signing of an investment agreement by the two governments in La Paz on September 23, 1955. It is notable that by June 30, 1964, some $20 million in foreign investment was insured against expropriation under the program and that over 80 percent of this amount was in the oil industry. Other extractive firms so insured were gold and tungsten mining, and nonextractive investments included sugar and housing. There was a noticeable absence of guaranteed foreign investment in manufacturing.[69]

Another important and related development was the formation (with the help of U.S. experts) of a new petroleum code promulgated on October 26, 1955 that attracted more than a dozen foreign oil companies which undertook exploration in Bolivia. Foreign interest was further stimulated by the dramatic results of the government's oil corporation in quintupling the output of Bolivian crude oil between 1952 and 1961.[70] Early in 1962, for example, the government reported that private concessions covered some forty-one thousand square kilometers and investments totaled about $80 million.[71] But large oil strikes did not appear and

TABLE 2
AID LOCAL CURRENCY PROGRAMS IN BOLIVIA
1954–1964

Program	Disbursements (in Millions of Pesos)	%
Agriculture	168.5	11.89%
Industry and mining	253.1	17.86
Roads	61.9	4.37
Transportation and power	55.8	3.94
Education	25.1	1.77
Public administration	23.6	1.67
Health and sanitation	47.6	3.36
Community development	39.7	2.80
Budgetary support	659.4	46.54
General and miscellaneous	82.2	5.80
Total	1,416.9	100.00%

Source: U.S., Agency for International Development, *Economic and Program Statistics, Bolivia*, no. 9 (March 1968), p. 41.

most foreign companies had suspended their explorations by 1962 so that in 1964 (in one of his last acts as president), Paz sharply decreased the areas available for foreign concessions.[72] As a result, the state petroleum company (YPFB) produced about 90 percent of all Bolivian crude oil during the early 1960s. Foreign companies did not again find and export oil until after 1964, when Gulf Oil of Pittsburgh began shipments by a newly constructed pipeline to the Pacific port of Arica, Chile.

CONFLICT OVER MONETARY STABILIZATION

The next politically significant phase in U.S.-Bolivian relations was the political struggle over the economic stabilization program announced in December 1956. After the 1952 insurrection the government increasingly resorted to the printing presses to finance governmental operations as well as publicly owned economic enterprises. The groups that helped bring the MNR to power, such as the miners, organized labor, and the peasants, were relentless in their demands for a larger piece of the national pie. Once the government's modest reserves were exhausted (and in the absence of viable tax sources), the government resorted to printing new money as an expedient in fending off these pressures.[73] Unfortunately, the tin mines could not provide taxable surpluses, partly because of the declining yields of both tin and foreign exchange and partly because the politically powerful miner's organization had taken over management of the mines, where featherbedding, high government subsidies, declining output, and wage increases prevailed. An unrealistic exchange rate (190 bolivianos to the dollar, when in fact the dollar was worth many thousands of bolivianos) encouraged speculation, smuggling for resale abroad, and other illegal market operations. The most dramatic symptom of the crisis was runaway inflation, and the cost of living index, with a base of 100 in 1952, rose to 2,270 in 1956.[74]

In the face of what appeared to be impending political and economic collapse, the MNR government appealed to the United States for assistance, but the cash support initially provided was swallowed up in government deficits and U.S.-supplied commodities either found their way to the black market or were smuggled abroad. In the end, the United States made it clear that either the Bolivian government had to put its house in order or U.S. assistance would be cut off. As a result, the Bolivian government requested that the United States send a financial mission to assist in this housecleaning operation, and George Jackson Eder, a U.S. lawyer formerly with the Department of Commerce and the International Telephone and Telegraph Corporation, came to Bolivia in June 1956 as "an invited, but scarcely welcome, guest of the Bolivian Government."[75] Eder's studies began under President Paz Estenssoro, but his stabilization plan was implemented under the latter's successor, Hernán Siles Zuazo.

Eder reasoned that only a drastic program had any chance of success, and he recommended that a surgical operation be put into effect. The major elements of the new program were:

1. The establishment of a realistic single exchange rate with fixed compensation for the miners and others to compensate for the pro-

posed elimination of food and other supplies subsidized at artifically low prices

2. Consolidation of all government budgets and the achievement of an overall balance to eliminate further borrowing from the Central Bank

3. The simultaneous elimination of state subsidies, and restrictions and controls on foreign exchange transactions (except customs duties) and on prices (except rents) [76]

The International Monetary Fund, the U.S. treasury, and the International Cooperation Administration established a $25 million fund to stabilize the exchange rate of the boliviano.

One of the most significant aspects of the stabilization program with regard to U.S.-Bolivian relations was that the program itself, sponsored and, in a sense, imposed by the United States, became the single most important political issue in the administration of President Siles. Eder appears not only to have provided the diagnosis and the remedy of Bolivia's inflationary ills but also to have been one of the president's major advisers and supporters in the implementation of the stabilization plan. According to Eder, he made every effort on his arrival in Bolivia to secure the widespread participation of all cabinet officers, including Juan Lechín, in drafting and carrying out the program. Eder cites several instances of Lechín's participation in planning the program as well as his early publicly expressed support for it.[77] Yet Lechín and the vice-president, Ñuflo Chavez, led opposition to the plan on political and ideological, as well as economic, grounds. They charged that the program failed to promote Bolivia's economic development, bore more heavily on the poor than the rich, damaged public welfare on behalf of private interests, and constituted a renunciation of the MNR's revolutionary line.[78] Lechín sought to circumvent the line on wages by securing increases for his miners.

The struggle over stabilization concerned more than the additional burden of checking inflation; it became a struggle for control of the MNR. The crisis was intense, with President Siles wondering whether he might end up like ex-President Villarroel, hanging from a lamppost in the Plaza Murillo,[79] and Eder's insistence that U.S. aid would be cut off if the stabilization plan were not completely carried through.

In the face of U.S. pressure and apparently convinced of the validity of the plan, President Siles made a dramatic defense of stabilization, first by going on a hunger strike in La Paz and, later, by a courageous visit to the mines to confront personally the miners whose wages Lechín sought to raise. Meanwhile Lechín leveled an attack against Eder's "colonial attitudes" and "paternalistic effrontery." [80]

By August 1957 President Siles had broken the opposition to the stabilization program, and from that time through the 1960s Bolivia has had one of the most stable currencies in Latin America. In an address to Congress in August, President Siles said that the country had been "on the brink of civil war" and that the stabilization program "saved the country from disaster." [81] As a result of this episode, U.S. policy became even more clearly identified with the right wing of the MNR.

The implications of monetary stabilization were profoundly ideological, or, at least, they were so conceived by George Jackson Eder whose proud and personal dedication to a free-market economy seemed indisputable. Specific prerequisites which the Bolivians were required to fulfill in order to qualify for the loan reflect his well-known support for the laws of private property and free enterprise. He told the Bolivians, for example, that the U.S. State Department, Treasury Department, and International Cooperation Administration required, among other things, "satisfactory arrangements for resumption of payment on the foreign debt; [82] a mutually acceptable agreement on compensation for the Patiño interests; legislation providing prompt, adequate and effective compensation for expropriated private property; [and] fair mining and investment codes." [83]

The leitmotiv of Eder's approach to the stabilization program was his suspicion and disapproval of Keynesian economics and his dedication to the free-market economy as exemplified by Ludwig Erhard and the West German economic miracle. On the latter point, he wrote:

The essence of the stabilization program was a return to a free market economy, at least in the matter of freedom from price controls, foreign exchange controls, and controls on imports and exports. It was a constant battle, however, and one that had to be waged continually against those who could not conceive of any economic system not controlled by the government.[84]

However one judges Eder's views, the stabilization program was eminently successful not only in checking Bolivia's inflation,[85] as the statistics so eloquently prove, but also in directing the country toward a free-market economy despite the socialist and statist orientation of many of its political leaders.

United States-Bolivian relations continued to be close during the balance of Siles's presidential term. Vice-President Nixon received a relatively cordial reception on his visit to La Paz in May 1958 and voiced his approval of continued U.S. assistance to Bolivia. Later in the year when the Soviet Union began disposing heavily of tin stocks on the world market, the Bolivians denounced Soviet economic aggression and decried low tin prices.

In February 1959 the Latin American edition of *Time* quoted a U.S. embassy official in La Paz as jocularly calling for the abolition of Bolivia by dividing the country up among her neighbors. Latent anti-Americanism burst forth with rioting and substantial damage to U.S. government property. United States officials retired to the suburbs from the center of La Paz, awaiting the end of the Bolivian popular protest, which died down after determined efforts to stop it by Siles's administration and the U.S. Embassy. Later that year when Senator McClelland undertook an investigation of the U.S. aid program, the committee report charged "negligence, waste, and inefficiency" in the U.S. aid program and reprimanded the U.S. official in charge, but the committee's findings did not appear to jeopardize the level of U.S. assistance in fiscal year 1961. As the graph on page 77 indicates, U.S. economic assistance averaged about $20 million a year during the years 1953 through 1960. The figures were substantially below $20 million in 1953 and 1960 but well above in the intervening years, and, except for $4 million in development loans, the commitments were all for grants.

CONFLICT OVER ECONOMIC DEVELOPMENT

The MNR leadership was so deeply involved in the revolutionary changes introduced after the 1952 insurrection and in conducting defensive economic policies that it was not possible to mount an economic development drive until the 1960s. In the years 1952 to 1956 the major problems were preventing famine, economic chaos, and political disorder. During this period, which corresponded roughly with President Paz's first term of office in Bolivia and President Eisenhower's in the United States, U.S. assistance was concentrated on famine relief. During the years 1956 to 1960, corresponding to President Siles' first term and President Eisenhower's second term, runaway inflation was a major problem, and the achievement of financial and economic stability seemed a prerequisite to rapid economic development. Through this period U.S. assistance concentrated on the monetary stabilization program. An all-out effort to promote economic development per se only became feasible in the early 1960s. This third phase corresponded roughly with the second administration of Paz Estenssoro (1960–1964) and the presidency of John F. Kennedy.

After the 1952 insurrection the tin mines, which were still Bolivia's principal industry and the major source of foreign exchange, were looked to as a means of financing capital imports for economic development. Tin seemed to hold the key to Bolivia's economic development, but, as production plummeted, revenues from tin sales sank. Low yields of ore, the deterioration of mining equipment, and inefficient management and labor practices meant that the cost of production frequently exceeded the price tin brought on the world market. Rehabilitation of the tin industry required a two-pronged approach: (1) the revitalization of the industry through extensive capital investments and (2) reforms in the organization and operation of the government-owned mining corporation, COMIBOL.

But the type of reforms which foreign experts felt were necessary in management labor relations and labor practices constituted political dynamite. Because labor had control of management in the tin mines, many experts estimated that several thousand surplus workers were featherbedding, forcing a rapid rise in the payroll with a consequent rise in costs. Employment in the Big Three tin mines rose from 24,000 miners in 1951 to 36,500 in 1956 and dropped to 27,000 in 1961, but some 26,000 workers produced 34,600 tons of tin in 1949 as compared to 27,000 workers producing on 15,000 tons in 1961.[86] The miners also traditionally received subsidies in the sense that commissary stores provided food and other items to the miners below market prices. In addition, theft was common in the mines, and infractions of labor discipline were widespread. Measures to correct these practices, naturally, faced the stolid opposition of the tin miners, the very group which had been a major element in the insurrection which brought the MNR to power and was perhaps the largest homogeneous group behind the MNR.

Aside from the problems of management and labor practices, heavy investments were required in mining equipment. Up to that point the United States had refrained from providing economic assistance to mining and industrial activities in the public sector. Economic assistance for education, health, and agriculture was politically less controversial in the United States than the provision of funds from U.S. tax sources to support a nationalized industry.

The connection between reforms in the tin mines and economic development came sharply into focus just as the United States and Latin America were coming to a political crossroads. In the last year or two of the Eisenhower administration greater attention and resources were devoted to Latin America's needs generally, although there was greater skepticism about Bolivia. This trend of recognizing Latin America as a whole was intensified by the election of John F. Kennedy in 1960 and the announcement of the Alliance for Progress in early 1961.

Paz Estenssoro returned to Bolivia from his diplomatic post in London in the late 1950s and was elected president for a four-year term in 1960. Early in his term he tried to lead Bolivia out of economic stagnation and showed a willingness to assume the political risks that rapid economic development would entail. He sought the economic and social objectives for Bolivia which had been denied the MNR earlier, capitalizing on the new, more liberal economic assistance policy of the Alliance for Progress and the Kennedy administration. In a sense, the MNR's revolution had adopted objectives as early as 1952 which were incorporated into the Alliance for Progress a decade later.

In the meantime, the USSR had developed interest in Bolivia, and during his visit to the United Nations in 1960, Premier Khrushchev dramatically offered Bolivia the funds for constructing its own tin smelter so the nation would no longer have to depend on U.S. and European smelters. In December of the same year a delegation from the Supreme Soviet visited La Paz and announced a Soviet offer of credits in the amount of $150 million for the government-owned petroleum corporation, road building, railroads, and other public works, as well as the smelter; but, despite pressure from the miners and other leftist groups, the government postponed a decision. The United States opposed acceptance of the Soviet offer; therefore, President Paz considered the Bolivian choice clear, partly because prospective U.S. assistance was far more than he expected from the Soviets.[87] Faced with the Soviet bid, the United States overcame its reluctance to support the government-controlled mining corporation COMIBOL, and the Plan Triangular was presented as the United States's answer to the Soviet offer.

Formulated in early 1961 and implemented over the course of the succeeding years, the Plan Triangular was the initial motivating force of Bolivia's economic development plan for the 1960s. But achieving rapid economic development meant facing up to the tin problem and the political implications its solution involved. The plan sought to rehabilitate the tin mines by providing funds for investing in the exploration of new mineral deposits, for metalurgical work to increase the recovery rate, replacement of materials and equipment, commissary supplies, elimination of surplus labor, and technical assistance.

All this involved administrative changes in COMIBOL, greater labor discipline in the mines, and other politically sensitive issues. The United States, the Federal Republic of Germany, and the Inter-American Bank together pledged more than $37 million to the plan under conditions specified in the agreement with the Bolivian government. Like the earlier stabilization program, the Plan Triangular linked the United States with the Paz group in the MNR, thus bringing the United States once again into direct conflict with the tin miners' union and their leader, Juan Lechín.

Not surprisingly, the tin miners bitterly resisted the required layoffs of thousands of excess workers, and Paz faced a crisis and confrontation with the miners led by Juan Lechín similar to that of former President Siles in the stabilization controversy. He rose to the occasion, as Siles had, meeting the strikes, demonstrations, and other agitation with persuasion and coercive countermeasures. President Paz temporarily managed to survive the crisis over mine reform, but the miners' unrest continued, and his conflict with Lechín as well as other issues ultimately led to a serious split in the MNR and Paz's fall from office.

Meanwhile, U.S. commitments to Bolivia rose slightly above the average of the late 1950s through 1961 and mounted sharply to more than double the earlier level in fiscal year 1964. Obligations in that year amounted to nearly $60 million under AID programs (see the graph on page 77).

SEMICOLONY OR ALLY?

United States–Bolivian relations since 1953 have been, perhaps, closer than those of any two countries in the hemisphere. United States per capita economic assistance to Bolivia has been higher than to any other Latin American country during this period, and a large number of officials have been assigned to the U.S. mission in La Paz.

The U.S.-Bolivian relationship differs in several ways from that of other countries with which the United States has been closely associated. Most of the other countries under strong U.S. influence are located in the Caribbean region, physically closer to the United States. These countries have, as well, a much greater need for U.S. purchases of their export products and depend heavily on U.S. tourism to bolster their economies. Because Bolivia sends a large percentage of its tin ores to the United Kingdom to be refined, it does not depend solely on U.S. purchases and there is little U.S. tourism in Bolivia.

Official relations between U.S. and MNR leaders between 1952 and 1964 were so close that critics of the Bolivian regime have long accused the MNR of selling out to the North Americans. In 1960–1964 President Paz Estenssoro's critics charged that the administration was attempting to substitute U.S. economic and military aid for popular support, and, in fact, Paz did rely on increased levels of U.S. economic assistance to bolster his government in its struggle with Lechín and the miners. Thus arises the important question of whether the Bolivian revolutionary regime was forced to sacrifice its independence as a quid pro quo for U.S. economic assistance.

Few would seriously attempt to deny that the United States has had great influence in Bolivia since the beginning of the AID program in the early years of the revolution. The U.S. government has maintained a large staff in the embassy in La Paz, reaching a peak in 1959 of one hundred eighteen employees in the economic assistance mission alone, according to the Foreign Service List. Larger countries like Chile and Colombia had less than half that number, and Brazil, which in size literally dwarfs Bolivia, had only a slightly larger economic mission. By the early 1960s the size of the economic mission to Bolivia was stabilized at about seventy-two persons, operating an aid program involved in almost all major aspects of Bolivian life including agriculture, education, health, industry, and public administration. It must be remembered, too, that the influence of educated and trained officials could be much greater in a country where the population as late as 1950 was predominantly illiterate.

George Jackson Eder's account of the stabilization program contains some of the most authoritative and convincing evidence of the deep U.S. involvement in Bolivian domestic affairs. Eder, for example, drafted domestic legislation:

I was forced to take charge of the long process of a complete revision of customs tariffs and devoted considerable time to the elimination of nuisance taxes and to the question of social security taxes, matters that Freeman could have handled more effectively had he been fluent in Spanish. A much needed reform in the real property tax system, proposed by me, and an effective income tax, proposed by Freeman, went by the board solely because there was no one who had the time, the fluency in Spanish, and the persuasiveness to put the measures across. This was unfortunate, as it would have been simpler to reorganize the tax laws and administration under the temporary emergency powers of the monetary stabilization program than at any other time, before or since, in Bolivia's history.[88]

In addition, Eder was deeply involved in Bolivia's domestic politics and had great influence over and support for President Siles in the stabilization controversies and the struggle with Lechín:

When the tumult and the shouting died, Lechín, on behalf of the COB convention, presented a memorandum to President Siles containing a nine-point critique of the stabilization program and suggestions for its improvement, all of them as improvised, counterproductive, and politically motivated as any of the measures that had led the country to its 1956 crisis. Nevertheless, the memorandum had been released to the press, and the President and the Stabilization Council asked me to draft a reply for the President's signature, conciliatory in tone, but emphatic in substance. This was done, and a draft was presented to the council which approved it almost without change.[89]

At the same time it is important to point out that, although the stabilization program hung by a thread for many months, it ultimately achieved its objective of stabilizing the currency, and Eder's participation appears to have been an indispensable element in the program's conception and implementation.

TABLE 3
AID CONTRIBUTIONS TO BOLIVIAN CENTRAL GOVERNMENT REVENUE
1957–1966

| | INCOME (IN BILLIONS OF BOLIVIANOS) | | AID SHARE AS % OF | |
Year	Total of Central Government	AID Contribution	Central Government Revenues	Total AID-Bolivia Expenditures [a]
1957	267.0	85.5	32.0%	27.2%
1958	297.9	77.6	26.0	22.1
1959	342.8	100.5	29.3	29.3
1960	341.9	78.3	22.9	53.9
1961	413.4	105.5	25.5	32.1
1962	459.2	82.8	18.0	37.9
1963	439.4	65.0	14.8	12.2
1964	554.4	42.8	7.7	10.4
1965	737.8	30.0	4.1	22.5
1966	837.0	34.4	4.1	9.0

Source: James W. Wilkie, *The Bolivian Revolution and U.S. Aid Since 1952* (Los Angeles, 1969), tables 4 and 5.
    a. This column is based on a U.S. fiscal year. Other columns are based on a calendar year, so the two sets of figures are not strictly comparable. For methodology, see Wilkie (cited above).

One cannot overlook the active participation and influence of U.S. Embassy officials during Paz's last years as president. Leading Bolivians and North Americans have testified privately and at length about the intimacy and importance of their collaboration, an interaction marked by a heavy flow of demands and supports from both sides.

Another important indicator of the extent of U.S. influence was the large direct contribution the United States made in support of the central government's budget (table 3). This contribution amounted to 32 percent of the 1957 budget and gradually declined to 7.7 percent in 1964, the last year of the Paz administration. Thus, the Bolivian leadership was not only dependent on the United States to finance desirable programs of economic and social development but also for funds necessary to support the day-to-day operations of the national government. Since provision for direct budgetary support occurs only occasionally in U.S. aid programs, it is obvious that great weight was attached to the advice of U.S. officials while their government was footing a large share of the Bolivian government's bills.

After his fall from power, former President Paz Estenssoro described the tension in the U.S.-Bolivian relationship in a statement which in its comprehensiveness and authoritativeness merits full quotation:

One of the most difficult aspects in the foreign policy of the national revolution was relations with the United States of America, with the exception of the time corresponding to the government of President Kennedy, in which a much more understanding attitude was evident. The importance which these relations have for Bolivia, like other countries on the continent, was recognized, especially during the stage of the implementation of programs of economic development, and great attention was devoted to them. But, there was not always a coincidence between national interests on both sides. Laborous negotiations were necessary, therefore, in order to find in the detail of each agreement the means of harmonizing them or at least avoiding conditions which could prejudice the country, affecting its sovereignty or damaging Bolivian pride. Nevertheless, there were cases in which it was not possible to reach an agreement because of the existence of diametrically opposed positions, for example with regard to credits for the Banco Minero, which were conditioned on the suppression of the state monopoly in the purchase of minerals and for the approval of a new mineral code; obstacles for the securing of resources destined for exploration work for the YPFB; North American objections to the establishment of an antimony smelter offered by Czechoslovakia and of a hydro-electric plant for COMIBOL by the Yugoslavs. Also there were difficulties with the sale of other metals from the North American strategic stockpile for the checking of the rising tendency of the international market. Much to its sorrow, in many of these cases the government found itself obliged to assume a delaying tactic or to yield, for example with respect to the decree of August 22, 1963, because the alternative, communicated implicitly or explicitly, was the interruption of financing for development projects, which was very serious. The largest source of available resources was North America and only this source included the necessary funds for covering the transportation of machinery and local costs, indispensable for our country, because of an absence of our own funds for investment.[90]

Many of the points of friction to which Paz refers involve U.S. private as well as public interests. On the one hand, they also involve Bolivian legislation affecting actual or prospective U.S. investors, as in the case of oil and mining. The United States also opposed economic assistance from Communist countries for the construction of a tin smelter and power plant, both of which would have conflicted with existing foreign, including North American, interests. In general, the United States appears to have exerted its considerable influence over Bolivia to provide a welcoming climate to private foreign capital as a means of both promoting economic development and discouraging the expansion on competing publicly controlled agencies. United States reservations about public corporation have been based on the corporations' fairly consistent record of heavy deficits. However, the Bolivians have resisted the attempts to limit the public sector partly because such limitations would involve a loss of government control over certain strategic industries, not only vis-à-vis Bolivian but foreign corporations as well. Two important causes of the tensions have been different underlying conceptions of the proper role of a government in promoting economic development and conflicting emphases on political versus economic considerations.

For example, the Bolivians have resented U.S. pressure to eliminate the government monopoly on the domestic purchase and foreign sale of tin ore through the Banco Minero. Since the late 1930s, the leaders in the MNR government had been strong proponents of such a monopoly as a means of controlling the Big Three mining companies. Under the stabilization program, however, Eder attempted with partial success to make the use of the bank's facilities voluntary rather then compulsory.[91] The U.S. arguments were made on persuasive economic grounds, whereas the Bolivian opposition was in part political—based on fear that the political gains of the revolution would be eroded.

Some of Paz's objections mentioned above are not ideological at all but rather reflect simple conflicts of interest, such as the U.S. requirement that Bolivia spend U.S. loans in the United States. Although most U.S. loan agreements contained this requirement, Paz deeply resented the restriction, which was implemented through import-control regulations discriminating in favor of the United States.[92] Similarly, U.S. sales of tin from its strategic stockpile caused friction.

In his list of the problems in U.S.-Bolivian relations, Paz did not refer to U.S. pressures regarding Bolivia's position in international organizations. On crucial votes related to international communism and Cuba at inter-American meetings, Bolivia has taken positions directly opposed to the United States. Bolivia has consistently resisted the United States in its Cuban policy, voting against the Cuban government's expulsion from the Organization of American States in January 1962. Similarly, Bolivia refused to break relations with Cuba in August 1963 or to vote sanctions against her in July 1964 in connection with charges of Cuban aggression against Venezuela. Bolivia's refusals to break with Cuba appear to have resulted in the failure of a Bolivian mission to secure U.S. economic assistance.[93]

At the same time, the Bolivian government has modified certain positions to mollify the United States. At the Caracas conference in 1954 the Bolivian delegate, Wálter Guevara Arze, voted to support Secretary of State John Foster Dulles's resolution condemning international communism. Guevara Arze in his speech to the conference, however, took a notably different view of international communism than did Secretary Dulles, indicating Bolivia's preoccupation with its own domestic problems and making clear his own view about the dangers of an exaggerated anti-Communist crusade. Bolivia also supported the United States in the missile crisis of October 1962 and broke relations with Cuba in August 1964 to help insure continued U.S. support.

No doubt it is naïve to inquire whether any two nations of such disparate resources and political power can be allies on an equal basis, but it is equally difficult to prove that the United States economically exploited Bolivia during the years 1952–1964, whatever U.S. motives may have been. Bolivia simply has not had that much which could be profitably exploited. In fact, given the hundreds of millions of dollars which the United States has poured into Bolivia, one might make a case for the opposite. Nor do North American firms come out as rapacious money grabbers, since, in the case of oil, the millions invested in exploration and equipment appear to have far exceeded the possible profits on the modest quantities of petroleum actually exported.

Yet, one cannot overlook the pernicious effect that U.S. influence has exerted in Bolivia, at least in psychological terms. The late Sergio Almaraz Paz, an emotional and ideological figure committed to the left, was one of the most severe critics of the United States. He offered a perceptive view of Bolivia's predicament:

The assumption of power by the North Americans brought us a more general and less precise phenomena: Bolivians began to feel uncomfortable with each other. If a foreigner imposes himself as a permanent intermediary; if plans as diverse as those for electrification, highways and schools depend on him; if he has to tell us how we must live and think; if local functionaries don't know how to deal with their colleagues from another office because they don't know the latters' relationship with the foreigner; if, in the final analysis, what is done or what is not done depends on the interest of a foreign nation, then citizens are left segregated, incomunicado and suspicious that [national] unity is impaired, that the nation is beginning to dissolve. This fragmentation takes place at the administrative levels, in the press, and in cultural activities; it is visible at the highest levels of a population where little groups dispute the privilege of being friends of the foreigner; it descends to the people when the desperation of poverty causes one to consent to achieving an advantage by the sacrifice of dignity. If the spectacle of the bourgeoisie pressing themselves upon an ambassador and smiling servily in order to secure a credit is repulsive, it is painful to see peasants presenting a bouquet of flowers as an expression of their gratitude for a little school or a well received as a gift. Extreme poverty facilitates colonization; men in Bolivia have a lower price. There is a certain level at which poverty destroys dignity; the North Americans have discovered this level and work on it: in their eyes and for their pocketbook, a Bolivian costs less than an Argentine or a Chilean.[94]

The MNR government has had few opportunities to play the USSR against the United States, and it never exchanged diplomatic representatives with the Soviet Union. In the late 1950s there was a flurry about the Soviet dumping of tin in the international markets to drive down prices at the expense of Bolivia and other tin-producing countries. The Soviet offer of credits for a tin smelter and other proposals in 1960 never materialized, mainly because the Bolivians preferred the Plan Triangular. The Bolivian Communist party has long been weak and many Bolivian Marxists have been of Trotyskite rather than Stalinist persuasion. For the most part, there has been little contact or evidence of mutual interest between the two countries,[95] although Bolivia has had diplomatic relations with the Eastern European socialist countries, such as Czechoslovakia, Hungary, and Yugoslavia and Marshall Tito visited the country in 1963.

THE BOLIVIAN MILITARY AND U.S. POLICY

Despite the entreaties of the party's left wing, the MNR leadership did not completely dismantle the armed forces in the years immediately following the 1952 insurrection. The new regime did destroy the capability of the army to act as an independent political force, and the armed forces were ruthlessly purged of all elements considered hostile to the revolution. According to one authoritative estimate, about 80 percent of the armed forces were demobilized within a matter of days.[96] The MNR regime deliberately denigrated the armed forces, and military expenditures dropped from 23 percent of the national budget in 1952 to 6.7 percent in 1957 (table 4). The MNR thoroughly reorganized the

TABLE 4
BOLIVIAN DEFENSE EXPENDITURES AND U.S. MILITARY ASSISTANCE

Year	Defense Expenditures (in Billions of Bolivianos)	% of Central Government Budget	U.S. Military Assistance (in Millions of Dollars)
1952	1.0	23.0%	—
1953	1.2	13.7	—
1954	1.7	11.4	—
1955	3.3	12.8	—
1956	6.7	8.7	—
1957	17.8	6.7	—
1958	28.0	8.6	$0.1
1959	37.9	10.6	0.3
1960	38.8	10.9	0.0
1961	50.9	12.2	0.4
1962	61.3	13.5	2.2
1963	68.3	13.5	2.4
1964	80.3	13.9	3.2

Source: James W. Wilkie, *The Bolivian Revolution and U.S. Aid Since 1952* (Los Angeles, 1969). The first column is calculated from table 7 and appendix N; the second column is from appendix N; the third column is from appendix A.

military and took steps to insure its complete loyalty to the party machine; in fact, army officers took their oath to the party and not to the state.

As a counter to the army's future resurgence, the MNR gave more responsibility to the reorganized police, whose leader, General Antonio Seleme, had conspired in the April insurrection. More important the MNR permitted, even encouraged, the seizure of arms by insurrectionary units and the development of peoples' militias among the peasants, miners, and factory workers. According to one estimate, the militias achieved their greatest strength (fifty thousand to seventy thousand armed men) toward the end of President Paz's first term in 1956. President Siles began rebuilding the armed forces after his conflict with Juan Lechín and Ñuflo Chavez over the stabilization program when the resulting strikes, demonstrations, and violent encounters threatened the public order. At that time Lechín was political leader of the miners' militias and Chavez of the peasant militias. Thereafter Siles began to conceive of the armed forces as a major prop for the MNR government and a counterpoise to the militias. Military expenditures rose sharply in 1958 and steadily thereafter, while the militias were permitted to deteriorate and the number dropped in early 1963 to probably no more than sixteen thousand men.[97]

In 1956 the United States and Bolivia renewed the agreements for the army and air force missions which continued to permit the assignment of U.S. military officers to La Paz. In the 1950s the United States did not provide extensive military assistance to the MNR government, but in 1956 the economic mission began providing technical assistance to law enforcement agencies.

Faced with similar problems and even more intense conflicts within the MNR then his predecessor, President Paz Estenssoro continued the military buildup in the 1960s, as the expenditures on table 4 indicate. Military assistance from the United States also increased especially sharply in the last three years of the MNR regime. Note that the level of military assistance was slight by U.S. standards but quite enough to have political impact in a small, developing country like Bolivia.

In addition, Paz encouraged extensive efforts to improve the training and equipment of the armed forces and gave them through the Civic Action program what he considered an important role in the social and economic development of the country. The Civic Action program was introduced in Bolivia before it was generally adopted by the United States in its foreign military programs. Under the program the military worked on development projects such as the construction of schools, roads, and agricultural and industrial works, receiving new material from the United States, which, according to Paz, "was not difficult to obtain because they [the United States] always showed interest in the existence of order in the country." [98] United States Army records showed that by early 1964 twenty out of the twenty-three senior officers of the Bolivian army had either attended the U.S. School of the Americas in Panama or had visited the United States.[99] It is probably more than coincidence that the Bolivian army officer and former West Point student who led the Civic Action program under Paz Estenssoro, Lt. Col. Julio Sanjinés Goitia, was first minister of economics and later ambassador to the United States under the succeeding military government. Interestingly, the air force general who led the successful coup against Paz Estenssoro in 1964, René Barrientos Ortuño, was among the military officers associated with the Civic Action program.

THE UNITED STATES AND THE FALL OF THE MNR

Many of the causes, probably fundamental ones, of the MNR's fall from power and Paz's exile are domestic in origin. One of these was that Paz served as president of Bolivia from 1952 to 1956, again from 1960 to 1964, and a 1961 constitutional amendment permitted him to run for a third term in 1964. In doing this he pressed his luck too far.

In the 1960s Paz aimed to break the development impasse, something neither he nor Siles had been able to do previously. Central to this effort were the cost-cutting programs coupled with the efficient management and production of the tin mines through investment financed by foreign assistance. He hoped thereby to provide a firm base for economic development, to be financed in large part through the Alliance for Progress. Meanwhile, he relied increasingly on U.S. assistance to complete his domestic objectives and on the military to counter political opposition.

Modernizing the tin mines brought Paz into direct conflict with organized labor, and his unwillingness to step aside in favor of new leaders divided and weakened the MNR, his political base. Sensing Paz's vulnerability, the traditional political groups, whose enmity to the revolution had been smouldering so long, seized their opportunity to move against Paz in concert with his labor opposition within the MNR. At this point the role of the military became crucial, indeed decisive, when the armed peasants did not rally to Paz's defense. A combination of his MNR opposition, a resurgence of parties on the right, and the power and ambitions of a revivified military toppled Paz on November 4, 1964, a fate from which U.S. moral and economic support could not save him.

In retrospective appraisal of the MNR period, Paz attributed the "prolonged political stability" of the 1952–1964 period to the "equilibrium existing between the armed forces, the police, and the popular militias." [100]

But, in explaining his overthrow, Paz said his greatest mistake was placing his trust in the loyalty of the military. Paz explained that the leaders of the army had been close collaborators with the MNR leaders during the Chaco War and the Busch and Villarroel presidencies. When these older officers retired, they were succeeded by younger men who, though formally pledged to the MNR regime, lacked the personal ties with the political leadership.

Paz's continued strengthening of the armed forces in the 1960s disburbed the equilibrium of the political and military situation by providing them with sufficient strength to challenge his rule, especially after he forfeited support from a key bulwark of the regime—organized labor. What he had counted on to checkmate the armed forces, and what failed to materialize, was armed support from the peasant militias.[101]

Although the foregoing explanation has emphasized domestic factors, President Paz's association with the United States was so important to him that U.S. influences may not be ignored. Because critics of the United States and Paz have written so much against U.S. involvement and they have been so widely believed, the subject must be dealt with even if the allegations are only partly true. Paz's decision to run for a third term was intimately connected with his calculations about U.S. and other foreign economic assistance.

In the opinion of many U.S. observers, including sectors of the U.S. press and the State Department, Juan Lechín was the bête noire of the Bolivian Revolution. Yet, he was a prime candidate for the presidency in 1964; indeed, from the early 1960s there was wide discussion within the leading circles of the MNR about his probable candidacy. In an effort to establish himself in the good graces of the U.S. government Lechín traveled to the United States and, curiously, to Formosa to pay a call on Chiang Kai-shek. By 1963 it was clear that Lechín had not succeeded in his task and was emphatically not favored by the North Americans for the presidency. So, with some justification, President Paz concluded that he himself was probably the only figure in the MNR capable of denying Lechín the office.

Paz's decision to run for the presidency again was made after his return to Bolivia from a visit in October 1963 with President Kennedy on the eve of the latter's assassination. Many considerations affected that decision, not the least of which were his own personal aspirations and interests. Moreover he concluded that the only way to insure the continued flow of needed external resources from the United States and from the international agencies in which U.S. resources predominated was to continue as president.[102] There is no available evidence that any U.S. spokesman in Washington or La Paz attempted to dissuade him from this analysis or its implications. However, the widely held belief that the United States played a role in his decision is difficult to substantiate since both Paz and the U.S. representatives have wisely avoided going on record on the subject. The explanation of this role is that U.S. spokesmen pointed out their opposition to Juan Lechín, the damaging effect Lechín's election would have on foreign assistance, and the desirability of Paz's running again. Later, Paz explicitly stated that the assassination of President Kennedy and subsequent shifts in the U.S. policy toward Bolivia changed the grounds on which his decision was based and that he erred in not taking the changed circumstances fully into account.[103] An inference of this statement is that changes in the U.S. government contributed to his fall—an inference difficult to substantiate.

President Paz was closely associated with the last two American ambassadors accredited to his government, Ben S. Stephansky and Douglas Henderson, and this association was widely known and publicized in Bolivia. The completion of many Alliance for Progress projects, at the inauguration of which the U.S. ambassador was properly invited to participate, happened to coincide with the presidential campaign of 1964. This resulted in criticism by anti-Paz groups that Henderson was being used in the MNR election campaign. Later, after Paz's election, Henderson is widely believed to have done everything he properly could to support the constitutional president in the tense days before the coup.

What has been in doubt, in the eyes of both the Paz group and the opposition, is the role of the U.S. military in the MNR's demise. The U.S. military has been charged with collusion in the political ambitions of Gen. René Barrientos Ortuño, at least as early as his successful campaign for the vice-presidency.[104] Barrientos turned the tide in his favor for his nomination as Paz's vice-presidential running mate in 1964 after a mysterious and little explained "attempt on his life" at which time he was whisked away to Panama for treatment in a U.S. hospital. The furor created by this incident forced Paz to withdraw his handpicked vice-presidential candidate, Federico Fortún, in favor of Barrientos. It is also widely believed in La Paz that the U.S. military attaché, Lt. Col. Edward Fox, encouraged Barrientos to launch a coup at the very time that Ambassador Henderson sought to sustain Paz in the presidency.[105] Paz has stated that Fox publicly expressed his hostility to him at a dinner in

October some time before the coup.[106] This, incidentally, appears to be the same Col. Edward Fox whom Antonio Arguedas Mendieta, former minister of interior, accused of involvement in his recruitment as a CIA agent in 1965.[107] Accounts of contradictions in U.S. policy refer darkly to the fact that these events occurred during General Curtis LeMay's assignment as Air Force Chief of Staff.

Such conflicts between the State Department and the Pentagon have occurred in the past, and it is well within the realm of possibility that they occurred in this case. Colonel Fox's affection for and collaboration with General Barrientos on military matters was not necessarily improper in view of the nature of their relationship. Whether a representative of the U.S. military encouraged Barrientos in the conspiracy, however, is another question and, short of records of actual conversations, difficult to prove. It is significant that no evidence is available either that Colonel Fox attempted to discourage Barrientos. Of special interest, however, is a pamphlet on Civic Action written by the military engineer, Lt. Col. Julio Sanjinés Goitia, and containing a foreword by Col. Truman F. Cook of the military assistance mission. Colonel Cook made the statement, remarkable in the light of later events, that "the military organization is perhaps the only institution endowed with the organization, order, discipline, and self-sacrificing attitude towards objectives for the common good." He continued, "Should political and economic institutions fail . . . then there is a real possibility that the military would move in against graft and corruption in government." He called it "naive to assume that they might not move to power in a classic sense." [108]

The United States recognized the new military government on December 7, 1964, a month after Paz fell. Economic assistance to Bolivia fell off markedly in the next three years, but after a year's lull military assistance returned to about the level of the early 1960s.

CONCLUSIONS

Bolivian perspectives. Bolivian attitudes about the relationship with the United States follow classic patterns. Not unexpectedly, the leftist critics of the MNR government attacked its collaboration with the United States as a sellout to imperialism, while the rightist opponents claimed that the MNR had misused economic assistance and bitterly resented U.S. support of their rivals. Caught in a maelstrom of conflicting pressures, ex-Presidents Siles and Paz may sometimes have asked themselves whether close collaboration with the United States was worth the anticipated rewards. But, in the end, did they have any other choice than to seek and accept U.S. assistance? Both Paz and Siles were realists, if nothing else, and they correctly assessed Bolivia's extreme economic dependence. If Bolivia could not sell her exports, especially tin, it would not have the resources to import food and other national necessities. Even with satisfactory trade relationships, Bolivia has had difficulty in locally accumulating sufficient capital to sustain a minimal rate of economic growth. Thus, its development has been inextricably tied to foreign sources of capital and technology as well as to foreign markets, and even *with* access to these sources the Bolivian economy nearly collapsed in the 1950s. *Without* such access, total economic collapse would probably have been inevitable. The revolutionary government could hardly have expected to survive under such circumstances; in fact, Presidents Paz and Siles both have indicated that their governments would not have survived without U.S. assistance.[109]

If Bolivia's extreme economic dependence dictates access to foreign markets and capital, why necessarily must it be in the United States? Would not the Soviet Union do? Castro was willing to accept, perhaps encouraged, a complete break with the United States, gambling on Soviet assistance which came through; thus Castro won in the sense that he made a revolution and stayed in power. Bolivia's geographic and strategic position, however, is vastly different from Cuba's. In the first place, Bolivia has no ocean ports; nor does it control rail or river access to such ports since, unlike Cuba, Bolivia's lifelines are in the hands of hostile or potentially hostile neighbors. In addition, Cuba's insular position makes it less vulnerable to military pressure from regular or guerrilla forces than Bolivia whose borders are surrounded by five nations. More important, the Soviet Union did not offer economic assistance at the crucial junctures in the 1950s; nor did it press its offers of loans on Bolivia in the early 1960s in the face of Bolivian reluctance. The MNR government correctly judged that the United States was willing and able to supply assistance of greater quantity and better quality than the Communist countries.

The most controversial and difficult issue then is not so much whether Bolivia needed, or should have sought, external assistance, but whether the MNR paid an unnecessarily high price for that assistance by permitting the United States to help determine the nature and course of the revolution.

U.S. perspectives. Why did the United States become a major bulwark of the Bolivian Revolution when it had so promptly opposed other Latin American revolutions such as the Mexican, Guatemalan, and Cuban, not to mention those in Europe and Asia? Some observers believe that since U.S. citizens owned virtually no property which was expropriated under the land reform and only about 10 percent of the nationalized mining interests, the United States had few private interests threatened by the revolution. United States financial interests were, of course, far smaller than in the three other Latin American countries. It is noteworthy, however, that the United States attached great importance to property rights and compensation in the event of expropriation, and diplomatic recognition of the MNR government was granted only after assurances had been made about respect of these. In subsequent years these same issues returned many times to haunt the MNR government with the specter of compliance or economic collapse. The U.S. economic aid program was not begun in 1953 until after the Bolivian government had reached an agreement with the Patiño interests about compensation. This is not to say that U.S. stockholders in Patiño necessarily had great political influence in Congress, especially since U.S. citizens had a claim of only about 10 percent of the $20 million paid in compensation. As a result, U.S. insistence on compensation appears to have been less attributable to the political influence of interested parties in the United States than to an established principle which linked compensation for expropriated property with congressional authorization for economic assistance. The MNR leadership from the outset demonstrated full awareness of the importance of this issue and time and again committed themselves to compensation, also stressing the importance of the private sector of the economy.

A great part of U.S. interest in Bolivia should be attributed to humanitarian considerations, that of heading off imminent famine and chaos in Bolivia as a result of the collapse of Bolivia's tin revenues. (This becomes apparent most vividly in the writings and personality of Dr. Milton Eisenhower.) In addition, the United States could not forget that Bolivia was a major source of tin during World War II so that to beat down tin prices below Bolivia's production costs or to shut down the Texas tin smelter would have seemed a cruel and ungenerous act to a wartime ally. In fact, in the early 1950s it may have been easier to provide Bolivia with economic assistance in the form of surplus agricultural commodities than to meet its price demands for tin which were well above the world market level.

Politically more significant were fears in the United States about the spread of communism in the western hemisphere aroused by alleged Communist influence on the Arbenz regime in Guatemala. The MNR government effectively used these fears about communism in Bolivia, and a U.S. official's rationale for the aid program presented to Congress emphasized security issues. Just as the United States had opposed the MNR for fear of Nazi Germany in the early 1940s, the United States supported Bolivia in the 1950s and 1960s for fear of communism. Also, the flexibility of the United States's Bolivian policy made it easier to defend the rigid and repressive policy toward Guatemala in the early 1950s. Nor should one overlook the tact, flexibility , and persuasiveness of the MNR leadership in both La Paz and Washington, particularly as contrasted with the sensitive, combative, and proudly unyielding Guatemalan revolutionary leadership. Víctor Paz, Hernán Siles, and Wálter Guevara Arze all were skillful analysts of the U.S. position and capitalized masterfully on their U.S. opportunities. Ambassador Víctor Andrade, experienced and urbane, made Bolivia's needs known to Washington's inner circles. The Bolivians skillfully developed personal as well as professional relationships with such U.S. leaders as Dr. Milton Eisenhower, Henry Holland, and John F. Kennedy. Most of the American ambassadors who served in La Paz were strongly sympathetic to the MNR's appeals.

An important and related question is whether U.S. economic assistance achieved its major objectives. The initial objective of averting famine and total chaos was met by the emergency assistance program and later the monetary stabilization program. The second objective was the U.S. hope of saving the country from communism. That the Communists have never even come close to dominating Bolivia was most dramatically illustrated by the comparative ease with which Che Guevara's guerrillas, with basically foreign composition and leadership, were politically isolated and destroyed. Whether U.S. assistance was responsible for the failures of the Bolivian Communists both before and after 1964 or, indeed, whether a genuine Communist threat ever existed is another question with so speculative an answer that it will not be treated here. As stated earlier, the Communists have always had one of the country's smallest and weakest parties, and the Soviet Union and other Communist countries have shown relatively little interest in Bolivia.

The U.S. government appears to have had a third objective, more implicit than explicit, of moderating or deradicalizing the revolution. From the beginning U.S. influence has tended to check the nature and extent of revolutionary change. United States insistence on compensation for expropriated mining properties and support of private ownership and control served to prevent nationalization beyond the three major tin mining groups. United States policies consistently sought to limit or decrease government participation in the economy, such as control over foreign exchange and management of extractive industries, and to promote expansion of the private sector. Under U.S. influence the petroleum code, the mining code, and other measures helped to improve the investment climate for foreign capital.

Stabilization in 1957 and the Plan Triangular in 1961, both conceived and implemented with U.S. support, brought the MNR government into head-on conflict with organized labor, especially the tin miners. Although U.S. representatives may not have felt politically or personally friendly to the tin miners, it might be difficult to prove that U.S. policies were directed against organized labor as such. Even so, the effect of U.S. influence was to make the United States an ally of the MNR center and right and the enemy of the labor left. Thus, the effort of U.S. policy was to bolster the position of the Bolivian middle classes against organized labor.

A well-known expression of tension between the miners and the United States was the latter's persistent antagonism toward Juan Lechín, an articulate, agile, and durable protagonist of the miners' interests. Yet even some of his closest associates would not deny a prevailing U.S. view that Lechín has been personally irresponsible and politically unreliable. Few, however, believe that Lechín is a Communist agent for a number of reasons, one being his extreme opportunism. The MNR organization's (and Paz Estenssoro's) rejection of Lechín for the presidency in 1964, a decision to which U.S. opposition may have contributed, meant the continuing alienation of the miners from the centers of formal authority and a postponement of the reconciliation of a major contending force within the MNR. More than any other person, Lechín had the capability to make a politically and economically viable arrangement with the miners, thereby promoting the political integration that the MNR always lacked. In fact some miners feared Lechín's rise to the presidency, since that could be the one circumstance which would cause him to agree to subordinate the miners' cause to broader national interests.

Economic and social development has been a fourth objective of U.S. economic assistance and the dominant one since the Alliance for Progress was announced in 1961. Bolivia's record in this respect has been mixed. The output of tin ore, lead, and zinc has been especially disappointing, not having reached prerevolutionary levels by 1968, but the output in agriculture and manufacturing has steadily increased and, in the case of petroleum and natural gas, dramatically. From 1961 to 1967 the per capita gross national product appears to have risen more rapidly in Bolivia than in Latin America as a whole.[110] Exports are much larger now than during the 1950s and have surpassed 1952 in value, and dollar reserves are much above the late 1950s. Proponents of the revolution will interpret these and other figures as indicating that, although economic indicators deteriorate in the initial phases of a social revolution, as they did in Bolivia, economic performance in the last years of the MNR government and since fully justifies the revolution on economic grounds. On the other hand, critics of the revolution maintain that the economic growth that has occurred recently is small for a country which averaged more than $50 million in U.S. aid annually from 1961 through 1964 and has continued to receive lesser, but considerable, sums since.

Champion of the latter view is George Jackson Eder, an authoritative and committed spokesman of the conservative point of view. After mentioning certain positive factors, such as continuing monetary stability and higher foreign exchange reserves, Eder charged that

the country is racked by civil strife, corrupted and pauperized by fourteen years of U.S. aid which, far from promoting Bolivia's economic development and social progress, served only to maintain in power a government that proved unworthy either of American or Bolivian support and which, without American aid, would admittedly have fallen almost at the inception of the Revolution. It was a government, itself incompetent and corrupt, which has corrupted the great masses of the Bolivian people by permitting violence and robbery to go unpunished; by arming mobs under the euphemism of a 'People's Militia'; by teaching labor that the rewards of loafing are greater than those of hard work; by discouraging thrift through the debasement of the currency; by inculcating the idea that prosperity and progress must depend upon government action (whereas, in Bolivia at least, nothing could be farther from the truth); and, above all, by reducing a once sovereign nation to the indignity of a truculent mendicancy, with the government claiming as rightful compensation for fancied wrongs what is patently nothing more than a gratuity motivated in part by blackmail and threats of communism, and in part by the compassion of the American people coupled with a feeling of guileless guilt for our prosperity in a world of poverty.[111]

Although representing opposing extremes of the political spectrums, Eder and the Bolivian Marxist, the late Sergio Almaraz (quoted on page 92), both are concerned about the corrupting and degrading psychological

effects of U.S. aid. It is difficult to see how any country which has received so much foreign assistance for so long could avoid showing signs
of the effects they describe.

Eder asserts that U.S. assistance has been far too great and misspent
as well. Between 1952 and 1964 the United States extended some $380
million of economic and military assistance to Bolivia, over half in
grants.[112] That's more than a third of a billion dollars for a population
which reached four million in 1964. Whether economic assistance was
too great is, of course, quite a different question.

Eder documents his charges that U.S. aid was misspent with an AID
report which allegedly holds that much of U.S. assistance, perhaps 70
percent, has merely covered deficits of Bolivian government agencies
rather than financing economic development.[113] However, that report was
published in 1963 and much of Bolivia's economic growth has taken place
since that time as the economic indicators referred to earlier indicate.
Eder's charge is a serious one indeed and requires examination beyond
the scope of this study.

Almaraz's and Eder's emotional charges of the U.S. role in the revolution, both of which should be read with caution, suggest that one's
evaluation of U.S. policy toward Bolivia depends as much on subjective as
objective factors, namely on one's own political values. One aspect of this
is that the significance assigned to different factors—economic, social,
and political—varies widely. Eder, for example, puts heavy stress on
economics, especially productivity and efficiency criteria on the basis of
performance in the late 1950s and early 1960s. Yet U.S. assistance did
not have exclusively economic objectives, and an assessment of progress
towards these objectives must also take into account the performance of
more recent years. Moreover, social and political factors figured as well.

The MNR is especially proud of its achievements in the latter fields.
Thanks to the revolution, the Bolivian peasant participates more fully
and more independently in the national economic and political life than
any of his Indian brothers in the Western Hemisphere, with the possible
exception of those in Mexico. Many own and cultivate their own small
plots of land and are entering the national market in ever-growing
numbers. Suffrage has increased from one hundred twenty-six thousand
in 1951 to about nine hundred thousand in the 1960s. More important,
since electoral practices still leave much to be desired, peasant and worker
organizations, though often led by "bosses," are active and influential
participants in national politics. The revolution caused political power to

pass from the hands of a small traditional elite, based primarily on the big tin mines, to a new revolutionary elite which was probably more broadly representative of peasants, workers, and sectors of the middle class. In both ideological orientation and political practice the Bolivian government since 1952 has, for the most part, shown a greater concern for the peasant, the miner, the urban worker, and the dispossessed at the expense of the more affluent social sectors. Moreover, living standards and the economy generally have improved steadily in recent years.

One's evaluation of the Bolivian Revolution and U.S. assistance depends greatly on the value one attaches to these achievements in the direction of greater economic, social, and political equality. For some, and particularly those who place high value on economic and social stability, and whose material interests were damaged, the revolution and U.S. assistance have been a tragedy. For others, especially for those who have claimed to represent the downtrodden, and who had few vested interests in the old regime, almost no price would have been too much.

The MNR leadership is primarily responsible for the revolution, its achievements, and its fall from power. But the United States came to the aid of the MNR government in its worst moments, and U.S. representatives were intimately involved in the events surrounding Paz Estenssoro's exile. Thus, the United States shares with the MNR the credit or blame for the Bolivian Revolution, depending on one's judgment of that unique historical occurrence.[114]

NOTES

1. U.S., Agency for International Development, *Overseas Loans and Grants and Assistance from International Organizations, Obligations and Loan Authorizations, July 1, 1945–June 30, 1967* (March 29, 1968), table 1. Comparisons were made for the years 1953–1964 inclusive. In Latin America, Chile came closest to Bolivia in per capita economic assistance. A selective review of this publication suggests that the only country to receive more per capita economic assistance than Bolivia during this period may have been Israel.

2. United Nations, Department of Economic and Social Affairs, *Foreign Capital in Latin America* (New York, 1955), p. 44.

3. Herbert S. Klein argues persuasively that the charge against the companies is unfounded (*Parties and Political Change in Bolivia, 1880–1952* [Cambridge, 1969], p. 53).

4. Bryce Wood, *The Making of the Good Neighbor Policy* (New York, 1967), chap. 7.

5. Luis Peñaloza C., *Historia del Movimiento Nacionalista Revolucionario 1941–1952* (La Paz, 1963), p. 21.

6. José Felman Velarde, *Víctor Paz Estenssoro: El hombre y la revolución* (La Paz, 1954), p. 88–89.

7. Alberto Mendoza Lopez, *La soberanía de Bolivia estrangulada* (La Paz, 1952), p. 159.

8. Alberto Ostria Gutiérrez, *Una revolución tras los Andes* (Santiago, Chile, 1944), pp. 133 ff.

9. Ibid., p. 134. The text of the alleged letter is also contained in Elías Belmonte Pabón, *Justificativos de nuestra rebelión, 1942,* pp. 268 ff. Neither the publisher nor the place of publication is shown, but the latter is believed to be Germany.

10. Belmonte, *Justificativos de nuestra rebelión,* chaps. 21–24.

11. U.S. Department of State, *Foreign Relations of the United States, Diplomatic Papers, 1941* (Washington, D.C., 1963), vol. 7, p. 436.

12. In an article now being prepared for publication, I will support these conclusions based on documents from the U.S. and German archives, written accounts, and recent interviews with some of the principals. I believe that the Nazis exerted ideological influence over some of the precursors of the MNR (such as President Busch), over some of the earlier military associates of the MNR leaders, and probably over some of the MNR civilians (see note 16).

13. See Professor Thorn's chapter in this volume.

14. U.S., Department of State, *Foreign Relations of the United States, Diplomatic Papers, 1943* (Washington, D.C., 1965), vol. 5, p. 536.

15. The summary was published in U.S., Department of State, *Foreign Relations of the United States, Diplomatic Papers, 1944* (Washington, D.C., 1967), vol. 7, pp. 431 ff. Ostria Gutiérrez published a document purporting to be the full text of this memorandum in *Una revolución tras los Andes,* pp. 220–37.

16. Klein, *Parties and Political Change in Bolivia,* pp. 337, 372–73. Charles H. Weston, Jr., "An Ideology of Modernization: The Case of the Bolivian MNR," *Journal of Inter-American Studies* (January 1968), p. 101, distinguishes sharply between Nazi influence and control.

17. This contention is elaborated in the document mentioned in note 11.

18. *Movimiento Nacionalista Revolucionario,* signed June 7, 1942, by the Comando del Movimiento, Víctor Paz Estenssoro, chief. The date and place of publication are unknown, and page 42 was missing from the copy examined.

19. U.S., Department of State, *Consultation Among the American Republics with Respect to the Argentine Situation* (Washington, D.C., 1946), p. 1.

20. *New York Times,* April 20, 1952, p. 22.

21. M. M. Whiteman, *Digest of International Law* (Washington D.C., 1963), vol. 2, p. 259.

22. *New York Times,* April 13, 1952, p. 1.

23. Whiteman, *International Law,* p. 262.

24. *New York Times,* April 19, 1952, p. 3.

25. *New York Times,* May 4, 1952, p. 29.

26. Whiteman, *International Law,* p. 262.

27. See Professor Goodrich's chapter in this volume.

28. *New York Times,* June 3, 1952, p. 10.

29. (La Paz, n.d.). So did Edmundo Vázquez, *Bolivia en la encrucijada comunista* (Lima, 1955).

30. Víctor Paz Estenssoro, *Discursos parlementarios* (La Paz, 1955), pp. 220–22.

31. Ibid., pp. 41 ff.

32. Alberto Cornejo S., *Programas políticos de Bolivia* (Cochabamba, 1949), p. 393.

33. *Fourth International,* January–February 1953, p. 16.

34. Ibid., pp. 187, 286.

35. Paz Estenssoro, *Discursos parlementarios,* p. 221.

36. Ibid., p. 277.

37. Augusto Céspedes, *El presidente colgado* (La Paz, 1966), pp. 135 ff.

38. Miguel Bonifaz P., *Bolivia, frustración y destino* (Sucre, 1965), p. 168.

39. Akademiia Nauk SSSR, Institut Latinskoi Ameriki, *Politicheskie Partii stran latinskoi ameriki* (Moscow, 1965), p. 85.

40. Ibid., p. 87. See also Bonifaz, *Bolivia, frustración y destino,* p. 177.

41. Akademiia Nauk SSSR, *Politicheskie Partii stran latinskoi ameriki,* p. 87. See also Mario Rolan Anaya, *Política y Partidos en Bolivia* (La Paz, 1966), p. 453.

42. Cándia, *Bolivia, un experimento comunista en América,* pp. 70 ff.

43. I. E. Ershov, "Osvoboditel'no revoliutsionnoe dvizhenie v Bolivii," in *Osvoboditel'noe dvizhenie v Latinskoi Amerike,* ed. Akademiia Nauk SSSR (Moscow, 1964), p. 272.

44. U.S., Department of State, *World Strength of the Communist Party Organizations* (Washington, D.C., 1953).

45. Partido Comunista de Bolivia, *Primer congreso, documentos* (La Paz, 1959).

46. Wálter Guevara Arze, *Planteamientos de la revolución nacional en la décima conferencia inter-americana* (República de Bolivia, 1954), p. 21.

47. Ibid., p. 19.

48. Paz Estenssoro, *Discursos parlementarios,* p. 291.

49. Peñaloza, *Historia del Movimiento Nacionalista Revolucionario,* p. 41.

50. Víctor Andrade, *Bolivia—Problems and Promise* (Washington, D.C., 1956), p. 12, from an address given by the ambassador on November 15, 1952. Andrade, usually associated with the center or right wing of the MNR, expressed the opinion in an interview in La Paz on July 1, 1969, that the MNR sought political *not* economic ends in nationalizing the three large tin companies. He said the MNR did not think the state could operate the mines any more efficiently than private industry, perhaps the contrary, but the purpose was to eliminate the pernicious influence of the tin barons over the state.

51. U.S., Congress, Senate, Committee on Foreign Relations, *Hearings on the Mutual Security Act of 1953* (Washington, D.C., 1953), p. 368.

52. Andrade, *Bolivia—Problems and Promise,* p. 15.

53. *U.S. News and World Report,* June 5, 1953, pp. 69–70 (text of an interview with President Paz Estenssoro). I have been unable to locate any other authoritative evidence that U.S. citizens had interests in the Patiño Company.

54. Ibid., p. 68.

55. *New York Times,* June 17, 1953, p. 26.

56. U.S., Department of State, *Bulletin,* July 20, 1953, p. 82.

57. Milton Eisenhower, *The Wine Is Bitter* (New York, 1963), pp. 67–68.

58. Ibid., p. 68.

59. Ibid., p. 194.

60. Interview, 1969 (name of source withheld).

61. U.S., Department of State, *Bulletin,* November 2, 1953, pp. 584–87.

62. U.S., Department of State, *Bulletin,* October 26, 1953, pp. 554–55.

63. John Moors Cabot, *Toward Our Common Destiny* (Medford, Mass., 1954), p. 186.

64. Interview, La Paz, July 27, 1969.

65. U.S., Department of State, *Bulletin,* October 26, 1953, p. 555.

66. Interview with Andrade, La Paz, June 27, 1969. Andrade reported that Bob Hope started out with the presidential foursome during the subsidy incident and asked the president about the golf stakes. The president reportedly replied he would bet only one dollar, "I just lost three million to the Bolivian ambassador."

67. U.S., Congress, Senate, Committee on Banking and Currency, *Study of Latin American Countries,* report no. 2 (Washington, D.C., 1954), p. 63.

68. U.S., Congress, House of Representatives, *Hearings Before the Committee on Foreign Affairs on the Mutual Security Act of 1955* (Washington, D.C., 1955), p. 306. Mr. Holland's testimony was on June 14, 1955.

69. U.S., Department of State, International Development Agency, *Investment* (Washington, D.C., 1966), p. 3. This is a cumulative report of all specific risk investment guarantees issued since the beginning of the program through June 30, 1964.

70. Cornelius H. Zondag, *The Bolivian Economy, 1952–65* (New York, 1966), p. 114.

71. Dirección Nacional de Informaciónes, *Bolivia diez años de revolución* (La Paz, 1962), pp. 120–36.

72. Zondag, *Bolivian Economy,* pp. 113–14.

73. An authoritative explanation of the inflation problem is contained in George Jackson Eder, *Inflation and Development in Latin America: A Case History of Inflation and Stabilization in Bolivia* (Ann Arbor, Mich., 1968), pp. viii–ix, and chaps. 5, 6, and 7.

74. Zondag, *Bolivian Economy,* p. 56.

75. Eder, *Inflation and Development in Latin America,* p. ix.

76. Ibid., chap. 7.

77. Ibid., pp. 234 and 720.

78. The opposition's criticism of the Plan is contained in Ñuflo Chavez, *El signo del estaño* (La Paz, 1961), pp. 109–55.

79. Eder, *Inflation and Development in Latin America,* p. 177.

80. *Hispanic American Report,* no. 7 (1957), p. 375.

81. *New York Times,* August 7, 1957, p. 9.

82. This is an interesting sidelight since the foreign debt had been in default since 1931. Agreements were worked out with the Foreign Bondholders Protective Association to resume payments on the debt, thus fulfilling one of the requirements qualifying Bolivia for loans from the World Bank (IBRD) as well as for the stabilization loan. Many of Bolivia's defaulted bonds were not in the hands of the original owners but had been bought up by speculators. Payments on the debt have been suspended and resumed several times since the agreement was announced in 1957.

83. Eder, *Inflation and Development in Latin America,* p. 148.

84. Ibid., p. 220.

85. Since 1958 the Bolivian peso has been stabilized at slightly less than twelve pesos to the U.S. dollar.

86. Zondag, *Bolivian Economy,* p. 90.

87. Interview, Lima, Peru, July 7, 1969.

88. Eder, *Inflation and Development in Latin America,* p. 163.

89. Ibid., p. 460.

90. Víctor Paz Estenssoro, *Contra la restauración por la revolución nacional* (Lima, March 1965), pp. 35–36.

91. Eder, *Inflation and Development in Latin America,* pp. 175–76.

92. Supreme Decree 06556, August 22, 1963.

93. Sergio Almaraz Paz, *Requiem para una república* (La Paz, 1969), p. 20. Víctor Paz confirmed this version in an interview in Lima, Peru, July 9, 1969.

94. Ibid., p. 27.

95. See, for example, Akademiia Nauk SSSR, Institut Latinskoi Ameriki, *Strani latinskoi ameriki v sovremennykh mezhdunarodnykh otnosheniiakh* (Moscow, 1967), pp. 125 ff.

96. U.S. Army, *Area Handbook for Bolivia* (Washington, D.C., 1963), p. 688.

97. Ibid., p. 660.

98. Paz Estenssoro, *Contra la restauración*, p. 44.

99. William H. Brill, *Military Civic Action in Bolivia*, Ph.D. dissertation, 1966, p. 121. Available from University Microfilms, Ann Arbor, Mich.

100. Paz Estenssoro, *Contra la restauración*, p. 44.

101. For more details see William H. Brill, *Military Intervention in Bolivia: The Overthrow of Paz Estenssoro and the MNR* (Washington, D.C., 1967).

102. Interview with Víctor Paz, Lima, Peru, July 7, 1969.

103. Ibid., July 9, 1969.

104. Almaraz, *Requiem para una república*, pp. 301 ff.

105. *New York Times*, November 22, 1964, p. 26. For official denials and other information regarding Lt. Col. Fox, see Christopher Rand, "Letters from La Paz," *The New Yorker*, December 31, 1966, p. 54.

106. Interview, Lima, Peru, July 7, 1969.

107. See the *New York Times*, August 18, 1968, p. 18, for a partial text of Arguedas's published statement.

108. Julio Sanjinés Goitia, *Civic Action* (Bolivia, 1964), pp. 2–3.

109. An AP correspondent quoted Paz in *El Mercurio*, Santiago, Chile, April 8, 1955, that "my government would not have lasted without North American aid." The *New York Times*, August 7, 1957, carries a statement by Siles that the stabilization program "saved the country from disaster." The foregoing is quoted by Eder, *Inflation and Development in Latin America*, pp. 79, 513. The quotes have been verified in the original source; *New York Times* source is 1957, not 1959.

110. *Estadísticas Económicas*, 10 (La Paz, 1969), p. 5, shows the per capita GNP for Bolivia increasing from 1961 to 1967 by about 23 percent as compared to an average of 10 percent for eighteen Latin American republics. This handbook contains statistics on agriculture, manufacturing, petroleum, trade, etc.

111. Eder, *Inflation and Development in Latin America*, pp. 609–10.

112. See the graph on p. 77.

113. Eder, *Inflation and Development in Latin America*, p. 605. Eder bases this conclusion on figures and analyses found in Anthony M. Solomon et al., *The Finances of the Public Sector of Bolivia* (Washington, D.C., March 1, 1963), mimeographed.

114. Readers are also referred to Laurence Whitehead, *The United States and Bolivia, a Case of Neo-Colonialism*, a pamphlet published in 1969 by the Haslemere Group, London. It was not received here until after the manuscript had gone to press.

JAMES M. MALLOY
University of Pittsburgh

Revolutionary Politics

THE INSURRECTION

The rising of Easter Week 1952 was brief (lasting three days) and relatively unbloody as contemporary insurrections go. Like most such conspiratorial efforts there was a plan behind it. No sooner had the first shots been fired, however, than the plan was submerged by actual events, and the leaders of both sides were forced to react to a situation largely outside their control. When the smoke had cleared, the leaders of the *Moviemieno Nacionalista Revolucionario* (MNR) found themselves in charge of the Bolivian government. Within days Bolivia was plunged into a process of social, economic, and political change the like of which Latin America had not seen since the Mexican Revolution. The Bolivian national revolution was underway.

Although all of the aspects are not clear, a brief analysis of the insurrection is important to put the revolution that followed into perspective. There is good reason to believe that the original plan of the insurrectionaries did not envision a mass rising but rather a civil-military coup d'etat. The blow was to be delivered by the MNR's civilian irregulars, elements of the national police headed by the minister of government Gen. Antonio Seleme, and, hopefully, elements of the regular military to be delivered by the army chief Gen. Torres Ortiz. The coup was to result in a government similar to that headed by Gualberto Villarroel between 1943 and 1946, that is, a civil-military alliance aimed not at revolution motorized from below but at structural reforms imposed from above.[1]

111

Plans went awry almost immediately. Torres Ortiz, who had never given a firm commitment to the plotters, after some vacillation rallied the army behind the ruling military junta of Gen. Hugo Ballivián. Seleme and his police did come into the streets, but on the second day when he judged the effort to be doomed, Seleme deserted the cause. Isolated and surrounded, the MNR irregulars in the capital under the leadership of Hernán Siles Zuazo continued to resist. Later, on April 10, fighting broke out in a number of the cities in the interior, and in some areas armed workers joined the ranks of the insurrectionaries. Events took a dramatic turn when one contingent of armed miners seized a munitions train near the capital while another surrounded potential reinforcements in the city of Oruro. On the eleventh the junta surrendered, and the MNR assumed formal governmental power. What began as a civil-military coup ended as a broad-based insurrection in which one of the chief components was armed workers.

Throughout the country the army collapsed. Garrison commanders either joined the revolution or abandoned their posts leaving their armories to the insurrectionaries. As the army faded, a populace in arms appeared, and, in the interior, civilian irregulars seized control in the name of the MNR. Within days relatively well-organized militias appeared throughout the country; they were particularly quick to organize the mining camps and areas of worker concentration. Shortly thereafter the formation of a *Confederación Obrera Boliviana* (COB) was announced. Under the leadership of Juan Lechín Oquendo it established itself as the singular voice of Bolivian labor. Although it backed the MNR, the COB made it clear that its support was based on anticipation of a rapid and profound overhauling of Bolivian society and not simply piecemeal reforms. The COB also made it clear in mass demonstration after mass demonstration that such an overhauling had to be based on the nationalization of the mining industry and a meaningful agrarian reform. In effect the COB was telling the MNR that, like it or not, there was going to be a revolution; it was soon apparent that some segments of the MNR did not like it at all.[2]

THE MOVIMIENTO NACIONALISTA REVOLUCIONARIO

The MNR was formed officially in 1941, but its antecedents are directly traceable to manifestations of political dissent which appeared as early as the late 1920s when a general political movement sprouted up among students and young professionals. Although ideologically vague the movement was based on a conscious rejection of the "Liberal" political economy which had held sway in Bolivia since the civil war of 1898. By far the bulk of the participants in the movement were drawn from middle- and upper-class youth.

Two rough ideological and tactical orientations appeared in this early movement. One group adopted the Marxist-Leninist ideological framework and began to project a mass-based revolution from below. The other adopted a vague ideological posture of national renovation and was oriented to achieving office within the existing political framework and imposing structural reforms from above. This latter group, among whom Carlos Montenegro and Augusto Céspedes were important figures, formed the Nationalist party which supported the reforming efforts of the then president (1925–1930) Hernando Siles. A number of Nationalist figures held office under Siles, but they were eclipsed when he was ousted by a military coup in 1930. The activities of both groups were then submerged in the frenzy of the Chaco War period.[3]

The youth movement, buttressed by disaffected young army officers, reappeared with new vigor following the Chaco debacle. After some abortive attempts at forming a united front, the previous Marxist-Nationalist division reoccurred, and the two groups went their separate ways. The Nationalists participated in the reform military governments of Toro and Busch, and in the new daily, *La Calle,* they developed an ideological position which they dubbed "state socialism." This position was heavily influenced by the current European scheme of corporate states and reconfirmed the group's predisposition to immediate occupancy of governmental office and reform imposed from above. When the quixotic Busch killed himself and the old parties reasserted control, the Nationalist group was again pushed to the side.[4]

One of the more important factors operative in the post-Chaco period was the political mobilization of the urban middle-class, the artisans, and the working-class groups. The urban-middle sector was the most immediately relevant group politically, since it was most affected by national inflation. The artisan and labor groups, while important to the political conflicts of the 1936–1939 period, were still too poorly organized and ideologically divided to directly shape the flow of events. The important point is, however, that this period saw the mobilization and politization of sectors previously excluded from political participation. The upshot was that the scope of political conflict was expanded beyond the narrow boundaries of the pre-Chaco political system, and human numbers became an important element of political power. The chief political problem became how to organize these mobilized publics and to give shape and form to this new element of political power.

It was against this backdrop of mobilization and the expansion of political conflict that the two youth countermovements in existence since the late 1920s organized themselves into permanent formal organizations. The bulk of the Marxist wing of the movement formed the *Partido de la Izquierda Revolucionaria* (PIR) while the bulk of the Nationalists formed the Movimiento Nacionalista Revolucionario (MNR). Both parties assailed the "restoration" government of Enrique Peñaranda, but they adopted different programs and pursued different political tactics.

The PIR projected and planned for a mass-based revolution from below; for them, nationalization of the mining industry and agrarian reform were cardinal programatic principles.[5] The PIR, thus, sought to broaden and organize its popular base and to this end sought direct contacts with artisans, workers, teachers, and, to some extent, peasants. These efforts were, in the main, successful, and the PIR established itself as the major political spokesman of the Bolivian lower classes. Throughout the early 1940s the political demands of these groups were increasingly expressed through the symbols and rhetoric of Marxism.

The MNR sought to build a popular image but did little at this point to organize public support. Its open political activity was primarily propagandistic, and its major appeal was to the increasingly restive urban middle class. Like the PIR the MNR managed to seat a number of its members in the national Congress. Under the leadership of the rising figure of Víctor Paz Estenssoro, the party flailed away at the "Liberal" order and developed its own ideological orientation.

The MNR claimed to have formulated a nationalist position uniquely appropriate to Bolivia. As part of its nationalist stance the MNR attacked all groups with an international orientation including imperialists, masons, Jews, and leftist groups such as the PIR.[6] Its leaders argued that, while politically independent, Bolivia was economically a vassal state. This vassalage was the result, they claimed, of the current Liberal capitalistic state model which allowed foreign financial penetration, dependence on mineral export, and monopolistic control of the vital tin industry. The MNR held that, due to the Big Three tin magnates' economic power, they formed a state within the state. This superstate ruled Bolivia through an upper class which the tin barons bought and controlled. This group was known as *La Rosca,* an oligarchy which exploited Bolivia for its benefit and that of its imperialist cronies thereby impoverishing the nation, alienating its patrimony, and submerging its national culture.

Thus, in the MNR's Bolivia, the problem was not the internal exploitation of one class by another (of which the PIR spoke) but the oppression of the nation as such. The issue was not class versus class but nation versus antination. The instrument of struggle could not be a party like the PIR because a party is the expression of a class. There had to be a movement which would draw together within it the essential elements of the nation, e.g., the impoverished middle class, the workers, and the peasants. As the true base of the nation all of these groups were equally oppressed and had, therefore, a common set of interests. Yet an analysis of the situation demonstrated that the workers and peasants, through no fault of their own, were nonetheless too underdeveloped to shape a course of action. Hence the movement had to be led by the most advanced and progressive sectors of the society—the middle- and upper-class intellectuals of the MNR.[7]

The MNR declared its intention to liberate Bolivia economically and, thereby, to create a truly self-defining nation. Its watchwords were *nation, state,* and *development.* The state would be used to foment development, thereby liberating and consolidating the nation. The state would achieve these ends by: a) regulating the tin industry, particularly in matters of foreign exchange, b) sponsoring economic diversification and agricultural development, c) controlling public utilities, d) protecting small- and medium-sized private enterprises, e) giving a decent standard of living to all, and f) freeing Bolivian jobs for Bolivians. In this period there was no official party call for universal suffrage, nationalization of the tin industry, or agrarian reform.[8]

Despite its rhetoric the early MNR hardly constituted a multiclass movement. It remained an electoral and parliamentary cabal seeking quick access to governmental office through which it intended to impose reform. While it openly pursued electoral methods, behind the scenes it followed the path of conspiracy. Its conspiratorial efforts led to the coup of 1943 which put the group back into the realm of formal governmental control. The basic orientation of the early MNR was, in short, reformist, statist, and elitist.

When the hapless Villarroel was toppled in 1946, the MNR was again out in the cold; clearly, it was time for a postmortem. The members of the MNR had touched formal power three times by following a strong man; but when the strong man went down, so did they. After a bitter debate which resulted in a number of splits, a new tactical line began to emerge.[9] This line, identified with the exiled Paz Estenssoro, was based on three conclusions drawn from the past experiences of the party: a) the MNR could not achieve its goals alone, b) future governments had to be anchored in a popular base, and c) the political teeth of the mine magnates would have to be extracted. After 1947 the MNR, therefore, began an attempt to broaden and organize its popular base.

Attempts at organization met with considerable success particularly in the cities among middle groups, artisans, and marginal elements of the working sector. The MNR formed a national structure ascending from local cells through regional commandos to a national political committee. The organization was almost exclusively urban and, due to communications difficulties, was poorly coordinated. This primary organization was, therefore, relatively small in numbers, mainly middle class in both leaders and followers, and dominated by a political committee more or less isolated in La Paz.

During this period the MNR also made a concerted effort to draw into its fold the more organized working groups such as miners, railway workers, and factory workers. However, by this time these groups, which formed the basis of the Bolivian labor movement, had developed fairly coherent and self-conscious organizations led by an internally generated working-class elite. Moreover, due to their previous connections with the PIR and the smaller *Partido Obrero Revolucionario* (POR), these groups had come to express themselves politically in the rhetoric and symbols of revolutionary socialism. Finally the leaders of these groups made it clear that, despite having cooperated with middle-class radicals in the past, they were fundamentally suspicious of all petit bourgeois politicians, whatever their rhetoric.[10]

Thus the labor public which the MNR sought to mobilize after 1947 was not an unled, unoriented mass like the other groups which the MNR pulled into its orbit. Unlike the unorganized urban middle, artisans, and the marginally employed, the workers were not directly available for mobilization. The local *sindicato* ("labor union"), the functional federation, and a loose national confederation stood between the individual mine, railway, or factory worker and the MNR. As a result the MNR never directly incorporated organized labor into the party but became, rather, its chosen political instrument. Labor leaders, who formed around the increasingly powerful figure of Juan Lechín Oquendo, began to make up a leftist labor sector of the MNR separate from the largely middle-class primary organization. Thus, while the MNR broadened its popular base after 1947, it did not become a centrally directed mass movement. It was transformed instead into an alliance between the bourgeois-dominated political committee and the more radical leaders of organized labor. This alliance was precarious and fraught with mutual distrust and hostility.[11]

The impact of this dramatic shift in the composition of the MNR was demonstrated in the election campaign of 1951 when the party, for the first time, became publicly associated with a program embodying the goals of universal suffrage, nationalization of tin, and agrarian reform. But it is evident from later events that a number of the original MNR leaders either viewed this program as tactical rhetoric or had limited conceptions as to what these measures would entail.

As a result of its impressive showing in the 1951 elections, the MNR became a magnate for the disaffected of both the Left and the Right, and the party, thereby, grew in strength. Most of these newcomers were leftist in orientation, however, and the existing labor-left sector of the party was strengthened considerably.

It is important to note that, up to and including the insurrection of 1952, the MNR had little organizational contact with the peasant mass. The peasants remained marginal to the political process until the post-insurrection period. Hence, up through the rising of 1952, the MNR, despite dramatic internal changes, remained a movement of the urban-oriented, tin-dominated sector of Bolivian life.

The purpose of this brief recounting of the MNR's pre-1952 growth and development is to make clear that on the eve of the insurrection the party was a multicephalic mélange of conflicting elements held together by tactical realities. For purposes of analysis it is useful to distinguish three different leadership groups in the MNR at this stage of the revolutionary process. The bulk of the leaders of the national political committee actually on the scene maintained the original MNR's elitist and essentially reformist vision of a new order; for this reason they can be classified as right wing. The labor-left sector, in contrast, had a definite revolutionary socialist vision of the society it expected to create. Many in this sector were ex-*PIRistas* or *PORistas* who entered the MNR under a strategy known as *entrismo* ("infiltration")—to join the party and radicalize it from within. A third rough grouping was made up of older MNR leaders in exile such as Paz Estenssoro. This group adopted what can be called a pragmatic nationalist position with a basic goal of national development. To achieve that goal, it was willing to be flexible in bowing to the ascending power of the left, but, ultimately, it sought to keep the left within a national development framework dominated by the core MNR elite.[12]

Between 1936 and 1952 one of the most important processes taking place in Bolivia was that of mobilization, which led to a steady expansion of the scope and intensity of national political conflict. During this time the grouping with the greatest growth in power potential was the relatively autonomous and highly politicized labor movement. Although it alone could not mount a revolutionary drive, it did, after 1946, set the major tone of conflict. Throughout this period the MNR was transformed from a small, elitist cabal oriented to reform from above into the formal directorate of a broad-based revolutionary movement. The MNR core elite's ability to control this movement was, at best, problematic.

THE REVOLUTION

PHASE I

As the old structure of power literally collapsed throughout the country and armed civilian irregulars assumed control in various population centers, Hernán Siles Zuazo assumed interim control of the presidency in the name of the MNR. As part of his interim duties, Siles staffed an amplified cabinet which included members of all sectors of the party. A critical precedent was established when Siles appointed three COB members as *ministros obreros* ("workers' ministers"), Juan Lechín Oquendo as minister of mines and petroleum, German Butron as minister of labor, and Ñuflo Chavez Ortiz as minister of peasant affairs. On April 17, 1952, Paz Estenssoro returned from exile, assumed the presidency, formalized the interim cabinet, and designated Siles as vice-president. Joyous street demonstrations ratified this first official government of the national revolution.

A common characteristic of modern revolutions, beginning with the French, is an effort at a total break with the past in political concept as well as in social and economic deed. New political principles, new religions, new rhetorical styles, new modes of dress, etc., have all been common features of these attempts to build from scratch a new social universe. It is of more than passing interest that the core leadership of the MNR proclaimed no such radical break with the Bolivian past. Paz and Siles claimed their right to govern not on the basis of revolutionary legitimacy but on the grounds of existing constitutional authority.[13] They claimed to be assuming the mandate given them in the elections of 1951. In other words the insurrection was a means to reestablish the constitutional norms abrogated by the coup of 1951. By this and a number of other acts too numerous to go into here, it is clear that the core MNR group drew on the past for its right to rule and never claimed to be the source of right in itself.

The first major political act decreed by the revolutionary government—universal adult suffrage—should be seen in this light. Undoubtedly the enfranchisement of the Indian peasant mass has had a profound impact on the distribution of power in Bolivian society. But without the agrarian reform which came over a year later (and then only after bitter struggles in the party), the implications of the vote could have been quite different. Landowners could have controlled the new peasant vote and used it to buttress their power. The vote was not necessarily a revolutionary act in terms of preexistent political norms but could be viewed, rather, as an act broadening the citizen body that would participate in those norms.

This process of openly proclaiming its continuity with pre-existent political morality is probably a reflection of attitudes that ran deep in the original founders of the MNR. No matter how profound were the changes in the structure of Bolivian society, the core MNR leadership remained, in spirit and orientation, essentially reformist. Moreover, the dimension of society that they were most concerned with reforming was the economic. Social and political changes were secondary, but instrumental, to the goal of economic development.[14] That the MNR presided over (as opposed to directed) an important revolutionary process was more a result of circumstances than intention. The Old Guard of the MNR was, at best, a reluctant band of revolutionaries. This basic orientation, which was shared by the pragmatic nationalists as well as the right, was a permanent factor in shaping the relations between the MNR core and its labor-left allies.

This fact was not missed by the left. Immediately after the insurrection the COB declared itself in a state of permanent vigilance lest the bourgeois MNR seek to hold back the revolution.[15] The style and rhetoric of the labor-left leadership jarred that of the MNR leadership. The two elite groups obviously differed profoundly in their basic views of the meaning of the revolution and what the new society should look like. Through its organ, *Rebellion,* the COB warned that MNR reactionaries were attempting to either totally block or, at least, dilute programs such as mine nationalization and agrarian reform.[16] The MNR right wing, through its organ, *En Marcha,* countered by warning of a COB-based plot to communize Bolivia. Intense and bitter behind-the-scenes struggles were carried out in party and cabinet meetings. The COB took to the streets, utilizing mass demonstrations to exhort its followers to seize the mines and the land. In policy debates the COB demanded nationalization of tin without indemnification and land expropriation without repayment.

It was in this context of bitter ideological conflict and intense factional struggle that the revolutionary process unfolded. The great structural changes decreed by the revolutionary government were not the result of the implementation of an agreed-upon program. Rather they represented consciously engineered compromises among the conflicting factions operating under the penumbra of the MNR. The big loser in these measures was undoubtedly the party's right wing, which found itself more and more isolated from the central drama. In the main the compromises were hammered out between the MNR pragmatic nationalists around Paz and the leftist entristas around Lechín. In these early battles the older centrist leaders following their long-standing interest in economic development and diversification were concerned mainly with state control of capital sources and means of reinvestment, while the newer leftist leaders were mainly concerned with property relations and the redistribution of economic and political power.

The first major structural change decreed by the new government was the tin nationalization order. Historically the MNR had always wanted to get a hold on tin profits for the state but, prior to 1951, had not identified itself with a policy of nationalization. Sentiment remained strong among the older party stalwarts to restrict action to a policy of controlling, rather than expropriating, tin.[17] The COB, however, was adamant on the question of nationalization. When the continual pressure of the COB was combined with the feeling in some party circles that the political power of the tin barons definitely had to be destroyed, the decision to nationalize the mines was pushed through. The decree itself was a compromise between the position of the pragmatic center and the labor left.

In the first instance, the scope of the decree was restricted to well-defined limits. The only property to be nationalized was that of the Big Three consortiums of Patiño, Aramayo, and Hochschild. Small- and medium-sized operations and those owned by foreign capital, such as the Grace Company, were not affected. Moreover, the decree neither challenged the principle of private property as such nor, for that matter, foreign capital as such. It was a bill of particulars justifying limited and specific action against three companies for their specific antinational sins. Indeed the principle of private property was obliquely sanctioned by the government's commitment to foster the growth of small- and medium-sized private companies and to indemnify the companies losing their property.[18] These actions were taken as much to mollify Washington as to reassure the right wing of the party.

The decree, therefore, was not a socialistic measure. As the MNR ambassador to Washington explained, the nationalization decree did not reflect a general MNR approach to political economy but a special case.[19] From the core MNR point of view, therefore, the nationalization decree was not part of an integrated theory of revolution and social change. The decree embodied an expression of pragmatic nationalism measured in terms of the wealth and power of the state, which is seen as the locus and expression of the nation. The original MNR orientation, which separated it from other countertendencies, was showing remarkable persistence despite changing tactical realities.

Although these subtleties of conception reflected more of the MNR core view, the implementation of the decree was to reflect more the concrete power of the labor left. The major concession to the left was the provision known as *control obrero con derecho al veto* ("worker control with the right of veto"). At every level of the administration, worker-designated representatives were to participate in decision-making with the right to veto decisions deemed inimical to the interests of the mines and the miners. The effect of this decree was to create in the mines and in the new state mining corporation an independent locus of power under the control of the union organizations.

The reality of the situation in the mines was given dramatic demonstration during the decree-signing ceremony. The ceremony took place on October 31, 1952, in the María Barzola mining camp, a part of the historic Catavi Siglo XX complex which had been the lodestone of the Patiño empire. When President Paz arrived at the isolated camp, high in the reaches of the bleak Andes, he was greeted by a salute of twenty-one blasts of dynamite—the chief tool of the hard-rock miner and often his favorite weapon.

When the president affixed his signature to the paper, the thousands of miners assembled for the ceremony expressed their approval by firing round after round from their newly acquired rifles and machine guns into the thin Andean air. Paz signed as president of the republic and leader of the MNR. His signature was followed by that of Juan Lechín Oquendo, minister of state, leader of the miners federation, and chief of Bolivian organized labor. Lechín's hand on the document reflected much more than the countersignature of the appropriate state officer. It spoke of a reality comprehensible at a glance—the disparity between formal and concrete power.

Another critical issue in this first phase of the revolution was the status of the military in the new society. The left called for total destruction of the military, a demand which the MNR right resisted assiduously. Again a compromise was worked out. Contrary to some earlier reports, the military as an institution was not destroyed. It was purged, reduced in size, and downgraded in status; the purge was conducted by a military tribunal, not a revolutionary court, indicating thereby the essential continuity of the institution as such.

In addition to the purge, the role of the military in Bolivian society was redefined. The army was to be changed from an institution of control and repression into an institution of production. The idea was that the army would become a source of labor and technical expertise and a means of mobilizing resources for development. In this notion of the producing army lay the seeds of the later Civic Action programs undertaken by the Bolivian army.[20]

Whatever the intentions of the actors caught up in events, changes such as those we have been discussing cannot help but have a tremendous impact on a society's politics. From the political point of view the crux of the issue of revolution lies not in socio-economic changes per se but in the effect such changes have on the composition and distribution of the capacity to control and rule. Before a new society can be built to reflect the preferred images of any particular group, the would-be builders must have previously established their ability to rule.

In Bolivia the most immediate change in the pattern of control and rule was the dramatic emergence of labor as a key power group. Central to this fact was the continuing and accelerating process of mobilization which had been acting as a parameter of political struggle since the late 1930s. One immediate result of the insurrection was the rapid dispersal of weapons to the civil population. Sporadic and spontantous at first, the process was quickly organized in working-class districts and mining camps. A national system of workers' militias emerged with stunning rapidity. Nominally subject to the MNR, the militias were, in reality, under the effective control of the labor left on both a national and local basis.

As Max Weber has pointed out, one of the essential characteristics of the modern state is its ability to claim a legitimate monopoly on the capacity to use force within its boundaries. Likewise it seems axiomatic that in a revolutionary situation (which does not terminate with a successful insurrection) one of the chief immediate determinants of political outcome is the distribution of the capacity to organize and use force.

The MNR core elite was committed to the idea of national development measured in the increase of the power of the state. The MNR core sought to achieve this goal while keeping the existing form of the state largely intact. While formal continuity was maintained, an important functional basis of formal authority's operational reality was slipping away. The capacity to organize and use force was devolving to intermediate bodies whose relationship to both the party and the state was rather problematic.

Workers' militias, for example, were organized and controlled by the COB. Not only was the COB's right to be the only voice of Bolivian labor recognized, but the COB was also granted the right of cogovernment. Under this arrangement the COB had the privilege of naming the ministers of mines, labor, and peasant affairs. Thus three crucial state ministers were not national officers but direct representatives of the labor left.

With the nationalization decree the miners' federation, the most powerful group in the COB and the basis of Lechín's power, was given a significant voice in administrating the most important sector of the economy. This formal power was backed by the militias attached to the local unions. Before the new mining corporation could even be organized, the unions had become the real centers of authority and power in the camps.

During this first phase of the revolution, there developed an important divergence between authority and power. The COB, which included in its ranks not only the left-wing of the MNR but also leftist parties such as the PIR, POR, and Communists, became a government within a government. The COB had all the characteristics of a sovereignlike entity including executive, deliberative, and judicial organs; a defined area of authority and constituents; and, most importantly, armed forces. Allied with the MNR the COB demanded and received corporate status within the state. As such, it let the MNR assume the formal responsibility of government while it constituted itself as an unrivaled center of initiative and veto—it had governing power but no responsibility.

The COB was not a monolithic entity; it was wracked by ideological and group conflicts. Yet in these first days of the revolution it was able to present a relatively united front to the government of the bourgeoisie. In any event, in this critical period the labor left successfully established itself as the pivot of the national revolution.

PHASE II

Up through the insurrection of 1952 the revolutionary process in Bolivia was confined almost exclusively to the cities and mining camps. With the collapse of the old system of control the revolutionary drive began to break out of its previous sociopolitical confines. In the fall of 1952, reports reached La Paz of peasant protest activities in the Cochabamba valley. This protest activity later turned into land seizures and the invasion of rural towns. During the late winter and spring of 1953 the sporadic risings turned into a generalized Indian peasant drive against the existing rural order.[21]

By all accounts the question of land reform was the most divisive issue to be raised in the loosely knit revolutionary family. The MNR as such was not associated with the goal of a general agrarian reform until the elections of 1951. Even then a number of party leaders had very limited measures in mind. There is also reason to believe that in some quarters of the party any notion of a peasant movement was abhorrent.[22] Thus when the issue was raised in the context of open peasant violence, all semblances of party unity began to give way.

Behind the battle over agrarian reform were fundamental differences in both attitude and concept. In the first instance, the reform went to the heart of the property issue which had been so skillfully evaded in the tin nationalization decree. At stake was not simply the property rights of a few individuals but of an entire social class. For many Bolivians an agrarian reform implied the dispossession of white, Spanish-speaking "civilized" Bolivians in favor of the lowest creature in the Bolivian human scheme—*el indio* ("the Indian"). The agrarian property system of Bolivia was born in the Spanish Conquest and extended throughout the nineteenth century by an open and often brutal dispossession of Indian communities by the new Creole elite. The agrarian structure was a product of the conquest of one culture by another and, hence, continued as the nexus of a system of internal colonialism.[23]

Thus to threaten the agrarian structure was to threaten a complex system of values and a way of life traceable to colonial times. The organization of man and land within the *hacienda* was not simply a means of accruing wealth; it was the concrete root of a family and its name.

The values associated with the landed status were shared by many in the middle sector who patterned their own lives as much as possible on that of La Rosca. That these people resented the upper class is evident, but their resentment grew out of an inability to share fully in the upper class's way of life, not a rejection of it. They were the impoverished middle, but they were not indios; and they wished to be *buena gente* ("good people").

Finally the issue of agrarian reform awakened fears that ran deep in Spanish-speaking Bolivia. The relationship between the Spanish-speaking culture and the suppressed Indian culture was pervaded with mutual hate, distrust, and fear. To many, the city was the repository of civilization and the hacienda its outpost. With the hacienda destroyed, what was to stop the hate-filled Indian horde from sweeping over the cities in a paroxysm of revenge? [24]

Agrarian reform, therefore, was an emotional issue which raised questions regarding property rights, the distribution of power, cherished values, and race. The MNR was committed to do something about the agrarian system, but what that something would be was far from clear. The enfranchisement of the Indian was a nod in that direction. Agrarian reform as a goal was spoken of in the early days of the revolution, but little was done beyond talk of the need to study the problem. Once the peasant movement was under way, however, the question could no longer be put off.

The origins of the Bolivian peasant movement are cloudy and the subject of much academic dispute, particularly over the question of whether it was a spontaneous movement from below or a controlled thrust organized from above. As yet there is not enough information to clarify the situation completely, but a few general comments can be made. The movement originated in the peasant center of Ucureña located in the Cochabamba valley. Peasant organization in this area can be traced to the post–Chaco War period when a union type of organization was founded on the *finca* ("farm") of Santa Clara. Modified versions of this early organization survived throughout the 1936–1952 period. During those years the union had contact with non-Indian outsiders, but it remained a relatively autonomous entity. It was this organization, along with a few others, that was involved in the first land seizures of 1952. It seems legitimate, therefore, to look upon the movement as a self-generating, if not wholly spontaneous, phenomenon. [25]

While it was the peasants who conducted the seizures, it is clear that they did so with the active encouragement of the labor left. Representatives of the COB and the POR were very active in the valley during the risings. Outside influence was, therefore, rather marked in these first activities. This external influence became even more evident as the movement spread from the Cochabamba valley to the rest of the country. Given the topography of Bolivia, the notorious isolation of most rural communities, and the absence of national communications, it is difficult to account for the rapid spread of the movement in terms of a spontaneous imitation of the valley pattern. If it had not been for other factors, most Indians would not have heard of the risings for months. Someone had to carry the word. That word was spread by the POR, the MNR left, and, perhaps most importantly, by the ministry of peasant affairs controlled by the *COBista* Ñuflo Chavez.

Under Chavez, organizers fanned out across the country organizing unions and promising land reform. The POR and COB, meanwhile, warned of reactionary cliques in the MNR and counseled the peasants to follow the example of the miners. As these organizing and propaganding efforts spread so, too, did rural violence and land seizures. As the movement spread, landowners and town dwellers fled the countryside bringing with them tales of Indian vengeance.[26]

The MNR split deeply over the issue of rural violence. While the left pushed the movement, some elements of the right actively sought to repress it. The center first condemned the movement, then equivocated, and, finally, declared its support for a thoroughgoing reform. As the bulk of the party swung behind the movement, the right, in a last-ditch effort, attempted a coup d'etat on January 6, 1953. The attempt failed miserably, and on January 20 a commission to adopt an agrarian reform law was formed.

As the commission deliberated, rural violence continued unabated. Indeed, it was soon evident that whatever role national actors had played in fomenting the movement, it had taken on its own dynamic thrust and was not in the control of any national organization. In most of the country the old structure disappeared, and the countryside was in a total state of flux. When the agrarian reform was promulgated on August 3, 1953, it amounted to little more than the ratification of a *fait accompli*.

Whatever its roots, the following conclusions seem legitimate in regard to the peasant movement after 1952:

  a. The immediate stimulus was the collapse of national control brought about by the MNR-led insurrection.

b. The rapid spread of the movement was aided by the active support of the labor left.
c. Once underway, the movement developed its own dynamic and slipped out of the control of all national actors.
d. The movement definitely ruptured the old links between rural and urban Bolivia and left the countryside in a state of total disarray.

Again formal authority and concrete power diverged. Neither the MNR nor the COB was able to step into the rural vacuum and reorganize it on a national basis. The sindicato became the new basic unit of rural Bolivia, and alongside of it there appeared well-armed peasant militias. While the sindicato became universal, its level of organizational maturity varied considerably from region to region. In many regions political activity subsided and peasant communities lapsed into isolated subsistence. In these areas the sindicatos remained at a low level of development, and militias did not become a significant local factor. These areas also tended to remain marginal to national political developments over the next decade.

In other regions another pattern of rural development occurred. Local sindicatos and militias were consolidated into centrally controlled regional groupings which in some cases covered almost an entire department. This pattern was particularly important in the Cochabamba valley and in the Altiplano region around Lake Titicaca. In both areas a newly emergent peasant elite gained control of the sindicatos and the militias.

It should be added that since the agrarian reform, the Bolivian countryside has been marked by a bewildering array of patterns with variations both among and within regions. Moreover, knowledge of recent rural Bolivia is far from complete. The papers in this volume by Professors Carter, Léons, and Burke, however, give the reader a broader feel of the diversity of the situation. The new peasant elite sparked the formation of a national confederation of peasants which aspired to a status similar to that of the COB. This national organization, however, never really established itself as the singular voice of the Bolivian peasant. Effective peasant political organization remained essentially a regional phenomenon, the most important of such regions being the Cochabamba valley and the lake area.

The most important form of regional peasant organization was the unit known as the central—twenty to thirty sindicatos tied to a command center located in or near a town. In the valley, Ucureña, Cliza, Punata, and Totora were among the more important centrals; on the Altiplano

Achacachi, Warisata, and Huarina were strong centers. Each central was dominated by a *dirigente campesino* ("regional strong man"). Over the years these dirigentes continuously struggled amongst themselves for regional power and jurisdiction. At one point the centrals of both the lake and valley areas were consolidated under the control of two dominant *caciques* ("regional bosses"), Toribio Salas who controlled the bulk of the Altiplano and José Rojas Guevara who held sway over the valley. These caciques battled each other for national control, and each had to fend off the incessant threats of local challengers. Both regions experienced protracted intrapeasant civil wars.

The political effects of this revolutionary spill over into the rural sphere were profound but extremely variable. The most immediately important general effect was the disappearance of institutionalized ties between the national urban arena and the vast rural realm. In some areas these ties were not reestablished, and the inhabitants slipped into a state of atomized subsistence marginal to the national political struggle. In other areas the peasant was to become a political actor of prime importance, but he did so on the basis of autonomous, personally controlled local organizations that entered national political disputes within a localized and particularistic frame of reference.

Like the workers' unions and militias, the peasant sindicatos were nominally a part of the MNR. The national party organization, however, had minimal control over the sindicatos. Where the unions were strong, peasant political behavior was not determined by national elites but by the interests, views, and whims of the local dirigentes. The centrals and regional confederations like the COB became sovereignlike units ruled by the princelike caciques. Through the militias they monopolized force in their areas. Some centrals established barracks manned by compulsory levies on individual sindicatos. The centrals mobilized financial resources by taxing their members, imposing fines, and extracting tribute from regional commerce. With these resources they bought weapons and maintained staffs. Within their *de facto* jurisdictions the dirigentes made rules and punished transgressors. Thus the rural revolution expanded the general process of the dispersion and localization of concrete power.[27]

REVOLUTIONARY ALLIANCES, 1953–1960

The coup attempt by the MNR right was a last-ditch effort to stem what it considered a leftist takeover of the revolution. The coup brought to an end a ten-month period of intense internal struggles in which many old MNR stalwarts saw their ability to influence events and enjoy the perquisites of office systematically reduced. To their minds the individuals responsible for their eclipse were Paz and Lechín, two Machiavellians who had entered into a pact to communize the revolution.[28] That Paz and Lechín were responsible for the right's decline is unquestionable, but the motives behind their actions are another matter.

The labor left emerged from the insurrection as a much stronger and more purposeful wing of the revolutionary movement. Since the Thesis of Pulacayo (the Trotskyite document propounding a workers' revolution) and the beginning of entrismo, the labor left had been developing an elaborate ideological picture of what it wanted from the revolution. Moreover, its overall strategy was predicated on the anticipation of a clash with what it called the bourgeois right of the MNR. The speed with which the workers' militias and the COB were organized was a definite indication of the left's readiness and willingness to push its line against all comers.

The MNR right, in contrast, never formulated a clear image of what it expected from the revolution. It had no program and proffered little more than vague abstractions and emotive symbols. It had almost exclusively focused on the problem of seizing power and had given little thought to what would come after. The right's power was based on its control of the largely middle-class primary organization and urban paramilitary units, which numbered no more than five hundred.[29] Measured against the labor left, the real power of the right in terms of numbers, guns, and determination was unimpressive.

The pragmatic center around Paz had no real base. On his return in 1952 Paz was confronted with a situation radically different from that which he had left six years earlier. The power manifested by the labor left could not be ignored; in fact, when the question of counterrevolution was considered, it was a welcome resource. The problem of the MNR center boiled down to how to tread the middle line between the threat of counterrevolution and the strident demands being raised in the COB for an immediate leftist takeover, in other words, how to utilize the power of the left within an MNR-led framework of national development.

For ten months the MNR center partially gave in to the left's demands at the expense of the right. The MNR right was being consistently pushed to the sidelines, but so, too, was the POR-dominated left wing of the COB. In a real sense the MNR center was co-opting the bulk of the COB by demonstrating the correctness of the entrista strategy—that the revolution could be radicalized from within.[30] The upshot of this was the steady emergence of a center-left axis dominated by the figures of Paz and Lechín. This trend solidified into an active coalition with the abortive rightist coup of January 6, 1953. In the wake of the coup many right-wing leaders (including such notables as Luis Peñaloza and Jorge Rios Gamara) were purged, but none were killed and the involvement of some was covered up. By the same token the POR rump lost influence in the national COB but retained its bases in the sindicatos and particularly in the mines. An operative coalition was formed, but it continued to be flanked by right and left wings. Beyond this the *Falange Socialista Boliviana* (FSB, a right-wing party formed in the late 1930s and modeled on the Spanish Flange) put itself at the head of all those hurt by the revolution and grew rapidly into an intransigent vanguard of counter-revolution.

The Paz-Lechín center-left axis dominated the next three years of the revolution. But the MNR center had all it could do to hang on to formal power. In addition to the great revolutionary reforms, the left pushed through decree after decree favoring labor. Thousands of miners who had been fired between 1946 and 1952 were hired back by the state mining corporation, COMIBOL. Wages were raised, bonuses decreed, rents controlled, ceilings on prices established, and so on. The government intervened on labor's behalf in disputes with management. It became virtually impossible to lay off or fire a Bolivian worker. The social security system was expanded, schools were built, and in the mines the *pulperiás* ("company stores") were maintained by government subsidy.[31]

These measures, along with other reforms, constituted a tremendous process of wealth redistribution and increase in popular consumption. At the same time the government sought to realize its long-standing dream of economic diversification, particularly in agriculture. Public investment in economic projects increased dramatically. During these first years the revolutionary government was trying to follow a consumption and investment policy simultaneously. That would have been a tricky course to strike out on in any underdeveloped environment; in the unibased Bolivian economy it was a most hazardous route. Unfortunately, before the government was even firmly on route, tin prices dipped precariously. The result of all these factors was uncontrollable inflation.[32]

The brunt of the inflation fell on the economically dependent urban middle stratum—the sector which had backed the MNR due to its inflation-pressed position in the old regime. The rise in power and status of the workers and peasants and the grinding effects of the new inflation drove this middle section from the MNR to the ranks of the FSB. The FSB launched a series of violent risings to which the government responded in kind. Violence begat violence and the revolutionary government became more and more repressive. A *control político* ("political police") was formed, dissidents were banished to isolated camps, and a general air of personal insecurity pervaded the country. In hopes of cowing its opponents, the revolutionary coalition trucked thousands of workers and peasants to the capital in pointed demonstrations of the revolution's armed might. These demonstrations made their point but hardly reawakened the urban middle's loyalty to the revolution.

In the preelection convention of 1956 the battle between the right and the left was rejoined with new vigor. Wálter Guevara Arze, a figure of long-standing prominence in the party, became the spokesman for the right and openly attacked Lechín and the COB. The COBistas demonstrated their power by forcing through a censure of Guevara, but the party was shaken deeply. To ward off another open split, a compromise ticket was formulated. Hernán Siles Zuazo, considered to be of center-right sympathies, was given the presidential nomination with the prominent COBista Ñuflo Chavez as his running mate. More importantly the COB dominated the drawing up of the party's legislative list. Only a last-minute threat from Siles to resign blocked the left from stacking the lists too completely in their favor. The MNR ran away with the elections of 1956, but the FSB held up well in the major cities, confirming the diss-affection of the urban middle.[33]

Siles declared the major goal of his government to be an institutionalization of the revolution. Central to his scheme was his avowed intention to rely on U.S. economic aid. The rub, from the point of view of both the United States and Siles, was the inflation; before anything else could be done the inflation had to be stopped. A stabilization plan was drawn up by a U.S. economic advisory team headed by George Jackson Eder. The plan was based on strict monetary logic and called for a return to a free market in which all price controls would be removed and further increases in consumption power restricted.[34] Not surprisingly the labor left viewed this as a direct attack on the workers' revolutionary gains. Siles, however, announced his intention to implement the plan, thereby forcing Lechín (who had offered cautious support for a modified plan) to take a stand.

The plan had variable impact on workers' groups. Some were relatively unaffected, while others, particularly the miners, were scheduled to be hurt seriously. The miners' federation was the single most important wing of the COB and, of course, the bedrock of Lechín's national prominence. Therefore, when the POR and the *Partido Comunista de Bolivia* (PCB) cadres whipped up the feelings of the miners against the measure, Lechín had little choice but to declare his implacable opposition as well. By playing on old ideological distinctions and the variable impact of the plan, Siles was able to engineer the first serious split in the COB. A pro-Siles wing was formed, but the bulk of the key organizations lined up behind Lechín. The struggle over the stabilization plan dominated the four years of Siles's presidency, and during the battle a number of important factors were added to the political equation.

The battle between Siles and Lechín ruptured the center-left coalition that had controlled the revolution since 1953. As part of his drive against Lechín, Siles returned to office a number of right-wing figures including Peñaloza, Rios Gamara, and Guevara Arze, and Lechín's supporters were ousted from important party and governmental posts. In 1958 Siles scored an important victory when he managed to redesign the legislative lists in favor of MNR figures loyal to him. These actions resulted in the substitution of a center-right coalition for the previous center-left alliance at the national level.

Siles took two other steps which were ultimately to have critical significance in the future of the revolution. He appointed José Rojas Guevara as minister of peasant affairs, thus permitting the first Indian peasant in Bolivian history to hold a cabinet post. In addition, Siles began, with U.S. help, to rebuild the army and to dust off its public image.[35] Siles then used units of the army to intervene in Rojas's behalf in an intracampesino war in the valley, thereby aiding Rojas to establish his control over the area. Behind these moves was a concerted effort on Siles's part to establish the army as a counter-weight to the miners' militias and to woo the peasants to his cause rather than to the Lechín labor left. Under Siles, the army grew but was still no match for the militias. Siles gained the support of the valley peasant groups for his drive against the left, but the Altiplano areas under the control of Salas threw their weight behind Lechín.

By 1959 Siles appeared to have Lechín and his supporters on the ropes, but the costs of the battle were high. Violent demonstrations, bitter strikes, and political assasinations had wracked the country from 1957 to

1959. After a particularly bloody clash in the mines in early 1959, Siles, perhaps in fear of open civil war in the revolutionary family, slackened his pressure on Lechín and reduced a full implementation of the stabilization plan. This action amounted to a political stand-off, and 1959 drew to a close with a shaky peace between the Siles center-right coalition and Lechín's bloodied but still powerful labor-left sector. Both sides licked their wounds and looked for ways to shape the future more to their liking.

All sides were focusing on the upcoming conventiion of 1960. The left, obviously remembering the better days of 1953–1956, called on Paz to return and lead the party. He did so, and, after a particularly bitter internal struggle, Lechín was chosen as his running mate for the 1960 electoral campaign. The left also received assurances that Lechín would assume the presidency in 1964. The center-left axis appeared to be back in business with the additional proviso of a definitive leftist ascendency in 1964. Tasting victory, Lechín reestablished his control of a unified COB. This time the party's right wing would make no compromises and, following the lead of Guevara Arze, left the MNR to form a rival party, the *Moviemiento Nacionalista Revolucionario Auténtico* (MNRA).

REVOLUTION AND DEVELOPMENT

The leaders of the MNR, particularly those in the pragmatic nationalist center, saw themselves as developers and modernizers. They justified their violent seizure of the Bolivian state as the only means to achieve rapid national development in a country ruled by an intransigent, parasitic oligarchy. Their movement would embrace all sectors of the nation in a drive to sweep away La Rosca and establish an economically viable, independent national existence.

The MNR is a case of what many have come to call "national popular movements." [36] Such movements have appeared recently in underdeveloped countries where the incomplete development of society has led to contexts in which single, class-based reform parties have not been possible. In these environments national popular movements represent broad multigroup alliances aimed at removing blockages to reform and development. These movements have at least three factors in common:

(1) An elite placed at the middle or upper-middle levels of stratification impregnated with an anti-*status quo* motivation

(2) A mobilized mass formed as a result of the revolution of expectations; and
(3) An ideology or a widespread emotional state to help communication between leaders and followers and to create collective enthusiasm [37]

The leadership of these movements constitutes a counterelite drawn from the preexisting elite and subelite strata of society. Counterelites such as these usually arise from a generation frustrated by a shortage of career outlets and are reinforced by a desire to catch up with the advanced industrial states. The mobilized mass can be drawn from a variety of social sectors reacting to the contradiction between the desired levels of consumption and the real possibilities of realizing their aspirations in an underdeveloped context. The ideologies which usually develop from these are generally vague and reflect both the counterelites' development aims and the mass's desire for concrete betterment.

Looking at the MNR from this perspective, it becomes evident that the Bolivian national revolution is not an isolated phenomenon but a manifestation of a more general process which could be called *modern revolution*. In the contemporary context of underdevelopment, the goal of rapid state-sponsored economic development has become such a pervasive, normative standard of behavior that all elites are forced to proclaim it, at least publicly, as a primary collective goal. The orienting power of the development goal is a particularly strong motivational factor in the counterelites' behavior. The aim of the counterelites to seize and to use the state as a means of achieving rapid development is a defining characteristic as well as a limiting factor in the modern revolutionary situation. As a result, once the old elite has, as in Bolivia, been eliminated by force and when the counterelites inevitably array against one another, the major issue posed is that of finding alternative means to reach the goal of rapid development. The chief issue of the postinsurrection phase of modern revolution is that of opposing political models of state-sponsored economic development. [38]

The battle over political models is joined in an environment characterized by two critical factors. The first is the underdeveloped context itself in which, by definition, there is an acute shortage of investable resources in the broadest sense of the term. The second is social mobilization, a process usually accelerated by the activities of the counterelites in their drive to power. While talking the language of development, the counterelites also express the pent-up frustrations of various sectors of the populace for immediate concrete betterment. The extreme marginality of existence experienced by some groups confers as explosive air of urgency to the unfolding situation. Three factors—a) development-oriented elites, b) an environment of scarcity, and c) a mobilized expectant mass—interact to set the boundaries within which the struggle over contending political models must be played out.

There are three major dimensions of conflict and tension in the modern revolutionary situation as defined here. The first involves the situationally derived tension between the elites' developmental goals which demand the deferral of consumption by at least some sectors of the society in the name of an investable surplus and the demands of mobilized groups for the immediate and concrete betterment of their life situation. The second springs from the multiclass nature of national popular movements such as the MNR. Ideological pronouncements not withstanding, groups as diverse as a dependent urban middle, workers, and peasants have different interests arising out of different problematic situations. In an underdeveloped environment these differences eventually lead to clashes over the distribution of rewards and costs in the movement.

The third line of conflict derives from the tension between what we may call political versus economic logics. The first order of business that contending new elites must face in a revolutionary situation such as post-1952 Bolivia is to gain support for a new political order and to implement specific governments to operate it. In so doing they must resolve the timeless political problem of balancing the demands made and the supports offered by significant sectors of the populace. Force is a possible means of inducing supportive behavior, but it is unstable over the long run and, more importantly, presupposes, not always correctly, that the elite has the ability to use force. Revolutionary elites can and do seek support by playing upon revolutionary fervor, but such emotional states are usually based on the expectations of immediate material gratification. A final means could be to satisfy the demands of the supporting publics; this is a policy which in the contemporary context implies increasing levels of consumption. Thus, where force is not a viable means of achieving support, political logic forces elites along a consumptionist policy line. Such a policy, however, collides with basic economic logic which in the underdeveloped context calls for a policy of accumulation for investment.

A successful insurrectionary effort such as the one the MNR conducted, then, does not eliminate conflict; it tends to increase it. The formulation and implementation of a political model of development is of necessity, therefore, a difficult and at least potentially violent process. Any such model must be fashioned out of the resolution through struggle of at least two critical issues: a) which elites identified with which publics shall assert control and define the new system and b) which group or groups will pay the costs of the society's collective economic advance. To resolve the twin issues of control and social costs, an alliance of groups sufficiently powerful to impose a development solution on the society must be formed. Until this is achieved, the revolution continues.

As shown above, the insurrection of 1952 resulted in an MNR seizure of power only in the most formal sense. While the MNR elite was established in the Presidential Palace, two important processes were taking place: the involvement of workers in the insurrection and the spread of the revolution to the countryside increased the process of mobilization and resulted in a precipitous increase in the quantity and quality of demands pressed on the new government. Furthermore, as weapons found their way into the hands of the civil population and the army was pushed aside, there developed a dangerous divergence between authority and concrete power. The state lost its legitimate monopoly on force, and this critical form of political power passed to intermediate, nonauthoritative regional and sectoral bodies. Formal ties with the MNR created the image of a powerful, single party state, but reality belied the image.

Very quickly after 1952 Bolivia degenerated into a collection of semisovereign fragments only tenuously tied to the national governmental center. The COB took on the characteristics of a diminutive state. In the Cochabamba valley and the Lake Titicaca region powerful peasant fiefs were established. In much of the rest of the country the Indian peasants withdrew into atomized subsistence. This centrifugal process also extended to the huge eastern portion of the country which takes in the departments of Pando, Beni, and Santa Cruz—well over half the national territory. Geographic and cultural barriers had always separated these areas from the national reality. After 1952 these regions were brought under the personal control of two modern-day *caudillos* who, despite fictive ties to the MNR, ran their domains as they chose. Ruben Julio Castro established his hegemony over the Pando and Beni, while Luis Sandoval Morón subjected the rich department of Santa Cruz to his will. It would not be an exaggeration to say that, at times, effective national authority stopped at the city limits of La Paz.

Almost from the beginning then, the possibility of a national center controlled by the old MNR elite imposing its image of a new Bolivia, by force if necessary, was out of the question. In truth the small coterie of Movimientistas around Paz and Siles could do little more than cling to the symbols of formal power. In order to rule, accommodation had to be made with concrete power. In the immediate post-1952 situation this meant with the COB and the labor left. It was in this context that the center-left coalition which was dominate from 1953 to 1956 was formed. During this period the national government followed a dual policy of investment and consumption. The costs of this course were paid first by the old upper class through expropriation and later were shifted to the dependent urban middle through the mechanism of inflation. These cost allocations were enforced by the real power of the left measured in terms of the workers' and peasant militias. The middle, thereupon, turned increasingly to active opposition.

With these developments the MNR center lost its original support base and found itself increasingly reliant on autonomous, armed sectors over which they had little or no direct control. Support from these groups was gained through the satisfaction of their demands, and loyalty to the MNR became rooted in the party's willingness and ability to "pay off." As indicated by the inflation, the wherewithal to continue this policy was limited. At this point the question of foreign aid as an extra source of capital became crucial.

The left urged a policy of collaboration with the USSR, but this was a line the MNR center was neither willing nor, given the economic realities of Bolivia, able to support. Thus, through its foreign aid, the United States began to loom large in the future development of the revolution, but as the Eder report made clear, continuance of that aid was predicated on the party's adopting economic and political policies acceptable to the United States. The first economic move demanded by the United States was the control of inflation by means of a strict monetary policy. Such an economic move, however, carried within it a set of unavoidable political implications.[39]

The loss of the urban middle, U.S. pressure, and his own predilections put Siles into a situation where controling inflation meant doing battle with the bulk of the labor left. By shifting to a center-right coalition, courting the peasants, and starting a buildup of the military, Siles was able to stem the power of the labor left and halt the inflation. Through the mechanism of the stabilization program, pressure was taken off the middle class and social costs shifted to labor, particularly the miners.

The battle between Siles's center-right coalition and Lechín's labor left was basically an ideological conflict stemming from the differing views of the core MNR and the COB leaderships concerning a new sociopolitical order. It was a battle between opposed political models of development. The model held to by the core MNR was most often expressed in the concept *sociedad democrática burguesa* ("democratic bourgeois society"); that of the left, in the concept *el gobierno obrero campesino* ("government of workers and peasants"). The first envisioned the establishment of a state capitalist framework dominated by a middle-class elite in which the market would play a role allocating social costs; the second pictured a state socialist system dominated by the labor-sector elite in which the market would be abolished and cost allocations made through central planning. In the Bolivia of the 1950s the first looked back to Mexico, while the latter, in a sense, anticipated Cuba.

Siles's political strategy blocked the movement toward the leftist model, begun in 1953, but Siles was either unwilling or unable to form a sufficient power base in order to begin a definitive move in the opposite direction. Siles's term ended in a political stalemate. Neither side was able to impose its solution, and the country slipped into political immobilization. On the economic front the inflation was stopped but was followed by economic stagnation. Economically and politically the revolution ground to a halt.[40]

From 1952 to 1959 the MNR core elite was seldom in control of the events taking place around it. Having lost the ability to use force, the party's center had to rely on demand satisfaction in its desperate struggle to hold the various sectors of the society at least nominally in its orbit. The policies of the first three years strengthened the left, set off a wild inflation, and alienated the middle. The policies of the next three years achieved monetary stability at the price of economic stagnation and, more importantly, called into question labor's loyalty to the party. The MNR was now as fragmented as the society over which it presided, and no national elite was able to assert real control over the party, let alone the society as a whole.

THE FALL OF THE MNR

The reelection of Paz in 1960 and the ascension of Lechín to the vice-presidency appeared to mark a return to the center-left axis of 1953–1956. However, during the Siles period a number of important factors had been added to the Bolivian political equation. The organized sectors of the peasantry had emerged as political actors of significant magnitude. The army, although not a dominant political force, was larger, better equipped, and more organized. With the tin industry infirm in the extreme, the country had become exceedingly reliant on U.S. foreign aid simply to keep its head above water. Paz declared his intention to devote the next four years to the problem of economic development.

It is of no little consequence that in 1960 John F. Kennedy was elected president of the United States and shortly thereafter announced his intention to launch the Alliance for Progress in Latin America. In the men around Kennedy, Paz saw a band of kindred souls who understood what core MNR leaders such as himself had always wanted for Bolivia—a reformed capitalist system in which the state would regulate, but not totally dominate, the workings of the economy. State capitalism within a formal constitutional framework was acceptable both to the definers of the U.S. alliance and to the MNR pragmatic nationalists. The new government in Washington, therefore, saw in revolutionary Bolivia a potential showcase of the Alliance and pledged its wholehearted support to Paz. United States economic aid within the framework of the alliance would become the basis of Bolivia's new forward surge.[41]

Despite the apparent return to the pre-1956 coalition, Paz, like Siles, was moving on a collision course with the labor left. In order to begin the movement toward the state capitalist model implied in the concept of the alliance, Paz had to break the economic and political immobilism that gripped the country. To do this, he had to resolve at least three exceedingly difficult problems. He had to 1) assert the authority and control of the national government over local decision centers, 2) discipline the unwieldy MNR party apparatus, and 3) assemble an effective power bloc to impose the state capitalist model.

Any national development policy implies the existence of an effective national decision-making center, which in the Bolivian context of the early 1960s meant bringing the local caciques to heel. Paz, therefore, began an attempt to break the hold of the independent power centers. Unable simply to assert national control, he followed a strategy of playing off the local leaders against one another. In the east he supported Ruben Julio against Sandoval Morón. In the Cochabamba valley area he helped José Rojas beat back the threat of his rival, Miguel Veizaga. On the Altiplano he encouraged new peasant leaders such as Felip Flores to challenge the hegemony of Toribio Salas. The threatened caciques responded vigorously to the challenge, and in all these regions the level of violence escalated rapidly.

The party apparatus presented a different type of problem. Between

1952 and 1960 the party had swollen to gigantic proportions as the job hungry traded a party oath for a bureaucratic sinecure. Thus the struggle for jobs was added to the other conflicts wracking the party. As a result the party divided not only along ideological lines but also into factions of job-seeking cadres. Even with the defection of Guevara the huge and unwieldy MNR was by 1960 one of the major drains on the nation's meager resources. Paz openly attacked the situation but could do little to remedy it.[42] For this as well as ideological reasons, Paz, unlike Siles, did not turn to the old right to help him in the struggle brewing with the left. Rather he gathered around him his own faction made up largely of new, young, post-1952 figures such as Reynaldo Venegas and Carlos Serrate Reich. Paz installed his new band in a number of key governmental and party positions. The excluded began to attack bitterly the *camarilla Paz Estenssorista* ("the Paz gang"). Hence, although Paz appeared to dominate the party, in reality his control was superficial.[43] Below the national level, large sections of the party were becoming increasingly hostile to Paz, the man.

Paz's difficulties in the party were part of a more profound problem posed by the socioeconomic makeup of the Bolivian urban middle sector —a dependent service stratum composed largely of bureaucrats and liberal professionals. Taking the old upper class as its major reference group, it had developed an imitative, consumptive life style. Due to its makeup, it produced little concrete wealth and was almost totally lacking in modern technological skills. But, as Helio Jaguaribe has pointed out, the state capitalist development model is predicated on the predominance of a middle-class technocratic elite.[44] The cadres of the MNR as well as the general urban middle, while pressing claims on the nation's resources, hardly constituted a stratum of technocrats, let alone entrepreneurs. One of the prime reasons for this was the existing university system which produced, above all, classical lawyers.

Thus, in addition to his battle with the caciques and the job-hungry factions of the party, Paz moved to take on the bastion of middle-class social supremacy, the autonomous university system.[45] Assailing the university system as an archaic roadblock to development, he established the *Instituto Tecnológico Boliviano*. The ITB was staffed with many foreigners, run on strict standards, and, most importantly, was put outside the governing system of the autonomous university. This attempt to create technocrats overnight provided an issue around which the urban middle could unite. The universities became the focal point of middle-class resistance to Paz, and the university students emerged as its shock troops.

It should be evident by now that Paz was moving on a broader front than was Siles when he clashed with the Lechín left. Moreover, when the clash between Paz and Lechín came, it sprang from even more fundamental factors. Siles and Lechín fought over the specific issue of the stabilization and the threat it carried to the gains of some workers' groups. Although the Paz-Lechín clash ultimately was joined in the mines, the roots of the battle derived from the overall development strategy of Paz and the United States. Behind this strategy was the view which had developed over a period of years that, aside from all the technical problems, the major roadblock to Bolivia's development was labor.

The negative role of labor, it was argued, derived from the negative relationship between productivity and labor costs. High labor costs, in turn, were due to labor undiscipline and the lack of managerial authority. Hence labor costs in the fullest sense (size of work force, wages, fringe benefits, etc.) had to be scaled down. To do this, labor had to be disciplined, e.g., the relative power of unions and management, both public and private, reversed. But the bargaining power of the unions was directly related to their political power organized in the COB. Therefore, the political power of labor had to be broken. This strategy then not only implied a shift of social costs to labor but a redefinition of its entire status within the ongoing revolution. Since the mines were Bolivia's major source of exchange, the first step was to reorganize COMIBOL. This was to be accomplished by the implementation of the Plan Triangular, in which the United States, West Germany, and the Inter-American Development Bank would provide capital and know-how while the Bolivian government would guarantee a pruned and disciplined working force. The first group to be broken, therefore, was the miners' federation. But the left saw that this attempt was part of a more general thrust, and when Paz moved to assert control in the mines, he found himself challenged by a reunified labor-left sector.

Every move to cut wages, lay off workers, or close pulperías was met by strikes and demonstrations. To bolster his position, Paz abrogated the *control obrero* ("workers' representation") and paid no heed to the COB's demands for its cogovernment rights. By late 1963 the situation began to get out of hand, and Paz, acting under the umbrella of an alleged Communist coup plot, arrested important mine union leaders. The miners responded by taking seventeen hostages, whom they threat-

ened to kill if their leaders were not freed. Paz, in turn, surrounded the
mining complex of Catavi Siglo XX with army units and contingents of
Rojas's peasant militia. After a few days the besieged miners capitulated
to the superior force mobilized by the government. The successful siege
of Catavi Siglo XX was a historic moment; it marked the waning of the
Bolivian labor left and the emergence of the peasants and military as
critical political forces.

Paz, even more than Siles, leaned on the peasants and the military to
underpin his political strategy. He courted both groups assiduously. Rural
investment was increased, and the signing of land titles was stepped
up.[46] He told the peasants that they were the true base of the revolution
and warned that a leftist takeover would result in collectivization of
agriculture.[47] With U.S. help he continued the process of rebuilding the
military and refurbishing its image as an important and legitimate national
institution.[48]

The increasing significance of the peasants and the military was, in
part, a result of the political intention of the MNR center to use their
strength as a counterweight to the labor left. There were, however, deeper
factors behind this development. The basic strategy of development which
again came to the fore in the early 1960s was predicated on a shift in
emphasis from the Altiplano and its exhausted mines to the interior
where, presumably, agriculture and oil lay waiting to flourish.[49] The mining plan sought to remove the basic roadblock preventing this diversification. In that context the miners appeared not only as a political liability
but also as an economic anachronism.

In this picture, through the program known as *Acción Cívica* ("Civic
Action"), the new military became the spearhead of the drive by building roads, colonizing land, constructing schools, etc.[50] In the early 1960s
a school of high military studies aimed at turning out a modern breed of
officers was founded. Political and economic strategies coalesced not only
to restrengthen the military but also to widen its role and the range of
functions it would perform. In the Santa Cruz action against Morón, in
the intervention in the valley, and during the mine strikes, the military
regained its role as an instrument of national control. Through Acción
Cívica it acquired, in addition, the functions of mobilizing developmental
resources and providing a source of technical leadership. As distant regions
of the country began to feel, many for the first time, the presence of the
national state authority, they did so through the soldier who carried a
shovel and axe as well as a gun.

When the eyes of the national leadership turned from the mines, the peasant loomed large as the human base of a new, modern Bolivia. Through improved techniques he would increase production in the old agricultural areas, and through colonization schemes he would open up the Alto Beni, the Chapare, and Santa Cruz. At the same time he would provide the psychological and physical support for the new revolution of development.

Backed by the resources of the United States and surrounded by a new generation of stalwarts, Paz sent out to break the political and economic immobilization and assert the authority of the national center. The peasants and the military would provide the economic and political muscle to back the push, and the labor left would pay the political and economic costs.

By 1963 the economic picture brightened considerably. Santa Cruz was booming as rice and sugar production increased markedly. Bolivia became self-sufficient in oil and the GNP growth rates were more than respectable. But everything still turned on Paz's ability to maintain the political initiative, and the political picture was uncertain. By 1964 there was a disparate, broad range of groups looking for some way to stop Paz. It included remnants of the groups dispossessed by the revolution, the bulk of the urban middle, the universities, the MNR factions excluded from jobs, and the entire labor left—a rather impressive array. At this point the critical question lay in Paz's ability to control the military and to turn out armed peasants on command.

The gathering political storm was brought to a head by Paz's decision to run for the presidency again in 1964.[51] Faced with four more years of Paz, his opponents had little choice but to actively seek his defeat or to submit to defeat themselves. During the convention of 1964 the party fell apart. Lechín bolted to form a new leftist party, Siles declared his implacable opposition to Paz, and the factions making up the party rump struggled among themselves over the vice-presidency. An important portent of the future occurred when Paz was forced to jettison his own vice-presidential choice and accept the popular air force chief René Barrientos Ortuño as his running mate.

The emergence of Barrientos, who had gained prominence in the Santa Cruz and Cochabamba interventions, had significance not only in relationship to the influence of the military. For over a year important peasant leaders had been booming his name as a presidential possibility. José Rojas Guevara, who was reappointed minister of peasant affairs in the new government, was openly known to be a Barrientos supporter. Barrientos's prominence, in effect, confirmed the new power of both the military and the peasants (who had entered into an anti-Communist alliance) and, more importantly, indicated that neither group was under Paz's thumb.

In the late summer and early fall of 1964 the miners again initiated a series of strikes. These actions were reinforced by a national teachers' strike. The university students supported both these actions and hit the streets. The mines stopped, the schools shut down, and, with the streets of the capital in chaos, Paz called on the military and the peasants to restore order. In the midst of all of this, Barrientos repaired to Cochabamba and declared himself in rebellion; meanwhile, all the opposition parties drew together for the kill. The question was, What would the peasant leaders and the military officers do? As might be expected they split in a variety of directions, but, in the main, the bulk of both groups either actively or passively opposed Paz.

Key peasant leaders in the valley such as Rojas, Jorge Soliz, and Macedonio Juarez supported Barrientos by letting it be known that they would sit the entire affair out. Some Altiplano contingents remained loyal to Paz, but others such as Warisata followed Rojas's lead. Finally, assured of minimal or no peasant resistance, the anti-Paz sections of the military moved, and late on November 3, 1964, the army chief of staff Gen. Alfredo Ovando Candia informed Paz that the military would appreciate his withdrawal from the country. Guaging the realities of the situation, Paz accompanied Ovando to the airport and departed for Lima, Peru.

With Paz off the scene, the MNR faltered and then collapsed into a bewildering array of impotent factions. On the evening of November 4, Ovando and Barrientos, after a day of hectic bargaining, arrived at the Presidential Palace and declared themselves copresidents. But the crowds gathered on the square wanted only the popular Barrientos and said so over and over. Bowing to the crowd, Ovando allowed Barrientos to assume the formal title alone. As Barrientos stepped onto the balcony to receive the accolades of the throng below, Ovando and the other generals stood close behind the windows, thinking, perhaps, of the real difference between the disparate voices shouting vivas to the air force general and the well-equipped army units returning to their barracks after a job well done. In any event, as far as the MNR was concerned, the revolution was over, temporarily at least. But the eclipse of the MNR did not do away with the basic questions of power and social costs that had brought it to grief.

LA REVOLUCION RESTAURADORA

From November 1964 until August 1966 Bolivia was governed by a military cabinet with first Barrientos alone and later he and Ovando together acting as chief executive. In July 1966 Barrientos waged a successful electoral campaign and on August 6 was installed as the constitutional president of the republic; Ovando assumed the post of commander in chief of the armed forces. Throughout this period both stressed that their rule did not constitute a counterrevolution. Their aim was to restructure the revolution and return it to its rightful path from which it had been led by Víctor Paz and his rapacious *camarilla* ("clique of loyal followers"). Actually, in many respects Barrientos and Ovando followed much the same overall strategy initiated by Paz in the early 1960s. The main difference was that they did so with much more ruthless efficiency.

The labor left was an important part of the coalition which helped to bring down Paz and install the military in power. It was soon to learn, however, that the pressure on its political and economic status went deeper than the policy preferences of a single individual. Like Paz, Barrientos looked to the United States as his major source of economic aid and in so doing accepted the logic of the previous alliance program. In turn, the United States, after making the requisite formal complaint regarding the military supression of civil power, embraced Barrientos. Actually many felt that the military was in a better position to make the thorny political moves that the development plan demanded, for as long as Bolivia was following the state capitalist model, the resolution of the mining problem remained the first order of business. The major obstacle to such a resolution continued to be the political power of the labor left.

It was not long, therefore, before the new government moved against Lechín and the embattled left. The state mining corporation was put under the control of a military director (ironically, named Colonel Lechín Suarez). The new directorship announced that previous plans for layoffs, salary reductions, and the reduction of pulperiá privileges would not only be enforced but broadened. The miners predictably reacted violently. The military moved into the mines in May 1965 and after a brief but bloody encounter smashed the strike and disarmed the militias. The major union leaders were rounded up and dispatched to exile.

When the rest of the left protested, the military did not hesitate. Juan Lechín was exiled, the COB smashed, and all major union leaders hustled out of the country or driven underground. After these first actions the military continued to impose a *mano fuerte* ("strong hand") on labor. In September 1965 the army again entered the mines shooting, and the major mines were put under permanent military occupation. Every major union in the country was purged, and where unions still functioned, they did so under a docile government-imposed leadership. Every attempt at an independent labor organization was smashed. Thus the once all-powerful labor left exists today only in isolated pockets of clandestine opposition.

During the period of open military rule, Barrientos set out to organize from above a mass base for an eventual civil regime. Much to the chagrin of the major anti-MNR party, the FSB, Barrientos rebuffed its offers of support and began to build a new organization. With an eye to the developments in neighboring Chile, Barrientos named his new organization the *Movimiento Popular Cristiano* (MPC, Popular Christian Movement).[52] The organizing cadres for the party were drawn from a variety of sources with the largest single source being from the old anti-Paz factions of the MNR. From the beginning the movement was artificial and existed almost solely on governmental largess. The major organizational target of the MPC was the peasant masses, but, like those of the MNR before it, the MPC's relations with the peasants were tenuous and problematic.

It is indisputable that the rise of Barrientos was directly tied to his successful cultivation of peasant support. His favorable relations with the peasants stemmed in part from the fact that he was from Cochabamba, had an Indian mother, and spoke Quechua. One must not lose sight of the fact, however, that through the valley interventions of the early sixties and by means of the Civic Action program, Barrientos made important contacts with peasant leaders which later ripened into alliances. To the extent that the peasants were political, and this was by no means the general case, they were so in terms of the directives of a number of powerful caciques. Hence, the real source of Barrientos's peasant support was not an in-depth commitment in the peasantry as such but his ability to maintain alliances with key peasant leaders. The nature of these alliances undercut all attempts to pull the politically active peasant pockets into a national political organization.

Barrientos's ties with the peasant leaders were direct and personal. Jealous of their independent power the dirigentes rejected all sources of organization and authority other than that of Barrientos himself. They looked upon Barrientos and only Barrientos as their leader and refused to recognize all intermediary links. Thus after an early flirtation with the MPC the major peasant leaders declared their organizational independence as a *bloque campesino* ("peasant bloc") and demanded parity with all other groups. The MPC, therefore, never became more than a collection of job-hungry cadres without a base.

Confronted with this fact, Barrientos was forced to organize on a broader base his attempt to achieve the presidency by electoral means. After negotiations with a number of political groups, he put together a rather heterogenous *frente Barrientista* ("Barrientos front") composed of the MPC, the bloque campesino, the Guevara-MNR rump (now the PRA, Authentic Revolutionary party), the remnants of the old PIR, and the *Partido Social Demócrata* (PSD). (The last party dated to the pre-1952 period when it constituted a mildly reformist wing of the old elite.) Given the ideological diversity of this front, it seems safe to argue that its reason for being was the desire of these little bands of politicians to ride into office on Barrientos's coattails. And little bands they were, with none of them representing any real electoral strength other than themselves. The real basis of the front was the personality of Barrientos who was running with the sanction of the military and the direct assurance of the peasant vote. The rest was gloss.

Barrientos won the election of 1966 handily by carrying a good part of the urban middle class and peasantry. The FSB ran second with almost all its votes coming from the cities.[53] Two wings of the MNR directly contested the election while a third supported a leftist position of voting in blank. While the total of all three was small (including blank ballots), the MNR showed surprising strength in the working-class sections of the cities and in the mines. Of the 677,805 votes received by Barrientos, only 105,361 came from the cities; by far his vote strength lay in the peasantry, a bloc vote which, since 1952, had always been cast on the command of the dirigentes.

Of the other groups the FSB polled 138,001 and the two open MNR factions a surprising 148,897. The leftist campaign of voter protest resulted in 60,505 blank votes. Putting aside the peasant bloc vote, then, Barrientos, working through four ostensible political parties (MPC, PIR, PRA, PSD), did not really defeat the opposition. The most significant result of the election was that the strongest single civil party formations remained the FSB and the divided MNR. Behind the multiparty facade Barrientos's new government rested mainly on the military and the peasants.[54] The old strategy first initiated under Siles of using a coalition of peasant and military power to break the political power of the left and impose social costs on labor was still quite alive. Lacking any real party organization Barrientos's continued stay in power rested upon the continuance of the coalition and his ability to maintain the personal loyalty of the military officers and the independent peasant leaders. Barrientos assiduously courted both and, in addition, strove to mobilize the support of the urban middle class. The salaries and perquisites of the military went up consistently, and the process of the granting of land titles did likewise.

The basic policy of controlling the mining industry while at the same time opening up agriculture and oil in the east was also still in effect. Thus while the names of the prominent national players changed, the basic political and economic dynamics set in motion when Paz Estenssoro and the United States set out to impose the state capitalist model were still the major motors of the situation. The basic political question which remained was who would drive the machine. In spite of his successful crushing of the Che Guevara movement (essentially an aberration in the Bolivian context), Barrientos's hold on power was precarious. In most respects Barrientos found himself in much the same position that Paz had.

The working sectors of the population, particularly the miners, were unalterably opposed to the regime. They were, however, in no position to challenge the regime alone, and soon there were increasing signs that they were no longer alone. The universities, for example, manifested a decided shift to the left and became a continual source of harassment to the regime. Barrientos also found himself in increasing difficulty with another old Paz enemy—the teachers' union. By 1968 both rural and urban teachers were pressing heavy economic demands on the government. Pleading economic difficulties, the government rejected the demands, and the teachers also began to employ a variety of harassing tactics.

Two of the most important structural weaknesses of the regime were the facts that it had no political organizational base and it excluded the two most potentially powerful civil political groups, the FSB and the MNR. There were increasing signs that the realities of opposition were moderating the hatreds between these two old enemies and that important sections of both were seriously discussing the possibilities of common action. There were also indications that Paz, Siles, and Lechín had set their differences aside and that the bulk of the old MNR was again relatively unified. As the elections of 1966 indicated, a good part of labor now found the MNR more preferable than Barrientos and a more realistic alternative than the POR or the Communist party. In short, the possibility of a grand nationalist coalition which would include a good part of the old labor left was a distinct possibility.

One of the more important elements strengthening this possibility was the belief among the opposition that either Barrientos would cling to power after 1970 or he would be replaced by Ovando, but in either case, his opponents would continue to be excluded. Given this perception they not only were drawing together but were increasingly inclined to adopt the conspiratorial road. Feeling himself embattled, Barrientos dropped the niceties of constitutional politics and assumed a more repressive stance.

The two big question marks in the equation were the military and the peasants. By the summer of 1968 Barrientos had dropped all pretense of ruling through the political parties that made up his frente. He began talking of a new single party (*Partido Único*) and, at the same time, drawing closer and closer to the peasants. In the crisis sparked by the appearance of Che's diary in Cuba, he spent inordinate amounts of time in Cochabamba with the valley dirigentes. At a number of points he went so far as to intimate a racially tinged civil war if any opposition groups moved against him.

With regard to the peasants the important question was, Were they willing and, more to the point, able to defend their ostensible leader? Large sectors of the peasantry were still unorganized and politically passive. There were also signs that the once powerful Altiplano organizations had disintegrated greatly. It now appeared that the only real source of organized peasant power was in the Cochabamba valley. But it is not clear how strong these unions were, especially when one considers that their weapons were, in the main, early 1950s vintage. Finally, it was still not at all clear for whom or for what the peasants would fight.

Thus far the peasants had shown remarkable fickleness in their loyalties to national political leaders. They also showed little concern with either national issues or ideologies. Their political stance had been couched in a defensive posture oriented to the protection of their particularistic interests and, above all, to their individual landholdings. Was it not then possible that the same peasant leaders who sat on their hands when Paz fell could do so again, particularly if they received assurances regarding their personal and sectorial interests? There were more than a few in Bolivia asking these questions, and many began to conclude that, just as Paz could not produce the peasant masses when the chips were down, neither could Barrientos. Further, many believed that, while peasant voting power could swing an election, peasant armed power was a paper tiger.

The real key to the situation in Bolivia was the revived and revitalized military. In the first place, the military was the only real national organization in the country. Secondly, the military was now the most important single institution with the capacity to organize and deploy force. The nature of the political issues still to be resolved was such that the capacity to use force was still the most relevant form of political power. Yet the military had to face the fact that it was not strong enough to take on all relevant groups in the situation at once, and, even if it took formal power, it could not govern and solve Bolivia's basic problems alone. The military also had to consider the delicate problem of forming viable power coalitions.

It must be pointed out that the military hardly constitutes a monolithic body of opinion driven by a singular will. Like every other grouping in Bolivia the military is riddled with factionalism. Divisions in the military cut along a variety of lines including generational, ideological, and personal differences. The most profound recent experience of the military is its almost complete annihilation in the early 1950s. Since that period a strong sense of institutional survival has developed. There exists a definite feeling that, if the institution were subjected to either personal or group political ambitions, it could again be led into another confrontation with the general populace and would be destroyed once and for all.

Throughout the summer and fall of 1968 Barrientos's position became increasingly precarious. He was particularly hurt when it was revealed in July that his close friend and minister of government, Antonio Arguedas, was the person who sent Che's diary to Cuba. Events took an even more serious turn when Arguedas, after successfully escaping, returned in August and announced that he had been a CIA agent and that this pernicious organ of U.S. imperialism had penetrated all levels of the Bolivian government. A wave of nationalist indignation swept the country, and a cloud of suspicion settled over Barrientos.

Things became even more confused when Vice-President Luis Adolfo Siles Salinas began to attack Barrientos for subverting the constitution. Few failed to grasp the irony of Barrientos's being publicly assailed by his vice-president. Rumors of a coup became rife and there was at least one serious attempt in August under the leadership of Gen. Vasquez Sempertegui. Barrientos fought back, but, as the country moved into 1969, everyone believed that his hold on power depended on the pleasure of General Ovando and in turn on Ovando's ability to keep control of the restive military.

On Sunday, April 27, 1969, the question was resolved. The former air force general, who over the years had cultivated the image of a dashing and invincible *macho* ("he-man"), was destroyed when one of his innumberable trips to the interior to cultivate peasant support ended with his helicopter colliding with a high-tension wire.

Ovando, who was in Washington when the news of Barrientos's death broke, scurried to return to Bolivia. In La Paz the pivotal role of the military was confirmed when Siles Salinas felt forced to journey to the army high command to request permission to assume his mandate. The generals gave their nod, but it was clear that Siles would be little more than window dressing and that the man of the hour was Ovando. It was generally assumed that Ovando wished to assume the presidency by constitutional means, and, as elections were scheduled for July 1970, everyone sat back to watch Ovando's maneuvers and, perhaps, to find a way to jump on his bandwagon. Although a powerful man, the dour general could not spark the public imagination as Barrientos had done. His bland figure remained the center of attention, but serious doubts began to crop up in important places. By midsummer of 1969 the word was out that Ovando was slipping.

At the same time the removal of Barrientos from the scene sparked new activity in the deposed MNR and other opposition groups. Political figures who had wisely stuck close to their homes in recent years began to be seen on the main streets or huddled with cronies in coffee shops—long the centers of conspiracy and intrigue. It was open political wheeling and dealing of a kind that Bolivia had not seen in years. The MNR, scenting a chance to return, strove mightily to resolve its internal disputes and unite behind Paz. Slogans such as "The MNR lives" and "We shall return with Víctor Paz" appeared scrawled on walls or painted in the streets. Every day new stories of deals between the MNR, the FSB, and other groups to form electoral alliances were batted around in the papers, the streets, and the coffee shops. There was some talk of restive sectors of the military supporting a grand nationalist coalition. Some even spoke ominously that, while the army would indeed rule, there was no reason that it might not be led by younger, more aggressive officers.

In addition to political fluidity in the capital, important developments took place in the *campo* ("countryside"). Many dirigentes deposed by Barrientos reappeared and challenged government-supported figures. In the valley there were major clashes reminiscent of the late 1950s and early 1960s. Although many leaders declared for Ovando, it was clear that he could rely on the peasants even less than Barrientos. In short, the situation opened up very quickly and was showing definite signs of getting out of hand.

However, as bland as he was, no personality of sufficient stature had as yet challenged Ovando. This changed in July when the popular mayor of La Paz, Gen. Armando Escóbar Uria, announced his candidacy for the presidency. Ovando began to run scared, and, in a bid to preempt nationalist sentiment, his rhetoric took on an anti-U.S. flavor. He also expressed his general agreement with the new Peruvian government and attacked the Gulf Oil Company which in recent months had become a focal point of attack from all sides.

Would Ovando wait for elections or out of fear move against the government illegally? The latter option was helped along considerably with the reemergence of the guerrilla movement that had been prematurely written off with the death of Che Guevara. This time, centering its activities on the capital, the revived *Ejercito de Liberación Nacional* (ELN) carried out a series of terrorist raids which revealed the complete weakness and vulnerability of the Siles regime. Ovando declared the need for national pacification, at the same time calling for a true nationalist political program.

Under this umbrella Ovando moved and on Friday, September 27, 1969, overthrew Siles and established himself in the presidential chair. In his first public statements, Ovando self-consciously styled his regime in the new modern military mode adopted by his Peruvian counterpart, Velasco Alvarado. To back up this image, he suspended the government's contract with Gulf Oil and announced a new civil-military cabinet of the "national left." This new cabinet has a large civilian contingent made up of young and well-known independent nationalists.

Exactly what kind of course Ovando will follow remains to be seen. One can assume that as long as the civilian ministers remain in the cabinet, they will push an aggressive nationalist line. This will probably be reinforced by the young institutionalist army officers anxious to legitimatize yet another army intrusion into politics and to avoid any hint of personal or institutional self-seeking. Moreover, the ambitious and agile Ovando who, no doubt, intends to rule for some time will feel the political wind and follow its drift. Thus odds are that Bolivia will take its place alongside Peru as a case of a new and important form of military involvement in politics in Latin America.

NOTES

1. For an account of the planning behind the coup, see Luis Peñaloza, *Historia del Movimiento Nacionalista Revolucionario* (La Paz, 1963).

2. Tensions over a program are discussed at length in Lydia Gueiler Tejada, *La mujer y la revolución* (La Paz, 1959), pp. 119 ff. For the MNR right-wing version, see Alfredo Candia, *Bolivia: Un experimento comunista en America* (La Paz, 1955).

3. For an account of the nationalist position, see Augusto Céspedes, *El dictador suicida* (Santiago de Chile, 1956), pp. 81–96; for the Marxist position see Miguel Bonifaz, *Bolivia: Frustracion y destino* (La Paz, 1965), pp. 120–40.

4. While there is general agreement now that Busch killed himself, the popular view at the time (still held by some) was that the hapless leader was murdered by agents of the tin barons.

5. The first ideological statement of the PIR is reprinted in Alberto Cornejo S., *Programas políticos de Bolivia* (Cochabamba, 1949).

6. The first official statement of the MNR appeared in a pamphlet entitled simply *Movimiento Nacionalista Revolucionario*. In Bolivia the pamphlet is referred to as *El libro verde*. A late statement appears in Cornejo, *Programas políticos*.

7. This view of the lower classes was expressed in an early speech of Paz Estenssoro in which he argued:

But my respected colleague forgets or doesn't want to mention who are the ones who make the great transformations of history. It is a general law that the men of the oppressed class never are the ones who achieve gains for their own class and this is for a simple reason; those of an oppressed class do not have the economic means to even raise themselves culturally and develop their personality let alone be able to make a great reform or a revolution. (Víctor Paz Estenssoro, *Discursos parlamentarios* [La Paz, 1955], pp. 316–17)

8. Individual MNR leaders such as Paz and Guevara did publicly discuss the issue of agrarian reform, but it was never included in a party platform.

9. For a discussion of the struggle, see Peñaloza, *Historia del MNR*, pp. 153 ff.

10. The suspicion of the labor leaders is made clear in Augustin Barcelli S., *Medio siglo de luchas sindicales revolucionarias en Bolivia* (La Paz, 1956), p. 155. The radical orientation of the mine workers was clear in its first ideological statement known as *la Tesis de Pulacayo*, reprinted in Carnejo, *Programas políticos*.

11. The distrust between the two wings is made clear in Peñaloza, *Historia del MNR*, which is a history from the bourgeois group's point of view.

12. For a fuller discussion of the development of the party, see James Malloy, "Revolution and Development in Bolivia," in *Constructive Change in Latin America,* ed. Cole Blasier (Pittsburgh, Pa., 1968), pp. 177–232.

13. Robert J. Alexander, *The Bolivian National Revolution* (New Brunswick, N.J., 1958), p. 46.

14. The basic economic orientation of the core MNR was pointed out to me by one of the more important original leaders, Wálter Guevara Arze, in a 1966 interview in La Paz.

15. Lechín openly stated, for example, "The right [wing] of the MNR allied with the most reactionary elements of the Army has attempted to stab the revolution in the back" (*Lechín y la revolucion nacional* [La Paz, n.d.], p. 72).

16. For an excellent discussion of these early battles, see Gueiler Tejada, *La mujer y la revolución,* pp. 119 ff. The following quotes give some of the flavor of the left's position at this time:

Only the proletariat supported by the peasants can avoid an abandonment of the revolution by the petty bourgeoisie.

The proletariat wishes to push the revolution to its ultimate consequences.

The best guarantee of the defense of these conquests consists in the participation of the worker in government, worker control with a veto and the unionization and militarization of workers and peasants. (*Programa ideológico y estatutos de la Central Obrera Boliviana* [La Paz, 1954], pp. 24–25)

17. This view was pointed out to me by one of the stalwarts of the Old Guard Armando Arze, in a 1966 interview in La Paz.

18. Relevant sections of the decree embodying these points are reprinted in *Bolivia: 10 años de relvolución* (La Paz, 1962), p. 35.

19. Alexander, *Bolivian National Revolution,* p. 103.

20. The new role of the military was outlined in a speech by its new commander in chief Coronel Inofuentes, reprinted in *El Diario,* June 5, 1952, p. 4, col. 3.

21. These developments were fully reported during the period in *El Diario.*

22. This view is expressed in José Fellman Velarde, *Víctor Paz Estenssoro: El hombre y la revolución,* 2d ed. (La Paz, 1955), p. 228.

23. From the time of independence to the 1920s, the story of land in Bolivia has been punctuated by the continual, ruthless expropriation of Indian land. This story is recounted in many studies, among the most important of which are Abraham Maldonado, *Derecho agrario* (La Paz, 1956); Arturo Urquidi Morales, *El feudalismo en America y le reforma agaria boliviana* (Cochabamba, 1966); and Rafael Reyeros, *El pongueaje* (La Paz, 1949). For a detailed study of how one community of Indians was disposed of in the early twentieth century, see Edmundo Flores, "Taraco: Monografía de un latifundio del Altiplano Boliviano," *El Trimestre Económico,* 22, no. 2 (1955), pp. 209–29.

24. There are many novels of mutual race hate and fear in Bolivia. One of the most moving is the famous novel by Alcides Argüedas, *Raza de bronce* (Valencia, 1923).

25. The best discussion of the development of this union is Jorge Dandler-Hanhart, "Local Group, Community, and Nation: A Study of Changing Structure in Ucureña, Bolivia," Master's thesis, University of Wisconsin, 1967.

26. These developments were reported fully during the period by the La Paz daily, *El Diario.* This interpretation was confirmed further in a 1966 personal interview with Ñuflo Chavez Ortiz in La Paz.

27. The following partial chronicle of events will give the reader some idea of the autonomous power of the regional bosses: shortly after the reform, *campesinos* ("countrymen") from Achacachi blocked truck traffic along the lake in a demand for higher food prices, *El Diario,* August 19, 1953, p. 7, col. 1. In 1954 armed

peasants invaded Achacachi and freed the peasants held in the local jail, *El Diario,* May 5, 1954, p. 7, col. 3. On January 27, 1959, campesinos stopped, held for eight hours, and then robbed Víctor Paz Estenssoro, *El Diario,* January 28, 1959, p. 7. Again in 1961 Altiplano peasants blocked traffic and cut transportation to the city, *El Diario,* November 8, 1961, p. 4, col. 6. Shortly thereafter the city was totally cut off, and Salas forbade all persons except the president, the minister of peasant affairs, and newsmen to enter the *campo* ("rural area") under threat of arrest, *El Diario,* January 13, 1962, p. 5, col. 1.

28. For a statement of this view, see Alfredo Candia, *Bolivia: Un experimento communista.*

29. The ideological vagueness of the right is pointed out in Gueiler Tejada, *La mujer y la revolución,* pp. 115 ff. Miss Gueiler reiterated the point to me in personal interviews in La Paz, 1966.

30. The logic of the entrista strategy was spelled out for me by one of its foremost proponents, the ex-PORista, Edwin Moller, in 1966 interviews in La Paz.

31. For an analysis of labor's new position, see U.S., Department of Labor, Bureau of Labor Statistics, *Labor Law and Practice in Bolivia,* report no. 218.

32. For data on the Bolivian inflation, see *Análisis y proyecciónes de desarrollo económico IV: El desarrollo económico de Bolivia* (Mexico, 1958), p. 62.

33. For a detailed analysis of these events, see Lois Deicke Martin, *Bolivia in 1956,* Hispanic American Studies Series (Stanford, Calif., 1958).

34. For a detailed analysis of the plan, see *Análisis y proyecciónes,* pp. 80–82.

35. United States military aid to Bolivia was resumed in 1958. *Report Submitted to the House Committee on Appropriations,* 88th Cong., 1st sess., p. 624.

36. See for example Torcuato Di Tella, "Populism and Reform in Latin America," in *Obstacles to Change in Latin America,* ed. Claudio Veliz (New York, 1965), pp. 47–74.

37. Ibid, p. 53.

38. I use the term in the same sense as does Helio Jaguaribe, *Desarrollo económico y desarrollo político* (Buenos Aires, 1962).

39. For a breakdown of various aspects of U.S. economic aid to Bolivia, see appendix tables 1 and 2.

40. For a discussion of economic immobilism under Siles, see David G. Green, "Revolution and the Rationalization of Reform in Bolivia," *Inter-American Economic Affairs* (Winter 1965), pp. 3–27.

41. A brief glance at appendix tables 1 and 2 will show the tremendous increase in U.S. economic aid after 1960.

42. One speech in which he attacked the situation is reported in *Presencia,* January 18, 1964, p. 5, col. 6.

43. For a discussion of the camarilla and its effects on the MNR, see Mario Pando Monje, *Los movimientistas en el poder* (La Paz, 1968), pp. 236–39.

44. Jaguaribe, *Desarrollo económico,* p. 68.

45. In an important speech Paz attacked the university and called for the creation of a technocratic middle class. See *El Diario,* January 25, 1962, p. 5, col. 5.

46. Between 1955 and 1960 some 47,746 titles were signed; then, in a burst of activity, Paz signed over 200,413 between 1960 and 1964. See James W. Wilkie, "Bolivian Land Reform Since 1952: A Statistical View of Title Distribution," UCLA paper, 1968, appendix A.

47. This line was developed in a number of speeches. For an example see *El Diario,* August 25, 1963, p. 4, col. 5.

48. The increase in U.S. military assistance is documented in appendix table 2.

49. The idea of achieving development by means of economic diversification to be achieved by a shift to the east goes back at least to the early 1940s. It was expressed most clearly then in a U.S. Embassy paper called the Bohan report.

50. For a discussion of Acción Civica, see William Brill, "Military Civic Action in Bolivia," Ph.D. dissertation, University of Pennsylvania, 1965.

51. Paz was able to do this under the terms of a new constitution adopted in 1961. Many charged that Paz specifically included an article permitting succession in order to further his own political designs.

52. There was already in existence a Christian Democratic party. The Barrientos group sought to supplant this previous group, but its requests for recognition by the international Christian Democratic movement were rebuffed. Thus the small Christian Democratic party headed by Remo di Natale remains the officially recognized group.

53. It is generally agreed in Bolivia that the FSB negotiated with Barrientos to play the role of "official" opposition. This general belief has besmirched the FSB's image as an independent opposition force and seriously weakened its political position.

54. Results printed in *El Diario,* July 4–15, 1966. The FSB contested the election as the Christian Democratic community. The two MNRs were the officially recognized MNR led by Víctor Andrade and a group calling itself the *Movimiento Revolucionario Paz Estenssorista.* The Andrade group received 88,392 votes and the Paz group, 60,505.

RICHARD S. THORN
University of Pittsburgh

The Economic Transformation

INTRODUCTION

The Bolivian Revolution was primarily a national revolution, more political than economic in its orientation in spite of its frequent references to Marxist imagery and terminology. The nationalistic goals of the revolution, largely stated in negative terms, were described by Víctor Paz Estenssoro as antifeudal, antiimperialistic, and dedicated to eliminating Bolivia's economic backwardness.[1] While these objectives carried important economic implications, they were largely conceived as political requirements for achieving Bolivian national sovereignty. Therefore, it is not surprising that a search of the statements from the leaders of the Revolutionary National Movement party (MNR) fails to reveal any comprehensive statement of the economic objectives of the revolution. Nevertheless, the economic and political events of the revolutionary epoch were inextricably entwined, and this is the story that I shall try to unravel. In doing so, the economic developments that occurred in the dozen years between April 1952 and October 1964 shall be assessed to the extent that they were successful in promoting the political objectives of the revolution.

The economic theme of the MNR's political pronouncements was that of devoting the resources of Bolivia to Bolivians. The MNR, along with other national and foreign observers, was struck by what the UN's Keenleyside mission was to call the Bolivian paradox: "Bolivia has within its boundaries all the resources necessary to provide a sound economic foundation for a national life distinguished by a wide diffusion of culture, by progress and prosperity, but these results have not been achieved." [2]

Bolivia is larger in size than France, Italy, and West Germany combined but at the outset of the revolution was inhabited by only a little over three million people. Silver, gold, tin, zinc, antimony, tungsten, lead, copper, and other valuable minerals occur in large quantities in the highlands. The fertile central valleys and broad eastern savannahs are well supplied with good soil suitable for cultivating rice, corn, sugar, tea, citrus fruits, and cocoa. The less fertile western high plateau, the Altiplano, produces potatoes, barley, wheat, quinoa, and other agricultural products. Two-fifths of the country is covered with rich forests producing lumber and wild rubber. There are extensive pastures for cattle and sheep in the northern plains and valleys and for sheep and llama on the highlands. The lakes and rivers provide fish.

Agriculture, at the beginning of the revolution, accounted for about one-third of the gross national product and engaged almost three-quarters of the population but utilized only 2 percent of the land area. Mining provided only 15 percent of the national product but 95 percent of the foreign exchange. Mining, however, determined the national pattern of urbanization, transportation, trade, and government revenues. The transportation network consisted of a few railroads connecting the mining areas with the seaports, but the rest of the country was left virtually without modern roads. The urban-monetized economy in 1952 probably consisted of not more than six hundred thousand persons with a purchasing power of less than that of an American city the size of Charlotte, North Carolina, with a population of one hundred thirty-four thousand persons.[3]

At the outset of the revolution, the MNR had no master plan for the reorganization of economic activity and the acceleration of economic development in Bolivia, but, to the extent that the party leaders did have any economic model in mind, it was essentially a capitalist one. Indeed, in many respects it appears that the MNR was trying to establish the institutional arrangement of nineteenth-century capitalism, depending on free competitive forces to propel the Bolivian economy into the twentieth century:

It is the existence of anachronistic and unjust structural organisations; it is the existence of an economy tied fundamentally to foreigners and which suffers a permanent drainage of its wealth. Interrelated with these two characteristics, and in a certain sense as a consequence of them, the country lingers in a permanent state of economic backwardness which extends itself to the social field.[4]

But the MNR did not adopt the nineteenth-century capitalistic model completely—references were traditionally made to the benefits to be obtained through national planning. It was through this national planning (never clearly defined) that the resources of the country were to be marshaled in order to bring about the transformation of the Bolivian economy. The MNR, unfortunately, was so thoroughly occupied with the problems of seizing and maintaining political power that it was never able to formulate a well-defined program of how planning was to be organized under the new society that it was to create. As a consequence, when in power, it had to resort to foreign models and technicians to give the planning form and content. Although the MNR's planning efforts began to produce some results in the closing days of the party's stay in power, planning never was integrated into the political and administrative processes of the government.

The MNR suffered from great misunderstanding abroad, at various times it was labeled socialistic, fascist, communistic, and, ultimately, pro-Yankee. It was, in fact, nationalistic; it never deviated from this basic orientation, even though in its tortuous journey to power it made various alliances with many different national and foreign political powers, which to distant (and suspicious) eyes abroad appeared to tint the color of the party. These nationalistic goals, however, brought the MNR into conflict with economic realities, a conflict which was never fully resolved, right up to the party's deposition by the coup d'etat of November 1964. Its failure to develop an economic program consistent with its nationalist political objectives was, in fact, one of the principal factors leading to its downfall.

Paz himself, a professor of economics, declared that, above all else, economic development was the key to Bolivia's emergence as a truly independent nation, even if such growth meant sacrificing some of the immediate political goals of the revolution. He, as Professor Malloy comments in his essay, made economic development the ultimate criterion of the revolution, defining an antirevolutionary as one who stood in the way of economic development.[5] Paz stated, "If the government of the national revolution can consolidate itself with a sufficient economic and social base, the reactionaries, the *Rosca,* and their servants will have lost all hope of returning to power in Bolivia." [6]

THE REVOLUTIONARY ECONOMIC REFORMS

The three great economic reforms of the revolution—agrarian reform, nationalization of the mines, and the implementation of the 1939 labor code of President Busch—were not taken as part of a socialist philosophy but, rather, in the spirit of a national liberal philosophy.

NATIONALIZATION OF THE MINES

The nationalistic and capitalistic tenor of this program is apparent from the provisions of the nationalization decree.[7] The large mining corporations, Patiño, Aramayo, and Hochschild, were nationalized so that their profits would be employed in the national interest and their political influence destroyed. The small- and medium-sized mines, which were largely in Bolivian hands, were not nationalized but were required to sell their minerals to the state *Banco Minero* (Mining Bank). This was required of the medium-sized mines so that the state might share more fully in their profits; for the small mines, it was, ostensibly, to prevent their being exploited by the middlemen to whom they formerly sold their output. In 1961, however, the medium-sized mines were again authorized to sell their minerals abroad and were taxed according to a new schedule based on the price of the minerals. The operation of the small mines was to be modernized by means of loans and technical assistance from the state Mining Bank in order to increase their productivity and improve the subsistence conditions under which the *mineros pequenos* ("small miners") lived. Although substantial loans were made by the State Mining Bank, the modernization program of the small mines was never implemented. The loans were granted largely on a political basis, and the administration of the bank proved inefficient and corrupt.

AGRARIAN REFORM

The object of the agrarian reform was to liberate the country from an outmoded form of economic organization which denied the riches of the Bolivian soil to the Bolivian people. As Paz stated: "It does not imply a socialist viewpoint; it is a liberal viewpoint. It represents the rejection of the feudal regime already achieved in many nations but which still persists in the economically backward countries of Latin America. The subdivision of land is the classical hallmark of agrarian reform of a liberal type. . . . A socialist reform implies the nationalization of the land not its subdivision into small plots to be tilled individually."[8]

The fact that this liberal type of land reform would do little to solve the basic problems confronting Bolivian agriculture, namely, the low productivity of farmers and the concentration of agricultural exploitation in the poorer agricultural regions of the country, was not dealt with extensively by the MNR before it came to power.[9]

After seizing power in April 1952, the MNR gave priority to the nationalization of the mines over agrarian reform. Meanwhile, as the peasants began to seize the land and homes of the large landowners, many of the landowners fled their properties for the relative safety of the cities. To stop violence and anarchy from ruling in the countryside, the government established a commission headed by Vice-President Hernán Siles Zuazo to prepare a study and to make recommendations within four months for an agrarian reform law. The commission, advised by the Mexican economist Edmundo Flores, attempted to introduce some economic considerations into the agrarian reform. On August 2, 1953, before one hundred thousand armed *campesinos* ("countrymen") at Uruceña, in Cochabamba, the president promulgated Decree Law 3464, proclaiming that date as "the Day of the Indian." The decree set forth six fundamental objectives:

1. Redistribution of the land
2. Abolition of unpaid labor
3. Promotion of Indian communities
4. Stimulation of agriculture
5. Preservation of national resources
6. Promotion of internal migration to the less populated eastern regions

Far from confiscating all the property of the former landowners, the law permitted the continuation of medium-sized properties from six hundred to fifteen hundred acres and agricultural enterprises from two hundred to five thousand acres, depending on the region of the country where the land was located. For stock-raising purposes estates as large as one hundred twenty-four thousand acres were permitted. However, the spontaneous seizure of the land went much further than that authorized by the ex post facto law, and few of the owners who had abandoned their properties attempted to assert their legal rights under the law. Thus, an unintended result of the law was to delay the issuance of new titles to the present occupants of the land, because the original owners still had a legal right to the property. The law provided that the former owners of expropriated land were entitled to compensation in the form of bonds paying 2 percent interest for twenty-five years, while the new owners were expected to pay off the assessed value of the land within the same period. In practice, inflation and usage made these latter provisions inoperative, although in a surprising number of cases the new owners voluntarily agreed to make some payment to the former owners, often in the belief that this would guarantee the legitimacy of their title, the agrarian reform law notwithstanding. The attempt of the law to protect the efficient agricultural producers, however, was a failure for the reasons mentioned. Although many formerly uncultivated properties were brought under cultivation, many properties that formerly were efficiently operated must have been less efficiently exploited, since total production was adversely affected. To make matters worse, the amount of produce going to the market was sharply reduced as the new owners took part of the increased income from their new holdings in the form of a better diet. The immediate effect of the land reform was, therefore, to improve the distribution of income, but it did little to promote the revolutionary goal of economic growth. Land reform also created new difficulties, such as the creation of *minifundia* ("extremely small land plots") and new obstacles to the transfer of part of the population from the poorer Altiplano area to the richer eastern regions.

The revolution did, however, destroy irrevocably the *latifundio* ("large landholding") by eliminating the key element that had sustained it, namely, the rendering of personal service as payment for the land.[10] The independent farmer became a fact of Bolivian economic life.

LABOR CODE

The basic labor code of Bolivia (drafted under President Toro) was enacted under President Germán Busch in 1939. An excellent piece of legislation, it stressed both the duties and the rights of workers and employers and specifically permitted workers to organize. The law, however, in practice, had been implemented in many different manners, depending on the government in power. In 1943 a joint U.S.-Bolivian labor commission, formed at the request of President Villarroel, reported that, although the right of the workers to organize was guaranteed by the constitution and the labor code, in reality the practices of employers, often tolerated and supported by the government, prevented workers from voicing their grievances either collectively or individually.[11]

The MNR was to change the situation radically. The workers' rights under the Labor Code were emphasized and those of the employer suppressed or ignored. The Labor Code forbade unions to participate in political activities, but this provision was universally ignored, especially since the MNR encouraged unions to engage in politics. This situation created a great deal of disruption in the limited industrial sector that did exist in Bolivia. In many cases, legally compulsory arbitration panels made awards that disregarded the economic viability of the enterprises. Labor strikes were rampant, averaging over three hundred fifty a year between 1952 and 1957, rising to fifteen hundred in 1958 but dropping to twelve hundred in 1959 as a reaction to the stabilization decrees. Businesses were abandoned, requiring the government to appoint administrators who usually executed the *coup de grâce* to the enterprise, since they were not normally provided with any resources to continue its operation. More than any other factor, labor conflicts led to the near paralysis of industry until 1960, when a combination of improved economic circumstances and a tougher government policy toward illegal strikes resulted in some measure of labor peace. In 1960 only 150 strikes were recorded.[12]

The MNR had long advocated the policy of giving workers a share in the management of business. It introduced this principle in article 17 of the nationalization law in the form of the *control obrero* ("workers' control delegate"). The miners elected the control obrero to represent them in matters concerning the efficiency of the enterprise, working conditions, workers' welfare, and personnel problems. He could veto management decisions if they violated labor contracts or legal provisions granting social benefits but was to refrain from using the veto in cases involving technical decisions. In practice, this latter restriction had little meaning, and, in fact, the control obrero and eventually the *directores obreros* ("worker directors"), both of whom were represented on the board of directors of COMIBOL (The Bolivian National Mining Corporation), interceded in all matters affecting the Corporation. The control obreros, representing the *Federación Sindical de Trabajadores Mineros de Bolivia* (FSTMB) under the control of Juan Lechín Oquendo, exercised their functions largely on the basis of political considerations and, eventually, were able to alienate the miners from both the MNR leadership and the management of COMIBOL.

The responsibility for the lack of labor discipline which existed in COMIBOL must be shared among the management, union leaders, miners, and the MNR itself. The apportionment of the blame is beyond the scope of this work. There is little doubt, however, that the failure of the MNR to create an efficient management for COMIBOL and to enlist the cooperation of the miners and their leaders was one of the major failures of the revolution.

The lack of labor discipline and managerial inefficiency in COMIBOL meant that the large mines, which offered the one possibility that the economic development of the country could be independently financed from national resources, became, in fact, a major economic problem and forced the MNR to seek capital for national development almost entirely in the form of economic aid from abroad.

The other side of the story was explained with much candor by the director obrero, Sinforoso Cabrera Romero, on the occasion of his resignation. He pointed out that the control obrero was elected without receiving a basic orientation concerning his functions and objectives. He complained about the lack of responsibility in COMIBOL's management and the indifference of the miners themselves to issues affecting the profitability of COMIBOL and, indirectly, their own welfare.[13]

The inefficiency of COMIBOL is supported by the author's personal observation of the central office of COMIBOL in 1960 and 1961. At that time it presented a picture of incredible disorder and inefficiency which left him wondering how COMIBOL managed to function at all, not to say well. Through the years no accurate set of accounts and records was kept. A proper balance sheet of the corporation, even as late as 1970, did not exist; reasonable income statements have only been prepared since 1964. As late as 1970, after eighteen years of operation, there was still no uniform system of accounting.

THE GRAND STRATEGY

The fundamental obstacles to Bolivia's economic development were long known and commented upon by numerous writers. All recognized the country as one with enormous wealth in natural resources. They pointed out that the agricultural population was concentrated in the Altiplano (one of the poorest agricultural zones in the country) and immobilized by a feudal structure. They also saw that the domestic market was too small to support any but the lightest consumer industry. The foreign exchange necessary to purchase machinery and other imports was derived almost exclusively from the export of minerals, principally tin. A legion of critics, the MNR among them, called for the liberation of agriculture from the dead hand of feudalism and the freeing of the country from the tyranny of tin. Yet no comprehensive program was put forth to rescue the economy from its backwardness, beyond the all-important first steps of destroying the feudal structure and eliminating the hegemony of the tin barons. Bolivian economic thought rarely proceeded beyond this fundamental first stage. It was almost as if these steps were an impossible dream that Bolivian intellectuals dared not venture beyond for fear of being accused of fantasy. When the MNR put forth its first comprehensive statement on its economic program (drafted by Wálter Guevara Arze, minister of foreign affairs and culture and chief theoretician of the MNR), it turned to an earlier foreign report for its grand design.

The main outlines of the MNR's development strategy were inspired by the Bohan mission from the United States. On January 28, 1942, Bolivia severed relations with the Axis powers, and, simultaneously, the United States announced the signing of an agreement providing for $25 million through the Export-Import Bank to promote Bolivian economic development.[14] Merwin L. Bohan, a State Department official, was sent to head an economic mission to Bolivia to investigate that country's financial needs for development. The program he recommended was essentially that incorporated into the MNR's detailed economic program drafted by Guevara Arze.[15] Bohan recommended that first priority be given to projects which would increase exports or decrease imports, if self-sustaining development was to be achieved,[16] but the main emphasis was to be on import substitution. He recommended that the population be shifted from the poor lands of the Altiplano to the fertile lands of the east. To accomplish these objectives, the *Corporación de Fomento de Bolivia* (Bolivian Development Corporation) was established with a $10 million loan from the U.S. Export–Import Bank; the first project announced under the loan was the construction of the Cochabamba-Santa Cruz highway.[17]

Under Bohan's plan Bolivia was to become self-sufficient in petroleum by December 1942 and to attain self-sufficiency in sugar, rice, cotton, livestock, and lumber by 1947. To promote exports, technical and financial aid was to be granted to the mining industry. None of the objectives set forth by the Bohan report were accomplished before the 1952 national revolution. Even the Cochabamba-Santa Cruz highway, originally to have been completed in 1946, was finally opened by President Paz in 1954. By 1964, however, the only one of Bohan's objectives not achieved was self-sufficiency in cotton, and, even there, a substantial start was made under private Bolivian auspices to accomplish the last of the mission's "short-term goals"—some seventeen years later than anticipated. Thus, the economic story of the revolution, like so many Bolivian stories, started off in the wrong direction, although it ended happily. It was, however, not until the end of the MNR period of administration that the happy ending came into sight.

Economists often like to employ the aeronautical analogy of the "take-off" to describe the process of economic development. The image this is supposed to conjure up is that of a powerful airplane lumbering down a concrete runway until it reaches a critical speed and then takes off gracefully into sustained flight. The Bolivian takeoff was more like those which used to occur at the old El Alto airport before the new jet runway was built in 1964. The airport was perched on the high plateau overlooking the city of La Paz, which is located in the gorge below. The runway was unpaved and ran slightly downhill so that a plane could achieve a little extra speed for its final assault into the thin air. The plane would race noisily down the dusty, bumpy runway; in contrast to the dull routine of the modern jets, every takeoff had an air of excitement to it, not completely unjustified. Once airborne, the ride in the mountain air was often so rough that one wished he had never begun the journey. In retrospect, it seems that the takeoff at El Alto was a better analogy to the way economic development occurs than the more aesthetic image I had thought of when I first heard the word "takeoff" applied to it.

The main outlines of the Bohan report were subscribed to later by the UN's Keenleyside mission in 1950 and by the Bolivian Ten-Year Development Plan of 1962–1971, and again reaffirmed in the Plan Bienal of 1963–1964. The question of why the objectives which Ambassador Bohan thought could be attained by 1947 were not yet achieved by 1952 would make a fascinating story, but this must be left for another time and place. This narrative concerns itself with the question of why these objectives were not attained until almost the downfall of the MNR, leaving the fruits of this progress to be reaped by other hands.

The economic developments of the Bolivian National Revolution of 1952 can be divided into four major periods as shown in table 1 each marked by a major event: April 1952, the coming to power of the MNR; December 1956, the introduction of the stabilization program by President Hernán Siles; August 1961, the inauguration of Operation Triangular to rehabilitate the Bolivian National Mining Corporation; and November 1964, marking the overthrow of President Paz and the MNR

TABLE 1
AVERAGE ANNUAL RATE OF GROWTH IN GROSS DOMESTIC PRODUCT
IN CONSTANT PRICES
1951–1968

	1951–56	1956–61	1961–64	1964–68
Gross domestic product	−1.3%	1.5%	5.7%	5.6%
Agriculture	−2.4	4.8	2.1	0.2
Mining	−4.3	−3.9	8.6	4.0
Petroleum	44.2	0.2	7.5	27.7
Manufacturing	0.6	−2.5	7.4	8.3
Construction	7.6	20.0[a]	15.5	18.4
Transportation	8.1	2.4	5.9	4.2
Commerce	0.4	−1.3	5.4	5.0
Government	1.5	4.6	7.1	5.8

Source: Appendix table 1.
a. For period 1956–60 only. Construction activity fell drastically in 1961. See appendix table 1.

and the installation of a military junta (and later President Barrientos). The story ends with the dramatic death of Barrientos in April 1969.

The first period, from 1951 to 1956, is marked by an inflation and absolute decline in national production resulting from the sharp decline in mineral output and agriculture which was only partially offset by the great expansion of the petroleum industry. This period was followed, from 1956 to 1961, by a program of economic stabilization. The decline in national production was checked as a result of a sharp increase in construction activity, largely public roads, which gave a strong impetus to increase agricultural output, particularly in the province of Santa Cruz. Mining and industrial output, however, continued to decline as the stabilization program removed the artificial stimulus to domestic industry. The government sector grew steadily. The period 1961 to 1964 was marked by high levels of foreign aid, which benefitted the state mining corporation, agriculture, and construction, and a continued increase in the rate of government expansion. As a result of the high-level activity in the public sector, there was a revival of domestic industry and commerce. The overall expansion resulted in a sharp rise in the rate of growth to an average of 5.7 percent per annum. The post-MNR period, 1964 to 1968, experienced continued high levels of foreign aid and a sharp rise in both petroleum production and prices which offset the slower rate of growth of mineral output. A building boom in residential and commercial construction in the large cities further helped to maintain the growth rate at its former satisfactory levels. The only dark spot in the picture was the virtual stagnation which occurred in agriculture and the economic disruption associated with the *golpe* ("coup d'etat") which occurred in September 1969 and the subsequent nationalization that same month of the Bolivian Gulf Oil Company.

MORNING AFTER THE REVOLUTION

A great optimism pervaded the MNR as it took power. The impossible dream had come true through a rare combination of persistence, skill, and luck that brought all the dissident forces in Bolivian society into sharp focus for one brief moment during Easter Week 1952. The unity of purpose that accompanied the MNR's triumphal march to the Presidential Palace was never to be seen again. Soon the campesinos would seize the land, and both the latifundia and feudalism would disappear before the MNR could take steps to dispose of them legally.

NATIONALIZATION OF THE TIN MINES

The first task in the economic domain to which the MNR turned its attention was the nationalization of the large tin mines. The revolution took place on April 9, 1952, and a month later, on May 13, President Paz Estenssoro established a commission under the direction of Vice-President Hernán Siles to study the problems involved in the nationalization of the mines. The commission presented its report, but it met with opposition from the *Confederación Obrera Boliviana* (COB), which was led by its executive secretary, Juan Lechín Oquendo. Controlled by Trotskyites, the COB urged the government to nationalize the mines without compensation and turn them over to the miners.[18] The report did not recommend either of these actions. The MNR, however, regained control of the COB, causing it in the following week to reverse itself. The Bolivian National Mining Corporation (COMIBOL) was created on October 2; on October 7 the mines were nationalized; and on October 31, 1952, the "Act of Bolivia's Economic Independence" was signed and promulgated by President Paz at Campo de Maria-Barzola at Catavi, nationalizing the three largest mining enterprises—the Patiño Mines and Enterprises Consolidated Incorporated, the Mauricio Hochschild S.A. Minera Industrial, and the Compania Aramayo de Minas en Bolivia. All were put directly under the control of the *Corporación Minera de Bolivia* (COMIBOL), the newly created state mining enterprise.[19]

The priority given to the nationalization of the great mining corporations can readily be understood in that they were responsible for 85 percent of the country's tin production, 95 percent of its foreign exchange receipts, and about 50 percent of the central government's fiscal receipts. There was not an enterprise in Bolivia that did not have business with the large mines. The predominant economic importance of mining in the economy and the key political role that the miners played in the revolution made the move inevitable. Somewhat more surprising was the decision to grant compensation to the former owners, especially in view of the famous Thesis of Pulacayo which was presented to the first congress of the *Federación Sindical de Trabajadores Mineros de Bolivia* (FSTMB) in 1946, which called for the nationalization of the mines without compensation. It was this same congress that elected Juan Lechín Oquendo executive secretary of the FSTMB.

The decision of Paz and Siles to grant compensation to the former mineowners can be explained by the overwhelming priority they gave to achieving economic independence:

We declare the economic plan has primacy. If we develop the economy now, we will see its effects in the social field, in legal, cultural, and welfare matters, etc. Therefore, our plan has to give heavy preponderance to the economic aspect.[20]

Secondly, the United States and the United Kingdom, the chief purchasers of Bolivian tin, strongly expressed their belief in compensation for the confiscated properties. Thirdly, Paz desired early recognition from the United States, not only to legitimize his position but also because he was aware that Bolivia would need outside assistance to overcome its backwardness.

This central fact, that the social goals of the revolution could not be achieved without economic progress—which itself could not be attained without external assistance—was the central political problem of the MNR throughout its dozen years in power. In spite of all the political compromises and side roads that it was to take, the MNR never did depart from its central belief that economic development was a prerequisite for social development. Its failure to establish a rapid growth rate early enough and its sacrifice of other revolutionary goals in the attempt to accomplish more rapid growth gave its political opposition sufficient ammunition to eventually overthrow it. Lechín was destined by political events to play the antagonist in this drama.

The tin mines, since their development at the end of the nineteenth century, exhibited a steady decline in the assay of the ore. Beginning with ore assays of 16 to 18 percent fine tin content at the turn of the century, by the thirties the mines were utilizing ores of around 2 and 3 percent, and by the end of World War II they were down to 1.25 to 2.50 percent.[21] At the time of the revolution, the mines were beginning to exploit ores containing around 1 percent tin (table 2). The large mines

TABLE 2
AVERAGE TIN CONTENT OF ORE
IN CATAVI MINE
1925–1964

Year	%
1925	6.65%
1935	3.76
1940	3.07
1945	2.46
1950	1.28
1953	1.06
1955	0.84
1957	0.86
1960	0.73
1964	0.54

Source: National Planning and Co-ordination Department (Secretaria Nacional de Planificación y Coordinación), "Plan decenal: Sector minería," mimeographed. Reprinted in United Nations, "The Economic Policy of Bolivia in 1952–64," *Economic Bulletin for Latin America*, 12, no. 2 (October 1967), p. 69.

had tried to keep abreast of the declining quality of the ore by introducing new technological methods in mining and concentration, as necessary. In the thirties, in response to the low demand for tin resulting from the worldwide depression, the large tin mines relaxed their pace of investment as shown in table 3. Their postdepression peak was achieved during World War II, when 42,500 tons of tin were produced. The strong sellers' market that persisted in the postwar period encouraged continued high levels of production and exportation as shown in table 4. The Korean conflict and then the Suez crisis permitted the mines to continue to operate at a profit. The declining assay of the ore, however, would have required ever larger amounts of capital investment in order to maintain

TABLE 3
AVERAGE ANNUAL IMPORTATION OF MINING AND
INDUSTRIAL MACHINERY (*In 1950 Prices*)
1925–1955
(*In Millions of Dollars*)

Years	Mining	Industry
1925–29	$3.0	$7.4
1930–34	1.6	3.8
1935–39	2.4	5.4
1940–44	3.0	5.2
1945–49	2.9	5.7
1950–52	3.1	6.2
1953–55	4.4	5.6

Source: United Nations, Economic Commision for Latin America, *Análisis y proyecciónes del desarrollo económico IV: El desarrollo económico de Bolivia* (Mexico City, 1958), p. 54.

production. The large mines, confronted with declining ore reserves of increasingly lower tin content and with the fact that Bolivia was a high-cost producer, declined to undertake the necessary steps to maintain output, and tin production fell to 34.3 thousand tons in 1952 (appendix table 6).

Bolivia was unlucky in that the rise in tin prices which occurred in 1951 and 1952 as a result of the Korean conflict proved to be temporary. In 1953 tin prices returned to their pre-Korean level. In spite of the frequent protests of the MNR about tin prices in the fifties, prices remained

TABLE 4
AVERAGE ANNUAL EXPORT OF TIN
1900–1949
(*In Metric Tons*)

Period	Tin Exports
1900–09	14,908
1910–19	24,710
1920–29	35,455
1930–39	26,330
1940–49	38,820

Source: United Nations, Economic Commission for Latin America, *Análisis y proyecciónes del desarrollo económico IV: El desarrollo económico de Bolivia* (Mexico City, 1958), pp. 7, 12.

at their favorable pre-Korean levels fluctuating between ninety cents and one dollar a pound with the exception of 1954, when prices dipped to eighty cents (table 5). Tin production rose briefly in 1953 to 35.4 thousand tons but was never again able to attain this level. Following the nationalization of the mines approximately one hundred seventy of the some two hundred foreign mining engineers employed by the large mines,

TABLE 5
COMIBOL TIN PRODUCTION
1951–1968

Year	Tin Production (in Thousands of Metric Tons)	Cost (Cents/lb.)	Market Price (Cents/lb.)	Difference (Price/Cost)	Employment (in Thousands)
1944	39.3 [a]	$0.56 [b]	$0.61	0.05	n.a.
1948	37.8 [a]	0.87 [b]	0.94	0.07	24.2 [c]
1951	28.4	n.a.	1.26	n.a.	24.0
1952	27.3	n.a.	1.17	n.a.	29.0
1953	26.0	n.a.	0.93	n.a.	30.8
1954	25.8	n.a.	0.88	n.a.	32.8
1955	23.5	n.a.	0.90	n.a.	34.2
1956	23.0	n.a.	0.98	n.a.	35.7
1957	21.6	0.91	0.91	0.00	32.1
1958	17.4	1.03	0.94	−0.09	27.9
1959	15.8	1.16	0.98	−0.18	27.2
1960	15.2	1.25	0.97	−0.28	27.4
1961	14.8	1.44	1.17	−0.27	26.4
1962	15.3	1.46	1.08	−0.38	25.5
1963	15.4	1.49	1.16	−0.33	24.0
1964	17.7	1.63	1.53	−0.10	23.8
1965	16.5	1.70	1.70	0.00	24.6
1966	18.4	1.42	1.59	0.17	n.a.
1967	18.6	1.43	1.49	0.06	22.7
1968	18.6	1.35	1.40	0.05	n.a.

Source: (Production), *1944, 1948:* Ricardo Anaya, *Nacionalizacion de las minas de Bolivia* (Cochabamba, 1952), p. 76; *1951–1957:* René Ruiz González, *La administration empirica de las minas nacionlizadas*, p. 142; *1958–1968:* U.S., Agency for International Development, *Estadisticas economicas*, no. 11 (La Paz, 1970). (Cost), *1944, 1948:* Ricardo Anaya, *Nacionalizacion de las minas*, p. 76; *1951–1968:* Inter-American Committee on the Alliance for Progress (CIAP), *Domestic Efforts and the Needs for External Financing for the Development of Bolivia*, mimeographed (Washington, D.C., 1969), p. 34. (Prices), *1944, 1948:* Ricardo Anaya, *Nacionalizacion de las minas*, p. 76; *1951–1968:* COMIBOL. (Employment), *1948:* Ricardo Anaya, *Nacionalizacion de las minas*, p. 85; *1951–1964:* Table 10 (p. 193); *1965–1969:* COMIBOL.
Note: n.a. = no data available.
   a. Tin exports.
   b. Aramayo mines only.
   c. Employment in *mineria grande* ("large mines"). Not exactly comparable to COMIBOL properties.

together with most of the managers, left the country. The heavy utilization of foreign engineers by the large mines had been one of the criticisms leveled against the tin barons, and the full effects of their departure were felt by the MNR leaders who had to find skilled replacements for these men. In the period from 1946 to 1952, the *sexenio* ("six-year" exile of party leaders in MNR lore), numerous workers were fired from the mines for political reasons. When these former workers began to concentrate in the cities in 1952, the MNR, worried about the political repercussions of a growing army of unemployed, issued a decree that all miners dismissed for political reasons during the sexenio were to be reinstated in their jobs. This decree was utilized by Lechín to consolidate his political control of the mines. Meanwhile, the labor force in the national mines rose from twenty-nine thousand in 1952 to almost thirty-six thousand in 1956 (table 5), a period during which many mines were incurring losses and some were forced to close down.

In addition to the creation of a large number of supernumeraries, many additional benefits were granted to the miners, including continuation and extension of the pre-1952 practice of subsidized sales of feed products and other items through *pulperías* ("company-run commissaries").[22] The cost per worker rose from $3.64 per man/day in 1950 to approximately $10.00 per man/day in 1953.[23] The production cost of tin rose from less than a $1.00 per pound before 1952 to $1.25 per pound in 1960.

Production and labor productivity fell sharply in COMIBOL after 1953 with serious consequences for the balance of payments and government revenues. Output per worker fell from 2,338 kilos of fine metal in 1952 to 1,598 kilos in 1955.[24] These results were widely ascribed, even by the MNR, to the technical incompetence of COMIBOL's management and the lack of labor discipline on the part of the miners. What is often not recognized is the strong contribution of the MNR's policies to these results.

Before the stabilization program of 1956 COMIBOL was compelled, under the system of multiple exchange rates, to sell its foreign exchange earnings to the Central Bank at rates considerably below the free-market rate. COMIBOL had to exchange its dollars for bolivianos at a rate of 230 in 1953, 325 in 1954, and 570 in 1955. For the same years, the rate of exchange in the free market was approximately seven hundred, fourteen hundred, and three thousand (see appendix table 4). The cost of living and the free-market rate of exchange in the same period rose approximately four times, but COMIBOL's rate of exchange rose only two and one-half times.

If COMIBOL had sold its exchange at the free-market rate, it would have registered a profit of $35.4 million in 1953, $34.2 million in 1954, and $34.2 million in 1955,[25] instead of the cumulative loss for these three years of 10.2 billion bolivianos that was actually registered.[26] Ford, Bacon, and Davis, a team of U.S. consulting engineers, utilizing an exchange rate of 2,100 bolivianos to the dollar, calculated that COMIBOL had a profit of $17.5 million in 1955.[27]

The MNR's multiple exchange-rate policy forced it to transfer income from the most profitable mines to the least profitable ones and either to borrow from the Central Bank or to receive subsidies from the central government, in order to cover COMIBOL's necessary expenses. Politically these procedures placed COMIBOL at the mercy of the central government. Economically it resulted in a shortage of funds for the replacement and expansion of plants and equipment which were necessary to maintain the level of output. It also resulted in a shortage of working capital which interfered with the regular payment of wages and the stocking of the miners' commissaries, all of which promoted labor unrest and a sharp fall in productivity.[28]

While it is not possible to absolve either the management or the miners of COMIBOL for the decline in productivity, COMIBOL cannot be held responsible for the inflation that occurred. What the MNR did was to systematically divert from COMIBOL, through the exchange system, large amounts of resources to finance other projects, particularly the development of the national petroleum industry, the only sector of the economy which had the potential for a large rapid development in the short run. The diversion of COMIBOL's resources into the national petroleum company *Yacimientos Petrolíferos Fiscales Bolivianos* (YPFB) was a calculated risk which, in retrospect, did not pay off. In the period following the revolution, the MNR government invested some $140 million in the form of exchange and tax privileges in the reorganization of the YPFB, to be headed by President Paz's brother, José Paz.[29] A geological department was formed, and over two hundred wells were drilled, resulting in the discovery of a major oil field in Camiri. Production rose fivefold to 3.6 million barrels of crude oil in 1957, which was sufficient to meet domestic demand and permit a small surplus for export. The Camiri wells were less productive than anticipated, and by 1961 the import of a small amount of crude oil from Argentina again became necessary.

Realizing that the capital necessary to finance additional petroleum explorations was beyond the government's, or, perhaps more correctly, COMIBOL's resources, the government turned to private foreign capital and, in 1955 with the assistance of U.S. advisers, drew up and enacted a petroleum code. The gamble that oil would provide the financial resources to permit Bolivia to follow an independent economic policy free of foreign interference had failed. Mineral exports, which had provided over 50 percent of the government's revenues by 1955, had dropped to less than 5 percent, forcing the government to change the structure of taxation away from export duties toward import duties (table 6). The

TABLE 6
TAXATION BY SOURCE
1950–1968

Type of Tax	1950	1955	1964	1968
Foreign trade	65%	45%	52%	47%
Exports	(58)	(4)	(9)	(4)
Imports	(7)	(41)	(43)	(43)
Direct taxes	22	11	21	25 [a]
Indirect taxes	5	30	19	19 [a]
Others	8	14	8	8
Total	100%	100%	100%	100%

Source: 1950: United Nations, *Report of the United Nations Mission of Technical Assistance* (commonly called the Keenleyside report) (New York, 1961), p. 73; *1955–1968:* Various reports of the International Monetary Fund.
  a. Preliminary estimates.

national petroleum company paid little or no taxes, and, although it was estimated by the Economic Commission for Latin America that domestic petroleum production saved Bolivia $44 million in foreign exchange through reduced imports and new exports in the period from 1953 to 1957, it cost YPFB $38 million in foreign exchange to accomplish this.[30]

The problems of COMIBOL, which led to the MNR's economic downfall, were the result of a variety of factors:

1. Insufficient fixed and working capital
2. The exhaustion of mineral reserves
3. Technical and administrative incapacity resulting from the appointment of officials primarily on the basis of their party militancy without regard for their competence

4. Lack of labor discipline in the working force, many members of which owed their loyalty to political officials rather than COMIBOL

5. Excessive employment of workers who, in many cases, did not perform productive functions

6. Lack of a well-thought-out plan of exploitation of the mines

7. Excessive centralization of decision-making and authority in La Paz and no delegation of responsibility

8. The intervention of the control obreros in matters beyond their jurisdiction and competence

With the wisdom of hindsight, it appears that a financial policy of not squeezing COMIBOL so hard but, rather, placing more investment in it might have produced superior results. The real failure of the period, however, was President Paz's inability to reach a political compromise with the miners' leader, Juan Lechín, for such an agreement would have permitted a more balanced policy of development between COMIBOL and YPFB. As a result of this failure, COMIBOL became a state within a state, an ironic parallel to the prerevolutionary situation.

AGRICULTURE

The situation in agriculture, while not as unsuccessful as that in COMIBOL, could not give the MNR much hope of achieving its goal of economic independence. The agrarian reform consisted largely of the distribution of land and, in this area, must be considered as the most thorough program of land distribution carried out in Latin America. However, little consideration was given to the problem of increasing output and productivity. The agrarian reform law, when it belatedly appeared, made some attempt to preserve the more efficient agricultural producers. It came, unfortunately, after most landowners of medium- and large-sized estates had already abandoned their properties. In addition, the possiblity that was left open to some owners to reclaim their property legally often delayed the final disposition of the land and adversely affected output. Total agricultural output fell by 13 percent between 1952 and 1954 (see appendix table 1). Even more serious than this was the fact that the flow of agricultural foodstuffs to the market fell drastically as many of the new landowners enjoyed their higher incomes in kind. The distribution system was disorganized; the function of collecting and marketing the crops, performed by the former landowners, was temporarily dislocated. The result was a sharp increase in the imports of food products, particularly wheat, flour, butter, and sugar, which created serious balance of payments problems.

THE BALANCE OF PAYMENTS AND EXCHANGE CONTROL

Falling tin production and prices and a reduction in the flow of agricultural products to urban markets made it necessary to import food and contributed to an aggravation of the balance of payments. Between 1952 and 1954 the Central Bank's foreign exchange reserves declined from $29.3 million to $11.6 million (see appendix table 3).

Since 1937 Bolivia had experienced a continuous inflation, which was

TABLE 7
COST OF LIVING IN LA PAZ
1931–1968

Period	Administration	Average Annual Rate of Increase
1931–35	Chaco War, Salamanca administration	16.5%
1936–39	Presidents Sorzano, Toro, Busch	50.7
1940–43	Peñaranda administration ⎫ World War II	23.7
1944–45	Villarroel administration ⎭	7.7
1946–51	Gutiérrez, Hertzog, Urriologoitia	18.3
1952–56	Paz administration	147.6
1957–61	Stabilization program, Siles	26.2
1962–64	Alliance for Progress, Paz	1.7
1965–68	Barrientos administration	6.3

Source: 1931–1956: United Nations, Economic Commission for Latin America, *Análisis y proyecciónes del desarrollo económico IV: El desarrollo económico de Bolivia* (Mexico City, 1958); *1956–1968:* Banco Central de Bolivia, *Boletín estadistico*, nos. 181, 182.

dealt with largely by devaluing the boliviano, depending on the fortunes of tin. In 1934, under the government of President Daniel Salamanca, Bolivia introduced dual exchange rates; [31] these were unified in 1938 and reintroduced in 1947. The purpose of the system was twofold: 1) to hold down the cost of living by allowing foodstuffs and other necessities to enter at the official rate and 2) to discourage imports of luxury goods by selling exchange for their import at a higher rate in an attempt to reduce overall imports. The cost of this system was borne by the mining companies, which were required to surrender part of their export earnings at the low official rate. The MNR inherited this system, and with it the inflation which had been rising continuously since the Chaco War (table 7). The continuous inflation combined with the inefficient system of exchange control made it necessary from time to time to devalue the boliviano.[32] Under the MNR, however, the system broke down completely when the nationalized mines could no longer be taxed further by an artificially low exchange rate and, in fact, required large additional amounts of bolivianos to continue running.

The continuance of the multiple exchange-rate system without a much larger devaluation of the rates than was actually made, besides resulting in the loss of the nation's foreign exchange reserves, also served to reduce the government's revenues and intensified both the domestic inflation and the balance of payments situation. In 1950, 7 percent of the government's revenues resulted from import revenues and 58 percent from export duties on minerals (see table 6 on page 175). Putting an arbitrarily low boliviano value on imports resulted in smaller receipts for the treasury than would have been achieved with a more realistic exchange rate. On the other hand, giving the small- and medium-sized private mines a lower boliviano price for their minerals than a more realistic exchange rate would have indicated resulted in a reduction in their production and export of minerals.

The multiple exchange-rate system with grossly overvalued rates, therefore, resulted in an acute balance of payments crisis involving the loss of the nation's exchange reserves and a reduction in tax revenues, thus increasing the government's deficit and intensifying the inflation. In addition, it provided a mechanism for the wholesale corruption of large elements of the MNR and discredited the party in the eyes of the nation's educated young people.

The exchange-control system and the failure to introduce efficient management into the mines were the two most important errors that the MNR was to make in the area of general economic policy. Fortunately, the exchange system problem was easier to correct than the situation in COMIBOL.

The destruction of the profitability of COMIBOL had a profound effect on the structure and incidence of taxation as well. In 1950 export duties had provided more than half of the government's income. Direct taxes, which also were largely paid by mining corporations, accounted for a fifth of total government revenue (see table 6 on page 175). After 1953, when COMIBOL no longer had sufficient resources to pay taxes, these two sources of revenue, which formerly had accounted for four-fifths of total revenue, declined, by 1955, to less than a sixth. In order to maintain the level of revenue, it was necessary to raise the taxes on imports and consumption from 12 percent of total revenue in 1950 to approximately 70 percent of total revenue in 1955. Whereas, previously, the burden of taxation had been largely borne by mining, now it was largely borne by the middle and urbanized working classes.

The reluctance of the MNR to deal with the accumulated problems of budget imbalance, inflation, and balance of payments disequilibrium resulted in the loss of whatever momentum it had achieved in the economic field in 1953 when tin production actually increased. The official exchange rate was increased to 191.9 bolivianos to the dollar in 1953 when the free-market rate was 682 bolivianos (see appendix table 4). Importers who were able to obtain import licenses to buy exchange at the various official rates were able to make enormous profits. Bolivia became a major point of origin for smuggling into neighboring countries. The exchange system was probably the major source of corruption in the early period of the MNR and, in large measure, destroyed the pristine revolutionary image of the party. Where previously the excesses of the MNR had been those of a government dispensing jobs and favors to consolidate political support, the exchange system opened up the opportunity for a spoils system that rivaled the worst excesses of the past.[33]

By 1954 Bolivia had reached a dead end. The government was bankrupt. Foreign exchange earnings had declined as a result of lower tin prices and output. There was a shortage of food in urban areas as a consequence of the agrarian reform and no foreign exchange to import food. Inflation was rampant. The government now had to either follow a policy of austerity and national sacrifice or seek foreign assistance on a large scale. Paz had set economic development ahead of his other social goals, and recognizing that there was only one major source of foreign capital, he made whatever compromises were necessary to achieve the minimum economic stability necessary to preserve his party in power. The MNR was never again able to develop an independent economic program.

The government's choice was made in its emergency economic plan addressed to the United States and presented in late 1954 in which it stated:

The country is not able to survive with its dollar income provided exclusively by the exportation of minerals. It is necessary to continue to keep the mines producing, financing the difference in the cost of production and the price of minerals with loans from the Central Bank to the national mining corporation and to the private medium and small mines. This type of financing is one of the principle causes of the inflation. . . . There are two steps to follow in the process for economic stabilization. The first consists of immediate measures to contract the internal money market. The efficacy of these measures depends on the amount of aid the American government is able to grant in food and capital goods; the second consists of diversifying the economy and producing more in the shortest possible time.[34]

This was the policy line that was to be followed consistently throughout the remainder of the MNR period: reliance on U.S. foreign aid to deal with the problem of the budget deficit and inflation while at the same time trying to diversify the economy and seeking new bases for economic growth. The primary weakness of the program was that it did nothing to stabilize the deteriorating financial position of COMIBOL. The declining tin content of the ore placed constant pressure on the finances of COMIBOL; large-scale capital investment, reduction in the working force, and a rise in the price of tin were required to put an end to the drain on the government's fiscal resources. Only the granting of large-scale foreign assistance by the United States to Bolivia in 1954 and 1955, totaling approximately $52 million, averted economic collapse (see appendix table 9 on page 390).

ECONOMIC STABILIZATION, 1956–1961

Bolivia's foreign exchange system had not functioned well since 1929 when the country went on the gold standard and established a Central Bank. Faced with chronic budget deficits and internal inflation, the exchange rate was constantly overvalued. Before 1929 the budget deficits were often financed with foreign loans which moderated the deficits' inflationary impact. After 1931, however, when Bolivia left the gold standard and stopped service on the foreign debt, foreign financing was no longer available, and the government continuously resorted to borrowing from the newly created Central Bank.

The Chaco War (1932–1936) established a pattern of public finance and inflation that was to continue with little interruption until the revolution (see table 7 on page 177). The permanent feature of the inflation was the chronic appearance of a public deficit and the financing of public investment with Central Bank credit. During the Chaco War, in spite of the large budget deficits incurred, the rise in prices was restrained to an average annual rate of only 16.5 percent by reducing public investment and subsidizing the cost of basic consumer products with the introduction of multiple exchange rates. The multiple exchange-rate system, as already explained, was a form of indirect taxation of the mining sector.[35] The mining companies were required to sell a varying percentage of their foreign exchange earnings at differing rates below the free-market rate to the Central Bank, which sold the foreign exchange at the same, or lower rates, to the importers of essential consumer articles. In a classic piece of understatement, the Bolivian economist Eduardo Lopez Rivas has commented, "Since its introduction in 1935, the system of multiple-exchange rates has done nothing but create a long series of monetary problems for the country." [36] The exchange rate was unified in 1938, but multiple rates were again introduced in 1947. At the time of the revolution, the official exchange rate varied between 60.6 and 101 bolivianos per U.S. dollar, while the free-market rate was 173.3 bolivianos to the dollar (see appendix table 4 on page 376). The average rate of inflation in the five years prior to the revolution was 18 percent a year. Inflation, chronic budget deficits, and overvalued multiple exchange rates were not inventions of the MNR but were an established tradition of Bolivian financial policy or, more properly, the tradition in an absence of a well-defined financial policy. With the single exception of the years 1944–1945, Bolivia had experienced severe inflation for the two decades before the revolution. This one exception is of particular interest.

THE ABORTIVE 1943 STABILIZATION ATTEMPT

In December 1943, following the Bohan mission, the government of President Villarroel, with none other than Víctor Paz as his minister of finance, instituted an antiinflationary policy based on monetary orthodoxy. A ceiling was placed on Central Bank loans to the public sector and to the private banking system. The legal reserve requirements which private banks had to maintain at the Central Bank were raised, and the volume of deposits that banks could receive was made a function of their capital and reserves. The budget deficit was reduced, and by 1945 the budget was almost balanced. Production, imports, and foreign exchange receipts all rose substantially. The credits of the state-controlled Mining Bank and Agricultural Bank both rose. Prices rose an average of only 8 percent during 1944. This brief interlude of economic stability was soon shattered by a sharp rise in the government deficit. This was caused, in part, by large-scale investments in public works financed by the Central Bank, and large loans made by the same institution to public enterprises.[37]

A large part of this rise in government expenditure on public works resulted from agreements with the U.S. Import–Export Bank arising from the financing of projects suggested by the Bohan report. In order to utilize the U.S. funds, the government was required to contribute substantial sums of dollars to the projects. For example, in the initial agreement concluded with the Export–Import Bank in December 1942 for $15.5 million in credits to be made available to the newly established Bolivian Development Corporation, $3.5 million was to be contributed by the government.[38] This sum was equal to 14 percent of the total government expenditures in 1943. The government deficit rose from the equivalent of $326,000 in 1943 to $2.5 million in 1944. The Bolivian budget simply could not absorb such a substantial increase in expenditure as required by the Export–Import agreement and other similar agreements concluded with the United States. On the other hand, the government could not ignore the opportunity of receiving such a large credit under such favorable terms. The result was a continued resort to the printing press and renewed inflation. This entire scene was to be replayed many times after the revolution in 1952. As increases in U.S. assistance required increased governmental contributions, extreme pressure was placed on the budget, often more than it could stand without resort to inflationary financing or external budget support.

Given this history, it is difficult to understand why the MNR failed to follow a more decisive policy in combating the inflation and establishing domestic financial stability. The continuation of the multiple exchange-rate system by the MNR is particularly hard to explain in terms of economics. The original purpose of the system was to reduce the cost of living by subsidizing the cost of essential imported consumer goods, placing a hidden tax on the mining sector with the prejudicial exchange rate. President Paz was well aware of this, since he had been a member of the Board of Directors of the Central Bank in 1935 when the multiple exchange-rate system was originally introduced. The rationale of the multiple exchange rates was largely destroyed with the nationalization of the large mining corporations.

While there is no direct information on the matter, circumstantial evidence indicates that the multiple exchange rates held the same attraction as they had had when they were instituted in the prerevolutionary period, namely, they were a form of indirect taxation on mining. It appears that Paz was unwilling to institute a more efficient policy of taxing COMIBOL directly for fear that the move would be politically unpopular and, worse yet, administratively unenforceable. He, therefore, chose the indirect system of taxation of multiple exchange rates with its undesirable side effects of subsidizing consumption and offering enormous opportunities for political favors and graft.

THE 1956 STABILIZATION PLAN

The government outlined a stabilization program in 1953 in a memorandum presented to a mission headed by Milton Eisenhower in which the government indicated it would balance the budget and eliminate the multiple exchange rates.[39] The rate was unified and devalued to 190 bolivianos to the dollar, but as the free-market rate at that moment was 750 bolivianos to the dollar, the new measure was doomed from the outset.

In the middle of 1954, the government made an attempt to bring the inflation under control and to check the outflow of foreign exchange reserves, which had reached alarming proportions. The system of "revertibles" was introduced which was, in fact, a variable tariff on imports. The idea was to bring the local cost of imports more into line with the value of the boliviano on the free market. The revenues obtained from this tax were employed to subsidize the prices of basic consumer goods, establish minimum purchase prices for the producers of certain articles, finance investment, and cover the general expenses of the government. The rationale of the system of revertibles was sounder than that of the multiple exchange rates; administration of the system, however, was placed under the ministry of economy and required that an individual rate be established for every product. The obvious temptation for political manipulation and graft that such a system entailed was too great a challenge to the Bolivian administration. The abuses that were associated with the multiple exchange-rate system were simply shifted from the ministry of finance to the ministry of economy. At the same time, preferential exchange rates for sales of dollars were granted to the state mining corporation and the state oil corporation. This system, in the words of the Economic Commission for Latin America, resulted in monetary anarchy and aggravated the rate of inflation.[40] Foreign exchange reserves fell by more than $23 million following the introduction of the system of revertibles, and, at the end of 1956, only $2 million of foreign exchange remained in the Central Bank. Bolivia was at the brink of bankruptcy, and the life of the MNR was endangered.

It was under these conditions that President Paz negotiated a stabilization plan with representatives of the United States and the International Monetary Fund. However, the difficult task of implementing the stabilization plan fell to President Siles, who took office in September 1956. In December 1956 President Siles announced his stabilization program which, although generally believed to have been imposed by the International Monetary Fund and the United States, was strongly reminiscent of the December 1943 program of President Villarroel and his minister of finance, Víctor Paz. The plan provided for the following:

1. Government expenditure was to be reduced 40 percent; taxes and tariffs were to be raised. The budget was to be balanced with the assistance of counterpart funds generated from the sale of U.S. surplus agricultural commodities to the public. This money had formerly been directed toward financing development projects in the country.
2. The deficits of the state enterprises were to be eliminated and the subsidization of their commissaries abolished.
3. The exchange rate was unified at the rate of 7,700 bolivianos to the dollar, and all exchange, import, price controls, and subsidies were abolished.
4. Cost-of-living increases for wage and salary earners were to be granted for the anticipated increase in prices resulting from the proposed tax increases and abolition of price controls and consumer subsidies. After one year there was to be a freeze on all wage increases.
5. Legal reserve requirements on commercial bank deposits were raised, and deposits were to be limited by the capital and reserves of the private and state banks.[41]

In support of the stabilization program, Bolivia was to receive a total of $25 million: a loan of $7.5 million from the International Monetary Fund, plus a $7.5 million loan and a $10 million grant from the United States for development projects. A crucial difference between the 1956 stabilization plan and the earlier 1943 plan of Paz was the willingness of the United States to provide budget support as well as economic aid.

The MNR was saved from economic disaster, but whatever economic sovereignty Bolivia had achieved by the nationalization of the mines was now surrendered. The dominant economic role played by the tin barons in Bolivian economic life was now replaced by the more benevolent, but equally foreign, International Cooperation Administration of the United States, later to be succeeded by the Agency for International Development. The impression that the United States, in a sense, "bought" the stabilization program must have conjured up, in the minds of many Bolivians, the day of January 28, 1942, when the Bolivian government severed relations with the Axis powers and the United States announced a $25 million agreement for Bolivian economic development. Even the sum, coincidentally, was the same as that of the stabilization program.

The MNR had lost a great amount of prestige with its failure to control the inflation, the incompetence of its administration, the corruption that surrounded the exchange control system, and finally, the compromise of its recently won economic sovereignty. While the stabilization program of 1956 marks the beginning of Bolivia's long struggle to achieve sustained economic development, it also was the beginning of the decline of the MNR. Víctor Paz had recognized that, in order for the revolution to carry forward its social and political programs, he had to give priority to the economic spheres. This priority only became effective with the intervention of the United States into Bolivian economic planning. The Bolivian "takeoff" had brought the country to the brink of economic disaster, and now a *deus ex machina* was sought.

The success of the stabilization program was described by Robert Alexander:

Within a short time, the *boliviano* fell from 15,000 to the dollar to 7,500 to the dollar and, during the following months, again rose, but only to 8500. Goods which had been hoarded by shopkeepers and producers began immediately to appear on the market, and shortages of consumers' goods—which had been chronic and acute—disappeared. Prices went up in short order by about 100 percent and then began to decline. Prices of primary essentials particularly began to go down.

The impact on the various sectors of the economy varied greatly:

One of the hardest-hit groups was the manufacturers, who had been turning over a large part of their output to dealers in contraband for surreptitious sale in neighboring countries. With the stabilization program, the manufacturers found their raw material costs rose immediately from the 190 bolivianos to the dollar rate which they formerly enjoyed to the 7500 to the dollar rate. . . .

The banks also suffered from the stabilization program. Their ability to extend credit to business and industry was severely restricted. . . .

The peasants probably benefited from the stabilization program. The prices of their goods went up with everything else. Since the peasants were not sizable buyers of imported goods, or, indeed manufactured goods of any kind—tending to hoard their income—they did not feel the effect of the increase in these commodities to any great degree.[42]

The main losers from the stabilization program were all those groups who had benefited from the former exchange system, who had been able to import goods at artificially low exchange rates and sell at least part of the goods they imported to the public at a price which reflected the free-market exchange rate of 15,000 bolivianos to the dollar. The chief beneficiaries of this system were politicians and trade-union leaders closely associated with the government and their middle-class friends.

One of the groups hardest hit by the inflation was the government workers. This impact resulted not only from the failure of government revenues to grow in real terms but also from the growing share that invest-

TABLE 8
WAGE INCREASES FROM 1956 TO 1958

Employment	Percent Increase
Government employees	54% (to October 1958)
Bank employees	73 (to March 1958)
Private enterprise	30 (to October 1958)
Teachers and judges	50 (to August 1958)
Railroad workers	15 (to August 1958)
Construction workers	50 (to October 1958)
Mine workers	44–56 (to March 1959 retroactive to October 1958)
Memorandum Increase in cost of living in La Paz	24

Source: Prepared by the author from information supplied by the Ministry of Labor.

ment was taking in the government budget.[43] The results of these developments were disastrous for the efficiency of the government which was unable to attract the talent necessary to carry out its greatly increased responsibilities.

The impact on the working classes was even more varied. Between 1956 and 1958 the cost of living rose approximately 24 percent while wages for most organized workers rose approximately 50 percent (table 8). However, between 1955 and 1956 prices had risen 132 percent and there are no data available as to how successful the unions were in obtaining wage increases in this period. It seems likely that in the period preceding 1956 the real wage of the working class declined, and, following stabilization, it experienced a real increase.

The most important exception to this generalization, however, was the miners. Even though their wages also rose during this time about 50 percent, the elimination of the company stores represented a substantial reduction in their real wages.[44] Besides being able to buy consumer goods at low prices in the commissaries, the miners had also made it a custom to sell part of their *cupos* ("quotas") on the free market for additional cash income. They threatened to go out on a general strike on July 1, 1957, and it was only a dramatic tour of the mines by President Siles which prevented what would have been a disastrous blow to the economy. The railroad workers also failed to obtain any substantial wage increase due

TABLE 9
LABOR STRIKES
1956–1961

Year	Number of Strikes	Number of Workers Directly Affected
1956	220	60,000
1957	310	90,000
1958	1,570	147,000
1959	1,272	40,000
1960	336	18,000
1961	144	n.a.

Source: Ministry of Labor, Social Security Institute, *Política social, 1958–1960* (La Paz, 1961). 1961 figures are the author's estimate.
Note: n.a. = no data available.

to the poor financial condition of both the British-owned system and the state system.

While a major labor crisis had been averted, the workers' failure to strike did not mean that labor peace followed. The number of strikes rose dramatically following the stabilization program (table 9). It was not until 1960, when the government took a harder line toward paying wages for illegal strikes, that some measure of labor tranquillity was restored. However, following the frequent strikes and work stoppages of 1958 and 1959, many employers were able to achieve labor peace through local arrangements with their own workers and union leaders.

The U.S. economic assistance program administered by the International Cooperation Administration (ICA) following the stabilization program was now to become the main force in Bolivia's economic development. Early U.S. assistance programs in 1953 and 1954 had largely been in the nature of an emergency relief program consisting of grants of surplus foodstuffs, the sale of which was employed to support the government's budget, the development effort, and technical assistance. The only major development projects sponsored by the United States in this period had been the construction of the Cochabamba–Santa Cruz highway, which was completed in 1954 and paved in 1956, and the Guabirá sugar mill, completed in 1956 by the Bolivian Development Corporation. Both projects had resulted from commitments undertaken as a consequence of the Bohan mission in 1942.

IMPLEMENTING THE U.S. ECONOMIC ASSISTANCE EFFORT

It became apparent that Bolivia's economic problems were not of a transitory nature, and, starting late in 1954, the ICA began to launch a large-scale economic assistance program, concentrating mainly on transportation and agriculture. The means to administer this effort presented a problem in view of the widespread inefficiency and corruption in the administration of the Bolivian government and the low level of wages which prevented the recruitment of competent, honest Bolivian technicians. The Keenleyside report in 1950, confronted with the same situation, had recommended, and the Bolivian government had accepted, the employment of twenty-six foreign *asesores administrativos* ("administrative advisers") with executive authority, assigned to various government agencies. The MNR government renewed the agreement with the United Nations, but changed the title of the asesores administrativos to *consultores técnicos* ("technical consultants") and limited their role to an advisory one.[45] This solution was, politically, out of the question for both the MNR and the United States government. The United States resorted to the use of joint Bolivian-American *Servicios* ("services") for which there already was some precedent. Following the Bohan mission, the *Servicio Cooperativo Boliviano-Americano de Salud Publica*—SCISP (Bolivian-American Cooperative Health Services) was established in 1942, the *Servicio Cooperativo Inter-Americano de Educacion*—SCIDE (Inter-American Cooperative Educational Service) in 1944, the *Servicio Agricola Inter-Americano*—SAI (Inter-American Agricultural Service) in 1948, and the *Servicio Cooperativo Boliviano-Americano de Caminos* —SCBAC (Bolivian-American Cooperative Road Service) in 1955.

The servicios were formally attached to their cognate ministries but largely paralleled the functions of the ministries to which they were assigned. The servicios were to provide a framework in which U.S. technicians and their Bolivian counterparts could work together until such time as the ministry was prepared to incorporate the activities into their own regular functions. Both governments were to contribute funds in their own currency to the various servicio funds to pay for the cost of projects. In addition, the United States agreed to pay the salaries of its own technicians and the Bolivian trainees and for any commodities needed for demonstration purposes. The Bolivian "trainees" were often highly skilled technicians who, for financial and political reasons, could not find employment in the government or in the Bolivian private economy in their chosen profession.

Before 1956 the servicios were relatively small organizations, largely serving in an advisory capacity to their respective ministries. After 1956 they grew substantially in size and dwarfed the ministries they served, providing services that the government, financially, could not and undertaking new large-scale development projects.

The ICA, in addition, attempted to revitalize the group of agencies which was created as a result of the Bohan mission. The most important of these was the Corporación de Fomento de Bolivia (CBF, Bolivian Development Corporation), which was to become the main instrument of American economic assistance to the industrial sector, the sugar industry, and colonization efforts. The other institution was the *Banco Agricola* (Agricultural Bank) established in 1942 and reorganized in 1954. The Agricultural Bank was created to promote agricultural development through extending credit, organizing cooperatives, purchasing agricultural products, and financing the purchase of machinery, fertilizer, and seeds by farmers. A state Mining Bank, which had a monopoly on the sale of minerals produced by the *mineria chica* ("small private mines") as well as on the importing of machinery for the private mining sector, had been created in 1936 and was nationalized in 1939.

The Agricultural and Mining Banks were operated as political institutions with little consideration given to the economic ends for which they were created. In 1961, 91 percent of the Agricultural Bank's loans were in default, and its original $4.4 million capital had dwindled to $300,000. A similar situation prevailed in the State Mining Bank. As a result of the government's steadfast refusal to reorganize the two banks, U.S. economic assistance to agriculture was administered directly through a credit program controlled and supervised by the United States, and credits to the private mining sector were channeled through the Bolivian Development Corporation (CBF).

STRUCTURAL CHANGES IN THE ECONOMY

The outstanding structural change in the economy came as the result of large-scale investment in the road system and agriculture, particularly in Santa Cruz, financed by U.S. economic assistance. The highway improvement program was one of the most successful ICA programs ever undertaken in Bolivia. Employing equipment left in Bolivia following the completion of the Santa Cruz–Cochabamba highway, approximately two million dollars was spent in counterpart funds from the sale of U.S. Public Law 480 surplus agricultural commodities between 1957 and 1960 to improve the existing network of highways. In addition, approximately two million dollars more was spent in the less successful Caranavi–Alto Beni project, a penetration road through the Yungas destined to open up a colonization area on the Beni River. It was planned to extend the road eventually to Rurrenabaque, a port on a navigable tributary of the Amazon. The United States spent an additional $600,000 on maintenance of the Santa Cruz highway in 1959 because the Bolivian government was unable to provide sufficient funds to prevent its rapid deterioration. In 1968 the United States allocated $1.5 million for the resurfacing of the Santa Cruz–Cochabamba highway.

Dramatic results were obtained by the SCBAC program. The average monthly truck traffic on SCBAC roads rose from 11,755 trucks in 1956 to 48,705 trucks in 1960.[46] The average payload rose from two and one-half tons per truck to five tons per truck. Travel time on SCBAC-maintained roads was reduced 50 percent on the average in dry seasons and 80 percent in wet seasons. The amount of time that roads were usable rose substantially. Before 1956 there were no bus transport systems, but in that year an extensive system was developed with private capital, a development which brought profound changes in the Bolivian economy.

Agricultural production improved in this period, principally as a result of the large-scale AID-supervised agricultural program, in which credit was made available to farmers to buy seed, fertilizer, and machinery. Most of the improvement was accounted for by the increase in sugar production. The production of sugar rose from 4.4 thousand metric tons in 1956, to 41.1 thousand tons in 1961, and 93.6 thousand tons in 1964.[47]

But other types of agricultural production recorded only small increases or else none at all.

The improved roads and lower cost of transportation brought increased supplies of agricultural products to the markets of the city. The trucks brought not only food but also people. Every Bolivian truck had a high bar running the length of the body, and, after the truck was loaded, the cargo was topped off with people who, for a few pennies, could ride to the market. For the first time, the Indians from the countryside came in large numbers to the city, at the beginning only to sightsee and later to buy some of the goods. The roads, besides bringing food from the country to market, began to create a market for manufactured goods in the countryside, and by 1960 bicycles and transistor radios were invading the rural areas. The isolation of the Indian population was being rapidly broken down, and a national market economy was beginning to be established. The introduction of the transitor radio brought the Indian into contact with events not only in Bolivia, but also in the rest of Latin America and the world. The door for the integration of the Indian into Bolivian economic life had been opened.

PETROLEUM DEVELOPMENT

Oil production of YPFB, the state petroleum company, increased sixfold between 1952 and the peak production year of 1957. However, in spite of the strong internal demand for its products, the YPFB was not able to achieve sufficient earnings to maintain a level of investment necessary to expand output. The poor earnings performance of YPFB was largely due to the extremely low prices which were being charged for its products and which were being maintained for political reasons. Paz recognized that Bolivia's financial resources were not sufficient to continue the rate of expansion in petroleum production that had been achieved in the first three years of his administration. Therefore, with considerable political embarrassment to himself and the MNR, and with the assistance of North American advisers, he drafted the petroleum code of 1955 which offered concessions on favorable terms to foreign oil companies.

The economic wisdom of this decision became apparent when, under the new code, fourteen companies applied for concessions and invested more than $90 million in exploration. By 1961 all but two of the companies had abandoned their concessions, representing a loss in excess of $50 million. Of the two remaining companies, Bolivian Gulf Oil Company and Bolivian Oil Company, only Bolivian Gulf was to find a major oil field in the vicinity of Caranda in June 1961. Bolivian Oil began production in its Madrejones field in 1960 and, finding its field almost exhausted by 1964, ceased operations completely in 1968.

The MNR, unfortunately, was not to reap the benefits from its politically unpopular petroleum code. Oil exports reached a peak of $4.3 million in 1958 and declined thereafter, as production declined and domestic requirements left a smaller surplus available for export.

BOLIVIAN NATIONAL MINING CORPORATION

The financial situation of the Bolivian National Mining Corporation (COMIBOL) failed to improve during the stabilization period. Even though there was a substantial improvement in tin prices, costs rose even faster (see table 5 on page 172). The failure of COMIBOL to increase output masked the substantial improvement that occurred in both the private mining sector and agriculture. The two overwhelming problems of COMIBOL were the declining tin content of the ore, a perennial problem of Bolivian tin mining, and an almost complete breakdown of labor discipline. The tin content of the ore at Catavi, the largest mine, fell from a little over 1 percent fine tin content at the beginning of the revolution to less than 1 percent in the stabilization period (see table 2 on page 170). One indication of the breakdown in labor discipline is the fact that before the revolution the ratio of men on the surface of the mines to those underground was roughly one to one; by 1956 the ratio was greater than two to one (table 10).[48] Additional problems arose from operation of uneconomic mines for political and social reasons, continued existence of supernumerary workers in spite of a substantial AID-financed layoff program, continuous labor unrest, and the sale of goods in mine commissaries at subsidized prices.

Attempts were made following the adoption of the stabilization program to reduce the COMIBOL deficit. Several uneconomic mines were closed or given to the miners, and the labor force was reduced by more than seven thousand workers to a total force of twenty-seven thousand by 1958. In spite of these attempts, labor costs failed to decline and, beginning in 1958, actually began to rise again. Commissary losses rose from approximately $1 million in 1958 to $2 million in 1961. Labor discipline and managerial control continued to deteriorate. As a consequence of the tight financial situation, maintenance expenditures were sharply curtailed, and there was serious deterioration of the plant and equipment.

In 1960 the International Monetary Fund estimated that COMIBOL incurred a $6 million deficit, excluding depreciation charges. The deficit was financed in three ways: short-term credits were obtained from the English smelter, Williams Harvey Company (controlled by Patiño mine interests); commercial debts to domestic suppliers rose by $5 million; and labor-payment arrears rose by half a million dollars, contributing to the labor unrest. During this period, COMIBOL was paying former mineowners about $1.4 million annually in indemnification payments.

TABLE 10

DISTRIBUTION OF THE LABOR FORCE IN LARGE-SCALE MINING (COMIBOL) 1951–1964

Year	Inside the Mine		Outside the Mine		Total
	Number	%	Number	%	
End of 1951	13,200	55.0%	10,800	45.0%	24,000
1952	14,179	48.9	14,794	51.1	28,973
1953	14,410	46.8	16,352	53.2	30,762
1954	14,532	44.3	18,242	55.7	32,774
1955	12,608	36.9	21,569	63.1	34,177
1956	11,438	32.1	24,222	67.9	35,660
1957	11,200	33.7	20,931	66.3	32,131
1958	9,201	31.8	18,681	68.2	27,882
1959	9,171	32.0	18,009	68.0	27,180
1960	9,477	32.8	17,963	67.2	27,440
1961	8,552	30.2	17,872	69.8	26,394
1962	7,725	28.8	17,754	70.2	25,479
1963	9,391	36.8	14,615	63.2	24,006
1964	9,348	37.1	14,412	62.9	23,760

Source: COMIBOL. Reprinted in United Nations, "The Economic Policy of Bolivia in 1952–64," *Economic Bulletin for Latin America*, 12, no. 2 (October 1967), p. 68.

COMIBOL's financial problems (its gross expenditures of $63 million in 1961 exceeded those of the central government by some $33 million) jeopardized all the gains which had been achieved in the five years of the stabilization effort. The United States and the International Monetary Fund attempted to put increasing pressure on the government to do something in the state mines, but the fact remained that the government was powerless to act. This inability was illustrated dramatically when the vice-president of the republic, Juan Lechín, led a delegation of striking miners to the president in 1961 to demand higher wages and improved working conditions. In 1952 the state mines had not been in the best operating condition and in 1961, after nine years of inadequate maintainance and replacement, were on the verge of collapse.

COMIBOL's problem aggravated the finances of the public sector in numerous ways, as the government was forced to make fiscal transfers to COMIBOL to keep it from breaking down completely. COMIBOL, meanwhile, failed to make payments to other state enterprises such as the state oil corporation, which resulted in further transfers being made from these enterprises to the corporation. In addition, businesses which were not paid for goods and services were reluctant to pay taxes. The central government's cash deficit in 1961, excluding increases in its floating debt, totaled $7.1 million dollars, which was entirely covered by U.S. budget support grants. The entire fiscal situation was aggravated by the United States's attempt to cut back its economic assistance in 1960 and 1961 in an attempt to force reforms in the mines and to encourage the government to further improve its revenue performances.

The rise in COMIBOL's commercial debt was beginning to paralyze industry and created strong demands for additional bank credit. It was obvious by 1961 that, unless the corporation's growing deficits were halted, the stabilization program could only be maintained with an ever-increasing amount of U.S. budget support, a term charged with emotional overtones to the ears of an economy-minded Republican administration. Bolivia had roared down the length of the runway and still was not airborne, but it would make one last assault on the thin air of the Altiplano.

THE TAKEOFF, AUGUST 1961–1964

In 1961, just as financial disaster loomed up to dash the hopes of the revolution, a new president, who recalled that his country had also started its existence with a revolution, took office in the United States. Bolivia, in U.S. official circles, metamorphosed almost overnight from the role of a troublesome and difficult country south of the border to be recognized as one of the forerunners of the social revolution that was called for in the Alliance for Progress. The change in the wind did not go long unnoticed in Bolivia.

With Bolivia again politically respectable, a decisive event took place when President Kennedy sent a personal mission headed by Dr. Willard Thorp of Amherst to the country in March 1961. Thorp reported favorably on Bolivia's revolution, and in the same month the Inter-American Bank announced a joint loan sponsored by the U.S. and West German governments and the Inter-American Bank. Dubbed "Operation Triangular," the loan totaled $37.75 million to be spent over a three-year period to rehabilitate COMIBOL. In addition, Argentina and the United States each contributed an additional $1.5 million for social overhead expenditures in the state mines. However, the disbursements proceeded more slowly than planned, and the initial effect of Operation Triangular was only to slow down the rise in costs (see table 5 on page 172). The plan was saved from disaster only by the precipitous rise in the price of tin from $1.17, the plan price, to $1.70 a pound, which actually permitted some reduction in the operating losses. By far the most important result of Operation Triangular was to stop COMIBOL from absorbing all the available financial resources of the government. Public finances were regularized to an unprecedented extent, both salaries and merchants were paid on time, and COMIBOL's large floating debt was greatly reduced.

Although the Committee of Nine, the group set up under the Alliance for Progress to evaluate Bolivia's Ten-Year Development Plan, rejected the plan as unrealistic, it recommended that Bolivia be given $70 million in economic assistance in view of the tremendous social reforms the country had undertaken anticipating the Alliance's goals. As a result of this report and the changed attitude of the United States under President Kennedy toward radical social reform, the level of economic assistance almost doubled, from an average of $22.7 million annually in the period from 1957 to 1961 to $42.5 in the period from 1962 to 1964. This doubling of foreign aid, to use our previous metaphor, provided a jet-powered takeoff just at the moment when the economy was poised on the brink of disaster. If the United States had been prepared to provide development assistance of this magnitude during the first years of the revolution, capitalizing on the early fervor and dedication of the new government, what a different story might have unfolded! But, as related elsewhere in this volume, the chain of events, which, like a Greek tragedy, drove the government to its inevitable demise, had already begun, and no belated recovery in the economy could reverse it.

Whereas a level of foreign assistance of an average of $20 million a year produced a stabilized type of domestic chaos, an average level of $40 million produced domestic bliss. The results of the stepped up level of foreign aid were immediate and dramatic. The average rate of growth rose to 5.7 percent per annum, one of the highest rates experienced in Latin America. Every sector in the economy participated in this expansion; however, agriculture lagged behind considerably, in spite of the boom occurring in Santa Cruz based on sugar and rice. The poor performance of agriculture was largely due to the failure of the overall expansion to affect the subsistence agriculture on the Altiplano, where a third of the population was situated.

Domestic saving rose to an average of 7.8 percent of the gross domestic product in the period from 1962 to 1964, compared with 5.6 percent in the period from 1958 to 1961. The financial neutralization of COMIBOL and the greatly increased level of foreign assistance permitted the government, for the first time, to mobilize its resources for development, rather than to have to struggle with the overpowering deficit of COMIBOL.

TABLE 11
INDEX OF SALARIES
1959–1966

Year	General Index of Salaries	Cost-of-Living Index	Index of Real Salaries
1959	100	100	100
1960	118	111	106
1961	135	120	113
1962	144	131	110
1963	160	133	120
1964	167	146	114
1965	181	151	120
1966	195	163	120

Source: *1959–1962:* U.S., Agency for International Development, *Economic and Program Statistics*, nos. 4, 5, 9 (La Paz, 1963, 1964, 1968), and information supplied by the International Monetary Fund. *1962–1966:* Information supplied by the National Chamber of Industries, Bolivia.

The share of investment in central government expenditure rose from 1.8 percent in 1958 to 5.5 percent in 1962.[49] Revenues as a percentage of the gross national product rose from 5.9 percent in 1960 to 8.3 percent in 1964. Price stability was well maintained while real wages rose substantially, as shown in table 11.

NATIONAL PLANNING

In July 1961 the National Planning Council published the Ten-Year Development Plan which was drawn up with the assistance of the Economic Commission for Latin America and the cooperation of the UN Technical Assistance Board, Food and Agriculture Organization, and AID-Bolivia.[50] The plan projected a rate of growth of 9.1 percent annually for the national product during the period from 1962 to 1966, declining to 7.5 percent for the period from 1967 to 1971. These projections were based upon an average annual growth in population of 2.4 percent (which many experts now believe to have been, for population, on the high side). At the time, however, the plan estimated that this would permit a 45 percent increase in real consumption over the decade. The part of the plan which drew the most fire from foreign experts was the steep increase in gross domestic savings, which were to rise in the first year from 1.5 percent in 1961 to 8.1 percent in 1962, and then increase to 23.6 percent in 1971. With this sharp increase in saving, the need for foreign financing was to decline from $80 million in 1962—which represented an estimated 80 percent of gross investment—to about $3 million in 1971. The plan did not call for any sweeping changes in the structure of production but contemplated a faster rate of growth for mining, manufacturing, and services than for agriculture, with an emphasis on import substitution in both industry and agriculture.

The Charter of Punta del Este of the Alliance for Progress required that a country seeking aid offer a plan of action such as Bolivia's ten-year plan. But the Committee of Nine rejected the Bolivian plan largely because of the unrealistic estimates of domestic saving which it contained and the lack of detail on specific projects. The committee recommended that a two-year plan be prepared within the framework of the ten-year plan and recommended that the United States create a fund with which to finance the plan. In June 1962 the United States established a fund of $80 million to launch Bolivia's development effort. Of this figure $10 million was to be employed in an emergency public works program in the cities to relieve the intense labor unrest which was building up, and another $6 million was to be used for financing preinvestment studies to produce projects eligible for foreign loans.

The $80 million fund was only concurred to by the United States in the belief—which proved to be well founded—that Bolivia could produce investment projects at a rate only slightly higher than that at which the United States was already funding the AID program. While this was true, in the short run the preinvestment fund was eminently successful. Within five years the availability of acceptable investment projects was no longer the active restraint on Bolivia's ability to obtain foreign assistance.

In spite of the major effort that went into the ten-year plan and the subsequent Biennial Plan, which was produced in the middle of 1963 and contained the detailed projects which the Committee of Nine had requested, planning was never integrated into the governmental decision-making process. The National Stabilization Council and its successors, which had to approve all new government investment projects, had before them only one or two sheets of paper describing the project, which frequently lacked any quantitative information concerning the project's economic feasibility or its fiscal implications. Decisions were made largely on the basis of political considerations and of the availability of foreign financing.

Individual government agencies continued to deal independently with the external financing agencies, with the result that the administrative structure of the government was becoming chaotic. Nowhere was this worse than in agriculture, where in 1964 the ministry of agriculture was responsible for less than 20 percent of the government's expenditure in this sector. For example, in colonization the ministries of agriculture, rural affairs, defense, economy, the development corporation, and COMIBOL all operated projects financed by AID, the United Nations, the British Tropical Agricultural Mission, the Inter-American Development Bank, the Peace Corps, West Germany, and the International Committee for European Migration. A 1963 report on the second Biennial Plan stated:

The greatest obstacle to implementing planning in Bolivia is the lack of a clear definition of responsibilities and authority for the preparation and the implementation the economic sectorial plans. It is urgent to begin the reorganization of the responsibilities and jurisdiction of the various ministries and decentralized agencies with economic functions, so that each office corresponds to a sector or sub-sector of the economy.[51]

Without a more rational organization of government, it was not possible to conduct national planning simply because there was no authority to implement it at either the national or sectoral levels.

Once the financial instability provoked by COMIBOL had receded, all the positive work of ten years of the revolution began to emerge. The Bolivian economy was about to take off. The final boost was given with the sharp rise in tin prices which occurred in 1964. Although the people were still unaware of it, President Paz knew that with the rise in the price of tin and the volume of foreign grants and loans in the pipeline, Bolivia, for the first time since the beginning of the century (with the possible exception of the tin boom of the twenties) was about to experience the exhilaration of economic growth. The economy had lumbered downhill on the runway to the brink of disaster only to be saved at the last moment by the Alliance for Progress. Then, just as the economy was to become safely airborne, the pilot was jettisoned and a new crew took over. The frustration of this moment could perhaps be especially appreciated by the Bolivians, since, on a smaller scale, this kind of frustration continues to be a part of their daily experience.

THE REVOLUTION WITHIN A REVOLUTION, NOVEMBER 1964–APRIL 1969

The military junta which took power in November 1964 and, later, the administration of General Barrientos followed the same general economic program that had been laid down by the MNR, but what was notable was the vigor with which they pursued the MNR goals. President Barrientos's administration stated that the foundations of its program would be the moral education of the citizen and the economic development of the country.[52]

The changes that the Barrientos regime inaugurated were more qualitative than radical. Steps were taken to reorganize and rationalize the government. The ministry of agriculture recaptured most of the governmental functions in that sector. The development corporation divested itself of many of its operating functions, giving up its airline to Lloyd Aéreo Boliviano, the national airline, the maintenance of the Santa Cruz–Cochabamba highway to the national highway department, its milk factory to the minister of economy, and so on. The labor law of President Busch, which had served so many masters, was enforced more strictly with regard to employer rights. The prohibition of political involvement of the trade unions, which the law contained, was resurrected. And, perhaps, most important of all, the government once again was able to avail itself of the services of the middle class and professionals, who had stood at the sidelines during the period of the MNR. Well-qualified Bolivian técnicos were placed in important positions, and the rudiments of a government bureaucracy, which was not so intensely motivated by politics, began to appear. Many of these técnicos had found shelter in AID during the MNR years and were ready to participate in the government once the opportunity was offered to them.

The oft-heard cry that there was an insufficient number of technical people in Bolivia proved largely unfounded. As late as 1969 Bolivia had not been able to utilize fully its technical and professional people. Each year many young Bolivians returned from abroad and tried to establish themselves. Some stayed, many left. It is the author's personal observation over the past ten years that, under both the junta and, later, President Barrientos, the balance of this pattern in recent years was turning slowly in Bolivia's favor.

Perhaps the most dramatic indication of President Barrientos's determination to pursue a vigorous policy of economic development was his reaction to the problem of COMIBOL, the Achilles' heel of the MNR. Key members of the management of COMIBOL were replaced by the junta early in 1965, and Gen. Juan Lechín Suarez was named director general. Later, in April 1965 the army was sent to the mines. The miners were disarmed and several key labor leaders were exiled. The reduction of the labor force of COMIBOL, which had slowed down in Paz's second term of office, was accelerated (see table 5 on page 172), while the redistribution of the remaining labor force between underground and surface workers moved toward more normal ratios. For the first time since the beginning of the revolution, COMIBOL's production showed a rising trend, and in 1966 for the first time since the revolution, COMIBOL showed a profit. The political price of this profit was high. The mines, in many cases, resembled concentration camps, and as late as 1968 miners needed special permits to leave the mining areas.

Barrientos continued and defended strongly the mining and petroleum codes enacted by the MNR. In 1966 oil production almost doubled as Bolivian Gulf's Caranda field came into full production and oil again became a major export. By 1968 oil exports totaled more than $22 million and constituted 15 percent of the total exports. Petroleum became one of the major expansionary economic forces in Barrientos's administration.

Barrientos, with characteristic dash and impulsiveness, pulled off two economic coups that must have made the MNR envious. In 1967 he signed a contract with a private German company to build a major tin smelter, which long had been a Bolivian aspiration, to supplement the two small existing ones. It was done in spite of the fact that there were at least three major foreign studies and two Bolivian studies which concluded that a smelter would be uneconomical. Although the project was turned down by the United States and all international lenders, the new smelter was financed with a German supplier credit, without any foreign aid. It was a symbolic act, constituting the first major expression of Bolivian economic sovereignty since the signing of the stabilization agreement in 1956.

The second coup was the conclusion of the Natural Gas Agreement with Argentina in 1968, under the terms of which Bolivian Gulf Oil was to build and finance the construction of a gas pipeline from Santa Cruz to the Argentine frontier. The company would be repaid with receipts from the sale of gas to Argentina. While almost all the inputs into the gas pipeline and at least half the gas were to be provided by Bolivian Gulf Oil, Bolivia was able to secure joint ownership and to maintain the principle of its sovereignty over its natural resources. In addition, in 1968 YPFB entered into a joint contract with Bolivian Gulf for oil exploration on the Altiplano. Bolivian Gulf Oil was to bear all expenses if no oil was found, but again, the government was able to achieve recognition as a partner in the exploitation of Bolivian resources.[53]

The economy, spurred on by soaring tin prices, rising oil production, and increased foreign aid, boomed in the post-MNR period. Within a short time, however, two major weaknesses appeared: agriculture and public finance.

AGRICULTURAL STAGNATION

Agricultural production had consistently lagged behind in the early revolutionary period. It was only in the poststabilization period, when it benefited from large-scale highway improvements and heavy investments in the sugar and rice fields of Santa Cruz, that it ever achieved a satisfactory rate of growth. The average annual rate of growth in agriculture in the period 1961 to 1964 was only 2.1 percent, and this slowed down subsequently to only 0.2 percent in the period ending in 1968 (see table 1 on page 167). The low rate of growth in agriculture was the single most important reason that the GNP target of the ten-year plan was not attained.

The fundamental reason for agriculture's poor rate of growth since 1961 was the low rate of private and official investment in this sector. In 1966, the latest year for which information is available, only 3 percent of gross domestic investment and only 5.4 percent of public investment were made in agriculture.[54] Only nineteen million Bolivian pesos were budgeted for the ministry of agriculture in 1968, less than 2 percent of the total central government expenditure. Only 4.9 percent of U.S. development assistance and 15 percent of U.S. technical assistance expenditures up to 1968 were for agriculture, while only 16 percent of the Inter-American Development Bank loans to Bolivia were for agricultural purposes. In 1968 the World Bank made its first agricultural loan to Bolivia for $2 million for cattle development in the Beni.

Bolivian agriculture experienced low productivity because the majority of the agricultural population lived on the poorer lands of the Altiplano and valleys where problems of overpopulation and minifundia existed. Efforts as of 1969 to relocate the agricultural population through colonization projects in new areas opened up by the new major penetration roads, such as the Cochabamba–Puerto Villarroel and Montero-Yapacani highways in the Chapare, have met with little success, with the exception of the Santa Cruz region. Only one-fifth of the lands distributed in the colonization areas were being cultivated in 1967, and half the original colonists had returned home.

An unpublished 1967 World Bank report gave as one of the main factors retarding the development of agriculture the lack of infrastructure investments, primarily roads, in spite of the fact that transportation investments had accounted for approximately 30 percent of the total investment in recent years. One of the reasons for this paradox was the poor coordination of transportation investments with agricultural development. A striking example of this was the cattle-raising industry, which numerous reports cited as one of the most dynamic areas in the agricultural sector. In spite of this, the cattle industry in the Beni, as of 1968, had not benefitted from a single investment in transportation. Beef was still being slaughtered in the vicinity of makeshift runways which were inoperable in wet weather and flown to La Paz and the other large-consumption centers by World War II military aircraft.

One of the most important reasons for the limited resources devoted to agriculture in the MNR and post-MNR periods was that projects in this area required large amounts of governmental current expenditures and substantial administrative resources, both of which were in relatively scarce supply. In addition, the external financing agencies also exhibited a reluctance to undertake lending in areas in which heavy administrative and technical assistance inputs were required and where the risks of mismanagement and failure were greater (even though the rewards might have been still greater).

The government's reluctance to invest more in agriculture can be explained largely by the composition of investment expenditure in agriculture and the external lending agencies' bias against financing current budget expenditures. Most expenditures in agriculture, with the exception of large-scale irrigation works, require relatively larger amounts of current expenditures and smaller amounts of fixed investment than projects in other fields. Current expenditures are those which appear in the government's administrative operating budget, characteristically supporting salaries and similar costs. International lenders object to these on several grounds, namely, that noncapital expenditures do not create the ability to repay loans, and they are much harder to control. Since the external financing agencies were unwilling to finance current expenditure, it meant that Bolivia received a much smaller proportion of aid-financing for agricultural projects compared to other projects with a larger fixed investment component where up to 85 percent might have been foreign financed. Given the scarcity of government saving, it was understandable that the government sought out areas where it might receive the largest amount of foreign financing.

PUBLIC FINANCE

Since the turn of the century, the Bolivian government, with few exceptions, has run a chronic budget deficit which it has financed either through foreign borrowing or Central Bank loans.[55] Following the departure from the gold standard in 1931 and default on the external debt, recourse was made exclusively to the Central Bank.

At the outset of the revolution, the mining sector, through export levies and income taxes, was responsible for approximately 50 percent of central government revenues.[56] Between 1952 and 1956 government revenues were unable to keep up with the rate of inflation and declined by one-third in real terms, largely as a result of the declining revenues from mining, particularly COMIBOL. At the same time, however, the mining industry was taxed indirectly, through the requirement that it sell its foreign exchange to the Central Bank at the overvalued official exchange rate, and it is, therefore, difficult to present a clear picture as to the incidence of taxation. A reasonable conclusion is that the loss in central government revenues resulted from the declining mineral output, lower mineral prices, and the failure of the tax system to maintain the same effective rate of nonmineral taxation in face of the sharp rise in prices (with the relative importance of these factors being roughly in this order).

Following the introduction of the 1956 Stabilization Program, steady progress was made in the improvement of revenue collection, and by 1959 tax revenues as a percentage of gross national product were 5.6 percent—a figure slightly higher than they had been in 1952. By 1964 the central government revenues equaled 8.4 percent of the gross domestic product,[57] in spite of the steady and impressive rise in revenues, expenditures grew even faster. The rising central government deficit was financed by U.S. budget support in bolivianos resulting from the sale of surplus U.S. agricultural commodities and by Central Bank loans. Budget support reached a peak of 127 million bolivianos (an equivalent of $10.6 million) in 1962. Two major factors causing the rapid rise in budget expenditure were the necessity for making large transfers to public autonomous enterprises and agencies and the rising social expenditures, particularly for education. The major increase in revenues came from customs duties, with the duties on imports largely replacing the loss of duties on the export of minerals (see table 6 on page 175).

The consolidated deficit of the public sector reached a peak in 1963 and then improved sharply in 1964 as the deficit of COMIBOL was brought under control as a result of the sharp rise in tin prices and the cost controls brought about by Operation Triangular (see table 5 on page 172). Under the junta, the deficit of the public sector continued to decline, but the central government's budget deficit rose sharply as a result of large increases in expenditures on defense and education. As the military junta doubled its defense expenditures from 72 million bolivianos in 1964 to 138 million bolivianos in 1965, its share in the budget rose from 12.5 to 18 percent of the total. At the same time, educational expenditures rose further from 82 million bolivianos in 1961 to 138 million in 1964 to 283 million in 1967.[58]

In 1966 the price of tin began to decline, and this, plus lower mineral exports, created serious problems. The decline immediately resulted in the appearance of a large balance of payments deficit. The government, in its efforts to reduce the balance of payments disequilibrium, introduced a wide variety of measures to limit imports, including the outright prohibition of the importation of goods already being produced in Bolivia, a measure that was favorably received by the business community, which had been advocating greater protection for domestic industry. Import duties, however, constituted over two-fifths of total government revenues, and the reduction in imports resulted in a sharp fall in government income with the result that the deficit soared in 1968. The situation was compounded by the suspension of U.S. budget support in 1967 and the transfer of all the Bolivian-American joint services to the fiscal responsibility of the Bolivian government.

The government undertook to increase revenues by introducing several tax reforms; among them was a successful attempt to increase the income tax and an unsuccessful attempt to impose a tax on agricultural land. The most immediate impact of the reduction in the growth of revenues was the drastic curtailment of current expenditures in an effort to maintain a sufficient flow of government savings in order not to impede the flow of foreign aid, which required local currency contributions from the government. The major fiscal problem that the government faced in 1968 was to control the rate of growth of government expenditures to levels which could be financed domestically, in view of the United States's reluctance to engage in any further budget support. At the same time, it was necessary to change the structure of taxation, making it less dependent on the foreign sector, since it was likely that, in the future, imports and exports would not grow at the rapid rates that had been experienced in the past. Attempts to further reduce government current expenditures in order to maintain the rate of government saving were largely counterproductive, because they resulted in a sharp reduction in economic efficiency as the government failed to provide essential services and in the curtailment of critical development-oriented current expenditures, particularly in agriculture.

The story of Bolivian economic development is, of course, a story without an end. In 1968 the country was experiencing an economic boom resulting from the large-scale foreign aid expenditures being undertaken in transportation and other areas, the increased export of oil, and high rates of construction of both multistory apartment houses and office buildings in the cities. The economic prospects of the country also looked bright with the conclusion of negotiations for the construction of a gas pipeline to Argentina, to be completed in 1970, and the possibility of greater oil and nontin mineral exports. The balance of payments caused some concern because of the greatly increased debt service on foreign loans. The possibility, however, of large-scale import substitution in the area of agricultural imports, particularly wheat, gave some hope that even this problem could be resolved. If Bolivian economic development is to be sustained, the next great area of growth must be in the sector of agriculture. Much of the infrastructure in the form of roads, railroads, and electric power has already been created to make such a development feasible.

The key ingredient to the Bolivian takeoff, erratic and unorthodox as it was, was the element of relative political stability. In spite of the favorable growth experienced in recent years, the Bolivian business community, as of 1968, still had not shown the degree of confidence necessary to begin the slow transformation of Bolivia into a modern industrial country.

If relative political stability can be maintained over the next ten years, the "beggar on the throne of gold" could become the "Cinderella of Latin America."

Recent developments, however, cast some doubt as to whether political stability will be achieved. On April 27, 1969, President Barrientos was killed in a helicopter crash near Tocopaya and was succeeded by Vice-President Luis Adolfo Siles Salinas, half brother of the former president, Hernán Siles Zuazo. In September 1969 General Alfredo Ovando Candia, a candidate for president and former co-president with Barrientos following the military golpe of 1964, seized power in a bloodless palace coup.

President Siles, in his brief period in office, replaced many key officials, many of whom were former friends of either Barrientos or Ovando, with less competent politicians in an effort to diminish the influence of the military. The interregnum of Siles resulted in a substantial deterioration in the economic progress that had been maintained and strengthened by Barrientos. This was particularly true in the field of taxation, where failure to continue the program of fiscal reform begun under Paz and continued under Barrientos led to a sharply rising central government deficit in 1969.

General Ovando's first major act after taking office was to nationalize the Bolivian Gulf Oil Company in response to very strong internal political pressures. The move could not be justified in economic terms since the basic problem of insufficient capital to develop the nation's petroleum resources, which originally resulted in the institution of the petroleum code in 1955, still remained. While there may have been deficiencies in the contract with Bolivian Gulf,[59] it is questionable from an economic point of view whether nationalization, in the form in which it actually took place, was the most suitable remedy.

At the time of nationalization, Bolivian Gulf, in conjunction with the World Bank, was financing and supervising the construction of the gas pipeline from Santa Cruz to Argentina and had entered into a contract for joint exploration with YPFB for oil on the Altiplano. It is impossible for Bolivia to develop its oil resources without foreign capital; nor can Bolivia market the Gulf Oil output, two-thirds of which is exported, without the cooperation of foreign oil companies. In view of this, it is difficult to see where this latest development in the chaotic development of the Bolivian oil industry will lead.

In the early part of 1970 the Bolivian government began negotiations with Argentina and Spain for the completion of the gas pipeline, the export of petroleum, and the further development of the Bolivian petroleum industry. The United States did not protest the nationalization of Bolivian Gulf in view of the government's promise of indemnification, and U.S. foreign aid was not interrupted. It appears that the completion of the gas pipeline will be delayed until at least 1971. Whether or not this episode will have sufficient ramifications to break the momentum of Bolivia's present economic development cannot be determined. There is little doubt, however, that the rate of growth will slow down appreciably even though, luckily, the rise in the price of tin in 1969 and 1970 temporarily absorbed the loss of oil income for the government.

On October 8, 1970, as this book was going to press, Gen. Juan José Torres overthrew the government of General Ovando in a golpe. The new government was supported by members of the more extreme left and promised to introduce further nationalization measures. The renewed political instability following the death of Barrientos, reminiscent of the prerevolutionary governments, threatens to jeopardize the hard-won economic gains of the postrevolutionary period.

THE SUMMING UP

What was the economic contribution of the revolution? In retrospect, the 1952 revolution was more evolutionary than revolutionary in the economic sphere. Through a strange play of fate, the MNR was chosen from among the many radical parties in Bolivia to become an instrument of change. It accomplished this without any detailed master plan of how the change was to be brought about. The MNR was guided by its belief in the necessity for basic changes in the Bolivian social and economic order by three fundamental principles: 1) the necessity for the social, political, and economic integration of the Indian into the Bolivian nation, 2) the seizure of Bolivia's economic destiny from foreign influence, and 3) the primordial importance of economic development, if the preceding political and social goals were to be achieved. The necessity for changes in Bolivian society was so overwhelming that once the floodgates of change were opened by the revolution, the MNR was swept along by the great transformations that were taking place.

The unique contribution of the MNR was that it gave the country a dozen years of relative political stability under a popular government to work out its destiny. While the degree of popularity that the MNR may have enjoyed can be debated, there is no question that it provided by far the most broadly based government that Bolivia had ever experienced. That the government may nor have created the complete democracy that many Bolivian nationalists would have liked is beside the point. It was sufficiently popular (the word *popular* rather than *democratic* is used deliberately) to make irreversible the great economic transformations of the revolution: the integration of the Indian into national life, the land reform and the principle of economic sovereignty over the nation's resources. This was the greatest achievement of the revolution.

The basic economic strategy followed by the MNR was essentially borrowed from the Bohan report of 1942 and, as time has proved, was essentially a correct one. The great economic shortcoming of the revolution was the political failure of the MNR to reconcile the interests of the miners and enlist their political and economic cooperation. The reasons for this were largely questions of politics and personalities and are discussed elsewhere in this volume. The MNR attempted to solve this dilemma by taxing the state mining corporation through the multiple exchange-rate system before 1956 (much as President Salamanca had taxed the tin barons in 1931), in an attempt to develop the petroleum industry as an effective alternative source of growth to finance the other goals of the revolution. In this, the MNR gambled and lost. The petroleum industry proved to be too big a fish to be caught with the government's modest resources. In retrospect, a policy of more active encouragement of the development of the mines and political courting of the miners might have been better, particularly in the early days when revolutionary fervor was at its highest and a general willingness to make sacrifices to preserve the achievements of the revolution existed. Preservation of the system of multiple exchange rates was a serious error of judgment. In order to tax the mines through the exchange system, consumption was subsidized to an enormous extent. In addition, the exchange system gave rise to an image of corruption that was to cast suspicion on the MNR until its rejection by the people in 1964.

The loss of economic sovereignty by the MNR resulting from its overwhelming economic dependence on U.S. foreign aid from 1954 onward did not result so much in a change in the economic strategy since the United States had supported the Bohan strategy as strongly as the MNR. It did, however, result in a loss of creative impulse within the Bolivian government. The object became how to maximize the amount of foreign assistance from the United States, rather than how best to utilize Bolivian resources. While the objective results of this policy may not have differed significantly from that of the alternative, it destroyed a certain vitality within the government, the MNR, and the people that was necessary to maximize the mobilization of the country's human resources.

The second shortcoming of the revolution was its failure to attract to the cause of the revolution the middle and professional classes, particularly the young people from these groups. The failure to open up the revolutionary circle to these groups meant that the MNR had to run the government with a small group of trained people, many of them not competent to carry out the important responsibilities given them. The AID played an important role in this regard by providing a shelter for many Bolivian professional people and preventing even greater emigration than what took place.

In spite of these shortcomings, the success of the revolution in achieving structural changes in the economy is impressive. Mining, which in 1952 had accounted for 15 percent of Bolivia's gross national product and 97 percent of its exports, sixteen years later was to account for only 9 percent of the national product and 77 percent of total exports. While the role of mineral exports was largely taken over by petroleum exports, nonmineral exports also rose from 3 percent to 7 percent of total exports (see table 12). Petroleum production resulting from the enactment of the petroleum code, construction largely stimulated by aid-financed public works, and transportation responding to the greatly improved road system, all expanded their share in the gross national product. As a result of the large-scale investments in roads, the economic integration of the country improved enormously. Santa Cruz, in the Oriente, became a center of economic activity in its own right and in 1969 was the fastest growing region in the country. Agricultural production, on the other hand, with the exception of sugar and rice production in the Oriente, virtually stagnated under the MNR and post-MNR governments.

The midway results of the economy compared with those of what was regarded as the "impractical" ten-year plan were remarkably good, as demonstrated in table 13. While the actual rate of growth in 1966 of 6.9 percent fell 2.2 percent short of the plan's target, it was still one of the highest growth rates in Latin America. If the plan's growth rate had been adjusted downward for a more conservative estimate of the rate of population growth, the shortfall may actually have been less than 1 percent, even though only 70 percent of the amount of projected foreign aid was received. Exports and investment actually exceeded the plan's targets. The great shortfall in the plan's targets was the failure of the growth of

TABLE 12
STRUCTURE OF EXPORTS AND IMPORTS
1952–1968

	Distribution of Exports		
	1952	1964	1968
Minerals	97%	91%	77%
Tin	(63)	(67)	(51)
Other minerals	(34)	(24)	(26)
Petroleum	—	1	16
Other	3	8	7
Total	100%	100%	100%

	Distribution of Imports		
	1952	1964	1968
Capital goods	28%	27%	27%
Intermediate goods	33	46	40
Consumer goods	39	27	32
Total	100%	100%	100%

Source: 1952: United Nations, *Report of the United Nations Mission of Technical Assistance* (commonly called the Keenleyside report) (New York, 1961); *1964, 1968:* Inter-American Committee on the Alliance for Progress (CIAP), *Domestic Efforts and the Needs for External Financing for the Development of Bolivia,* mimeographed (Washington, D.C., 1969), p. 23.

domestic saving. The plan had called for domestic saving of 12.4 percent of the national product in 1966. The actual savings ratio rose from an average of 5.6 percent in the period from 1958 to 1961 to 7.8 percent in the period from 1962 to 1964, only to fall again in the post-MNR period (1965–1968) to 4 percent as increased military and educational expenditures cut heavily into the rate of government saving.

The target level of imports in the plan was greatly exceeded because the import substitution which had been projected by the plan failed to materialize. There was, however, some increase in the relative amount of intermediate goods imported and a reduction in the relative importance of consumer goods, as can be seen in table 12 above. The failure of the import substitution program was the result of the failure of manufacturing to increase its share in the national product and the poor performance of agriculture. This failure may be ascribed to the continued small size of the internal market in spite of the recent economic expansion and to the domestic entrepreneurs' lack of confidence in the Bolivian economy and government, despite substantial official encouragement in recent years.

TABLE 13
COMPARISON OF THE MIDWAY TEN-YEAR PLAN PROJECTIONS WITH
THE ACTUAL RESULTS OF THE ECONOMY for 1966
(*In Constant 1958 Prices*)

	In Millions of Dollars	
	Plan Target	Actual
Gross domestic product	$450	$397
Exports	111	129
Imports	122	168
Investment	81	90
Domestic saving	56	8
Total foreign aid, 1962–66	276	195

	Average Rate of Growth	
	Plan Target	Actual
GDP	9.1%[a]	6.9%
Agriculture	6.8	2.9

Source: Appendix table 1 and Junta Nacional de Planeamiento, *Plan decenal,* as reprinted in *Planeamiento,* nos. 3–5 (La Paz, September 1961). The plan's targets have been adjusted to take into account the January 1969 revision of the national accounts and the actual data for the last year before the beginning of the plan in 1962 which, in the projections, were only estimated.

a. Based on the plan's projected population growth of 2.7 percent per annum. If the actual rate of growth was less, as is widely believed, this figure should have been adjusted downward accordingly.

Even the extremely favorable attitude of Barrientos's administration toward business was not sufficient to induce any significant increase in manufacturing investment.

The data prepared for the 1968 revision of the national accounts indicated that there was a substantial reallocation of income in favor of farmers, artisans, and independent workers, whose share in national income rose from 29 percent in 1958 to 35 percent in 1966, without a substantial increase in the number of workers in these categories, as shown in table 14. The share of salaried employees rose only slightly from 43 to 46 percent in the same period while the share of proprietors of businesses fell from 28 to 19 percent.[60]

The year 1967 marked a historic turning point in Bolivian economic history; it represented the first time since the turn of the century that the economy was able to register significant economic growth in spite of declining tin exports. Tin will continue to play an important role in the

TABLE 14

DISTRIBUTION OF NATIONAL INCOME BY SOCIOECONOMIC GROUPS
1958–1966

	1958	1964	1966
Agricultural, independent, and artisan workers	29%	36%	35%
Salaried and other nonindependent workers	43	44	46
Proprietors	28	20	19
Total	100%	100%	100%

Source: Derived from *Cuentas nacionales*, p. 25. Reprinted in *Planeamiento*, no. 11 (January 1968).

Bolivian economy for many years to come, but its tyranny—and the days when the fate of the entire economy was determined by a single commodity's vagaries in price and output—appears to be over. In 1971, when the gas pipeline is planned to start operation, Bolivia will have three major export products and a hope for greater stability in its foreign sector. The signing of the contracts for the tin smelter along with gas and petroleum exports marks the emergence of a new Bolivian economic sovereignty. The MNR's goal of independent private and state capitalism was unrealistic because of the Bolivian economy's small capacity for saving and the revolution's objectives of improving the distribution of income. What is slowly emerging is a new sovereignty in which Bolivia is participating as an equal in the exploitation of its resources according to its own plan for national development.

The Bolivian economy, after its strange trip down the runway of the Altiplano, has taken off, and, although it may encounter some bumpy air ahead, it seems to be finally headed upward, provided a fight does not break out in the cockpit. Bolivia is slowly closing the economic gap that separates it from the rest of Latin America and is achieving a rate of growth that gives hope of allowing the social goals of the revolution to be implemented in the future. The one pessimistic cloud on the horizon is the failure of the rate of savings to rise despite the substantial increases in income that has occurred in recent years. The test that the government must now pass is whether it can slowly reduce its dependence on foreign aid. Movement toward this goal will require sympathetic understanding on the part of the United States and foreign lenders, so that the withdrawal of foreign assistance will not outrun the degree of progress being made and sweep away many of the hard-won gains of the past dozen years.

The Bolivian Revolution of 1952, in spite of its erratic course, was a great success. A measure of this success is the fact that the revolutionary changes in the society and the economic objectives set forth by the MNR have survived the counterrevolution of 1964, or what its supporters appropriately enough chose to call a "revolution within a revolution." If there were only economic factors to be considered, I would venture to predict that Bolivia is on the verge of a golden age. What is needed to realize this potentiality is another decade of relative political stability. Bolivia was the first in Latin America to rise up in the wars of independence and the last to become free. The economic progress which was sought by the revolution is now within reach. Let us hope that this opportunity does not become part of the history of frustration that has plagued Bolivia since its birth.

NOTES

1. Víctor Paz Estenssoro, *La revolución boliviana* (La Paz, 1964), p. 11.
2. United Nations, *Report of the United Nations Mission of Technical Assistance* (commonly referred to as the Keenleyside report) (New York, 1961), p. 2.
3. U.S. Army, Foreign Area Studies Division, Special Operations Research Office, *Area Handbook for Bolivia* (Washington D.C., 1963), p. 63.
4. Paz Estenssoro, *La revolución boliviana*, p. 9.
5. James Malloy, "Revolution and Development in Bolivia" in *Constructive Change in Latin America*, ed. Cole Blasier (Pittsburgh, Pa., 1968); and Víctor Paz Estenssoro, "La Revolución es un proceso que tiene raíces en el pasado," speech delivered in La Paz, February 1961.
6. Víctor Paz Estenssoro, *El pensamiento revolucionario de Víctor Paz Estenssoro* (La Paz, 1954), pp. 101–02.
7. Although the question of nationalization of the mines had a long history in Bolivia, it was not until the idea was incorporated into the Program of the National Conference of Students in 1928 that any group openly embraced it (see Ricardo Anaya, *Nacionalización de las minas de Bolivia* [Cochabamba, 1952]). Furthermore, it was not until 1940, when the idea became part of the platform of the newly formed Party of the Revolutionary Left (PIR), that any major political party espoused it. The MNR never officially included nationalization in its prerevolutionary political program, and, as late as 1951, Wálter Guevara Arze, principal theoretician of the MNR, stated that the MNR did not advocate the nationalization of the mines (René Ruiz González, *La economía y el comercio exterior* [Oruro, 1955], p. 108).
8. Víctor Paz Estenssoro, *Discursos parlamentarios* (La Paz, 1955), p. 310.
9. Víctor Paz Estenssoro and Wálter Guevara Arze, *Reforma agraria,* 2d ed. rev. (La Paz, 1945).
10. In 1968 the Barrientos government went even further and made sharecropping illegal. Henceforth, all payments for the use of the land in Bolivia had to be made for a monetary consideration.

11. U.S. Army, *Area Handbook for Bolivia*, pp. 541–42.

12. Bolivia, Ministerio de Trabajo, Caja Nacional de Seguridad Social, *Política social 1958–1960* (La Paz, 1961).

13. Sinforoso Cabrera Romero, *Informe de labores* (La Paz, 1960), pp. 121–50.

14. *New York Times*, January 29, 1942. In all fairness to U.S. motives, the question of a U.S. mission to Bolivia had been raised as early as 1938 when Merwin Bohan visited the country and made a preliminary report to Undersecretary of State Sumner Welles on the matter of economic assistance to Bolivia. Bohan's subsequent mission had been decided upon early in 1941, and he arrived in Bolivia on November 11, 1941, one month before Pearl Harbor.

15. Wálter Guevara Arze, Ministerio de Relaciones Exteriores, *Plan inmediato de política económica del gobierno de la revolución nacional* (La Paz, 1955). The MNR's debt to the Bohan plan was publicly acknowledged by President Paz in a speech delivered on September 29, 1954:

The plan of the government of the national revolution tries in general lines to achieve for the Bolivian people a better economic life. This plan was outlined by an outstanding American economist, Mr. Merwin Bohan, who is now in Bolivia. A plan so beneficial as this for the welfare of the Bolivian people could never be realized by the government of the oligarchy because it had no interest in improving the lot of the Bolivian people. (*La Nación*, September 30, 1954)

16. *New York Times*, May 24, 1942, p. 13. The Bohan report was never published. A summary may be found in Corporación Boliviana de Fomento, *La Corporación Boliviana de Fomento (sus orígenes, organización y actividad)* (La Paz, 1943).

17. Ibid., pp. 93 ff.

18. Robert J. Alexander, *The Bolivian National Revolution* (New York, 1958), p. 100; see also Inter-American Committee on the Alliance for Progress (CIAP), *Domestic Efforts and the Needs for External Financing for the Development of Bolivia*, mimeographed (Washington, D.C., 1969), pp. 121–22.

19. An interesting sidelight to the nationalization of the mines was the proposal made by the vice-president of the Patiño mines, Alberto Mariaca Pando, to the Paz government in July 1952. He suggested that the government participate in 75 percent of the profits before taxes of the Patiño mines in lieu of taxes. (See Manuel Carrasco, *Simón I. Patiño, un prócer industrial* [Paris, 1960], p. 280.) Mariaca estimated this would increase the revenue of the government over the next ten years by $9.5 million (in American dollars). If we assume that the average profit in the period he mentioned was the same as the average $3.14 million earned per year in the period from 1940 to 1948, this would imply that at the time of nationalization, the Bolivian government was already receiving approximately 58 percent of the profits before taxes of the Patiño mines. Cf. René Ruiz González, *La administración empírica de las minas nacionalizadas* (La Paz, 1965), p. 91.

20. Paz Estenssoro, *Pensamiento revolucionario*, pp. 79–80.

21. Cabrera Romero, *Informe de labores*, p. 52.

22. United Nations, Economic Commission for Latin America, *Análisis y proyecciónes del desarrollo económico, IV: El desarrollo económico de Bolivia* (Mexico City, 1958), p. 33.

23. U.S. Army, *Area Handbook for Bolivia*, p. 497.

24. Cabrera Romero, *Informe de labores*, p. 48.

25. United Nations, *Análisis y proyecciónes*, p. 46.

26. Cabrera Romero, *Informe de labores*, p. 15.

27. United Nations, *Análisis y proyecciónes*, p. 47.

28. Cabrera Romero, *Informe de labores*, p. 11.

29. Bolivia had passed its first law nationalizing oil exploitation in 1916 but was forced to repeal it in 1920 in order to encourage foreign investment, since local capital was both unwilling and incapable of undertaking investment in this area. Production was inaugurated in 1922 when Standard Oil of New Jersey acquired the concession held by Richard Levering and Company. In 1937 the government of President Toro expropriated the Bolivian subsidiary of Standard Oil, declaring the entire nation a national reserve, and established the YPFB (U.S. Army, *Area Handbook for Bolivia*, p. 504) to replace the Standard Oil operation. Bolivia thus became the first country in Latin America to nationalize its petroleum industry.

30. Ibid., p. 201.

31. René Gómez García and Rubén Darío Flores, *La banca nacional* (La Paz, 1962), p. 254.

32. Eduardo López Rivas, *Esquema de la historia económica de Bolivia* (Oruro, 1955) p. 124.

33. Gómez García and Darío Flores, *La banca nacional*, pp. 249–51.

34. Guevara Arze, *Plan inmediato de política económica*, p. 184.

35. United Nations, *Análisis y proyecciones*, p. 34.

36. López Rivas, *Esquema de la historia*.

37. United Nations, *Análisis y proyecciónes*, pp. 63–64.

38. *Corporación Boliviana de Fomento*, p. 95.

39. Alexander, *Bolivian National Revolution*, p. 206.

40. United Nations, *Análisis y proyecciónes*, p. 72.

41. Alexander, *Bolivian National Revolution*, pp. 208–09; and George Jackson Eder, *Inflation and Development in Latin America* (Ann Arbor, Mich., 1969), pp. 257–74.

42. Alexander, pp. 210–11; also Eder, pp. 275–307.

43. United Nations, *Análisis y proyecciónes*, p. 20; and Richard S. Thorn, "Foreign Aid as an Obstacle to Economic Development" (forthcoming).

44. The subsidization of the miners' commissaries was not an MNR invention but a traditional practice of the large mines. In 1948 it constituted 23 percent of labor costs, compared with 30 percent in 1955. (See United Nations, *Análisis y proyecciónes*, p. 33.)

45. U.S. Army, *Area Handbook for Bolivia*, p. 599.

46. Cornelius H. Zondag, *The Bolivian Economy, 1952–1965* (New York, 1966), p. 135.

47. Bolivia, Dirección Nacional de Coordinación y Planeamiento, Dirección General de Estadística y Censos, *Boletín estadístio*, no. 93, mimeographed (La Paz, 1967), p. 138.

48. Amado Canelas, *Mito y realidad de la Corporación Minera de Bolivia* (La Paz, 1966), pp. 126–31.

49. Bolivia, Secretaría Nacional de Plantificación y Coordinación, *Plan bienal de desarrollo económico y social, 1963–1964* (La Paz, 1963), p. 30.

50. Bolivia, Junta Nacional de Planeamiento, *Plan de desarrollo económico y social, 1962–1971* (La Paz, 1961).

51. Banco Inter-Americano de Desarrollo, *El segundo plan bienal, 1965–66*, mimeographed (La Paz, 1964), p. ii.

52. René Barrientos Ortuño, *Una doctrina boliviana para uso de los bolivianos* (La Paz, September 1966), pp. 6–7.

53. In spite of the favorable terms of the proposed contract, it was not sufficient to forestall the nationalization of Bolivian Gulf in October 1969.

54. Bolivia, Secretaría Nacional de Planificación y Coordinación, *Cuentas nacionales, 1958–1966* (La Paz, 1968).

55. United Nations, *Análisis y proyecciónes*, p. 11.

56. United Nations, *Report of the United Nations Mission of Technical Assistance*, p. 29.

57. Bolivia, *Cuentas nacionales*, table 4.

58. U.S., Agency for International Development, *Economic and Program Statistics*, no. 10 (La Paz, 1969), p. 39.

59. See Enrique Mariaca Bilba, *Mito y realidad del petróleo boliviano* (La Paz, 1966), pp. 151 ff.

60. Bolivia, *Cuentas nacionales*.

JAMES W. WILKIE
*University of California,
Los Angeles*

Public Expenditure Since 1952

Students of revolution may suppose that one of the first steps which a revolutionary government might take would involve a dramatic shift in the pattern of public expenditures. In two of the three Latin American major social and economic revolutions in this century, however, such was not the case. Mexico failed to achieve a significant shift in state budgetary policy until the 1930s (more than twenty years after the revolution of 1910).[1] In the late 1960s the pattern of Bolivian central government finances remained as it had been prior to the 1952 revolution. In the Cuban case (the third instance), the authoritative time-series data since 1959 remain unavailable and uninvestigated.[2]

In an interesting contrast to both the Mexican and Cuban experiences, the revolution in Bolivian public expenditure policy antedated by six years the seizure of power by the *Movimiento Nacionalista Revolucionario* (MNR) in 1952. Actually, the MNR altered the pattern of outlay in 1945 while participating in the government of Gualberto Villarroel. Though Villarroel fell from power in 1946, reactionary governments accepted the policy in expenditure established by the MNR. Thus, the MNR inherited its old policy when it came into full power after the revolution. Ironically, when the MNR was deposed in 1964, its policy of outlay again remained unaffected.

This twenty-five year continuous policy was made possible, to a large extent, by a lack of information available to policy makers. Because of their confusion as to the nature of budgetary categories (including especially the assignment of an important share of funds to a general category of "state obligations" without differentiation to function) and because expenditure accounts have remained unpublished, Bolivia's leaders have had remarkably little meaningful data with which to understand the thrust of state policy.[3] Also, since expansion of the role of the public sector (through the growth of decentralized activity and the influx of U.S. aid) has added to the pressures for developing new plans, few bureaucrats have had time to investigate past expenditures and suggest conceptual categories for comprehending the trajectory of the political economy in national development. The following brief examination of Bolivian central government and public sector policy in relation to U.S. aid will shed some light on this matter.

The silent revolution in budgetary policy was implemented in 1945 by the leader of the MNR, Víctor Paz Estenssoro, who served as finance minister for President Gualberto Villarroel. Responding to pressures of social disruption and economic inflation growing out of Bolivia's defeat in the Chaco War, Paz effectively fixed the pattern of central government expenditures, which had tended to be of a social nature during the late 1930s under President Germán Busch but had shifted to increased economic outlay under President Peñaranda in the early 1940s. Table 1 reveals that Paz rejected the Peñaranda approach and, like the Busch government, continued to cut back the traditional state expenditures for administrative functions (including support for the legislature, judiciary, police, military, and day-to-day administration of affairs) in order to emphasize the more social outlay (education, labor, public health, and, after 1952, housing, social security, and peasant affairs). Thus, the central government outlay for economic activity involving public works and agricultural development was deemphasized, and other economic outlay (including current and capital outlay as with administrative and social expenditure above) has remained inadequate for running the governmental agencies in charge of agrarian reform, colonization, communications, and mining and petroleum.[4]

The MNR's policy following the victory in 1952 became even more dependent upon sacrificing economic expenditure in favor of social outlay when it became apparent to Paz Estenssoro that great amounts of funds would be necessary to incorporate the peasant into the political life of the country (as well as into the national economic life) in order to create a rural counterbalance to the growing power of the tin miners.

TABLE 1
AVERAGE ACTUAL CENTRAL GOVERNMENT EXPENDITURE
1937–1966

Year	Presidential Term [a]	Years	Totals = 100.0%		
			Economic	Social	Administrative
1937–39	Busch [b]	3	12.6%	16.3%	71.1%
1940–43	Peñaranda	4	20.8	19.7	59.5
1944–46	Villarroel [c]	3	17.5	24.8	57.7
1947–48	Hertzog	2	10.5	28.7	60.8
1949–51	Urriolagoitia	3	8.7	29.2	62.1
1952–55	Paz	4	12.1	33.0	54.9
1956	Paz and Siles	1	12.5	50.8	36.7
1957–59	Siles	3	20.0	30.3	49.7
1960	Siles and Paz	1	15.7	37.2	47.1
1961–64	Paz	4	14.7	34.5	50.8
1965–66	Post-MNR [d]	2	11.8	37.4	50.8

Source: James W. Wilkie, *The Bolivian Revolution and U.S. Aid Since 1952: Financial Background and Context of Political Decisions* (Los Angeles, Calif., 1969), table 6.
a. Although several presidents may have served in these terms only the most influential in regard to budgetary policy are listed.
b. In 1939, President Carlos Quintanilla adopted Busch's policy of social expenditure.
c. Villarroel fell from power July 21, 1946, but his budgetary policy prevailed under his immediate successors.
d. René Barrientos Ortuño and Alfredo Ovando Candia.

Thus, political realities dictated a continuation of MNR budgetary policy even though the new government had committed itself to economic development.

Bolivia's post-1952 policy was revolutionary for the public sector in that the nationalization of the tin mines was expected to supply profits for national development funds. Such profits previously had been spent abroad. Unfortunately, however, Bolivia seized mines which were becoming less and less productive under conditions of declining ore content and lack of investment by owners fearful of expropriation. High cost operations of the nationalized mines contributed to the financial losses of the Bolivian Mining Corporation (COMIBOL), given in table 2, until 1966 when COMIBOL finally showed a profit. COMIBOL's success in 1966 resulted in a fifty million peso profit which dwindled to about five million pesos in 1967 and 1968, and none of these amounts left much for national development. Taking into account COMIBOL's production costs (see table 5 on page 172), the consolidated account of the public sector income, and expenditures for the years when data are available,

TABLE 2

CONSOLIDATED PUBLIC SECTOR FINANCES

1963–1967

(*In Millions of Pesos or Billions of Bolivianos* [a])

	1963	1964	1965	1966	1967
Income					
Central government	428.2	511.4	613.1	723.6	747.3
COMIBOL	548.4	814.8	983.6	944.8	920.0
Bolivian Oil Company	225.6	237.6	265.8	287.6	295.0
National railways	85.2	86.4	98.4	105.9	118.0
Other [b]	422.4	481.2	435.7	507.7	520.0
Total	1,709.8	2,131.4	2,396.6	2,569.6	2,600.3
Expenditures					
Central government	504.8	574.9	763.9	901.2	883.0
COMIBOL	780.0	915.6	991.2	895.1	915.0
Bolivian Oil Company	283.2	225.1	259.2	273.9	290.0
National railways	114.0	123.4	131.1	263.8	140.0
Other [b]	662.4	732.1	571.1	646.8	580.0
Total	2,344.4	2,571.1	2,716.5	2,980.8	2,808.0
Total deficit [c]					
Central government	−76.6	−63.5	−150.8	−177.6	−135.7
COMIBOL	−231.6	−100.8	−7.6	49.7	5.0
Bolivian Oil Company	−57.6	12.5	6.6	13.7	5.0
National railways	−28.8	−37.0	−32.7	−157.9	−22.0
Other [b]	−240.0	−250.9	−135.4	−139.1	−60.0
Total	−634.6	−439.7	−319.9	−411.2	−207.7

Source: AID/Bolivia, *Economic and Program Statistics*, 9 (1968), p. 31.

a. Bolivianos were converted to pesos in 1963 at a ratio of 1,000:1. These data include current and capital funds.

b. This includes, for example, Bolivian Development Corporation, Lloyd Aéreo Boliviano, National Social Security Institute, universities, and departmental and municipal governments.

c. Except in the six cases listed without minus signs.

we have a strong indication of the nature of COMIBOL's heavy losses during the 1950s.

COMIBOL might have shown a profit earlier if the government's currency exchange regulations had not, in effect, taxed tin mining production. As Harold Osborne has noted:

By establishing a state monopoly in the export of mineral ores the government also ensured control over . . . the foreign exchange earned by all mining exports. . . . A vicious circle was created when by the continued use of differential rates of exchange for imports the mineral exports were made to subsidize agricultural and other imports and the mining industry itself was kept short of the foreign-exchange capital necessary to maintain its own efficiency. In consequence the cost of tin production has been consistently above its selling price in the world markets.[5]

Because the decentralized sector failed to provide funds for national development after 1952, the Bolivian central government had to subsidize many public sector activities from its pool of tax revenues, as well as rely upon the foreign financing of public sector deficits. This subsidy placed great strain on the government, for the pool of income from taxes over which it has discretionary spending authority generally has been received from import-export levies while income from foreign loans generally has been consigned to autonomous agencies for nondiscretionary uses. Thus, the central government attempted to direct unprofitable national development with limited control over funds that it could allocate and reallocate at will. This problem was complicated even more, until recent years, by the Bolivian Congress's use of minutely earmarked taxes to further limit executive power. Fortunately, however, there are now plans to phase out these earmarked taxes which have tended to dissipate income into many small projects without giving any one program adequate funding.

Such restrictions on the Bolivian central government's ability to influence expenditure meant that, although formerly the government directly granted funds to such an autonomous agency as the Bolivian Development Corporation (as during the years 1942 to 1944 and 1954 to 1959), the central government decreased its subsidies as foreign funding took over during the 1960s. In this manner Bolivian tax revenues have increasingly been delimited to cover noneconomic aspects of development. As we saw in table 1 on page 219, the central government's budgetary policy was to direct its discretionary expenditure into the state's social functions while maintaining the basic administrative structure of national life. Theoretically, the central government should develop planning, but since it has no budget power over its autonomous agencies and no access to the many pools of funds with which the decentralized agencies conducted their operations, the central government had limited control over Bolivia's national destiny.

The central government could afford to concentrate its expenditures on social matters because U.S. assistance, beginning in 1954, was postulated on a program of economic aid. The United States supplied aid at low cost to its taxpayers by shipping to Bolivia surplus agricultural commodities purchased from U.S. farmers. Not only did such aid help to tide Bolivia over a food shortage in the cities following the rural upheaval in land ownership, but local currency, generated by the sale of those commodities, provided funds which could be programmed for economic development.

The extent of U.S. assistance is presented in functional terms in table 3 in order to compare the thrust of expenditure with central government policy. United States policy is characterized for two periods, 1952–1961 and 1962–1966. The first period, theoretically, was one of economic assistance ending in 1961 when the Alliance for Progress began to emphasize social assistance. In the latter period, also, sale of surplus agricultural commodities continued to be the major source of assistance.

It is apparent from a glance at table 3 that more than half of the actual expenditure by the U.S. Agency for International Development (AID and its predecessor agencies) as well as by the Peace Corps, Export-Import Bank, and military assistance programs during the first period was noneconomic in nature. Because local currency projects and direct budgetary support of the central government covered deficits as well as posivite contributions to economic development, the government in La Paz was free to spend its funds for continued social outlay.[6] Neither the Bolivians nor their U.S. advisers were fully aware, however, that a negative effect of manipulatable expenditure was to reinforce the Bolivian central government's frozen pattern of outlay.

To the credit of a 1963 U.S. mission to Bolivia, led by Anthony M. Solomon, officials recognized the noneconomic aspects of the AID expenditure, and from that date AID began to channel local currency from direct budgetary support of the central government into specific projects in order to stimulate economic development.[7] Nevertheless, AID's shift in policy was offset by the Peace Corps and military assistance programs, and there has been little change in the overall trend of U.S. assistance. Between 1962 and 1966 almost half of the total aid remained noneconomic in nature, even though the percentage of U.S. assistance for budgetary support declined from about 31 to about 18 percent.

As AID shifts its funding into more economically oriented projects, the central government faces a serious problem since it must increase its revenues to maintain the same amount of social services which had come to be expected by the Bolivian people during the last twenty-five years. The problem would not be serious if AID were not attempting to reduce funding because of the U.S. balance of payments crisis and the financial drain of the Vietnam conflict. As we have seen in table 1 on page 219, if post-MNR governments continue to channel the expenditures of the central

TABLE 3

FUNCTIONAL ANALYSIS OF AID, PEACE CORPS, EXPORT-IMPORT BANK, AND MILITARY
ASSISTANCE PROGRAMS, 1952–1966

Expenditure and Agency	1952–1961		1962–1966	
	Millions of Dollars	%	Millions of Dollars	%
Economic (AID except Export-Import Bank. See n. "a.")				
Food and agriculture	$ 9.4		$ 4.2	
Transportation and power	4.2		9.4 [a]	
Mining, oil, and industry	1.5		4.0	
Public works	— [b]		3.0	
Development loans	2.6		28.8	
Local currency projects [c]	34.8 [d]		34.8 [e]	
Subtotal	$ 52.5	46.9%	$ 84.2	50.5%
Social (AID except Peace Corps)				
Health and sanitation	$ 3.1		$ 0.7	
Education	3.6		1.7	
Labor affairs	0.2		0.9	
Community development	0.3		1.8	
Agricultural commodities (relief) [f]	6.6		3.4	
Local currency projects [c]	4.0		6.0	
Peace Corps	— [b]		8.9	
Subtotal	$ 17.8	15.9%	$ 23.4	14.1%
Budgetary support subtotal	$ 34.9	31.2%	$ 29.8	17.9%
Administrative (AID except military)				
Public administration and safety	$ 1.9		$ 3.4	
Planning	— [b]		1.9	
Other	2.0		5.1	
Local currency projects [c]	2.1		6.7	
Military assistance	0.8		12.1	
Subtotal	$ 6.8	6.0%	$ 29.2	17.5%
Total [g]	$112.0	100.0%	$166.6	100.0%

Source: James W. Wilkie, *The Bolivian Revolution and U.S. Aid Since 1952: Financial Background and Context of Political Decisions*, table 3 and appendix A; U.S. Operations Mission to Bolivia, *Point Four in Bolivia* (La Paz, 1960), p. 94; and Export-Import Bank, *Report* (June 30, 1963), p. 102.

Note: Table excludes Social Progress Trust Fund (administered by Inter-American Development Bank); cf. table 3 in Wilkie, *The Bolivian Revolution*, for figures limited to AID programs.

a. Includes a $4.6 million loan from Export-Import Bank for highway construction.
b. Not applicable.
c. Public Law 480, title I.
d. Includes $17.4 million for road construction, Public Law 480, title II.
e. Includes Public Law 480, titles II and IV.
f. Public Law 480, title III.
g. Amounts are for obligations (approximately equal to disbursements), except for local currency programs, Export-Import Bank loan, and military assistance, which are for disbursements. Data include at least $3.1 million for technical aid, 1942–1951.

government into social outlay and are not fully aware that funds from the pool of tax revenues (over which the central government has discretionary authority) must be reoriented to cover U.S. economic withdrawal, then the autonomous sector will gain in importance.

Given the economic growth of Bolivia during the 1960s, outlined in Professor Thorn's chapter, one might be tempted to conclude that the increasing success of the Bolivian national revolution does not necessitate any change in policy. Such a conclusion, however, would ignore the fact that the series of conditions which existed in the past may no longer exist as AID withdraws economic support. Although Bolivia's successful development under three different masters (the central government, the decentralized public sector, and AID) might suggest that centrally directed state planning has not been necessary, we cannot say that the same argument will always hold true. Perhaps all that can really be suggested is that the future development of Bolivia will depend more than ever before on an awareness of the extent and the nature of public expenditures.

As AID withdraws its support, the country will become increasingly more dependent upon foreign loans to stimulate new development; hence it is instructive to examine in table 4 Bolivia's post-1952 external debt. This outstanding debt, as of December 31, 1966, not only reveals the extent to which international funds have been available since 1952 to help finance deficits but shows both the source and recipient of the funding.[8] The total of AID funding was 37 percent of all loans, a share included in the functional analysis of U.S. assistance given in table 3. Deducting AID and Export-Import Bank loans, the total outstanding debt for the period 1952 to 1966 was about $82 million, all but about 6 percent of which probably went for economic functions. This latter small amount was provided by the U.S. Social Progress Trust Fund of the Alliance for Progress and administered by the Inter-American Development Bank. The Bolivian Development Corporation received about 44 percent of the Social Progress Trust Fund for colonization (an economic function).[9] It is interesting to note that total Social Progress Trust Fund loans came only to about 6 percent of all foreign loans during the period between 1952 and 1966. This explains why many feel that the fund has failed either to develop or to fulfill its social goals in Bolivia. As a matter of fact, the Social Progress Trust Fund made no new loans to Bolivia during the years 1966 to 1968, and it would appear that, as far as Bolivia is concerned, the fund is no longer active except in an advisory capacity.[10]

TABLE 4
BOLIVIA'S POST-1952 EXTERNAL DEBT AS OF DECEMBER 31, 1966
(*In Thousands of Dollars*)

Source of Loan	Amount	%
Inter-American Development Bank	$ 25.486	18.6%
International Development Association	10.827	7.9
AID	50.871	37.0
United Kingdom	0.591	0.4
Federal Republic of Germany	5.390	3.9
Argentina	12.658	9.2
Brazil	0.026	— a
Venezuela	2.000	1.5
Suppliers' credits	21,592	15.7
Export-Import Bank b	4.562	3.3
Other	3.363	2.5
Total	$137.366	100.0%

Recipient of Loan	Amount	%
Central government	$ 52.477	38.2%
Local government	0.190	0.1
COMIBOL	31.147	22.7
Bolivian Oil Company	11.443	8.3
Bolivian Development Corporation	14.826	10.8
Lloyd Aéreo Boliviano	0.277	0.2
National railways	0.346	0.3
Other public sector	3.072	2.2
Banks	16.562	12.1
Private sector with government guarantee	7.026	5.1
Total	$137.366	100.0%

Sources: Ministry of Finance; Export-Import Bank, *Reports* (June 30, 1963–June 30, 1966).
Note: The external debt is the amount outstanding after drawings, amortization, capitalization, and payment of interest. It excludes four major central government loans contracted prior to 1952: U.S. bond holders, $61,906,000; outstanding Export-Import Bank loans, $29,357,000; Argentine railway debt, $49,785,000; and Brazilian railway debt, $11,803,000.
a. Negligible.
b. Amount outstanding for Export-Import Bank remained the same ($33.9 million) between 1949 and 1966 despite new drawings and repayments.

The Inter-American Development Bank's regular operations have continued to support Bolivian development, and since 1964 the International Development Association has been active in stimulating power projects and livestock development. The Inter-American Development Bank shared with the Federal Republic of Germany and the U.S. government between 1961 and 1965 in the operation of Plan Triangular to rehabilitate Bolivia's tin mines. (Under this plan Argentina also supplied funds.) The only other large funding which Bolivia obtained between 1952 and 1966 was supplier's credits for goods purchased immediately following the revolution and during the inflation.[11]

As the United States switched from direct grants to loans to Bolivia beginning in the 1960s,[12] Bolivia's outstanding external debt began to increase. If we take the external pre-1952 debt (which was not repudiated) into account with the post-1952 amount (table 4 on page 225), we find that the total external debt of Bolivia reached about $290 million in 1966. This amount was only slightly more than the $279 million in U.S. assistance shown in table 3. Perhaps this explains why President Barrientos announced in 1966 that the public debt could not be permitted to go much higher and why the Bolivian government (at least through the 1960s attempted to allocate relatively large amounts to keep this total down.[13]

Reliance on foreign loans, in contrast to reliance on U.S. grants, means that Bolivia faces a new kind of dependence upon foreign decisions. Loans are approved only for specific purposes and tailored to the specifications and restrictions of foreign agencies. Since lending patterns often change according to the current vogue and international thinking about development, it is possible that this funding will delimit Bolivian policy more than U.S. assistance did as it was handled before 1961.

Although many critics claim that the MNR sold out to the United States or that the United States "bought" the Bolivian national revolution, an analysis of tables 1 and 3 (pages 219 and 223) leads us to conclude otherwise. Actually, during the 1950s the result of U.S. policy was effectively to support the MNR's social revolution. Although U.S. advisers attempted to influence Bolivian policy and, obviously, had some success, until 1963 U.S. officials did not seriously question U.S. budgetary support of central government policy.

In terms of Bolivian independence, the central government's control over policy suffered a serious setback when the United States began to deemphasize direct grants to cover public sector deficits and AID attempted to tighten control over expenditures. Though one may argue that this cutback was desirable for U.S. interests or a necessary concomitant for economic growth, we should note that such control did not help Bolivia gain the needed experience to run its own affairs or to learn from trial and error. Clearly, the merits of these approaches cannot be settled here, but identification of the issues may help us to understand the complexities of development.

There are several ironies in the analysis of U.S. assistance and foreign loans. First, Republican leaders in the United States such as President Dwight D. Eisenhower and Secretary of State John Foster Dulles, were apparently more permissive in regard to Bolivian development than was the Democratic president John F. Kennedy, who took a personal interest in Bolivian development. This difference in policy was related directly to a lack of U.S. understanding of the effect that U.S. aid had on Bolivia; it also demonstrates the unreliability of stereotypes.

Bolivia's desire to keep its debt down and promptly meet its obligations represented an awareness of its dependency on foreign loans. Between 1952 and 1966, however, central government expenditures on amortization and interest for the public debt never exceeded 5 percent of its total outlays, and such percentages came only after the stabilization program was initiated. Although developed countries may well exclude amortization of the debt from budgetary analysis, it is necessary to include it as an administrative expenditure in the accounts of developing countries. They must balance need-to-pay obligations in order to obtain new loans against need-to-expand social and economic shares in total outlay. Apparently Mexico has resolved this dilemma, as noted elsewhere, by devoting a high share of its outlay to repayment of its debt in order to obtain loans with which to inject massive doses of capital into national development.[14]

In regard to the effect of public expenditure upon Bolivian development since 1952, we must finally face the question of whether the Bolivian economy was helped or hindered by official programs. George Jackson Eder has taken the view that Bolivia has been

corrupted and pauperized by fourteen years of U.S. aid which, far from promoting Bolivia's economic development and social progress, served only to maintain in power a government that proved unworthy either of American or Bolivian support and which, without American aid, would admittedly have fallen almost at the inception of the Revolution. . . .

Subtract U.S. aid and Bolivia is less prosperous today than it was before the Revolution—further from the "take-off point" to economic progress, both by reason of the depletion of wasted resources and because of the degradation that has come from idleness and dependency.[15]

In Eder's view the monetary stabilization program which he instituted in 1956–1957 was responsible for somewhat repairing the damage done to development by the MNR's suppression of a free-market economy. Thus, to Eder, Bolivia's problems began with government attempts to relieve poverty by ever mounting expenditures for welfare and economic development, financed by the exhaustion of the nation's gold and foreign exchange reserves, by U.S. aid, and by borrowing from the Central Bank. The bank met the government demand for credit by constantly increased issues of unbacked paper currency, which in turn were followed by a drop in the foreign exchange value of the boliviano and higher and higher prices at home. Higher prices brought demands for increased wages and higher social security benefits, which were wiped out by the inflationary tide. At the same time, they raised the cost of government, increasing the deficits and making necessary still further borrowing from the Central Bank. Price controls were instituted, but these resulted only in shortages of goods, black-marketing, still higher prices, and a flight of capital, each consequence accentuating its antecedent cause in a vicious spiral that seemingly had no end. . . .

In desperation, the government called upon the United States for aid, which came in cash and commodities. But the cash was swallowed up in the deficits of the government and of a score of government enterprises, while the commodities largely found their way into the black market or were smuggled out of the country. The counterpart funds generated by U.S. aid became a major source of further inflation, while the distribution of cash and commodities aggravated Bolivia's chronic ills.[16]

Given the revolutionary situation in which the MNR took power, however, and given the party's need to demonstrate to the masses as well as its supporting groups that it could act to make the state responsible for national development, an "untrammeled" free-market model of development was almost automatically ruled out from the start. It is by no means clear, as Eder apparently assumes, that Bolivia's halting development, which only gained strength in the mid-1960s, could have progressed without a thoroughgoing revolution which attempted not only to incorporate the mass of Bolivians into the market economy in the first place but to make important financial activity responsive to national needs. In short, Bolivia needed national integration as a concomitant of social and economic development.

The first order of business for the MNR revolutionists was to remain in power and to protect themselves by any means possible. In Bolivia's case, this did not mean sending dissenters to the firing squad; rather, in one of the least bloody, major revolutions the world has yet known, Paz either exiled or sent to camps of detention those who threatened the new government. One regrets and cannot deny, of course, that political prisoners have died before, during, and since the MNR period from 1952 to 1964; nor can one deny widespread government corruption under the MNR. It is only realistic, however, to expect some administrators' illegal use of power and fraud in administering great amounts of money in a chaotic situation, especially following a violent seizure of power and the institution of widespread change.

Since Paz's policy of social expenditure had been implanted six years prior to the revolution, obviously Paz did not feel that the pattern of public expenditure needed to be altered. Thus, during his first term he simply expanded an established program by printing more and more paper money. A great deal of money was needed to begin the operations which would win mass support for the new government already threatened with internal division over the nature of development.

The problem which has faced the central government, especially since the United States began to phase out budgetary support, is how to rechannel funds frozen in a pattern of social expenditure. If the thrust of discretionary expenditure is limited to social development, then economic development will lie in the decentralized and autonomous sector beyond the government's direct control. If the central government can now expand the pool of funds over which it has discretion, perhaps it can successfully face this problem. Since the government will need to continue the well-established tradition of social expenditure, it also faces the need of expanding its income so that it may directly increase its economic functions in relative terms without disrupting social outlay in absolute terms. Although tax reform was not compatible with attracting private foreign capital to Bolivia in the years immediately after the nationalization of the tin mines or during the period of the great land reform under Paz Estenssoro between 1960 and 1964,[17] perhaps it now appears to be Bolivia's best hope of giving the central government real (rather than theoretical) control over the country's discretionary funds without upsetting the national economy.[18]

In a sense the nonrevolutionary policy which the MNR followed after 1952 may have been an important factor in the MNR's ability to stay in power, because it offered a stable system amid events which caused great instability. The MNR might not have been able to hold its power if it had wanted also to change the pattern of expenditure. Nevertheless, as the MNR's term in office wore on, ability to stimulate directly economic development became the key issue. As Eder has noted, social expenditure without an economic base cannot produce sound results for long. Not only was the Paz group seeking to gain control over the instruments of political power, as Professor Malloy points out in his chapter, but it needed also to gain control over public expenditure.

As we have seen, successor governments to the MNR did not change the central government's policy in terms of outlay, and, thus, they have faced the same issue that the MNR faced in reorienting expenditure: successful planning depends upon a clear understanding of the role of state policy in regard to the political economy of national development. In rational state planning designed to carry out the promises of the revolution, the central government cannot expect to leave the major share of economic development to autonomous agencies which supposedly are more efficient than the regular bureaucracy. In sum, not only should social development be managed with the same efficiency developed by some decentralized agencies, but the central government should extend its control over the entire public sector.

NOTES

1. For Mexico's case, see James W. Wilkie, *The Mexican Revolution: Federal Expenditure and Social Change Since 1910,* 2d. ed. (Berkeley, Calif., 1970), pt. 1.

2. According to the tentative data on Cuban projected outlay, however, between 1957–1958 and 1962 the social and administrative activities of the state were diverted into economic development in quite dramatic terms; see Dudley Seers, ed., *Cuba: The Economic and Social Revolution* (Chapel Hill, N.C., 1964), p. 41. Cf. also United Nations, Economic Commission for Latin America, "The Cuban Economy in the Period 1959–1963," *Economic Survey of Latin America* (1963), p. 288.

The Costa Rican revolution of 1948 might well be added to the list of Latin American countries which have undergone true revolutions in the twentieth century; however, since my investigations of the Costa Rican case are still in progress, I omit discussion here.

3. For data on Bolivia's central government expenditure, which are reorganized by function for historical consistency, see James W. Wilkie, *The Bolivian Revolution and U.S. Aid Since 1952: Financial Background and Context of Political Decisions* (Los Angeles, Calif., 1969). Discussion here is limited to the policy of expenditure rather than taxation.

4. Rationale, full definitions, and complete yearly data for subcategories of administrative, social, and economic expenditure groupings are given in Wilkie, *The Bolivian Revolution,* pp. 14 ff., and appendices G and M. The reader should note that the question of honesty in the expenditure of funds is irrelevant to this analysis which involves allocations of funds for policy purposes. Examination of funds in terms of policy is very different from analyzing efficiency in outlay (see "The Wastage Overhead Factor in Government Finance," in Wilkie, appendix O).

5. Harold Osborne, *Bolivia, a Land Divided,* 3rd ed. (London, 1964), p. 151. For a discussion of the decapitalization of the mines, see Professor Thorn's chapter in this volume.

6. Table 3 excludes losses and unexpended local currency; see Wilkie, *The Bolivian Revolution,* pp. 9 ff.

7. Anthony M. Solomon, Frank W. Krause, and Norman S. Fielike, "Informe acerca de las finanzas del sector público de Bolivia," unpub. manuscript, 1963.

8. Since year-to-year summaries for public debt operations are not available for the early years of the revolutionary era, data are presented in a lump sum total for 1966 (fourteen years after the MNR victory and two years after its fall from power) in order to give perspective on both pre- and post-1964 developments. For problems in reconstructing the debt during the 1950s, see George Jackson Eder, *Inflation and Development in Latin America: A Case History of Inflation and Stabilization in Bolivia* (Ann Arbor, Mich., 1968), pp. 143 ff., 408 ff. Cf. also the Alliance for Progress, Inter-American Committee on the Alliance for Progress, *Domestic Efforts and the Needs for External Financing for the Development of Bolivia,* mimeographed (Washington, D.C., 1968), p. 74, which estimates the external debt for 1952 to 1966 at about $100 million.

9. Sources for functional analysis include: Inter-American Development Bank, Social Progress Trust Fund, *Seventh Annual Report* (1967), pp. 424–25; International Development Association, "Financial Statement," June 30, 1968; Inter-American Development Bank, *Ninth Annual Report* (1968), pp. 91–92; Banco Central, *Memoria* (1966), p. 64; AID/Bolivia, *Economic and Program Statistics,* 9 (1968), p. 30; and International Monetary Fund, "Background Material for 1967 Article VIII Consultation," pt. II, appendix, p. 66. The Bolivian ministry of finance presented the data in table 4 to this IMF source.

10. Inter-American Development Bank, *Ninth Annual Report.*

11. For a discussion of supplier's credits see Eder, *Inflation and Development,* pp. 41, 43, 123 ff.

12. See Wilkie, *The Bolivian Revolution,* p. 48.

13. *El Diario,* September 16, 1966; Alliance for Progress, *Domestic Efforts and the Needs for External Financing,* p. 74.

14. Wilkie, *The Mexican Revolution,* pt. 1.

15. Eder, *Inflation and Development,* pp. 609–10. Cf. Laurence Whitehead, *The United States and Bolivia; A Case of Neo-Colonialism* (London, 1969).

16. Ibid., pp. viii–ix.

17. James W. Wilkie, "Revolution and Land Reform: Bolivia and Venezuela," in manuscript.

18. By 1960 the actual expenditure of the central government finally had caught up with inflation and population and in 1966 appeared to be at about thirty-four to forty standard bolivianos per person compared to twenty-three to twenty-six in 1952. Unfortunately, however, estimates of the per capita gross domestic product appear to be only about even with or below the 1952 figures; see Wilkie, *The Bolivian Revolution,* p. 29. For a further discussion of these matters, see Professor Thorn's chapter.

WILLIAM E. CARTER
University of Florida

Revolution and the Agrarian Sector

If Carter Goodrich felt fortunate to be in La Paz during the 1952 revolution, I was just as fortunate to be on the Altiplano the following year when the agrarian reform began. His vantage point had been La Paz, the administrative and economic heart of the country; mine was Kachitu,* a small cantonal capital on the northern shores of Lake Titicaca. While he dealt with officials at the national level, I dealt with a small town's petite bourgeoisie and elements of the surrounding Indian masses.

In 1953, Kachitu had approximately one thousand inhabitants. Then, much more than now, ruling whites concentrated in the large cities; mestizo "petite bourgeoisie" divided their ranks between cities and towns; and subjugated Indians clung to time-honored traditions in ancient, rural communities. Whites attended high school and university; mestizos took a few years of grade school; and the Indian was left illiterate. Whites traveled to other South American countries, to Europe, and to the United States; mestizos went to La Paz or, occasionally, to the Yungas and the Oriente; and the Indian traveled on foot to the local market, church, or, sometimes, to a contiguous region of the country. Whites made decisions of national importance; mestizos carried them out on the local scene; and the Indian obeyed.

The founding of Kachitu dates back to at least early colonial days. It

---

* Fictitious name for a real town.

has been attributed to two Aymara families, and throughout the town's history monolingual Aymara speakers have been in the majority. Mestizos grew considerably in number during the first half of the twentieth century, however, and so preempted local power that, by 1953, recency of arrival was directly correlated with social prominence. All the political and economic leaders in that year belonged to families who had migrated to the town after 1900, to the total exclusion of those who could claim residence there since colonial days. The attractions that had brought these ambitious newcomers to the town were varied and are best illustrated through brief life sketches of three of the town's leading citizens as of 1953: Doña Marina, Don Pedro, and David Murillo.

Doña Marina had migrated from Achacachi, the provincial capital, because her family owned some small estates just outside Kachitu. Subsequently a sizeable cash inheritance enabled her to establish the largest general store in the canton and to set herself up as a major *rescatadora* ("wholesaler") of products emanating from the surrounding indigenous communities. In proper fashion she traveled frequently, maintained a town house in a good suburb of La Paz, and was the most generous sponsor of fiestas in the whole region.

Don Pedro also came from Achacachi. As a young man, he decided that the contraband traffic filtering through Kachitu offered an unusual opportunity to amass a fortune. Over the years he acquired several medium-sized properties and served an unprecedented number of times as the town's *corregidor* ("chief official"). During his administrations a true plaza was laid out with plantings and fountain, sidewalks were built, the town's first school was opened, a library was formed, and a new town hall was created.

David Murillo came to head Kachitu's first school. As the town's most educated and cultured citizen, he quickly assumed the bearing of a local aristocrat and justified his actions by hanging in his study a geneological chart through which he claimed direct descent from Manco Kapac, the first Inca. He thus astutely recognized his Indian ancestry but at the same time set himself well apart from the unlettered masses surrounding Kachitu.

The lives of these three leaders are representative of what was happening in towns like Kachitu during the first fifty years of the twentieth century. Although there was no great spurt in development, such towns were experiencing a growing degree of sophistication and were establishing ever increasing contact with the outside world. This gradual evolutionary process, however, hardly prepared people living in Bolivia's small towns for the rapidity and violence of changes that were to accompany the country's agrarian reform. The 1952 revolution and the subsequent nationalization of the mines had caused apprehension among the town's mestizos (*"vecinos"*), but the direct effect on these people had been slight. Unpaid Indian labor continued to care for their own modest landholdings and to supply household servant needs, and scores of Indian families still asked for their sponsorship as godparents.

This version of the good life was destined not to last long, however. For the townspeople of Kachitu, the first news of violent change came from the Cochabamba valleys. There certain groups of peasants began to seize land, sack estate buildings, and attack the landlords. By the time reports of these events reached Kachitu, they had become tales of atrocities, each more terrifying than the last. Finally, in January 1953, the most feared step of all was taken by the national government; it declared its intent to implement a sweeping agrarian reform.

Almost overnight rumors swept the town that the countryside was being infiltrated with agents preaching peasant revolt. Confused stories were told of attempts to organize the rural masses into *sindicatos* ("labor unions") and militia, to confiscate estates, and to annihilate the townspeople. Indians who refused to join the new organizations were terrorized; one who resisted was shot to death on his doorstep; another was slashed with a knife and his mutilated remains set out on Lake Titicaca in a balsa boat.

Don Pedro, still the town's corregidor, rushed to La Paz to obtain defensive aid in any way he could. Some months previously he had secured the approval and tentative commitment of funds for the building of a new schoolhouse on the edge of town. Now he succeeded in having assigned, for construction purposes, a contingent of some seventy soldiers who, while ostensibly stationed in the town for the innocuous purpose of school construction, could also defend it from attack.

Don Pedro's actions initially calmed the fears of the townspeople. As the days went by, however, rumors grew ever more frequent and frightening, and it was not long before the peoples' tension was at a pitch even higher than before. Some feared that the military contingent itself—entirely Indan except for the officer—would rise up and join in a peasant revolt. The officer in charge, a man from Cochabamba, did little to allay these fears. He collected every piece of information he could find about the Cochabamba revolts and then retold it with obvious relish, dwelling on and exaggerating the most bizarre details. One of his tales had to do with an estate owner who, when he arrived at his country house, was taken prisoner by the peasants. Tied to a tree, he had to watch while one after another raped his niece. Then his tongue was cut out, his ears sliced off, his fingers dismembered joint by joint, his eyes gouged out, and finally he was beaten to death and quartered.

There was no doubt in the minds of the local vecinos that such brutality was actually taking place. They were convinced that they lived in the midst of unbridled savages, and they responded accordingly. Guns were polished and cocked, ammunition stores were augmented, and a twenty-four hour street patrol was instituted. Most vecino women and children locked their houses and fled to La Paz. At least half the town's stores were closed indefinitely. All able-bodied men were instructed to carry arms at all times, and if they had none, they were supplied weapons by the officer in charge of the military contingent.

Tension continued to mount. One afternoon in March, on riding out to a nearby estate, I found the joint owners, a pair of sisters, supervising the barley harvest with whips in their hands and guards at their sides. They were determined to extract profit as long as they could. In the same month a number of trucks, protected by well-armed bodyguards, came through the town carrying estate owners intent on defending their land. When one of these landlord groups did not return for several days, rumor raced through the town that they all had been massacred and eaten in a cannibalistic orgy.

With the populace in such a state of apprehension, imagination ran riot. One moonless night a guard thought he heard a gunshot, the attack alarm was sounded, and women and children ran for shelter, some almost plunging to their death when they tried to hide on the escarpment that rose behind the town. The following morning all was quiet; the "attack" had probably been an illusion.

Midafternoon a couple of weeks later, the officer in charge of the local army contingent came running into town shouting, "Sound the alarm; sound the alarm; we are being surrounded." A meeting of all vecinos was hastily called in the town hall, and there the officer explained how he had gone into a nearby Indian community to collect a delinquent fine imposed by the corregidor. When the accused peasant refused to pay and others began to gether around him in support, the officer fired in terror at their feet. In retaliation they began to stone him, and he fled to Kachitu with a growing contingent of infuriated men hot on his heels. By evening several thousand peasants were encamped on a plain just across the river from the entrance to town. All remained quiet until about ten o'clock, when the first shot was fired. Immediately all women took refuge in the church sacristy, and armed men began to shoot into the darkness. Many volleys went back and forth that night, but no one was killed, let alone injured. The rumor that the town would be sacked and burned never became reality.

A further violent incident occurred one windy afternoon, when a fleet of trucks that had passed through the town a few hours before on its way to La Paz returned with tales of a mammoth battle raging between there and Achacachi. The drivers estimated that at least ten thousand peasants were involved, the stakes being regional leadership for the sindicatos. The battle continued for the better part of a day, and at its conclusion peasants from the winning side looted the houses of those who had lost. Carrying a booty of doors, plows, chickens, weaving and cooking utensils—anything, in short, which was movable—they staged a victory parade around the main plaza of Achacachi. Mestizo authorities in the provincial capital were helpless; faced with overwhelming numbers of armed Indians, they simply watched the parade from the safety of their second-story windows and balconies.

Such a combination of experiences, compressed into only a few months' time, was sufficient to convince most of Kachitu's mestizos that they could no longer resist impending change, and an exodus to La Paz quickly ensued. Economic survival being of the utmost importance, the émigrés rapidly adapted themselves to city life by either continuing their roles as storekeepers or entering technical or professional careers. There were exceptions, of course. One of Don Pedro's sons continued in Kachitu, Doña Marina's sister took her place, and two of David Murillo's daughters continued to live in his old home. Yet real authority swiftly passed into new hands. Within a year, an Indian peasant who had completed grammar school in the local Protestant mission emerged as virtual *caudillo* of both the town and the surrounding region. His impressive accumulation of offices included that of keeper of the public records, president of the cooperative, local agent for the department of roads, commander of the local militia regiment, and chief of the regional militia division. Though a mestizo continued to occupy the office of corregidor, in the years immediately following agrarian reform, his office degenerated into little more than an honorary appointment.

In many ways events in Kachitu during 1953 were characteristic of the initial stages of agrarian reform throughout the northern Altiplano. Although revolt appears to have been spontaneous in certain parts of the Cochabamba valleys, it did not occur in most other sections of the country until sometime later when the peasants were formally organized and armed by agents of the MNR government. However, the prerevolutionary agrarian situation had been so repressive that once the peasants *were* organized, the MNR had considerable difficulty in controlling them.

ROOTS OF THE AGRARIAN REFORM

To realize why agrarian reform was such an urgent step for Bolivia, one must first understand the landholding system of prereform days. In one of the most exploitive processes in the history of agriculture, peasant and communal holdings had been whittled away until, by 1950, 4.5 percent of the country's population held 70 percent of its agricultural lands. Estates were managed on a labor intensive basis, with an almost total absence of capital investment. The situation has been described very succinctly by Joseph Thome:

Most . . . land was exploited in a semi-feudal system called colonato, under which the landowner would provide the usufruct of small parcels to the *campesinos* (or *colonos,* as they were known). In return, the *campesinos* would work three or more days a week, without compensation, on the lands reserved exclusively for the landlord, as well as provide household and other personal services. (Thome: 12–13)

The system was so inefficient that between 35 and 40 percent of the country's imports had to be foodstuffs for use in the cities and the mines.

Bolivia had vast reserves of empty land, but these meant nothing to poverty-stricken agricultural laborers in places like Kachitu, since about 90 percent of the reserves was located in the Oriente and the remaining 10 percent in the Montañas. None could be found on the Altiplano; whatever vacant land had once existed there had long before passed into private hands (Weeks:12). This situation placed the common man in the highlands in such a plight that as late as 1952 advertisements continued to appear in the La Paz papers offering to rent bound peasants as servants and suppliers of dung (*"Alquilo pongo con taquia"*) or to sell estates with specified numbers of laborers and animals (*"Vendo finca con 50 pongos y 400 ganado ovino"*).

Prior to agrarian reform, tenure rights on Bolivian estates tended to be exceedingly complex. Under the guise of a Spanish legal system that typed gross holdings by size alone, there functioned intricate empirical systems which involved numerous usufruct features such as *kallpas, sayañas, aynokas,* and *pegujales* (all varieties of small individual land-holdings).[1] These essentially indigenous units made landholding much more complicated than is generally implied in the customary references to the "old feudal system." In fact none of Bolivia's tenure systems appear to have been feudal, since they lacked many of the specialized political mechanisms and hierarchical relationships of feudalism.

Though coming into their own only during the nineteenth century, Bolivian estates clearly had roots in the preconquest traditions of both Spanish and Andean culture. In both these civilizations there had been regional and district lords, lands cultivated for these lords by servile peasant populations, usufruct subsistence plots set aside for the support of common laborers and their families, and specific task work imposed by turn or lot. The fusion that evolved from the encounter of the two types of land traditions varied in specifics from place to place. In general, however, it gave rise to the setting aside of large pieces of land that were populated by servile cultivators, who, for the privilege of remaining in their homes, were responsible to owners, whether absentee or resident, for certain political, social, and economic obligations. This servile population could live either in small, scattered clusters of huts or in one nucleated settlement. Each hut was customarily built on a small houseplot where the occupants could raise small crops and barnyard fowl and could tend their animals at night. Near the entrance to the estate was the manor house, where either the owner or his manager lived.

The bulk of an estate was generally set aside for cultivation or pasture or both. This area tended to be broken into large blocks within which individual owner and peasant plots were often indiscriminately mixed. On the plots set aside for owners, peasants would work together, pooling their resources to plow and harvest whole fields at a time; but on those assigned in usufruct, they generally worked on an individual basis.

In addition to usufruct rights to individual land parcels, the peasants often had proportional rights of common to pastureland, meadow, woodland, and wasteland. As with their other rights, these also were validated by giving labor to the estate owner, the amount varying in relation to the amount of land allotted to the individual peasant family. It was often sufficient, however, to occupy most of their waking hours, and additional commitments could include specific tasks on the estate at certain periods of the year. Although there were many gradations of status and service, there was no place for outright slavery.

Where this type of estate system developed, in both the Andes and in Europe, it was intended basically for subsistence production and could never support large-scale industrialization or urbanization. As Bolivia attempted to democratize and modernize its society, the system was found wanting, just as it had been when Europe encountered the Industrial Revolution.

The Agrarian Reform Decree of 1953 did not occur in a historical vacuum. Ever since the beginning of the Andean estate system, attempts had been made to rectify rural inequities. As early as 1591 a royal *cédula* ("decree") had been issued to insure that Indian communities be left with enough land to sustain themselves. Time and again, however, vested interests thwarted the intent of such protectionist measures. As a result, by the 1930s human exploitation had reached such a state in Bolivia that the drafters of the 1938 constitution found it necessary specifically to reiterate that slavery did not exist in the country and that no one could be required to give personal services without just retribution and complete consent.

Using Bolivia's many protectionist precedents as a base, President Villarroel, a forerunner of the MNR, anticipated agrarian reform in 1945 by issuing four decrees in which he abolished all nonremunerative domestic service, prohibited estate owners from requiring tribute goods from their peasants, authorized an agrarian labor code which, among other things, set a maximum of four days per week for peasant labor on estate owners' lands, and required that estate owners provide schools for peasant children. This last requirement made the owners particularly wary, for, as one foreign observer wrote in 1947: "It is lack of education rather than 'debt peonage' which holds the Bolivian *colono* on the land which he is legally free to leave if and when he can find an alternative means of livelihood. . . . The problem is, how to educate the *colono,* make his situation attractive, and at the same time benefit rather than harm the patrón" (Weeks:2–8).

Given the severity of Bolivia's agrarian crisis, hopes for such a gradualist transformation seem to have been unrealistic. A critical period in which the major castes of Bolivian society would be forced into open confrontation was an inevitability.

THE DECREE

Once the MNR decided to implement agrarian reform, it moved quickly; its agrarian reform study commission was given only ninety days in which to prepare a report. This limited amount of time left the commission little choice but to base its report on idealized Spanish concepts of access and tenure, and the few passages that did deal with traditional indigenous usufruct used concepts based more on myth and hearsay than on empirical research. In response to subsequent criticism, MNR leaders excused shortcomings of both the report and its companion decree by stating that they had been forced to move with great haste in the face of imperative peasant demand (cf. Wilkie:7). A more realistic appraisal would have been the admission that the party leaders felt reform to be a necessary political move. As exemplified by the Kachitu case, peasant rebellion did not occur in many parts of the country until it was actually encouraged and, to some extent, formally organized by agents of the government itself, for relatively few peasants had taken part in the original revolution. The fact cannot be disputed that, by moving into the field of agrarian reform, the MNR was making an unprecedented bid for political support from Bolivia's rural masses.

Of the tiny minority of peasants who had actually agitated for agrarian reform, most appear to have lived in the Cochabamba valleys and, particularly, in the Ucureña area near Cliza. These valleys contain Bolivia's densest concentration of Quechua-speakers, and there the colonial institution of the *reducción* ("Indian resettlement") [2] had been particularly successful. As a result, Cochabamba peasants had, for centuries, lived in villages rather than in semidispersed communities and had interacted with ruling Spaniards and mestizos much more frequently and intensively than had their counterparts in places like the northern Altiplano. Peasant-owned land parcels were widespread in the valleys and small estates the rule. Understandably, the Cochabamba Quechua long enjoyed the reputation of being much more open and flexible than the supposedly hostile and recalcitrant Altiplano Aymara. By the mid-twentieth century, many of them had become bilingual, had attained some level of formal education, and were increasingly mimicking mestizo ways.

In an attempt to get at the roots of the Cochabamba agitation, Richard Patch and Jorge Dandler have chronicled the experiences and impact of a group of young Chaco War veterans on returning to Ucureña in the mid-1930s. The experiences of the veterans appear to have been more than merely broadening; they gave these men the confidence to challenge the estate system and to cooperate with outsiders like José Antonio Arze in ridding themselves of their hated *patrones* ("landlords"). Soon after their return from the war they succeeded in organizing and renting their estate from the owners, a group of Cochabamba nuns. In retaliation, landlords in surrounding estates quickly banded together, outbid the peasants in the rental, and drove the ringleaders from the land. This action only hardened the returned veterans' resolve, and with the aid of socially conscious whites they began to work toward the establishment of formal peasant organizations on other estates in the valleys. By early 1953, these organizations, calling themselves *sindicatos* ("unions"), began openly to attack patrones and administrators, seize buildings, animals, vehicles, seed stocks, and machinery and threaten to attack towns, murder their mestizo and white inhabitants, and confiscate anything they desired.

Previous governments would have immediately sent military contingents, for they would have argued that such actions were insurgent and could result in a civil war. The MNR, however, exercised restraint and by its inaction confirmed the formal emergence and unification of a national peasant organization. It then made its stand explicit when it sent organizing agents into all parts of the country where active peasant agitation for agrarian reform did not occur, that is, into practically all of Bolivia except the Cochabamba valleys. These agents, often members of mining and urban labor unions, informed rural leaders of the purpose of the agrarian reform movement and of the need for organization in order to implement the reform. By the time such messages filtered into rural communities like those near Kachitu, they had been simplified into a dictum that everyone would immediately receive possession of the land on which he worked, and that no one would work any longer for landlords. Arms flowed into peasant hands both directly and indirectly from official government sources, giving substance to the message. As a result, many landlords and their administrators abandoned their estates weeks, even months, before the Agrarian Reform Decree was pronounced.

On Labor Day, May 1, 1953, tens of thousands of armed peasant leaders were transported to La Paz in railroad freight cars and trucks to celebrate the victory of the Bolivian workingman. Even larger numbers were brought into the city three months later when the signing of the Agrarian Reform Decree and the celebration of Bolivian independence nearly coincided. The remarkable fact of both these celebrations is that, although the city swarmed with heavily armed peasants and although these peasants bedded down in previously inviolable parks, plazas, and avenues, very few incidents of violence occurred. Few had dared predict that the newly liberated Indian would exercise such restraint. Significantly, from this time on, the word *indio* ("Indian") became a pejorative in Bolivia, and the substitute *campesino* ("countryman") officially took its place, except for Indian Day, a school holiday that was established in 1937. When the Agrarian Reform Decree was signed in Ucureña, it was before the watchful eyes of fifty thousand campesinos, not indios. This change in nomenclature still stands as a key symbol of the fundamental irreversibility of the act.

In its preamble, the Agrarian Reform Decree set forth six basic goals:

1. To provide adequate parcels of land to peasants with little or none, providing they work them, expropriating for this purpose *latifundia* ("excessively large properties") or other land not worked personally by large landowners but from which regular income is derived
2. To restore to corporate Indian communities those lands which were usurped and to cooperate in the modernization of their agriculture, so far as possible respecting and building on their collectivist traditions
3. To free peasant laborers from their condition as servants, proscribing gratuitous and obligatory personal services
4. To stimulate the increased productivity and commercialization of agricultural goods, encouraging the investment of new capital, respecting small- and medium-sized landholdings, encouraging agrarian cooperativism, giving technical aid, and opening possibilities for credit
5. To protect natural resources through the adoption of modern technical and scientific means
6. To promote internal rural migration from the overpopulated Inter-Andean zone, so that there might be a rational population distribution and an affirmation of national unity, and the Bolivian Oriente might be integrated with the rest of the country (Avendaño:46–47).

The decree specified that certain lands were not subject to expropriation. These included: 1) the family house, 2) the small property, 3) the medium property (though portions occupied by colonos prior to the Agrarian Reform Decree were subject to expropriation), 4) cooperative properties, 5) the agricultural enterprise (up to one-third expropriable if based on the colonato system), and 6) Indian communal holdings (ibid.:49–50, 56–58). For most of these, a maximum size was set for each geographical zone and type of exploitation, and land over and above these maxima was subject to redistribution. Latifundia, which in the highlands were invariably tied up with a manorial system of forced labor, were to be totally expropriated (ibid.:50–51, 56, 58). Preferential distribution rights were given to those peasants who had been forced to work in exchange for rights of usufruct on either latifundia, medium-sized properties, or agricultural enterprises. Until legal rights were settled, such peasants were allowed to possess usufruct lands without obligation (ibid.:56, 57, 68, 69).

In an attempt to promote the development of the Oriente, the Agrarian Reform Law also provided that every highland peasant be given the right of sixty hectares on the eastern frontier, over and above whatever concession he might receive in his home community (ibid.:71). Thousands of peasants, taking advantage of this provision, today commute between their highland and lowland holdings, and some have permanently settled in the Oriente.

IMPLEMENTATION

The mechanics for carrying out the reform proved to be unbelievably cumbersome. In setting up the policies for land redistribution, the moderate reformist majority of the MNR hierarchy had tried to give some protection to preexisting institutions. Thus, to receive title, peasants had first to present a petition and to follow this with evidence in a series of hearings to demonstrate that their landlord had not made efficient modern use of his holdings, i.e., that his was not an agricultural enterprise. Petitions originally had to be presented through a regional fact-finding commission known as the *Junta Rural de Reform Agraria*. Once this junta received a demand, it would prepare a report to a regional agrarian judge. This procedure was so time-consuming, however, that it was eliminated by law on December 22, 1956. Juntas thereafter ceased to exist, and their functions passed on to mobile agrarian judges who had power over entire departments, as well as authority to initiate cases ex officio. The judges tended to be more efficient and honest than the rural juntas had been. However, since they were given neither vehicles nor travel funds, their mobility turned out to be more theoretical than real, and they initiated very few cases on their own.

A major blockage in the redistribution process lay in the provision that each individual title be signed by the president.[3] Clearly such a procedure was not only highly inefficient, it was unrealistic (Thome:57). Yet at the same time it is a vivid example of the paralyzing centralization of government functions that plagues so much of the development activity in the country. Responsibility for the delays in processing titles may also be attributed, to no small degree, to the lack of financial support by the government. The Agrarian Reform Council's budget was one of the lowest for any government agency in Bolivia; by the mid-1960s it represented only 0.6 percent of the national budget. Salary scales for agrarian reform employees were scandalously low. In 1966 monthly wages ranged from $271.00 (in U.S. dollars) for the president of the council to $51.00 for mobile judges working out of regional offices and a mere $29.00 for topographers.[4] These may be compared to rural schoolteachers' salaries of $40.00 to $50.00 per month for the same year. Understandably, agrarian reform employees have often practiced extortion when dealing with title seekers.

The impediments placed before the council by the MNR government testify to the essentially political nature of the agrarian reform movement. The MNR seemed more interested in altering the basis of political power than in modernizing Bolivia's agriculture. In the vast majority of cases, delays in expropriation proceedings favored former landlords far more than they did tenant peasants. Yet these delays also forced the peasants to organize politically and kept them cognizant of the fact that, through the Agrarian Reform Decree, the MNR was the party that had abolished unpaid labor and promised them clear title to the land.

Had the peasants not been thoroughly convinced of the revolutionary importance of the decree, the frustration generated by its lethargic execution would have been intolerable. Out of 15,322 cases initiated between 1953 and 1966, only 7,322 were terminated, leaving approximately eight thousand pending. Approximately four thousand of this pending remainder were awaiting presidential signature, three thousand were being reviewed by the central office, and one thousand were still in the initial stages of inquiry. From five hundred to one thousand nearly terminated cases were going to have to be referred back to the provincial judges, since the final *Resolución Suprema* had changed the distribution pattern originally recommended at the provincial level.[5]

Researchers from the Land Tenure Center of the University of Wisconsin submitted several reports from the middle to the end of 1960s which brought the acute problem of title processing to the attention of both the Bolivian government and AID. In response, mobile brigades were instituted in April 1968 and have been actively at work ever since. The membership of each brigade consists of one judge, one secretary, seven topographers, one agronomist, and one soil analyst. Through the combined efforts of AID and the Bolivian government, the brigades have been provided with adequate transportation and supportive facilities. Titles, for example, are now handled with an IBM computer. Before this change was made, an average of only thirty-six titles were processed per day. Using the computer, the average has been increased to between three hundred sixty to four hundred per hour, enabling the Council on Agrarian Reform to process 19,154 titles between February and July 1970.

From 1954 to 1968, only about eight million of Bolivia's calculated thirty-six million hectares of agricultural land were processed by the National Agrarian Reform Service. At that rate, processing would have continued well into the twenty-first century. The creation of the mobile brigades has speeded things up tremendously. It is planned for eighteen such brigades to be in operation by January 1971, and with luck they will be able to finish all titling under the agrarian reform law by 1975. The latest figures available indicate that, as of June 1970, 21,303 cases had been initiated. Of these 12,327 are now completely terminated and account for 12,290,687 hectares—approximately one third of Bolivia's total calculated agricultural lands. Some 272,811 families have benefitted from the granting of 450,557 separate titles.

Under the agrarian reform law the actual granting of titles falls into five categories: affectation, restitution, consolidation, inaffectability, and outright grant. *Affectation* is by far the most common. Claims brought by peasant unions for breaking up latifundia generally fall into this category, and they present the most difficult legal and social problems. *Restitution,* a simpler process, is rarely practiced; it consists of the return to Indian communities of lands lost to confiscatory landlords after January 1, 1900. *Consolidation* occurs in cases of small- or medium-sized properties where no colonato system had ever developed, but the present occupants desire a clear title. *Inaffectability* is declared primarily in cases of capitalized and mechanized agricultural enterprises where the present owners desire the legal security of a clear title as well as a defense from encroachment by squatters. The final title category—*outright grant* from the public domain—has been activated mainly for lands in Santa Cruz and the Beni, though several such titles have also been issued for frontier regions in the departments of Cochabamba and Tarija (Thome:35). All these titles carry the same restrictions: the recipient himself must work the land within two years of receiving title, he may not sell it, and upon his death it may pass only to his legal heirs. In the absence of such heirs, it reverts to the state.[6]

An additional provision of the decree is that peasants receiving expropriated property must pay to the Agricultural Bank a compensation equal to five times the 1948 tax assessment on the property. Payments were to be made over a twenty-five year period; and should the grantee default for two continuous years, his land would revert to the state. This requirement has never been enforced, however, and for all practical purposes grantees have been relieved of it permanently. Theoretically the payments were to have reimbursed the government for twenty-five-year agrarian bonds issued to the former landowners. The bonds have never been printed, and landowners have not tried to exact them from the government. Not only did the extraordinary inflation of the mid-1950s completely erode any original value the bonds may have had, but since they were based on 1948 tax assessments, they would have represented only a tiny fraction of the actual property value even at that time. Should a former landowner try to secure indemnification today, he would probably spend more in legal costs than the bonds would be worth (Thome:18– 19). The greatest recompense for expropriated property has come in those isolated cases where a peasant, following a tradition of good relations with his patrón, has made unofficial, voluntary property payments to insure his new title to the land. The few titles that have been issued in recognition of such payment have, unfortunately, no legal standing.

Another difficulty in implementing the Agrarian Reform Law has arisen from the fact that the principles for the redistribution of land were oriented more toward the abolition of the latifundia than to its subsequent use. Though the law specified the limits for maximum holdings in different areas, it gave no directions as to how estates were to be divided among the peasants, except for stating that the land was for those who worked it. This has made it unusually easy for distribution to follow former usufruct patterns. On the Altiplano thousands of titles have been given for sayañas that were in the hands of individual families for generations. Aside from these and a limited number of new sayañas created for young married couples and for landless excolonos who had migrated to the cities, most of the remaining lands have usually been labeled "collective," even though large portions of this collective remainder often have been broken up into extremely fragmented kallpas in communally supervised areas for cultivation (aynokas). A single community may have more than thirty thousand such separate aynoka-bound parcels, all of which have been completely overlooked by agrarian reform administrators (Carter:passim). Where this occurs, a peasant may walk miles to till a parcel of land only a fraction of a hectare in size, since his holdings are still scattered "like the stars of the sky."

Frequently, additional small land parcels have been set aside for specific community needs, such as schools, cooperatives, soccer fields, and chapels. But the inequality of the size of individual landholdings which separated the poor from the rich peasant in prereform days has not been solved. If anything it is more acute now than before, since comparatively well-to-do peasants have been better able to afford the legal costs of claim presentation (Wilkie:8–9). Data on the amount of land distributed through the reform indicate the magnitude of the resulting disparities. Though averaging around ten hectares, many peasant properties today come to less than one, while many others exceed twenty-five. There is great variation also in the amount of land titled to the original patrón, which may range from nothing to many thousands of hectares (ibid.:11). A large part of the disparity may be traced to the manner in which properties were classed by agrarian reform judges. Of the land titled thus far, approximately 38 percent of the units and 6 percent of the area was declared small property, 39 percent of the units and 36 percent of the area, medium property, 5 percent of the units and 28 percent of the area, agricultural enterprise, 16 percent of the units and 29 percent of the area, latifundia, 0.1 percent of the units and 0.1 percent of the area, cooperatives, and 0.5 percent of the units and 0.2 percent of the area was left unclassified.

Agrarian reform has also left untouched the problem of future land shortages which may arise from traditional inheritance patterns. A common practice with many Bolivian peasants is to divide land among all offspring, although males receive a larger share than females. Excolonos who follow this practice and who live in densely populated parts of the Altiplano and valleys are beginning to discover that the subsistence parcels granted them under the reform give succeeding generations no room whatsoever for expansion (ibid.:10–11). Their plight can be desperate. As the Léons point out in the next chapter, young people in places like Yungas find it very difficult to purchase land. There is particularly strong resistance to selling to someone from outside the area—specifically to mestizos and campesinos from the Altiplano.

IMPACT ON REGIONS

THE ALTIPLANO

The specific impact of the Agrarian Reform Decree has varied significantly from one region to another. In some parts of the Altiplano, where the majority of Bolivia's agriculturalists have traditionally lived, prereform usufruct patterns have often simply been continued. In one study covering seven estates, it was reported that, on the smallest of these, colonos occupied all the available land even before agrarian reform, so that all authorities could do was to legalize the existing usufruct holdings. On the remaining six, usufruct holdings absorbed an average of some 70 percent of the total land area so that, even when the estates were declared latifundia, the bulk of the land titled to the peasants constituted parcels to which they already had usufruct rights under the old estate system (Carter:65–83). In contrast, in other parts of the Altiplano, total redistribution appears to have been more common. In the case of fifty-one separate properties recently studied by Ronald Clark, twenty-five—representing some 65 percent of the land area covered in the sample—were declared latifundia by agrarian reform authorities, and consequently the former owner lost all his land. The remaining twenty-six were declared medium or small properties, and the landlord was able to retain some land for his own use.

It is clear that there was a variety of responses, even in the same geographic region. Of the fifty-one Altiplano estates sampled by Clark, only twenty were completely idled by the reform. Seven of these were left unworked for two years, five for three years, four for four years, two for five years, one for seven years, and only one was permanently abandoned (Clark:16). The causes for idleness were multiple:

Many conflicting reasons were given why lands were left idle. In one case where lands have not been worked for 14 years the landlord was particularly abusive and the peasants say that he still wants them to work for him under the same system as before the land reform on the lands which he still has. In other cases the peasants say that either their local or regional union leaders prohibited them from working the landlords' land where the owners had been abusive, or where the new peasant union leader was trying to ensure that the landlords would not return. In some cases the peasants did not work the lands "on orders from La Paz" without specifying from where the orders came. Peasants say also that they were waiting to see to what extent the lands would be expropriated before beginning to work them; that is, they were awaiting official pronouncements from the National Agarian Reform Service before they dared to work the lands of the landlord. . . .

It seems that confusion within the ranks of the peasant unions on the one hand, and peasants who would not appropriate for themselves what was not yet theirs on the other, resulted in these lands remaining unworked. (ibid.: 16–17)

It is important to note that, of the thirty-one estates in the Clark study not idled by agrarian reform, nineteen constituted cases in which peasants voluntarily took the landlords' share of production (50 percent) to the Ministry of Rural Affairs in La Paz for varying periods of time through the offices of their local peasant syndicates.

THE YUNGAS

Save for the products involved, the situation in the Yungas is not terribly different from that in the Altiplano. Elaborate coca terraces had been maintained in the Yungas from before the time of the Inca. Their repair required huge inputs of labor, to say nothing of the tedious burdens of cultivation and harvest. As the Andean indigenous population increased, and the world demand for cocaine grew, Yungas estate owners became impressively wealthy, and taxes on the coca leaf came to represent one of the government's principal sources of income. The Agrarian Reform Decree provided that peasants continue working the fields of the patrón in exchange for cash compensation until final distribution could be made. In some cases the workers labored under this arrangement without enthusiasm. In others, they simply abandoned the estate lands. Today, therefore, much of the acreage previously worked for the estates has gone out of production entirely and many terraces are in ruins. Yet this loss has been compensated by the great expansion of terraces on the part of individual small landholders. The result is that coca production has made a remarkable recovery, even in the face of a governmental decree forbidding the construction of new terraces (Léons:699).

William and Barbara Léons, in their Yungas study, uncovered a pattern which may account for much of the variation observed from estate to estate across the country. In the region they studied, those estates nearest towns and along main access roads often contained a full capacity of peasants in prereform times, while those in more remote areas had land to spare. This distinction came to have considerable importance after the reform, when excolonos from the more accessible properties were granted only usufruct plots with perhaps a very small supplement, while those from the more isolated areas received the full ten hectares permissible under the Agrarian Reform Law (see page 244 of this volume). The general tendency in both the Altiplano and Yungas, however, has been to break estates up into very small plots, few of which are amenable to modern mechanization.

THE COCHABAMBA VALLEYS

Excessive fragmentation has also occurred in Bolivia's valley regions. In the upper valley of Cochabamba, around Cliza, the only land parcels that remain in excess of five hectares are either those held by a few former landlords or public plots such as experimental stations. In general, the same crops are grown in this region today as before the reform. Because these crops are wholly dependent on rainfall (and this is a semi-arid region), the limited size of peasant parcels is of serious concern. The breakdown of holdings into minimal size, however, *has* resulted in a more even distribution of income and *is* forcing many peasants into the mainstream of national life. People find that, merely to survive, they must either produce a marketable surplus or engage in activities other than farming (Saa:5).

Peasants in the lower Cochabamba valley, where the population is twice as dense as in the upper valley, are comparatively much better off. Ten miles outside the city of Cochabamba the Angostura Dam was built by Mexican engineers in the years immediately prior to the 1952 revolution. Its waters cover ten thousand hectares of good agricultural land but, in recompense, do provide year-round irrigation for the lower valley. Before agrarian reform was initiated, the principal crops grown there were the traditional ones of the highlands: potatoes, maize, and quinoa (a pigweed containing seeds used as a cereal), supplemented in some instances by dairy farming. But by 1966, in response to the Angostura irrigation waters, there had been a mass conversion to labor-intensive vegetables, especially onions and carrots. Carlos Saa, a Bolivian social scientist, has calculated that peasants in the lower valley today are producing at least ten times as much as their landlords did before 1953 (ibid.:15). The combination of a steady supply of water and relief from the bondage of the old estate system gave these peasants an opportunity to shift to a much more labor-intensive system than had existed prior to the agrarian reform. Peasants in the lower valley, although culturally identical to those of the upper valley, have benefited much more from the reform because of the ecological alterations resulting from the Angostura Dam project. Independently they can handle the complex task of marketing fresh vegetables much more efficiently than could the estate owners and managers under the old system. Given the high level of population density and their typically large number of offspring, such labor-intensive activities come as a great blessing.

Though the population of Cochabamba's upper valley is only half as dense, the lack of comparable productive outlets presents a serious problem. Corn and potatoes, the traditional crops for nonirrigated Cochabamba land, absorb such limited manpower that beyond a certain point labor becomes superfluous. Therefore when the destruction of the old estate system released time to upper valley peasants, they could put it to little profitable use. To no small degree, this may account for the fact that, since the reform, the upper valley has been the site of much political unrest.

Ucureña offers a prime example of the present upper valley stalemate. In a sample of holdings there, Saa found that their median size came to only 3.1 hectares and the mean to only a little more—3.3. Most holdings were broken up into two, three, or even four separate plots, each so small that mechanization is impossible. Commercial credit is almost nonexistent. When peasants need to borrow, they turn to friends and relatives, even though the savings of these people are basically in the form of animals, especially beef cattle. Despite these facts, agriculture continues to provide Ucureña peasants with their most important source of income, and some 31.5 percent of the community's agricultural products are sold. Supplementary cash is derived from activities other than farming; almost every peasant pursues at least one such additional activity and many two or more.

Although agrarian reform has not spectacularly increased the income of Ucureña's peasants, it has broadened their horizons. Young people are receiving considerably more formal education than their parents. In 1966 the average educational level for heads of households was 2.33 years, for their wives, 0.17 years, while for all sons and daughters, ages 13 and over, it was 4.35 years. Fathers state that they would like their children to be something other than farmers; of 142 interviewed, only three wished their sons to remain on the land (Saa:27).

Agrarian reform in the Cochabamba valleys, as elsewhere, has transformed the peasant into an important segment of Bolivian society. He now expects to be socially mobile. Prior to the reform, Cochabamba peasants formed a society of their own with practically no legal rights and little or no hope of mobility into another class. Although their diminutive landholdings today may assure them of no more than a minimum subsistence living, it gives them a dignity they never had before.

THE SOUTHERN VALLEYS

The impact of agrarian reform on Bolivia's valleys diminishes as one goes south from Cochabamba. In these southern areas, its major effect has been the abolition of obligations to former estate owners. Charles Erasmus, who made a survey of Chuquisaca and Tarija in 1963, concluded that most of the rural population was still running households, rather than business concerns, and that the tradition of spending savings on food and drink for religious festivities was still very much alive. In other words, life ways were still those of a basically subsistence-oriented society. He found properties in the region that conformed to all three major types as established in the Agrarian Reform Decree: large (latifundia), medium (mediana), and small (pequeña). In the cases of latifundia, all the land was expropriated and each tenant became owner of the plot or plots that he had used in usufruct before reform. Lands on such latifundia which had formerly been cultivated and maintained for the owner were usually set aside for collective management to the benefit of the former tenants. In the cases of medium properties, all tribute obligations were abolished, though the former owner was allowed to keep the land he directly exploited before reform. Tenants on the small holdings were generally allowed to remain, with no further obligation to former absentee landowners (Erasmus:350–52).

Before reform, the landholding system of the southern valleys shared a number of features with that system previously described for the northern Altiplano. Portions of large- and medium-sized estates worked directly by the owners tended to range from only one-third to one-fifth respectively. This meant that the owners traditionally relinquished two-thirds to four-fifths of their cultivable land to their workers in return for the latter's labor or cash rent. Since redistribution usually followed these traditional lines, the amount of cultivated land redistributed to the peasants by the reform was relatively small. For example, on the 335 properties Erasmus studied in Chuquisaca, only 14 to 17 percent of the cultivated land changed hands; most of this change affected that portion of the estate which had been the owner's demesne. Although collective management was the intent for such lands, seldom did it become the practice. In Erasmus's words:

While these lands were supposed to be operated as collectives by the former *arrenderos,* at all former *latifundios* I visited the collectives had been voluntarily disbanded and the land divided (often into very tiny plots) among the ex-*arrenderos'* landless offspring. (Erasmus:359)

He concludes by saying that "in most cases peasants simply went on working their old *arriendo* with no change other than emancipation from previous fee and labor obligations" (ibid.:359). This left the inequalities in peasant holdings untouched. In Erasmus's sample, such holdings ranged from 1.0 to 15.8 hectares, although there were a few extreme cases, some as small as 0.1 hectares and as large as 648 hectares.

Before the 1952 revolution, peasants in the southern valleys channeled a great deal of their surplus into cash rent. Agrarian reform totally eliminated these obligations, freeing as much as half of the peasants' productive time. Although this did not change their technological base (and thus make them modern farmers), it did enable them to spend more on their fiestas, to eat and dress better, and to enjoy many luxuries previously out of their reach.

Even in those cases where land was not redistributed, the break with the past seems to have been decisive. In Villa Abecia, the administrative head of a small grapegrowing region, elite landholding families, when faced with agrarian reform, quickly dominated its mechanisms and succeeded in keeping their lands as medium-sized properties. Peón labor, however, now negotiates not only for cash wage but also for the size and quality of usufruct plots. The dominance of the traditional elite continues, but a newly independent spirit on the part of the workers is eroding the foundations of traditional society. Now there is dissatisfaction on both sides. The landowning class complains that workers are no longer conscientious, and the workers complain that their wages are too low and that the patrones no longer care for their welfare. Furthermore, increasing numbers of the workers are engaging in seasonal migration to the Argentine cane fields, and when they return, it is to rest not to work (McEwen:passim).

THE ORIENTE

The experience of the Bolivian Oriente is radically different from that of either the valleys, the Yungas, or the Altiplano. Part of an enormous plain that occupies the heart of South America, the Oriente has many types of soils ranging from good to bad. The very best are found along the waterways and, in their natural state, support high forest growth. Between these waterways, much of the territory is covered by a soil type known as *pampa negra* ("black plain") supporting vegetation ranging from sparse pampa grass to small trees and bush in response to varying amounts of rainfall. Far larger sections of the territory, however—some 50 percent of the soils of Santa Cruz—are *pampa blanca* ("white plain") poor, dry, and sandy, barely sufficient for scattered clumps of coarse grass. Stories of the universal fertility of the Oriente are only myths.

Though the Oriente covers 70 percent of Bolivia's territory, it has been estimated that only a tiny fraction, less than one-thousandth of this, is under cultivation. Major exploitative patterns have changed little since the territory was first opened up: agriculture is still concentrated in northern Santa Cruz, raising cattle in the Beni, and collecting forest products in the distant Northeast. Practically no effort has been made to improve the land, and irrigation is unknown.

Although there has been significant expansion in commercial agriculture in the Oriente since the Cochabamba-Santa Cruz Highway was completed in 1954, it has not met the extravagant expectations that existed for the region. A British mission which recently studied the potential of Santa Cruz concluded that, because of shortcomings in soil and climate, subsistence farming will continue to be the predominant economic activity for some time to come (Great Britain Mission:15–17). The slash-and-burn method is still commonly employed in land cultivation, even though it is such a time-consuming technique that one man can work no more than a few hectares per year. The result is that after the first crop or two, the land yield seriously diminishes, forcing the cultivator to temporarily abandon it to fallow and to move on to other land. For northern Santa Cruz, the fallow period may average as much as eight years.

The subsistence cultivators who produce the Oriente's staples fall into four basic types: squatters, tenants, renters, and small farmers. The squatter type is self-explanatory; the tenant is a cultivator who enters into a shares arrangement with the landowner; the renter pays a cash fee for using the land; and the small farmer is an independent operator who, since agrarian reform, has obtained formal title to his parcel.

At the apex of the society are the *finqueros* ("landlords") whose traditional power comes more from their control over labor than over land, for land has always been an abundant resource. Before the Cochabamba–Santa Cruz Highway was completed, the value of labor was, proportionately, so high that a Bolivian economist could write:

Santa Cruz is one of the few places in the world where the work of a farm laborer is much more valuable—within a short time—than a hectare of land. The shortages of labor and the abundance of land are such that there is no one who would pay 10,000 Bolivian pesos for a league of good fertile land situated on the outskirts of the city, while, on the other hand, the same amount or more which a tenant had contracted in debt would be paid in order to have his labor. (Sanjines:393)

Actually then, prior to the enactment of the Agrarian Reform Decree, most finqueros were technically as landless as squatters, but lack of legal title did not prevent them from producing the bulk of the area's commercial agricultural goods. They intimately identified with their land and seldom resorted to the absentee exploitative pattern so common to the highlands. This closeness to the soil neither tarnished their self-image as superior "whites" nor detracted from their status as the wealthy elite (Heath 1960:54).

The finqueros stood in marked contrast to the other landholding minority, for they were the small, independent farmers whose holdings were scattered throughout the countryside, seldom exceeding twenty hectares. So limited were the resources and holdings of these individuals that their real income was often smaller than that of the squatters or renters attached to rich estates, but these farmers' freedom of action was much admired. Their basic problem has traditionally been inadequacy of storage facilities. Faced with imminent spoilage of their crops, they have frequently had to sell them cheaply only to repurchase them at inflated prices a few months later.

Of all the commercial crops of the Oriente, sugar cane has long been the most important. Its production was greatly stimulated during the 1950s when the Bolivian government gave top priority to the development of highly mechanized processing plants, so that the country would no longer be forced to use scarce import funds for sugar and beverage alcohol. Because these plants need quality control, dependable harvest size, and ready delivery involving costly transportation, most sugar cane today is grown on finquero lands. So rapid, in fact, was finquero response to the needs of the sugar refineries that, by the early 1960s, cane production had caught up with demand, and Bolivia actually had some sugar for export. Oriente growers, led to believe that the market was infinitely expandable, soon found to their dismay that they had to submit to fixed quotas imposed by the refineries, and many ended up with large unsalable surpluses. The established price paid for raw cane was too high for Bolivian sugar to compete successfully on the world market (Wessel:24). As a consequence, although cane production rose from a little over two hundred to more than a thousand metric tons between 1958 and 1964, it has, since that date, remained relatively constant (U.S. AID Mission:18).

Rice—the Oriente's second major product today—has been a staple food in the region for generations, though only recently has its production been commercialized. Rice commercialization began in the mid-1950s when a number of finqueros, with the encouragement of the Interamerican Agricultural Service, began to mechanize planting and harvesting procedures. None of their other techniques were modernized, however, so that, in the absence of crop rotation, fertilization, and irrigation, their yield came to no more than it had been when they had previously employed slash-and-burn methods. To complicate matters, the finqueros soon found themselves in competition with immigrant colonies of Okinawans and Japanese, both of whom brought to Bolivia a sophisticated knowledge accumulated through generations of ricegrowing. It was not long before these two groups monopolized the commercial market. Had this market been larger, the immigrants could have been used successfully by the Bolivian government as technical advisors in developing truly massive production. By 1962, however, production had begun to exceed the capabilities of the market. Most Oriente agriculturalists continue to produce some rice today, but, as with cane, their production has expanded only moderately during the present decade (ibid.:18).

Because of the Oriente's traditional labor shortage and its abundance of flatland, agricultural mechanization was looked upon as a great hope during the 1950s. Many finqueros had been traditionally reluctant to mechanize because of the cost of machinery which, for a fully mechanized estate, could come to more than six times the value of the land itself (Loza:66). One of the things that pushed them to reconsider was article 17 of the Agrarian Reform Decree (Avendaño:54), which stated that an Oriente landowner could retain up to two thousand hectares of cultivable land, provided he could prove it was an agricultural enterprise. Proof was to consist in evidence of large-scale investment of developmental capital, salaried labor, and the use of modern technology (ibid.:50).

At the same time that article 17 of the Agrarian Reform Decree was encouraging the finqueros to mechanize, the Point IV (precursor of AID) program of agricultural credit got under way. Using land and crop futures as collateral, finqueros found that they could easily qualify for large loans with which they began to tap a newly established agricultural machinery pool, renting at rates lower than actual operating costs. The simultaneous advent of uncontrolled inflation enabled them to realize enormous profits on goods produced with the rental equipment and to amortize their loans in only one year while still retaining a sum far greater than their usual annual income. By investing practically none of their capital, depending on the labor of others, and assuming practically no economic risk, many thus became wealthy in a single twelve-month period. Unfortunately most of this new wealth was quickly squandered on luxury goods; very little was reinvested for increased production and expanded markets (Heath, 1959:36–38). Reaction to a 575 percent increase in machinery rental rate, implemented in January 1957, indicates prevailing attitudes. By October of the following year, only four of an original twenty bulldozers remained in the region, and these were being used almost exclusively for roads. Land-clearing had largely reverted to hand methods (ibid.:41).

Certain other provisions of the Agrarian Reform Decree also had peculiar effects in the Oriente. A primary example is article 78 (Avendaño:68), which stated that servants, tributaries, squatters, bound laborers, outsiders, etc., were to be declared owners of the parcels that they presently occupied and worked.[7] Finqueros interpreted this as meaning that a landlord had to forfeit to his tenants or squatters any plot customarily held in usufruct. To prevent this from happening, many immediately withdrew all usufruct rights, and some actually fenced their holdings. Thus a provision that gave land to masses of peasants in the highlands tended to have the opposite effect in the lowlands (Heath, 1959:6).

As a region, the Oriente still has such a low demographic density that dispossessed squatters and tenants can easily find unused land, even along major roads and railways. The loss of the ready hands of these squatter and tenant families forced finqueros to look elsewhere for a labor supply. They found it in peasants from Tarija and southern Potosí—people who for years migrated to northern Argentina for seasonal canefield work. Finqueros pay twice as much for this type of labor as they did for their former *camba* ("native Oriente lowlander") hands,[8] but they justify this by arguing that the new hands are more productive and less demanding. The paternalistic responsibility finqueros previously had for their laborers has gone by the board. Relations binding finquero and employee have become impersonal and businesslike; once new workers complete their immediate task, they are paid and dismissed (Heath et al., 1969:339).

North of Santa Cruz, in Mojos and the Northeast, agrarian reform has had the least effect of all. Land there is so abundant in relation to labor that there is practically no fear of expropriation and division. An implicit objective of the decree had been that all Bolivian landholdings be registered and entered on the tax rolls. "Owners" in Mojos and the Northeast quickly learned that the only legal titles were those issued by the National Agrarian Reform Council. Yet many refused entirely to file claims. Their holdings are in such remote places that the cost of transporting and feeding agrarian judges and topographers, added to the cost of legal counsel, would come to more than the true value of the land (ibid.:354–55). What they preferred was to request an outright grant from Bolivia's vast national domain which exonerated them from the payment of delinquent taxes and saved them the trouble and expense of documentation. It also had the advantage of simplicity. Mojeños are convinced that outright grants are handled much faster by the National Agrarian Reform Council than are the supposedly simpler confirmations of title.

MIGRATION

The greatest impact of agrarian reform on the Oriente has probably been in the realm of colonization. The preamble to the reform decree fixed as one of its six basic objectives the stimulation of internal migration to promote a more rational population distribution and to advance national unity by linking the economy of the Oriente with that of the highlands (Avendaño:47). Title VII of the decree set aside selectd empty lands as primary colonization targets, including a belt twenty-five kilometers wide on each side of the country's railways, highways, and navigable waterways, a radius of five kilometers around each town of more than one thousand inhabitants in the tropical and semitropical lowlands, and any other lands that might be designated as such in the future by the government. In these zones preference was to be given to landless peasants, unemployed laborers, returning expatriots, veterans of the Chaco War, and the families of men lost in the 1952 revolution.

One of the first acts of the government in promoting this plan was to create a rural army regiment composed basically of conscripts from the Altiplano and the valleys. This regiment was sent to the area north of the city of Santa Cruz in 1955 to open up new lands for agriculture. Soldiers who wished to stay on as colonists after completion of their term of service were guaranteed free land. Though few of them took up the offer, other highlanders moved into the cleared territory, occupied abandoned barracks, and quickly began a new life by harvesting subsistence crops planted by the military.

In terms of the overall colonization movement, the regions most affected have been the Alto Beni, a region to the northeast of the city of La Paz; the Chapare, a series of convoluted valleys lying between Cochabamba and northern Santa Cruz; and the northern part of the Santa Cruz plain itself. Colonization in these regions may be said to have been of three types: spontaneous, semidirected, and directed. With the first, colonists occupied specific areas, usually along a newly opened road, and then applied for legal titles. With the second, certain infrastructure was provided either by the Bolivian government or by international agencies, but fundamental decision-making with regard to cropping, selection of specific parcels of land, and the building of dwellings was left to the discretion of the individual colonist. With the third, the government or some other agency took charge of selecting the site, choosing the colonists, and providing elaborate aid in the form of tools, seeds, cash loans, medical and educational infrastructure, and technical aid. Of the three types, semidirected colonization has had the greatest success. Spontaneous colonies seldom develop above a very low level of subsistence farming, and highly directed colonies tend to be overly dependent on the paternalism of the sponsoring agency.

As the colonization site nearest to both the Altiplano and the city of La Paz, the Alto Beni has appealed mainly to Aymara-speaking groups. It is a very roughly defined area, lying in a general northerly direction from the city of Caranavi and averaging around six hundred meters above sea level. The vast majority of colonist settlements in the area are of the spontaneous type, but migrants in the Alto Beni's directed projects net six times more annual income than their spontaneous counterparts. The hope is that the Alto Beni will develop into a major cacao-producing area. Success will probably never be more than moderate, however, because of the formidable transportation hurdles separating the colonists from the rest of the country. To ship products to La Paz, they must pay $.80 per hundredweight (Cusak:61).

Spontaneous colonization into the second major target area, the Chapare, began over sixty years ago, but received its greatest impetus in the years immediately following agrarian reform. From the first, settlers have been mainly Quechua-speakers from the Cochabamba valleys; today four-fifths of the area's population can trace its origins to this one ethnic group (Henkel:24–27).

As with their Aymara counterparts in the Alto Beni, most colonists in the Chapare have succeeded in maintaining themselves without any external administration, but productivity has been low, and the two zones stand at the very bottom of the colonization list in return per hectare cultivated (Cusak:51). High transportation costs are largely responsible for this state of affairs although, in the case of the Chapare, the hindrances are not so much impassable mountain barriers as undeveloped road systems. Until means of communication are improved, most of the agricultural production from these rich zones will never reach Bolivia's markets. Two important AID-financed roads currently under development promise to help the situation in the near future.

Since pronouncement of the Agrarian Reform Decree, the area of most intense colonization has been the department of Santa Cruz. Land immediately surrounding the city is more than inviting for it has a mild climate, good soil, and adequate rainfall. Here more directed and semi-directed colonies have developed than in any other part of Bolivia.

Though most government resources have gone into sponsored colonization projects, these have drawn only one-fifth as many people as have spontaneous projects. The resources of the Bolivian government are simply inadequate to cover universally the initial $1,000 per household needed for sponsorship. In order to alleviate population pressures in the highlands, therefore, the country will be forced to continue spontaneous colonization, in spite of its low productivity and chaotic development.

Regardless of where or how they have migrated, certain interesting generalizations seem to hold for all agricultural highlanders who move into the colonies. Nearly one-half learn about colonization possibilities from friends and relatives and only about one-third from governmental propaganda. Nearly one-half have lived in two or more places before finally settling in their colony, and approximately one-fifth have worked in Argentina or some other foreign country (Wessel:33, 47–48, 59–60, 82).

One of the principal objectives of colonization is to improve the level of peasant living, but recent studies indicate, unfortunately, that these levels often remain unchanged. Annual income in the colonies remains about the same, houses are just as poorly built and furnished, and clothing no better than it was in home communities. The only clear economic advantage that migration seems to offer, at least during the first years, is that of a constant food supply (ibid.:34).

The colonization picture would not be complete without some reference to groups of foreign colonists brought in after the 1952 revolution. During the 1950s, agreements were signed between the Bolivian, U.S., Okinawan, and Japanese governments allowing for the entry of several hundred Okinawan and Japanese families. The Okinawans were particularly successful, and it is they who have been largely responsible for the fact that Bolivia is now more than self-sufficient in rice.

Mennonities from the Paraguayan Chaco constitute the only other significant immigrant group. On recommendation of CEPAL (Economic Committee for Latin America), the Bolivian government has been conservative in its search for foreign colonists. Large-scale immigration of colonists could threaten the success of the limited program of internal colonization.

OVERALL IMPACT

Because Bolivia has had a chronic deficit of foodstuffs, agrarian reform was looked upon by many—particularly in the country's urban centers—as a grave threat to the very physical survival of the populace. The consensus among urban dwellers was that peasants were either too ignorant to manage land without direction or, were they to attain sufficient know-how, would be interested only in providing subsistence for themselves and would not make the needed effort to feed the rest of the population.

Correlations between Bolivia's agrarian reform and its level of production have been the subject of much debate, partly because the difficulty of measuring subsistence production on a wide and representative scale has always made statistics on Bolivian agriculture questionable. There is no doubt that the latifundia were inefficient as productive units. Yet, in spite of their antiquated tools and techniques, they *were* self-supporting and *had* for many years succeeded in supplying urban markets with the major portion of their food needs. Their destruction left an organizational vacuum, which, through the emerging rural sindicato network, the Bolivian government exerted considerable effort to have filled.[9] But in the months immediately preceding and following the issuance of the Afrarian Reform Decree, the situation in vast stretches of the countryside was truly chaotic.

Bolivia's five basic foodstuffs have traditionally been: potatoes, wheat, maize, rice, and sugar. There seems to be a general consensus that urban supplies of all these products, except rice and sugar, fell substantially in the years immediately following the decree. Yet by the end of the 1950s, through a reorganization of the productive and marketing systems, supplies of potatoes and maize began to surpass prereform levels, and rice and sugar supplies increased so dramatically that, in terms of value, they alone more than made up for all other alleged production declines.

Before agrarian reform, some goods from free peasant communities and from usufruct peasant estate lands had always filtered into the national economy, but they were of minor importance. The bulk of agricultural products shipped to urban markets came from those portions of estates which landlords operated for their exclusive use (as opposed to those portions—the majority of the land surface—allotted to the peasants in usufruct) and was customarily handled by such landlords acting directly as wholesalers. With agrarian reform, this key linkage in the country's marketing structure was practically eliminated, and the large cash sales previously made in the cities and mines dropped severely and rapidly. But, simultaneously, there mushroomed regional markets where peasants could barter and sell small quantities of produce. New middlemen, primarily from Bolivia's *cholo* ("urbanized Indian") group began to emerge, and independent trucking increased manyfold. A new market system was in the making. Clark is probably correct when he asserts that "the 'apparent' decline in agricultural production after 1952, while true in part, is better explained by marketing adjustments, transportation scarcity, and weather phenomena, with the former by far the more important bottleneck to be overcome during that period" (Clark:23). Indeed, interviews carried out in the Sucre market in 1963 by Charles Erasmus had anticipated these conclusions:

Vendors in the Sucre market . . . who had observed the full cycle of changes since pre-reform times claimed that as much food if not more was now available. While in pre-reform times food came to market in larger units, brought by *hacendados,* it was now being brought in small quantities but by so many small producers that the supply was greater than ever before. Moreover, the peasants could not afford to hold their crops off the market for prices to go up, as the *hacendados* had been accustomed to do, with the consequent periodic shortages and price fluctuations. Now there was always food in season and prices fluctuated less. (Erasmus:361)

Bolivia in general is an underpopulated country, its rate of demographic growth being one of the lowest in Latin America. Yet many pockets of the country have population as dense as that of Puerto Rico and Haiti, and in these places, even after land redistribution, newly married couples are finding that they must either leave their community or else satisfy themselves with a very small land parcel—often no more than a quarter of a hectare. They are thus forced to supplement their income with either cottage industry or outside employment (Saa:29–31). Under such circumstances even moderate demographic increase looms as a threat.

It is not surprising, then, that the major cities of Bolivia—particularly La Paz—are being overwhelmed by young rural migrants. The unfortunate fact is that industrial and urban services are not growing rapidly enough to absorb them. Downtown streets are packed with the unemployed and the underemployed. In keeping with such limited urban opportunities, the countryside, in spite of the scarcity of land, continues to hold many, and the problem of *minifundia* ("very small subsistence land plots") will probably continue for generations to come.

Yet the Bolivian Indian today experiences a freedom and power never before known, freedom that derives from not one but a series of measures related both directly and indirectly to the reform. These include: 1) the abolition of labor tribute and cash rent obligations, 2) the creation of a strong peasant sindicato movement, 3) the granting of universal suffrage, 4) the massive extension of educational facilities, and 5) the distribution, with titles, of millions of hectares of cultivable land to hundreds of thousands of peasant families. There has been much indirect spinoff from these measures. Institutions set up for implementing them, while sometimes falling far short of primary goals, have been extremely fruitful in fulfilling the latent functions of providing new organization and direction to rural communities (Wilkie:12–13).

For the peasant, direct control over one's own labor and increased access to land has not only brought about an enormous expansion of opportunities to earn cash, but it has also contributed significantly to the opening up of direct linkages with the national market and, thus, resulted in a new nationwide distributional system. Such reorientation has been consciously sought by some peasant leaders. In some communities, for example, residents have been obliged by their sindicato officials to bring produce to a central place once a week. Truckers and middlemen have then been persuaded to come into the community for purchasing (Buechler:51).

The 1952 revolution has shaken Bolivian society in an unprecedented way. The landed elite, deprived of their traditional manorial base, have either emigrated or else been forced to adjust and reorient their claim to power. Kachitu stands as an example of their changing destiny—very few of the original vecino families remain in that town today. Of these, some have adjusted and function well as wholesalers or middlemen, while others seem to have lost all hope. To a man, they are in a far weaker economic position than they were in 1952, in spite of the fact that Kachitu is busier than ever.

Those Kachitu citizens who have most benefited from revolution and reform are the Indian peasants who were educated in the local Protestant mission school. Resident North Americans, heading religious, medical, and educational work for the past twenty-five years, succeeded in giving these people skills that have enabled them successfully to manage wholesale businesses, tailor shops, hat making shops, a bakery, a hardware store, an agricultural supply store, and even a bookstore. Such practical uses for education have brought an awakening of interest on the part of many Indian parents who, formerly refusing to let their children go to school, are now the first to encourage them. Symbolically, their daughters are replacing the traditional bell-shaped *polleras* with pleated skirts, and their long braids with short hair. Radios have entered such households and connect the peasant daily with the outside world.

Bolivians do not easily forgive and forget; rather they learn to live with their problems. In today's Kachitu the new "Indian vecino" is accepted, even on the governing council, but in private conversation among the remnants of the old elite he is remembered for what he was before the reform. Because the contribution he makes cannot be ignored, direct interaction between him and the old elite regularly occurs but always with a certain degree of restraint.

The Kachitu case represents only one point along a continuum of responses to agrarian reform. What happened there, however, does demonstrate the importance of the reform for Bolivian society. Elimination of tribute labor freed the Indian from the monolithic hold of the country's small, landed elite, and evidence of this fact may be seen in the thousands of abandoned manor houses and tens of thousands of greatly improved peasant huts that can be found throughout the country today. The psychological dimension of the change has been tremendous, charged with the euphoria of entering into a great new adventure.

In spite of this euphoria, agrarian reform has not raised Bolivia's peasants far above the paleotechnic level of production that prevailed before the revolution, and the likelihood is that they will remain there for a long time to come. There will be gradual expansion into new lands of the Oriente, but this will involve only a small minority of the country's overcrowded highlanders. Rather, the prospect for most peasants today is a slightly improved standard of living combined with gradual cultural homogenization. Rural communities will become more involved in national politics and possibly more effective as major political pressure groups. As this happens, regional differences will become blurred and the peasant will be caught up in a growing proletarization or national popular culture. Deeply rooted in Amerindian tradition, it will be unique in the Americas.

Cultural patterns and prejudices die slowly, and former elites will defend their privileges as long as they possibly can. In the opening chapter of this volume Carter Goodrich describes a Cochabamba official who, just before the revolution, remarked that the only solution for Bolivia was to exterminate the Indians and replace them with European immigrants. In the 1960s a similar official attached to the Bolivian National Planning Board reiterated this feeling by telling me that Bolivia's only hope was to pile all the campesinos together and set fire to them. In spite of revolution and reform, then, campesinos continue to occupy the bottom of Bolivia's social heap. The ideals of the revolution revolved around the concept of an open society with equal opportunity for all. But, to cite only one example of how these ideals have been diverted, the school system set up by the revolutionary government to implement universal education became dichotomized between urban and rural and thus tended to institutionalize traditional caste boundaries. Even at their best, rural schools today tend to prepare individuals for provincial rather than urban leadership.

With all the changes that have occurred, either success in regional politics and commerce or absorption into the semiskilled urban labor pool, is about as high as a peasant can presently hope to climb (Hickman:2). If he aspires for more, the fruits of change can be bitter indeed. Because this is so, the euphoria of reform may eventually give way to widespread and corrosive frustration. Should that ever happen, Bolivia will not have seen the last of violent revolution.

NOTES

1. In almost all Altiplano estates, each peasant had a plot of land around his house, ranging in size from a few hundred square meters to several hectares. This plot, known as the *sayaña,* was usually unitary, though it could be fragmented

through inheritance. Not even the *patrón* ("landowner") dared challenge the peasant's right to it, short of grave cases of misconduct. Farther away from the house-plots were usually *aynokas,* or large sections of land for cultivation in the summer and fallow grazing in the winter. Each peasant, like the patrón, had one or more plots, or *kallpas* within each aynoka. The aynoka as a whole, rather than specific kallpas, was subject to regular crop rotation. *Pegujal* is a term used especially in Bolivia's valleys and refers to small peasant usufruct plots.

2. The *reducción* consisted of gathering together in colonial days of dispersed Indians for the purpose of prosyletization and easy administration. Many of the present-day towns in highland Bolivia trace their origins back to this institution.

3. The 4,000 cases pending in 1966, if conforming to previous established averages of 30 titles each, would have forced the president to sign 4,000 *Resoluciones Supremas* and 120,000 titles. On this basis, it was calculated that for the agrarian reform to proceed as it should, Bolivia's president would have had to have spent about three hours a day just signing resolutions and titles.

4. These figures are cited in Thome, p. 26, and based on sources in the Administrative Department of the National Council on Agrarian Reform.

5. The number that would be referred back to provincial judges was estimated by authorities in the National Council of Agrarian Reform (Thome:5).

6. Thome has noted (p. 18) that, though this inheritance principle derives from an interpretation of articles 2 and 33 of the decree, in practice transfers of property do occur, mainly among members of a grantee's family.

7. Article 78 of the decree granted squatter rights in the following terms:

Those peasants who had been submitted to certain conditions of work and feudal exploitation in the condition as servants, tributaries, squatters, small farmers, bound laborers, outsiders, etc., of 18 years of age or older, those married of 14 years of age or older, and widows with small children, are declared, with the promulgation of this decree, owners of the parcels that they presently occupy and work, until such time as the National Service of Agrarian Reform gives them . . . the rights that belong to them by the definition of small property, or compensates them with collective right to land which will permit them to support their family.

8. A camba may be loosely defined as a manual laborer native to the Oriente.

9. Supreme Decree 03375 of April 30, 1953, made peasant unions and their leaders responsible for the harvest that year and for the planting and harvesting of lands the succeeding years (Avendaño:32–37).

REFERENCES

Avendaño, Walter del Castillo. *Compilación legal de la reforma agraria en Bolivia.* La Paz: Editorial Fénix, 1955.

Buechler, Hans C. "The Reorganization of Counties in the Bolivian Highlands: An Analysis of Rural-Urban Networks and Hierarchies." In *Urban Anthropology: Research Perspectives and Strategies,* edited by Elizabeth M. Eddy. Athens, Ga.: University of Georgia Press, 1968.

Carter, William E. *Aymara Communities and the Bolivian Agrarian Reform.* Social Science Monograph, no. 24. Gainesville, Fla.: University of Florida, 1965.

Clark, Ronald J. *Land Reform and Peasant Market Participation on the North Highlands of Bolivia.* Land Tenure Center Reprint, no. 40. Madison, Wis.: University of Wisconsin, 1967.

Cusak, Patricia L. "The Evolution of Colonization in Bolivia." Mimeographed. Gainesville, Fla.: University of Florida, 1967.

Dandler-Hanhart, Jorge. *Local Group, Community, and Nation: A Study of Changing Structure in Ucureña, Bolivia (1935–1952).* Master's thesis, University of Wisconsin, 1967.

Erasmus, Charles J. "Upper Limits of Peasantry and Agrarian Reform: Bolivia, Venezuela, and Mexico Compared." *Ethnology,* 7, no. 4 (1967), pp. 349–80.

Great Britain, Mission to Bolivia. *La agricultura tropical en Bolivia; sus posibilidades y requerimientos de orientación técnica para su desarrollo.* La Paz, 1962.

Heath, Dwight B. "Land Reform in Bolivia." *Inter-American Affairs,* 12, no. 4 (Spring 1959), pp. 3–27.

————. "Commercial Agriculture and Land Reform in the Bolivian Oriente." *Inter-American Economic Affairs,* 13, no. 2 (Autumn 1959), pp. 35–45.

————. "Land Tenure and Social Organization: An Ethno-historical Study from the Bolivian Oriente." *Inter-American Economic Affairs,* 13, no. 4 (Spring 1960), pp. 46–66.

Heath, Dwight B.; Erasmus, Charles J.; and Buechler, Hans C. *Land Reform and Social Revolution in Bolivia.* New York: Frederick A. Praeger, 1969.

Henkel, Ray. "The Chapare Report: A Study of Directed Colonization in the Bolivian Tropics." Mimeographed. La Paz, 1967.

Hickman, John M. "Colonization and Social Mobility in Bolivia." Mimeographed. La Paz: Iglesia Metodista, 1966.

Léons, Madeline Barbara. "Land Reform in the Bolivian Yungas." *América Indígena,* 27, no. 4 (1967), pp. 689–713.

Loza, José Romero. *El algodón en Bolivia.* La Paz: Empresa Editora "Universo," 1958.

McEwen, William J., ed. *Changing Rural Bolivia.* New York: Research Institute for the Study of Man, 1969.

Patch, Richard W. "Bolivia: The Restrained Revolution." Land Tenure Center Reprint, no. 33. Madison, Wis.: University of Wisconsin, 1961.

Saa, Carlos Camacho. "Minifundia, Productivity, and Land Reform in Cochabamba," Land Tenure Center Reprint, no. 21. Madison, Wis.: University of Wisconsin, 1966.

Sanjines, G., Alfredo. *La reforma agraria en Bolivia.* 2d ed. La Paz: Empresa Editora "Universo," 1945.

Thome, Joseph R. "Problems Which Obstruct the Process of Title Distribution Under the Bolivian Agrarian Reform." In manuscript, 1966.

U.S., Agency for International Development, Mission to Bolivia. *Economic and Program Statistics: Estadísticas económicas no. 11.* La Paz: U.S. Agency for International Development, 1970.

Weeks, David. "Land Tenure in Bolivia." Giannini Foundation of Agricultural Economics Paper, no. 120. Berkeley: University of California, 1947.

Wessel, Kelso L. "Socio-Economic Comparison of Eight Agricultural Communities in the Oriente and the Altiplano." La Paz: Cornell University, 1966.

Wilkie, Mary E. "Report on Bolivia (On the Social Structure of Rural Areas in the Bolivian Altiplano)." Land Tenure Center Library. Madison, Wis.: University of Wisconsin, 1964.

MADELINE BARBARA LÉONS
Towson State College

AND WILLIAM LÉONS
Goucher College

Land Reform and Economic Change in the Yungas

THE PREREFORM YUNGAS

The most important and certainly the most controversial of the social reforms instituted following the accession to power of the *Movimiento Nacionalista Revolucionario* (MNR) in Bolivia in 1952 has been the program of agrarian reform. Through it the *hacienda* was largely destroyed as the dominant agrarian institution of the country while the *colono* ("tenant") laborers of the big estates were transformed into small, peasant landholders. This agrarian reform took place within a context of simultaneous social and political changes which resulted directly and indirectly from the reformist policies of the MNR government. These policies served to open up new opportunities for the peasant cultivators of the country.

The present study examines the economic implications of these developments on the peasant cultivators of the province of Nor Yungas in the context of the structural reorganization of group relations within the

The research upon which this article is based was largely completed during the period from September 1963 to November 1964 and was supported by a grant from the Foreign Area Fellowship Program. The views and conclusions expressed in this paper are those of the authors and not necessarily those of the program. A research grant from the National Science Foundation to carry out studies in the neighboring province of Sud Yungas made it possible to briefly revisit Arapata in 1968. This paper has benefited from the comments of Prof. Arthur Tuden as well as the other contributors to this volume.

total society. It contrasts the patterns of land tenure, labor organization, and marketing in Nor Yungas during the hacienda period with those patterns prevalent a decade after the land reform. By so doing, it demonstrates that the economic reorganization has been responsive to the restructuring of the regional and national society but has not been of equal magnitude in all areas.

In Bolivia the term *Yungas* refers to the semitropical mountain valleys cutting down from the eastern slopes of the Cordillera Real. The richest and most populous area of this extensive geographic zone is to be found in the two adjoining provinces of Nor Yungas and Sud Yungas of the department of La Paz. The Yungas provinces are divided into three major ecological zones, Altiplano, Yungas, and the tropics, dependent on altitude. The changes from one to the other are gradual, but the zones are distinctive. The Yungas zone, consisting of a number of narrow river valleys with rich soils, high precipitation, and lush natural vegetation, is economically the most important. It lies at altitudes between five and eight thousand feet.[1]

Less than one-half of the province of Nor Yungas may be classified in ecological terms as Yungas, however. The northern half of the province lies at lower altitudes and has a tropical climate with higher temperatures and precipitation than in the Yungas zone. This northern area is now a frontier region currently being colonized and has undergone rapid population growth and economic development following the penetration of a road in 1958.

According to the national census of 1950, the total population of the province was 20,635 of which 16,410 were listed as rural and 4,225 as urban. The urban population was concentrated in the old colonial towns of Coroico, the provincial capital, and Coripata. At that time the bulk of the population lived in the Yungas zone, and this continues to be the case despite colonization. Since 1950 there has been considerable population growth as a result of improved health conditions and migrations into the area from the Altiplano. In addition, considerable movement to towns has occurred in the past decade involving both the old colonial towns of the province and recently developed new towns.

The single most important cash crop of the Yungas has been and continues to be coca (*Erythroxylon coca*) from which cocaine is derived. The dried leaves of the coca plant are chewed habitually by the Indian population of the country and reportedly dulls the pangs of hunger, thirst, and fatigue. The production of coca has been declining somewhat in recent years due to a decreasing coca consumption on the part of the more acculturated *campesinos* ("countrymen") and the increasing feasibility of turning to citrus fruit and coffee as alternative cash crops. The production of coffee is largely centered around Coroico, where in recent years it has reportedly become the single most important cash crop.[2] Around the town of Coripata, however, where the land is more suited to its cultivation, coca is still king. The data for this paper are centered primarily around the canton of Arapata, which is politically dependent on the town of Coripata. Here coca is cultivated almost to the complete exclusion of other cash crops.

THE PREREFORM SOCIAL ORDER

Prior to 1952 the Yungas zone of Nor Yungas was a region of haciendas in which only a few communities of small, independent landholders were to be found. The *hacendados* ("hacienda owners") were the province's wealthiest and politically most important citizens. The hacendados rarely lived permanently on their estates but, rather, had establishments in either La Paz or in the provincial towns. Those in the towns often had commercial interests as merchants or owners of the presses for baling coca.

Traditional political conflict between the adherents of the Liberal and the Republican parties occurred between factions of the hacendados and focused on the problem of who should occupy office rather than on differences in the parties' programs. Hacendados as a group were organized into a property owners' society called the *Sociedád de Propietarios de Yungas* (SPY), which had great influence in the political life of the towns as well as in national politics. The hacendados and allied merchants (usually *blancos* ["whites"] but including some mestizos) were recognized in the towns as *la gente decente* or *la gente buena* ("the decent people" or "the good people"). They maintained the integrity and exclusiveness of their group through formal and informal social interaction, endogamous marriage, and education of their children in the capital. Those blancos and mestizos who were poor found work as hacienda administrators, shopkeepers, schoolteachers, artisans, and employees of the local government bureaucracy. They took very little part in local politics.

A further segment of the town's population was classified by the townsmen as *cholos*. Cholos are Indians whose behavior has become, as the local people say, "more refined." They are bilingual, although their first language is usually the Indian tongue, Aymara. The women dress as the Indians do in full skirts, shawls, and derby hats, but the men are indistinguishable from poor mestizos. Cholos are nor primarily agriculturalists but are active in commerce. In Coroico they dominated the town market and a few were artisans.

Although a small number of Aymara-speaking *indios* ("Indians") lived in the towns and cultivated nearby privately owned plots, the vast majority of Indians (and some Negroes as well) lived on haciendas where they occupied land in return for labor obligations. To the blanco and mestizo population they existed only as workers or clients in commerce. They were illiterate, economically exploited, and excluded from political participation.

Through the socioeconomic structure of the hacienda the hacendados controlled their workers and siphoned off the wealth from their estates with little expenditure of capital or effort on their part. The hacienda formed a social unit within which all authority rested with the hacendado or *mayordomo* ("overseer"). Internal disputes were settled by them or, more rarely, were referred to the town *corregidor*, the lowest political official in the national hierarchy. In Arapata he was selected from among the mayordomos by the hacendados and confirmed in office by the subprefect of the province. Outside influences on the estates, such as the permanent settlement of traders or the building of nucleated settlements, were all actively discouraged. Few hacienda workers had been to school or could speak any Spanish; even fewer had served in the army. Thus, the contacts which an Indian might have beyond the boundaries of his own estate were quite limited and usually of a commercial nature.

HACIENDA LAND TENURE

In the core of the canton of Arapata [3] the haciendas varied in size from 112.7 hectares to 2,727 hectares. Five of these estates were small with an average extension of 361.9 hectares, while the three remaining were over 1,000 hectares. The smaller estates all lay along the main access road of the province or were easily accessible from it, while the larger estates were more remote. The smaller and more accessible estates were densely settled; the more remote estates were much larger and relatively underpopulated.

In the canton, as elsewhere in the Yungas, only a relatively small proportion of the total land of each estate was under cultivation for the hacienda. The rest was uncultivated or assigned to the colonos in usufruct parcels. Of the smaller estates in the core area, the smallest had 14.7 percent of its land cultivated for the hacienda; the average for the rest was

4.7 percent. For the large estates this figure dropped to 1.4 percent.[4] Nevertheless, a considerable amount of labor was needed for the cultivation of these hacienda lands. The labor was procured by granting the use of parcels of hacienda land in return for a labor obligation under a variety of arrangements. The three most important tenure categories were those of the *colono,* the *chiquiñero,* and the *yanapero. Arrenderos,* who paid cash rental for plots of land, were uncommon. While the hacienda could also make use of wage labor, on the estates of the canton the employment of paid workers on either a temporary or a permanent basis was used sparingly, if at all.

Colonos.   Colonos, locally called *peones,* were the backbone of the hacienda labor force. These colonos were, for the most part, Aymara-speaking Indians, many of whom had recently moved into the area from the Altiplano. On one estate of the canton and scattered through a few more were Spanish-speaking Negro colonos. A colono received a house and land for his own use on which he could cultivate both subsistence and cash crops. In return, members of the colono's family were obligated to work a stipulated number of days per week on land directly cultivated for the benefit of the owner of the hacienda and to render certain additional personal services. The usual labor obligation was three days per week for both an adult male and an adult female representative of each family. It was possible for a peón family working less than the normal amount of land to work fewer days.

The most onerous of the required personal services was the obligation of the colono and his wife to serve as *pongo* and *mit'ani* respectively, house servants living for a week in the *casa de hacienda* ("estate owner's house"). These obligations were taken on by all the colonos in weekly rotation as was that of the *mulero,* who looked after the mules and livestock of the estate. The *camani,* who oversaw the drying and baling of the hacienda's coca for shipment, served for the four-month duration of a *mita,* one of the triannual coca harvest periods. Many hacendados also used the services of their peones in transportation, road building, construction, and as bearers of burdens.

The labor obligation had been reduced from eight days per family to six days per family in 1945 during the administration of Villarroel. Prior to this reduction in labor obligation, the *patrón* ("landlord") had distributed such foodstuffs from the Altiplano as dried meat and sacks of dehydrated potatoes to his colonos. With the reduction in labor obligation these distributions stopped. Also during the Villarroel administration an attempt was made to outlaw the personal services required of the colonos. In the Yungas this effort was largely unsuccessful; however, on some of the estates colonos were excused from regular hacienda labor the week after they had performed as pongo and mit'ani.

A peón family was generally able to expand its holdings provided the head of the household first obtained the permission of the patrón or administrator. Thus the holdings of the colonos were never equal but reflected the enterprise and labor resources of the different colono households, along with their ability to ingratiate themselves with the hacienda administration. The lands most suitable for the cultivation of cash crops, however, were normally reserved for the expansion of the hacienda's cultivation.

Usually the patrón would intervene in the colono's management of his usufruct lands only if a colono planted on reserved land or defaulted in any of his obligations. In the latter case the colono and his family might be summarily ejected from the estate. Since men and women were both obligated to the hacienda, a widow or widower had to make up the time owed by the deceased partner or risked ejection. To meet the obligation, half-grown boys often performed a man's work in place of their fathers. In those instances where there were no available family members, a substitute would have to be paid to do the work.

Hacienda discipline was often harsh, but the peón who felt himself wrongly or too severely punished could either appeal for supernatural retribution or escape to another estate. If short of hands, his new patrón would protect him. Without such assistance, former peones recount, it was often impossible for a colono to procure traveling papers from the local police, unless he could obtain a substitute who would be willing to assume his obligations to his former patrón. If he left without the proper documents, he was liable to be recaptured by the police or the hacendado's men and punished. If the consent of both the hacendados concerned was obtained, however, a peón and his family could move from one estate to another quite openly. By this mechanism accessible estates were kept from becoming overpopulated.

A consideration of the experiences of one ex-peón, Hernán Condori,[5] an old man at the time of the land reform, may help to flesh out the picture of hacienda life presented above:

Hernán Condori and his sister inherited the hacienda obligations of their deceased father. His sister married and left the estate. Hernán left to work on his own on available land in a nearby property which was difficult of access and barely populated. The administrator found out where he was and sent two retainers to bring him back. He was imprisoned, beaten, and forced to make up the time he had missed on the hacienda. On a subsequent occasion he was beaten by the administrator for failing to complete some task and this time was thrown off the estate. He went to live on a neighboring estate where he worked for a widow. He then received land from the owner of that hacienda and entered as a full-fledged peón. Over the years he was beaten many times and once had his arm broken by an administrator. He considered leaving on many occasions, but by this time he had extensive permanent crops planted on his own usufruct lands which he was reluctant to abandon.

Although the patrón owned all the land, the usufruct of the peones over their own parcels was quite permanent and was transferred to their heirs provided they did not leave nor were ejected from the estate. This was particularly true in the case of land planted in coca and coffee, both permanent crops representing considerable labor investment and standing wealth.

When a youth reached his late teens, certain fields from his parents' holdings would be turned over to his management. He could dispose of the produce as he wished. As long as the young man remained single and in the household of his father, he had no direct obligation to the hacienda. Marriage was the mark of maturity, not only in the eyes of one's fellow peones but also to the hacienda administration. The administrators, usually short of labor, would often put pressure on a grown young man to establish a household and inscribe himself as a full peón with the hacienda. Often the mayordomo would overrule parental objections to a marriage in order to acquire the additional labor of a new peón family. Or, if the young man were willing but the woman he desired reluctant, the mayordomo would try, often successfully, to coerce her by threats of imprisonment or beatings. On becoming a full-fledged peón in his own right, a young man was also entitled to receive additional land for both subsistence crops and *cocales* ("coca fields") from the hacienda. After his marriage he would be assigned more of his father's improved fields. On the death of the father the remaining family land would be divided among the heirs.

Chiquiñeros.[6]   The category of chiquiñero accommodated the small but steady stream of migrants from the Altiplano to the Yungas haciendas. An individual new to the area could be given a small cocal and some land for subsistence crops (but no house) by the patrón in return for one day of labor per week from both the head of the household and his spouse. This arrangement could be terminated at will by either party.

Should the individual desire access to more land, however, he would have to enter the hacienda as a full-fledged peón.

Some migrants used the chiquiñero arrangement as a trial period before permanently attaching themselves to a particular hacienda. Other migrants, however, conceived of it as a temporary arrangement from the start. They would develop a cocal only in order to sell it to a resident peón. The transfer of money represented compensation for the improvements on the land, not sale of the land nor of the usufruct rights per se.

Yanaperos.   The yanapero also received land for labor, but in this case the terms were formalized in a contract, since he did not live on the estate. The labor obligation owed by the yanapero was calculated in terms of so many days' labor per mita, based on the amount of land involved. This labor obligation might, on occasion, be cancelled by a money payment or the delivery of an equivalent value of seedling coca plants. Normally the land that the yanapero received was planted in coca. If the cocal had just been planted, the labor obligation was temporarily reduced until the field came into full production. According to the standard yanapero's contract for land on any of the estates of José Marie Gamarra, one of the largest landholders in the Yungas, the yanapero was also obligated to give one or two days of labor during each mita for general hacienda upkeep, such as road repair. The yanapero could terminate the arrangement at will by abandoning the land parcel or selling his contract to another who would compensate the outgoing yanapero for the improvements he had made on the land.

Both Indians and mestizos could be yanaperos. The Indians usually worked along with the colonos of the estate during their obligated time. Mestizos, on the other hand, usually rendered a different type of service to the hacienda, often involving the transportation of goods rather than direct work on the land.

LABOR ORGANIZATION

As the patrón was often absent, the day-to-day management of the estate fell to the administrator who was locally called either *administradór* or mayordomo. He in turn appointed one or two *jilicatas* ("overseers") from the ranks of the colonos to keep track of the quality of their work and the fulfillment of labor obligations. It was the jilicata who usually administered whippings to those who failed to maintain work discipline. The colonos all worked under this supervision the same days of the week, usually Monday, Tuesday, and Wednesday. This group labor was known as *faena*. The faena was given a festive character when new cocales were put in for the hacienda. At this time, while the men labored at this arduous task, the women would prepare a large meal supplemented with contributions of purchased items such as noodles and alcohol from the patrón.

The peón family had several means of mobilizing the labor necessary to fulfill its obligations to the hacienda and, hopefully, to expand its own holdings. One of the most basic of these was the manipulation of household composition. The larger the household, the more hands there were available to fulfill hacienda obligations. Consequently, families often had an extended character with attached relatives and *criados*, who were adopted children of semiservant status.

Among themselves the peón families utilized labor exchange in order to mobilize work groups larger than one household. The two important mechanisms for labor exchange were *aini* and faena. The aini group was a small, cooperative work group formed on the basis of a short-term labor exchange between relatives, *compadres* ("ritual kinsmen"), and neighbors. The assembly of a much larger group of men for a single task, such as putting in a new cocal for one of the colonos, was also called faena. Among the peones faena work would be done in a festive atmosphere with the host providing refreshments.

The hacienda colonos were not solely reliant on their own families and fellow colonos for labor. In Nor Yungas there has long been a tradition of temporary labor migration from the Indian freehold communities of the Altiplano. In these communities the land base was insufficient to support the population, and seasonal labor was one way of supplementing incomes. These migrants would work for Yungas peón families for periods ranging from a few weeks to several months. These workers, *utawawas*, would be compensated with room and board and a small daily cash wage. Except on certain estates where the hacendado was characterized as *malo* ("bad"), an utawawa could substitute for a peón in his required labor service to the hacienda. Temporary workers of this kind were not employed directly by the hacienda administration in this area.

MARKETING

Each hacienda had its own coca press for compressing the dried coca leaves into more compact bundles known as *tambores* for easier shipment. Hacendados usually sold their coca and other cash crops in La Paz, although sometimes middlemen would buy the baled coca in the Yungas and would themselves transport it out of the area. In the canton of Arapata the peones sold most of their coca to the owners of coca presses in the town of Coripata. They sold either directly or through the mestizo representatives of the presses, called *rescateros,* who toured the countryside. The press owners lent money to the colonos or extended them credit in the stores which they also frequently owned. A peón in debt to a press owner would be obligated to sell coca to him at somewhat below the prevailing price. In addition, Indian traders from the Altiplano, known as *cocatakis,* bought coca on a small scale from the peones. They did not have the coca baled but bought only as much as they could carry loose in large sacks on their back.

Within the memory of the oldest informants, crops have always been sold for cash, and many essential items purchased. Clothing, tools, soap, matches, and small manufactured items were bought as were non-locally produced staples such as lard, sugar, and noodles. Dried meat, dried fish, cheese, and potatoes in many forms were often obtained on a small scale from Altiplano traders, cocatakis, and utawawas. These items were also available in the town markets of Coripata and Coroico along with other normally purchased commodities.

THE POSTREFORM YUNGAS

Life in the Yungas was altered profoundly by the land reform and other social, economic, and political reforms instituted by the MNR government. From the standpoint of the peasant, the years after the revolution have witnessed a rise in his standard of living and a transformation in the quality of his life in a satisfying direction. The change in terminology from *indio* ("Indian") to *campesino* ("countryman") as an indication of the peasants' increasing social and political importance has often been noted.[7] For the Yungas peasants the introduction of schools into the rural communities and their increasing contact with the capital have made for more social mobility than was previously possible. The coincident development of the Caranavi and Alto Beni colonization regions has allowed for potentially greater spacial mobility. Nevertheless, despite the fact that the system has been relaxed somewhat, it must be kept clearly in mind that the campesino still remains at the bottom of the social and political hierarchies.

Following the land reform, that power of the old provincial elite based on land ownership was undercut but not entirely eliminated. Those former hacendados who remained in the province fell back on their commercial interests and social prestige, and those who left permanently reestablished themselves in the cities. Commercial interests came to dominate the towns, and the real beneficiaries on the provincial level were those mestizos and cholos who were in a position to take advantage of the new developments.

At the same time the peasants, under government sponsorship, were organized into *sindicatos* ("unions") through which they were given a political voice for the first time. Although the Yungas peasants did not play the politically independent role that peasants assumed in some other parts of Bolivia, they soon learned to use their influence on a national government which was growing more and more dependent on peasant support as time went by. Between 1952 and 1964 local government offices, although not occupied by campesinos, were held by men nominally committed to their interests. By this means, the influence of the national government's policy on the campesinos was no longer mediated by the hacendados. Although the old provincial elite was far from eclipsed, it was forced to reorganize its own bases of power, and there were now alternate political channels through which the peasants could pursue their own self-interest.

Following the counterrevolution led by the military in November 1964, a great part of the political gains of the peasantry was eliminated. The peasant sindicatos, while continuing to be important in the local communities, lost most of their leverage on the national level. Many of the landowners who had previously fled their estates returned to work them at this time, and the former hacendados began to resurface politically in the towns and cities. Most of the economic changes which the previous decade had witnessed, however, were not so easily reversible.

The peasant is now presented with a far greater range of alternatives among which he may make meaningful choices, and in no area is this more apparent than in the economic sphere. One of the primary manifestations of both the new level of aspiration on the part of the campesinos and the new potentialities for achievement has been the development of a series of nucleated campesino settlements throughout Nor Yungas, paralleling developments of a similar nature on the northern Altiplano. The largest of these new towns and one of the first to be developed is the town of Arapata which is located midway along the main road connecting Coroico and Coripata. Arapata grew from a handful of houses in 1950 to a town with a population of 751 full- and part-time residents in 1964. By 1969 the town had grown considerably over that number. The bulk of the town's population is drawn from the surrounding estates augmented by a number of shopkeepers and craftsmen from neighboring towns and the Altiplano. Because of its strategic position, the future of the town as a commercial and political center is assured.

THE LAND REFORM

In most of the canton of Arapata the agrarian reform proceedings affecting the estates were completed prior to 1963. All properties were judged to be medium-sized properties although, considering the traditional technology employed, the lack of capital investment, and the use of the colono system, they might equally well have been judged latifundia, subject to total expropriation. This decision meant that in all the estates, with one exception,[8] the ex-patrón was left with at least the lands which had been directly under cultivation for him. Many were given about twice as much as this. In one estate the hacendado was granted the full 150 hectares permissible as a medium-sized holding. Nevertheless, none of these ex-patrones stayed on in the immediate area and several entirely abandoned any effort to cultivate their land.

Since much of the land previously under cultivation for the hacienda was abandoned or poorly cared for, the quantity of coca reaching the market from hacienda sources was diminished considerably. However, this same period witnessed the resupply of the market through increased production on the part of individual peasants. Many peasants were able to expand their prereform holdings, and since their labor was no longer obligated to the hacienda, they could intensify the effort expended on their own land. Furthermore, the establishment of a local marketplace in the town of Arapata where a variety of subsistence crops could be purchased at a reasonable price resulted in a greater proportion of the land being devoted to cash crops. This expansion of cash crops has occurred on an individual basis since cooperatives have generally been unsuccessful.

On all but three estates in the core area of the canton, land was set aside for a campesino cooperative either from the abandoned hacienda fields or from uncultivated lands. Only in those areas where hacienda fields already in production were included has there been any attempt to maintain the cooperative. In all cases but one, mismanagement and lack of interest have combined to negate any potential profit. On the one estate where the cooperative was successful enough that the profits realized could be used to construct a large school and other public facilities, there is still no intention of persisting with the cooperative beyond the life of the standing cocales.

Around Arapata there has been some concern over government propaganda and so far unenforced legislation against coca cultivation. As a result, some peasants have made a conscious effort to diversify their cash crops through the augmentation of coffee and fruit cultivation. This contrasts with the prereform period when almost all the coffee and fruit produced was for home consumption. However, coca still provides the greatest return and continues to overshadow any competition.

The framers of the agrarian reform decree did not seek to remedy differences in wealth or landholdings which existed among the peones of the haciendas. Only on estates with an excess of land were the holdings equalized as each full-fledged ex-colono received the full ten hectares permissible under the law as a small property. In this respect the distinction between large and small estates assumed considerable importance after the reform.[9] Ex-colonos from the more accessible properties were generally granted title to the plots of land they previously held in usufruct with perhaps some supplementation of very small holdings. For example, in Santa Ana, one of the canton's estates, the average size of the land parcel granted was four and eight-tenths hectares, with a range from one-tenth of a hectare to ten and a half hectares. Individual wealth, however, is not directly correlated with the amount of land owned but rather with the amount planted in coca. In Santa Ana in 1964, the spread in the production of coca was equally dramatic ranging from about six *cestos* [10] per year to over two hundred seventy.

Internal differentiation within the community has increased in the past decade. The distinction between the well-off and the poor peasant has become more meaningful. Granting individual exceptions, wealthy peasants are more acculturated to mestizo norms, buy and sell more in the market, and are more likely to have *compadrazgo* ("ritual kinship") relations with traders and mestizos from outside the community. Poor peasants have correspondingly less access to these economic and political advantages.

During the hacienda period the fiesta system served as almost the only legitimate outlet for a display of wealth. At the present time such economic differences among campesinos are more readily translatable into differences in living standards and styles of life. The construction of modern houses with more rooms and better circulation of air and the purchase of material items such as radios, lamps, sewing machines, and even trucks have come to rival fiesta expenditures for the attainment of prestige. The drinking of beer among friends in Arapata on Sundays has similarly become an important channel through which prestige may be acquired.

Since the destruction of the hacienda system and the organization of peasant sindicatos, economic advantage can be translated not only into social prestige but also into political power and authority. On the local level campesinos now govern their own communities through the local sindicatos and staff the regional organization which is responsible for the articulation of these local political units with regional and national government. During the MNR period sindicato officials could not only work through the sindicato hierarchy but also operate informally in influencing regional and national politics through direct appeal to officeholders, agencies of the national government, and the president himself. In the canton of Arapata political authority as exercised through the holding of an important office in the local and regional sindicato structure is correlated, with certain exceptions,[11] with above average economic resources.

Despite these developments complete bifurcation between rich and poor in the countryside is inhibited by the fact that at present all the peasants own some land and are very reluctant to sell their small holdings to either fellow peasants or merchants. The conspicuous expenditures now required of both political authorities and fiesta sponsors function as leveling mechanisms as well.

LAND TENURE

One of the factors which apparently contributes to institutionalizing a gap between rich and poor peasants is the newly emerging land-tenure system. Although during the hacienda period the traditional claims on the use and inheritance of usufruct parcels were usually honored, there were also several sources of flexibility in land allotment built into the system. The first of these was the right of the hacienda administration to redistribute unutilized lands. The second was the movement of a colono from one estate to another upon which he lost all claim to the lands he had cultivated. This change in personnel, although infrequent, also worked to distribute the population somewhat more evenly among the several estates of the region. Finally peón families with sufficient labor resources frequently exercised their option to increase their holdings by petitioning the patrón for permission to work additional land. The agrarian reform transformed this flexible system of preferential land usufruct rights, within which the heirs had alternative sources of land and which was subject to the ultimate disposition of a higher authority, into a more inflexible system of private property.

Despite the fact that as a result of the agrarian reform land titles of outright ownership have been distributed, the amount of land a man actually has at his disposal cannot be ascertained simply by knowing the amount of land to which he has title. Most of the deviations which exist reflect the prereform patterns of land transfer among the colonos of the estate. Since the land reform, use of land can be acquired by a campesino in any of the following six ways: 1) inheritance, 2) assignment of usufruct rights, 3) marriage, 4) division of unassigned or communal holdings, 5) rental, and 6) purchase.

Inheritance. Inheritance is the single most important source of permanent land acquisition. The general rule of inheritance is that, upon death, a person's land should be divided equally among his heirs. The determination of heirs and the actual division, however, is influenced by many competing claims.

A woman who has been legally married has the right to inherit her husband's property after his death and vice versa. However, she does not automatically inherit all his land unless all her children are minors. If any of the children are grown, they will come into their fair share of the inheritance at this time. The portion remaining to the mother will depend on the number of minor children she has to support.

A *concubina* ("woman not legally married") has no legal claim to the property of her deceased husband, no matter how stable the union had been, unless a will has been drawn up which specifically names her as an heir. She may, nevertheless, be allowed to control the land which is the rightful inheritance of the couple's recognized children if the children are still minors. Should she remarry, her right to administer the land usually ceases and is assumed by one of the relatives of the deceased man. The concubina does have a legal claim to any land which the couple had purchased subsequent to their union and as a result of their joint effort.

Although it is recognized legally that sons and daughters should inherit equally, in practice the sons inherit most or all the land. The girl is felt to be partially compensated by inheriting her mother's implements, such as pots and other cooking equipment. A girl's inheritance rights in land remain ambiguous and influenced by the countervalent claims of the male heirs. Expectations of a dowry of land-use rights at a girl's marriage or an inheritance of land which is not forthcoming often generate considerable bitterness and ill feeling between a young couple and the wife's parents.

Theoretically all sons, at least, are expected to inherit equally, but a father may wish to divide the land unequally or to disinherit one of his sons entirely. The family of one of the officials of the regional campesiono sindicato illustrates a case of this kind. Since this official is economically better off and politically more sophisticated than his compatriots, this is not a typical case. It does, however, illustrate the intricacy of such inheritance tangles.

Arturo Choque lives in an extended family arrangement with his father. His brother quarreled with his father years before and relations between them were broken. Arturo maintained it would be illegal for a man to completely disinherit one of his sons to profit another. Therefore, he is arranging to buy his father's land during the latter's lifetime for a grossly inflated price. This is designed to prevent the brother from repaying half the purchase price and claiming half the land. Money may not even be expected to change hands in the transaction, but, if it does, Arturo will get all or most of it back at his father's death.

Although it is becoming increasingly common for a person to leave a witnessed will, most people as yet do not. In the absence of a will the *ancianos* ("older, respected men") of the local community gather together to decide on a fair division of the land, just as they did during the hacienda period. A variety of different factors are taken into consideration, such as who actually worked the land, who took care of the mother or father if they were incapacitated or infirm, and who assumed the burial responsibilities.

The criterion of who actually worked the land is a very important one. On this basis, unrecognized children and others who are not direct lineal descendants of the owner of the land have valid claims on inheritance. This category includes all the dependents of the household, such as stepchildren, adopted children, and criados. Theoretically, if they worked equally with the lineal heirs, they should inherit equally, but in practice they are not in a strong position to press their claim to an equal share.

Arranging for the wake and burial of the landholder is very important in establishing differential claims on the land. Expenses for food and alcohol consumed during the eight-day wake, purchase of a crypt, and payment for masses for the dead are very high, and he who takes on the responsibility for this final rite of passage often assures his claim to the property of the deceased as well. Even when a formal will is drawn up, inheritance is often made conditional on the performance of mourning duties and payment for requiem masses.

Assumption of the burial obligations is also used to legitimize transfer of land when there are no heirs. In this instance a man without heirs will, before his death, arrange with either a private party or the peasant sindicato of the community to pay for burial expenses and masses in return for the land title. In those few cases where this kind of transfer has actually taken place between individuals, the amount of land involved has been small and the expenditures were equivalent to the purchase price. In the one case in San Juan where the sindicato acquired land in this manner, several young men have divided the land among themselves with the approval of the sindicato. Although they have not yet paid the sindicato for this land, it is expected that they will do so.

Assignment of Usufruct Rights.   The practice of assigning land plots to unmarried boys still continues, and when a young man marries, it is now customary for his father to give him the use of some land, including cocales, from his own holdings. A father is not under the same obligation to provide a daughter with the usufruct of some land when she marries. Whether or not a girl does obtain such land depends on factors of personality, competition of claims of other siblings (particularly males), and the extent of land controlled by the father. These are much the same factors which govern female inheritance of land.

The case of Antonio Luna illustrates the diversity in sources of land actually worked by an individual. Antonio, thirty years old and from Santa Ana, works a total of four and a half hectares. Two hectares are his own, granted to him by the reform, and one hectare was assigned to his wife by her father when she married. Additionally, he works one and a half hectares of his widowed mother's land. His mother owns a total of five hectares and has five living children, some of whom are too young to control land on their own. Antonio anticipates, however, that the land will be divided equally among the five children at her death, and he will be obligated to give up one-half hectare at that time.

Land to which a man has received title or which he has cleared himself is indisputably his own, but land which he receives from his parents retains its character of usufruct until their death. They continue to retain a degree of control over the use to which the land is put. One young man wished to plant an improved type of orange tree which he had seen at an experimental station on such land and to irrigate them as well. His parents were opposed to this, and in order to avoid a quarrel he abandoned the scheme.

A legal spouse inherits or shares with the children all the property of a deceased mate. However, this right does not automatically apply to usufruct lands, if the parents who granted the land are still living. Nevertheless, the claims of the surviving spouse are strong, especially if there are living children. In such cases a compromise settlement is usually worked out.

Marriage.   Although females are at somewhat of a disadvantage in inheritance, there are circumstances under which a woman can control a considerable amount of land. The first of these is when there are no male heirs or when the brothers of an adult girl are still immature. The second occurs when a woman is widowed while childless or with immature children. In the latter case, the woman often inherits considerable land as her husband's heir. Marriage with a woman who controls land affords an opportunity for a local young man to augment his holdings and provides the only way, albeit an important one, for outsiders to acquire claims on land in the community.

Altiplano men who come to the community, either as traders or temporary workers, are often quite frank about their desire to marry local women in order to acquire land. Marriage into an established Yungas family has long been the mechanism by which much spontaneous permanent migration to the Yungas has occurred in the past. The marriage of widows to men often many years their junior is common in the Yungas.[12] Usually the junior male partner is from outside the community. The man wishes to acquire access to land, and the widow needs someone to help her look after her holdings. If they marry legally, the husband will inherit equally with the children; if not, he will at least control the land in the interim. Such arrangements often end badly, however, with the young man being charged with being lazy, not looking after the land properly, spending money on himself, and having extramarital affairs.

Marriage by an outsider with an unmarried girl provides less immediate return but has a greater chance of permanency. An outsider who marries into a family with an adequate land base will normally continue to live in the household and to work the land of the girl's father. When the couple finally receives land as a grant or an inheritance, the man will be considered to have established his claim to it through the labor he has contributed to the household.

Division of Unassigned Holdings. After the land reform, even on the more densely settled estates, some land still remained after the estates were divided on the basis of prior claim established by recent use. This land had been previously unexploited or used communally for pasture, and most of it was relatively poor and unsuited to the cultivation of coca. Despite this, it was not long before all such land had been claimed, either by young men or by mature men expanding their holdings.

Since little grazing land is now available, cows can no longer be kept in the community, although Santa Ana, one of the estates affected, supported seventeen head just prior to the reform. In San Juan, an adjoining estate, peasants are planting subsistence crops in land which legally belongs to the proprietors, but the owners have so far blocked attempts at the planting of permanent cash crops on their property. At the present time, now that uncultivated land is no longer available, young men are almost entirely dependent upon their fathers, or the head of the household in which they reside, for land.

Rental. It is possible for a campesino without enough land to rent some from another with more adequate holdings. Only land for subsistence crops may be rented, never land planted in cash crops. The rental may be in cash, but it is more likely to be paid in labor on the land of the renter. These rental agreements are of a short duration, because it is thought that, under the principle of the agrarian reform law, he who works the land has established a claim to it. By extension, a worker who has worked continuously for the same employer for several years has claim to part of the land that he has helped cultivate. Land disputes arising from the claims of workers and renters have occurred. Therefore, at the present time, rental and work agreements rarely last more than a year.

Purchase. Individual title to land as private property along with the concomitant right of control over the disposal of the property has, of course, been made possible as a result of the land reform. However, the conceptualization of land rights held by the local campesinos reflects the recent history of agrarian strife and falls somewhat short of absolute rights of disposal.

The actual control of the campesino over his land is modified by the effective interest which the peasant sindicato of the community continues to maintain over the land within its jurisdication. It is said that just as during the hacienda period the patrón owned the land, now the sindicato almost owns the land. The sindicato makes it its business to see which owner is cultivating his land and which one is letting it go. Following the slogan, "land to he who works it," noncultivation or neglect of the land weakens ones claim to it in the eyes of the community. When young men having title or claim to land leave the community to work in the city, for example, they have difficulty in reasserting their claim against those of their relatives who remain behind.

Similarly, the sindicato, acting in behalf of the community, is considered to have the right to expel persons from the community for gross breaches of moral conduct. Those expulsions which have taken place in recent years all have involved persons who have married into the community, but it is generally agreed that the sindicato also has the right to expel one who holds clear title to land in the community. In this eventuality, still hypothetical, it is said that the land would be sold to someone else in the community and the money delivered to the exile. Significantly enough, these same informants say that sindicatos which have been organized in *comunidades indígenas* ("free landholding communities") do not have the right to eject an unwanted neighbor in this way. As they see it, the ownership of land in these communities did not derive from the agrarian reform, and, consequently, the sindicato does not have the same authority over it.

The most common instance in which the interest of the sindicato manifests itself concerns the transfer of land. Everyone is aware of the fair going rate for different types of agricultural land. Outright sale of agricultural land is rare in the canton of Arapata, despite the fact that most campesinos feel they could, or would like to, utilize even more land than they have. Land ownership is considered good in itself; conversely, selling land is bad. One woman who sold some land which she owned in another ex-hacienda (land which was much too far away for her to work herself) was subject to considerable moral censure. The presently maturing generation of young men, as a result, cannot easily obtain land through purchase. When sale of land does occur, sindicato officials must be present, and the transfer must be approved in a sindicato meeting of the community. The transaction is recorded in the record books of either the local or the regional sindicato. In each land transfer recorded in these books the approval by the sindicato is directly noted. If a person should flaunt this procedure and sell land without prior sindicato authorization, which is unusual, he may be denounced to higher regional sindicato authorities. In the one case of this nature which occurred in San Juan the ex post facto transfer was allowed to stand. How far the community is prepared to go when directly challenged in this way is contingent on how outraged they feel by the particular case.

Sindicato approval would be obtained with little difficulty in the cases of intracommunity transfer and would meet with slightly more resistance in the case of transfer to a person from a neighboring community. However, there is much resistance to alienation of the land by sale to someone from outside the area—specifically the mestizos and campesinos from the Altiplano.

The above discussion does not apply to the land which has now been incorporated into the growing town of Arapata, although it, too, was granted to individuals as the direct result of the agrarian reform. House sites in the town are bought and sold with fewer restrictions than are involved in any other kind of land transfer. Sites may be routinely sold without prior sindicato approval and may be purchased by outsiders. However, the sindicato is still capable of blocking or holding up land transfers in Arapata in specific cases where objections arise.

ORGANIZATION OF LABOR

The expansion and intensification of cash-crop production in the canton has been possible not only because the ex-colonos have been freed of labor obligation to the hacienda, but also because of the increasing availability of both supplementary sources of labor and of the cash to pay for it. Before the agrarian reform, wage labor was much less common than at the present time. Wage laborers are divided into two categories, *jornaleros,* local, day laborers, and *utawawas,* who live with the family and receive room and board as part of their compensation. Most utawawas are seasonal migrants from the Altiplano; jornaleros are recruited from among the ranks of the poorest local peasants and unmarried young people. They are paid a cash wage of forty-five cents to sixty cents per day and are expected to provide their own food. Since they are local residents, no question of room and board arises. With the increasing fractionating of holdings and the closing of access to additional sources of land, there are now more jornaleros with more available time than formerly. Jornaleros have no permanent labor relations with any of the families they work for, often working only a few days with one family before hiring out to another or going back to their own work. At present there are a few local people who support themselves exclusively from wage labor. These are primarily unattached women who have come originally from the Altiplano or other parts of the Yungas.

The number of seasonal migrants from comunidades indígenas of the Altiplano seems to have increased in recent years. Some of the wealthier peasants may have up to ten of these utawawas living in compounds with them during the busiest time of the year. Only the poorest of the peasants do not utilize seasonal laborers, and during the peak agricultural seasons there are rarely enough laborers to meet the demand.

Seasonal laborers may enter into two forms of labor arrangements with a family. Under the first, accommodating both men and women, the worker agrees to work with the family in harvesting and other light work for which his compensation is based on the number of days he works. In 1964 the wage paid to utawawas was about forty-two cents per day plus room and board for men and was slightly less for women.

The second type of labor arrangement, open only to males, is *contrato* ("contract labor") in which one or several workers agree to perform certain heavy jobs, such as clearing overgrown land, making cocales, or weeding, on the basis of a fixed, agreed upon compensation for the task. Tasks performed by contract are quite arduous and the compensation is considerably higher. Jornaleros may also make contrato arrangements.

Charles Erasmus has reported for Latin America as a whole that, in response to the growing importance of a cash economy, there is a decline in both festive and exchange labor and a corresponding increase in wage labor.[13] This trend is clearly observable in the canton of Arapata at the present time. Faena work parties are becoming less and less frequent in agriculture. Aini, the traditional form of exchange labor, is still practiced among relatives, neighbors, and compadres, but it is being increasingly augmented by wage labor.

Campesinos often say they prefer wage labor to aini, because aini labor is less reliable. Often those with whom aini arrangements have been made do not work as long a day as a paid worker. Contract labor needs no supervision, and the employer loses nothing by work stoppages in inclement weather. Additionally, in aini, the necessity to pay back the workday in kind is often onerous. For these reasons there are several well-off campesinos with large holdings who no longer engage in aini but use wage labor exclusively.

Aini does not seem to be in danger of disappearing, however, as it is still an effective way of obtaining extra labor without cash outlay. Since land was not distributed equally after the reform, many families have small holdings which do not absorb their full time. For them, exchange labor continues to be preferable. In addition, a man is not likely to be able to fill all his labor needs through wage labor. The amount of labor available for hire, although more abundant now than formerly, is limited and labor shortage is a perennial cause for complaint. Wealthier peasants find aini unprofitable, but subtle social pressures from friends and compadres to engage in labor exchange are often difficult to resist. In this way aini may serve as a leveling function by counteracting the trend to petty landlordism among the wealthier peasants. As a result most families fulfill their need for outside labor through a combination of aini and wage labor. Individual work parties are often made up of workers recruited in both ways.

CONTEMPORARY MARKETING

Most changes in marketing patterns which have occurred since the agrarian reform have been directly associated with the growth of the town of Arapata. These changes revolve around the establishment of stores in Arapata, the establishment of a weekly market, and the expansion of large-scale coca-buying by Altiplano traders.

Consumption. Since the growth of Arapata, most of the purchases which the local campesinos may wish to make can be acquired in its stores or marketplace. This is in contrast to pre-1952 patterns where such purchases were made—in much reduced quantities—in the towns of Coroico and Coripata.

Stores. In November 1964 there were thirty-nine stores in Arapata, but the exact number shifts constantly as stores open and close. Of the thirty-nine, there were six establishments of craftsmen and an equal number of small restaurants. Most stores sell the same limited range of commodities. A medium-sized store would stock the following: alcohol, beer, soft drinks, matches, sugar, salt, noodles, rice, canned sardines, soap, kerosene, and dried hot peppers. Smaller stores sell only a selected few of these commodities, while a few larger ones also sell wheat, flour, spices, candles, chocolate, candy, cooking oil, fat, confetti, magical supplies, and bread. Only a few of the largest stores in the center of town have for sale, in limited quantities, manufactured items such as pots, dishes, razor blades, nails, batteries, school supplies, and other small items.

The largest stores in town are run by mestizos who came originally from the established Yungas towns and by campesinos of Altiplano origin. Many of the large storekeepers also buy coca and extend credit on this crop. Smaller stores are maintained by craftsmen and young men recently married into the community, all primarily of Altiplano origin. In 1964 only eleven of the shops were run by locally born persons, all of whom cultivated their own land in addition. Such stores are the smallest in town and are open only a few hours each day. Those campesinos who own small stores are not the most prosperous in their communities but are somewhat short of land and are seeking a source of supplemental income.

The Marketplace.   Each Sunday the Arapata marketplace attracts a variety of goods and sellers from many places. Market women, who buy the goods they sell wholesale in La Paz, bring in produce such as carrots, broad beans, turnips, cabbage, tomatoes, hot peppers, and fruit in season. These vegetables and fruits were little consumed by the campesinos before the agrarian reform.

From Coroico and Coripata come cholas and mestizos who sell lettuce, bread, and chocolate. Two Coroico cholo butchers sell fresh beef and have no difficulty in disposing of a whole steer each week. This weekly supply of fresh meat is a dietary innovation; previously, fresh meat was reserved for festive occasions.

From Caranavi, the more tropical region of Nor Yungas, come dried corn, rice, cooking bananas, and tomatoes in season. Cooking bananas are one of the staple foods of the region and previously the local campesinos were more or less self-sufficient in their production. Now they can be bought relatively cheaply in the Sunday market as bananas are more productive in the more tropical interior. In consequence, much of the land previously devoted to bananas is now being planted with a cash crop. Similarly, the cultivation of rice, which was grown on a small scale in favorable locations, has now been abandoned.

The largest and most important group which comes to the marketplace are the Indian *comerciantes* ("traders"),[14] who sell the products of the high Altiplano: potatoes, onions, dried meat in a number of varieties, dried and fresh fish from Lake Titicaca, cheese, and fresh lamb and pork in small quantities. Such Altiplano foodstuffs have always been an integral part of the diet of the Yungas population and were previously obtained from individual traders and in the markets of the old towns. Individual trading still goes on, but comerciantes now have a much expanded outlet for their goods in the Arapata marketplace.

Most of the comerciantes who now trade in Arapata come from the comunidades indígenas around Lake Titicaca. The land base of these communities has been so constricted that the inhabitants have long had to rely on supplementary economic activities and some have concentrated on trading. Many speak good or adequate Spanish as a result of their outside experiences or of the opportunity of attending the Protestant mission schools in the area.

The traders who sell weekly in Arapata, with one or two unimportant exceptions, do not sell goods which they themselves have produced. Rather they buy their merchandise in Altiplano fairs to sell in Arapata. Each week these men spend some four days engaged in traveling and trading and the rest of the week cultivating their own land in Altiplano villages.

The comerciantes who come to Arapata form a closed group for all intents and purposes. For example, one newcomer trying to sell in Arapata was beaten, and, although the assailants were reprimanded by local authorities, he did not return and the traders kept their monopoly. Close ties are maintained with Arapata. The comerciantes are called upon to contribute financially to community projects and in the past have brought a band and danced at the Arapata fiesta.

A local campesino who wants to purchase an item not locally available or is looking for lower prices or simply for greater variety and diversion may now take a truck on Sunday to Coroico or Coripata. If he has to make a big purchase, such as a radio, he must buy it in La Paz. He may also commission one of the larger storekeepers or a *negociante* ("merchant") to make the purchase for him in the city.

Marketing of Cash Crops. In contrast to the prereform period, the campesino producer now faces an array of competing middlemen falling into several categories. In increasing order of importance they are other local capesinos; Arapata cholos and mestizos; Coripata buyers, who may be blanco, mestizo or cholo; and Altiplano-born indio or cholo traders. Although coca prices vary considerably throughout the year, in any given week the middlemen usually are buying coca at the same price. Coca is cheapest during the three peak harvest periods and most expensive between harvests, especially during the dry months of August and September. One of the factors which keep prices from finding a stable level is that the coca cannot be stored for any length of time in anticipation of a rise in prices. If the coca is kept in the warm, damp climate of the Yungas for more than a few weeks after it is sun dried, its green color begins to fade and its characteristic odor changes to the point where its value is considerably affected. The choice made among the competing buyers by the individual campesino with coca to sell is a very complex one influenced by such factors as kinship (real or fictive), economic indebtedness or the potential future need to borrow money, and political allegiance.

Before the agrarian reform the colonos' own coca was sold, for the most part, directly to the mestizo and blanco owners of coca presses in Coripata. After the reform many ex-hacendados and town mestizos were forced to fall back on commercial interests of this sort. Until recently truck ownership in Arapata and Coripata was largely in the hands of blancos, mestizos, and cholos, most of whom bought coca as well. Now that picture has altered as campesinos are acquiring trucks.

Coripata coca buyers continue to maintain a paternalistic relationship with the campesinos, usually structured through the compadrazgo system. They also maintain stores in which they extend credit or lend money to their clients with the expectation that the debt will be canceled in coca. The ways in which coca buyers living in Arapata have attempted to consolidate their own position (not always successfully) closely conform to this model. Campesinos, both local and from the Altiplano, may also follow this strategy of opening stores, extending credit, and lending money.

Political figures may also be in a position to establish patron-client ties which have economic as well as political implications. For example, the local political boss who rose to prominence with the MNR (and who has been able to weather the changes of government since its fall) trades on his political influence in establishing and maintaining commercial ties. These ties may then be consolidated, for both political and economic ends, by means of compadrazgo.

After the social and economic stranglehold of the townsmen was broken, the Altiplano cocatakis, trading on a much larger scale and now referred to as negociantes, became the largest single group of buyers. Negociantes have taken over an ever increasing share of the coca buying. It was estimated by local campesinos in 1964 that they buy some 70 percent of the total crop in the canton of Arapata. Closer to Coripata, however, they have not made quite such substantial inroads into the economic sphere of influence of the townsmen.

It is no longer necessary to take coca from the canton of Arapata to Coripata to be baled as three coca presses, all owned by negociantes, are now operating in Arapata. Unlike the comerciantes the typical large-scale negociante has permanently migrated out of his local Altiplano community and now maintains his permanent residence either in Arapata or La Paz.

At the present time there is considerable hostility directed toward the coca negociante by the local campesinos. The negociantes are regarded as exploiters and are resented because of their prosperity. They have been accused, among other things, of collusion to rig the weekly coca prices and are termed "our new patrones." The negociantes, although only recently established as large-scale coca buyers, now do all they can to protect their position and ensure that the local campesinos do not effectively challenge them by becoming competitors. Although many local Yungas campesinos are discontented, it is difficult for them to either market their own product directly in La Paz or to become coca buyers in their own right. A coca merchant needs a special government license. Although a campesino taking his own coca to La Paz does not need such a license, it is difficult for him to prove to the authorities that he is selling only his own coca and he may wind up in jail. In addition, the established coca middlemen have found ways of evading much of the taxes levied by the national government on coca, and from this comes their large profit margin. However, at the same time they make sure that all Yungueño traders are required to pay the full tax.

Despite these handicaps, two or three of the better-educated, young local campesinos have taken out licenses and are buying on a small scale. However, the rapidly fluctuating coca prices create additional difficulties for them. Lacking good information a local person may buy coca in the Yungas only to find that the price has dropped by the time he gets it to La Paz.

Two additional cash crops are coffee and citrus fruits. Although the production of both has increased substantially since the agrarian reform, they are still of secondary importance and are marketed through channels distinct from those which absorb the coca. Coffee is sold in small quantities to small buyers such as shopkeepers, comerciantes, and the mestiza bread venders. There is less difficulty with coffee than with coca for a campesino who wishes to sell his own product in La Paz, but often the price advantage is not enough to make it worth his time. In recent years a coffee marketing cooperative has been organized under the auspices of the British mission, providing an alternative for some, but the price received by the producers has fallen due to internatonal market conditions. Citrus fruits are bought by comerciantes, shopkeepers, and campesino middlemen.

SUMMARY AND CONCLUSIONS

The past fifteen years have witnessed a transformation of the Bolivian countryside in the wake of the social, political and economic reforms of the MNR government that have brought about increased prosperity for many Yungas campesinos. As Professor Carter's paper in this volume demonstrates, all regions of the country have not been affected in the same ways; nor is there necessarily regional uniformity. Granting this at the outset, one may still generalize on the dominant trends observable in Nor Yungas.

In this province the most obvious structural aspect of this transformation has been in the replacement of the hacienda as a social unit by peasant communities of small landowners. This should not be taken to mean that the position of the campesino has changed much in relation to other segments of the society, although the ways in which they relate to those other segments have changed. The hacendado was but the primary local point of contact within a wider national system which itself has changed little. As the hacendado fled the countryside, he was often able to reorganize his social, political, and commercial bases for power in the towns and cities. Although, in the total picture of regional stratification, mestizos have improved their position vis-à-vis blancos, the campesinos remain at the bottom of the social ladder.

Nevertheless, the breakup of the haciendas has been profoundly important as new economic possibilities were generated by campesino land ownership and the removal of hacienda obligations. These included the possibilities of entering trade, increasing production, and educating their children—all of which may, in the future, lead to social mobility. The hacienda structure had effectively isolated the peón, whose contact with the national society was largely mediated by the hacienda owners and administrators. The removal or weakening of the hacendado as a monopolistic broker has permitted other representatives of the national society—coca buyers, storekeepers, truck owners, merchants, politicians, and bureaucrats—to affect the lives of the campesinos more directly. It is significant to note that on those Yungas estates in which the hacendado continues to be resident the social situation is much closer to the pre-reform model than is the case in the canton of Arapata where the peones were left to manage their own affairs. However, even where the hacendado remains on the scene his position has been weakened, allowing other types of brokers to effectively compete with him.

As one result of the current proliferation of potential brokers in comparison with hacienda days, the asymmetry inherent in the campesinos' relationship to the larger society has lessened somewhat. Altiplano middlemen, town mestizos, and regional politicians have, individually or as representatives of group interests, less power concentrated in their hands than did the provincial elite prior to the reform. Political, economic, and socially derived positions do not coincide to the degree that they did prior to 1952.

Furthermore, the peasants, by means of their sindicato, have become organized. They are in a better position to take advantage of the existence of competing broker groups and brokers have emerged from their own ranks in the form of sindicato officials. In a political sense they may now exercise counterpressure on their own behalf to secure communal benefits in return for political loyalty as national political conditions permit.

From the economic perspective, prior to 1952 the contribution of the peasants of the province to the national economy was primarily that of their labor contribution to hacienda production and only secondarily by their involvement in the market. Since 1952 a significant change in the dominant form of economic integration of the bulk of the peasants has occurred. At present the primary campesino contribution to the national economy is through his participation in the market, both as producer and consumer.

It is revealing that many of the newly important brokers derive their position from being economic middlemen and that political brokers use their position to gain economic advantage as buyers. The locus of control over the peasant as an economic agent has thus shifted from control over the peasant as producer to control over the distribution of peasant-produced commodities.

The nature and degree of change in postreform peasant economics are congruent with this shift in the nature of the peasant's economic integration. Despite possible expectations the least change has been in the actual patterns of landholding and inheritance which follow rather closely the usufruct tenure system of the hacienda. A more substantial shift has occurred in land utilization and labor organization away from the more extensive cultivation characteristic of the estates toward more intensively cultivated small holdings. There has been a decrease of production on lands previously cultivated for the hacienda and an increase in cash-crop production on the part of individual peasants. Increased availability and utilization of wage labor have accompanied this greater emphasis on cash-crop production. There has also been increasing economic and political differentiation among the campesinos themselves. These differences are most visible in the unequal ownership of land and distribution of income and the predominance of wealthier peasants in the sindicato political hierarchy.

The most substantial discontinuities are observable in the organization of the distributional system. A whole new set of economic middlemen, the Altiplano negociantes, have stepped in to set up local stores and to absorb much of the coca previously directed exclusively to town mestizos and blancos, while among the townsmen political brokers have joined the commercial elite.

To project possible short-range transformations of the system, one might suggest that some local campesinos may find a more secure position as economic middlemen. Further entrenchment of wealthy campesinos may occur, along with the continued expansion of cash cropping and increasing mobility out of the region. However, the range of possibilities for economic transformation has been limited by the fact that the campesinos have received no effective technical or credit assistance; therefore, the basic agricultural technology and resources with which they operate have remained unaffected. Neither have cooperatives or other forms of collectivization been effective. There has been little industrial development or creation of other urban opportunities to absorb on a large scale those campesinos who choose or are forced to leave the land, although colonization may serve as a safety valve in the immediate future. Given conditions as they are, we may only expect economic stagnation or retrogression for the majority, despite the increasing opportunities open to a minority, as landholdings fragment and the market fails to expand.

NOTES

1. Seltzer, p. 2131.
2. RISM, p. 108.
3. The core of the canton refers to those eight estates subsequently under the jurisdiction of the Arapata subcentral sindicato. The exact size of one of these large estates was unavailable.
4. This information and the preceding data on estate size are taken from the *expendientes* ("land affectation briefs") filed with the Consejo Nacional de la Reforma Agraria. Data for the amount of land cultivated for the hacienda were unavailable for one large estate and one small estate. The percentages reported here may be high due to the possible overreporting, in some cases, of the amount of cultivated land.
5. Names referring to specific persons and estates are pseudonyms.
6. The term chiquiñero can have a number of referents. On estates in the Coroico area, chiquiñero could also refer to a person who was given usufruct rights over a portion of the colono's parcel in return for a labor obligation to the colono. This was not the practice in the canton of Arapata except in the case of heirs. Thus a youth,

having usufruct rights over some of his parents' holdings, as previously described, could also be called a chiquiñero.

7. See, for example, Patch, p. 129, and Heath, p. 27.

8. The owner of the estate which constituted the exception was compensated with land in another of his many estates.

9. For a more detailed discussion of the variations in estate size within the canton, see Léons, 1967.

10. One cesto in the canton of Arapata equals 30 or 32 pounds.

11. Some wealthy men did not find such political roles congenial and did not want the responsibilities involved; several important officeholders were not rich but possessed other valuable qualities, such as the ability to speak Spanish or experience as intermediaries with outside authorities.

12. Harry Tschopik has noted the same marriage pattern for the same economic reasons among the Aymara of Chucuito, Peru (p. 173).

13. Erasmus, p. 173.

14. The terms *comerciante* and *negociante* are used interchangeably in the canton of Arapata. We use them here with separate referents for clarity of presentation and to coincide with usage in Sud Yungas.

REFERENCES

Buechler, Hans C. "Land Reform and Social Revolution in the Northern Altiplano and Yungas of Bolivia." In *Land Reform and Social Revolution in Bolivia*, edited by Dwight B. Heath, Charles J. Erasmus, Hans C. Buechler. New York, 1969.

Erasmus, Charles J. "The Occurrence and Disappearance of Reciprocal Farm Labor in Latin America." In *Contemporary Cultures and Societies of Latin America*, edited by Dwight B. Heath and Richard N. Adams. New York, 1965.

Heath, Dwight B. Introduction to *Land Reform and Social Revolution in Bolivia*, edited by Dwight B. Heath, Charles J. Erasmus, Hans C. Buechler. New York, 1969.

Léons, Madeline Barbara. "Land Reform in the Bolivian Yungas." *América Indígena*, 27 (1967).

———. "Stratification and Pluralism in the Bolivian Yungas." In *The Social Anthropology of Latin America*, edited by Walter Goldschmidt and Harry Hoijer. Latin American Center, University of California. Los Angeles, 1970.

Patch, Richard W. "Bolivia: The Restrained Revolution." In *Latin America's Nationalistic Revolutions*. The Annals of the American Academy of Political and Social Science (March 1961).

RISM Bolivia Project. *Changing Rural Bolivia* by William J. McEwen with the support of the Bolivia Project Staff. Research Institute for the Study of Man. New York, 1969.

Seltzer, Leon, ed. *The Columbia Lippincott Gazetteer of the World*. New York, 1962.

Tschopik, Harry. *The Aymara of Chucuito Peru I: Magic*. Anthropological Papers of the American Museum of Natural History, vol. 44, pt. 2. New York, 1951.

MELVIN BURKE
University of Maine

Land Reform in the Lake Titicaca Region

Bolivia's National Revolutionary party (MNR) seized power in April 1952 and a year and a half later in August 1953 promulgated the agrarian reform law, which redistributed the land of the haciendas to the former Indian tenants and others. This comparative economic study of the haciendas and ex-haciendas in the Lake Titicaca region of Bolivia and Peru was undertaken to answer three important, but largely unresolved, questions about land reform: (1) Which land-tenure system—large estates or small peasant farms—affords the agriculture laborers and cultivators the greater freedom of mobility, opportunity, income, and education? (2) Did the land-tenancy conditions of a typical *latifundio* ("large landed estate") land-tenure system [1] border on serfdom and preclude freedom and was this system largely responsible for the low standard of living and education of the rural population in a traditional agrarian economy? (3) Is there any validity to the contention that "land reform is not only a reform of the way land is held but just as much reform of the man who tills the land?" [2]

LATIFUNDIO LAND TENURE AND LAND REFORM

Prior to the MNR revolution, Bolivia was an underdeveloped country with a traditional agrarian sector, characterized by a latifundio system.

This chapter is an expanded version of my article, "Land Reform and Its Effect Upon Production and Productivity in the Lake Titicaca Region," published in *Economic Development and Cultural Change,* 18, no. 3 (April 1970), pp. 410–50.

The agricultural sector was clearly differentiated from the nonagricultural sector. The nonagricultural sector comprised the extractive industries and the transport, construction, and trading activities associated with, and dependent upon, mining. Each sector had its peculiar problems. It was the agrarian sector, however, which was usually singled out as being the most backward, unproductive, and stagnant. Although approximately 70 percent of the Bolivian population was engaged in agricultural production in 1950, this sector was the source of only 30 percent of the gross national product and less than 3 percent of the value of the exports. In addition, roughly 40 percent of imports were food and other agricultural goods, most of which could have been domestically produced.[3] A partial explanation for Bolivia's backwardness can be found in an examination of the prerevolutionary land-tenure system.

THE LATIFUNDIO LAND-TENURE SYSTEM

Before 1952 land concentration was very great. According to the 1950 agricultural census, approximately 6 percent of the largest agricultural units constituted 92 percent of the land, while 80 percent of the smallest held only 1 percent of the land. Three-fourths of the country's agricultural population had no property rights. Although 30 percent of the total land area was classified as arable, only 2 percent was cultivated. Also, there was an inverse relationship between the size of holding and area cultivated. While the smallest agricultural units cultivated 44 percent of their land, the largest estates, comprising 92 percent of all land, cultivated only 1 percent of their holdings.

These statistics do little more than reveal the fact that agriculture in Bolivia was dominated by large landed estates. The haciendas, moreover, were not only agricultural enterprises; they were social units. This is evident in the tenancy arrangement under which the land was operated and its product divided between the tiller and owner. The *colonos* ("Indian tenants") were traditionally, and often quasi-legally, tied to the haciendas. For the right to use a small parcel of the estate's poorer quality land, they were required in varying degrees to render to the landowner their labor, tools, animals, and servitude.

THE LAND REFORM

The concentration of landed property in so few hands, the less than progressive tenancy conditions, and the traditional methods of production combined to render the Bolivian latifundio land-tenure system an anachronism. Many Bolivians and others came to consider this land-tenure system as one of the major obstacles to both agricultural and general economic efficiency and progress. Among these individuals were the leaders of the *Movimiento Nacionalista Revolucionario* who were responsible for the agrarian reform law which states that the soil, subsoil, and waters of the nation belong to the state but guaranteed private property which fulfills a "social function." It also committed the state to an

TABLE 1
BOLIVIAN LAND REDISTRIBUTION
1953–1965

Year	Number of Legal Re-distribution Cases	Titles Dis-tributed	Family Heads Benefited	Hectares Distributed	Hectares Reverted to the State
1953	—	—	—	—	—
1954	—	—	—	—	—
1955	32	3,400	2,809	51,811	—
1956	75	4,463	3,863	46,604	579
1957	281	11,400	8,028	276,293	103
1958	216	9,193	5,709	201,631	367
1959	313	18,380	12,097	316,462	4,040
1960	904	38,897	22,410	825,871	26,899
1961	1,186	45,511	28,210	1,129,442	38,379
1962	1,880	50,227	28,843	1,255,791	24,950
1963	1,185	47,461	40,641	1,271,686	91,905
1964	626	18,317	11,295	531,946	33,497
1965	202	15,600	9,652	365,042	23,241
Total	6,900	262,849	173,557	6,272,579	243,960

Source: Bolivia, Departamento de Estadistica, Servicio Nacional Reforma Agraria (February 8, 1966), unpublished. Provided by the department head, Sr. Hector Mercado Negrete

"equitable" distribution of land. The land-reform decree further stipulated that small peasant farms, cooperatives, and indigenous communities were to be created and expanded by the redistribution of all the latifundio land and portions of "medium properties" and "agricultural enterprises." [4] The expropriation was to be accompanied by monetary compensation in the form of 2 percent, twenty-five-year, agrarian bonds ultimately paid for by the new beneficiaries of this reform, the *campesinos* ("countrymen").

Since the passage of the Bolivian land reform, substantial progress has been made in legally redistributing the land. A comparison of the figures in the 1950 agricultural census with those in table 1 shows that, of the

32,749,850 hectares surveyed in 1950, 6,272,579 or 19 percent of this amount had been legally redistributed to individual campesinos by the beginning of 1966. A number of *expedientes* ("files of documents") relating to the legal distribution of land are still being processed, but, more important, a substantial amount of land was illegally expropriated by the campesinos.

In the midst of the early revolutionary years, 1952–1953, the campesinos organized militant *sindicatos* ("labor unions"), obtained control of the countryside, and confiscated or redistributed the lands of many estates—some of which were not liable for expropriation under the new law. It is important to bear in mind that the actual Bolivian land reform is distinct from that expressed in the legal statute. Land reform in Bolivia destroyed the latifundio land-tenure system and created the small campesino family-operated holdings. The Bolivian landowners were never officially compensated by the government or the campesinos for their expropriated properties. The only compensation received was in the form of non-official payments made by the campesinos to a few fortunate landowners. President Víctor Paz Estenssoro expressed the sum and substance of the true Bolivian land reform when he said: "We made the agrarian reform. We took the land from the unproductive and absentee landowners, and we have given it to the *campesinos* who work it." [5]

THE LAKE TITICACA REGION

The Lake Titicaca region is unique, since it is probably the only area in the world where haciendas and expropriated haciendas existed side by side in a relatively homogeneous setting.[6] As such, it afforded a remarkable opportunity to conduct a comparative economic study of land tenure, land reform, and their effect upon human resources and the economy.

A sampling of four Peruvian haciendas and four Bolivian ex-haciendas had been chosen for examination and comparison. From a nearly complete list of all the large landed estates in the Peruvian sector of the region, four haciendas were selected. These were livestock and grain enterprises that were absentee owned and representative in size, production, and productivity. From the other side of the border, four Bolivian ex-haciendas with similar characteristics were selected for comparison. Every attempt was made to insure comparability in such areas as distance from the lake, elevation, water access, and climate. In short, every

Bolivian ex-hacienda investigated was matched as closely as possible with a comparable Peruvian hacienda.[6] Nevertheless, because all available data indicate that the prereform Bolivian haciendas were usually smaller in size and supported larger populations than their Peruvian counterparts, the four Bolivian ex-haciendas investigated possessed these different characteristics. (See table 2.) A partial explanation for the difference in estate

TABLE 2
SAMPLE OF PERUVIAN HACIENDAS AND BOLIVIAN EX-HACIENDAS

	Peruvian Haciendas				
	I	II	III	IV	Total
Area in hectares	4,850	5,719	4,244	16,310	31,123
Campesino families	35	23	23	94	175
Family heads interviewed	34	23	22	88	167
Percentage interviewed	97%	100%	96%	94%	95%

	Bolivian Ex-Haciendas				
	I	II	III	IV	Total
Area in hectares	5,591	2,348	1,518	5,221	14,678
Campesino families	287	65	108	209	669
Family heads interviewed	68	30	48	21	167
Percentage interviewed	24%	46%	45%	10%	25%

size and population density among the two sampled groups can be found in the locations of the major consumer markets in the two nations. The prereform Bolivian haciendas had a greater access to a large consumer market, the capital city of La Paz. Thus, these estates had a nearby market for bulky, high-cost transport products, such as potatoes, ocas, and similar foods which are both labor and land intensive in production. On the other hand, the lack of a similarly accessible market in the Peruvian sector has historically oriented production toward high-value, low-cost transport products, such as wool, for international export.

Because a hacienda is dichotomized into that portion utilized by and for the landowner and that used by the campesinos for their subsistence, and because an ex-hacienda is separated into those farmed cooperatively and those farmed individually by the campesinos, two different questionnaires were used in the field study. In both cases, the services of an interpreter were necessary, since the Indians chose to answer in their native Aymara and Quechua languages. Also, due to the large number of campesinos encountered on the Bolivian ex-haciendas, only a random sample was selected for interviewing.

The field research for this article was carried out in a sedentary agricultural and stock-raising area. The Lake Titicaca region is composed of the Altiplano portions of the department of Puno, Peru, and the department of La Paz, Bolivia, as seen in figure 1. Prior to 1953, the culture,

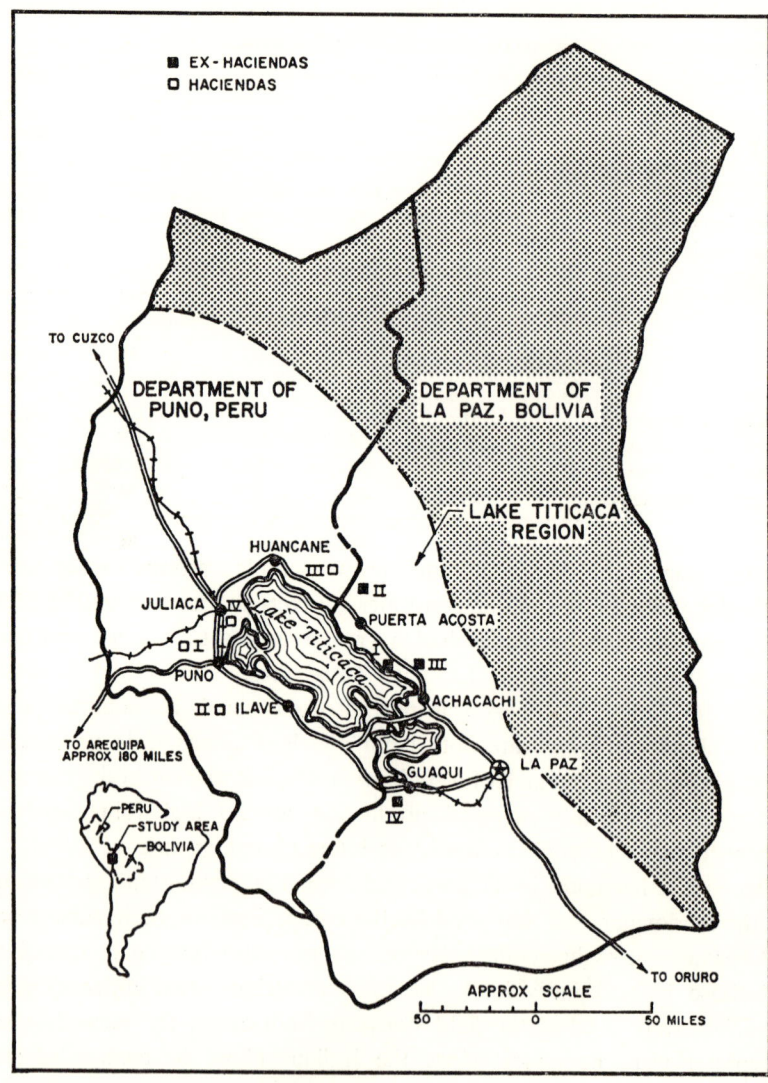

FIG. 1. LAKE TITICACA REGION

the economy, and, above all, the latifundio land-tenure system of the Bolivian sector were nearly identical to those of the Peruvian sector. For example, in the department of Puno, 80 percent of the smallest agricultural units owned 3.2 percent of the land while 0.2 percent of the largest units possessed 60 percent of the land. The same inverse relationship between size of holding and the area cultivated existed here as in La Paz. Nearly all the large estates were absentee owned, and the tenancy conditions resembled those of prereform Bolivia except for the differences discussed below. Finally, 70 percent of the Peruvian population was engaged in stagnant and unproductive agriculture.[7] Latifundio land-tenure systems are not dynamic, and in many ways the Peruvian haciendas investigated resembled the prereform Bolivian haciendas.

The Peruvian haciendas served only as imperfect proxies, however, since there were a number of notable differences between the Peruvian haciendas and the prereform Bolivian haciendas. The Peruvian Resolucion Suprema no. 14 of January 17, 1964, required all campesino laborers to be paid a minimum daily wage, and Resolucion Suprema no. 18 of May 21, 1965, formally designated the department of Puno as an agrarian reform zone.[8] Even though these decrees were either not fully obeyed or inoperative, they modified the Peruvian latifundio land-tenure system. First, because some money wages were paid to campesinos, labor was no longer a free resource. Secondly, if they exceeded the average productivity of haciendas in the department, the agrarian reform law enabled haciendas to retain between three thousand and eight thousand hectares of land. After the 1965 agrarian reform went into effect, the Peruvians have invested in capital equipment and livestock, as well as paid their laborers minimum wages. In short, these laws were instrumental in bringing about changes in the resource mix within the haciendas. Nevertheless, if one would ignore all of the cash income of the Peruvian campesinos, much of the newly acquired capital, and some of the international wool sales of the Peruvian haciendas, one would approximate the prereform Bolivian sector of the Lake Titicaca region.

As can be seen in table 2 on page 305 two important distinctions between the haciendas and ex-haciendas must be borne in mind. First, although the same absolute number of campesino family heads was interviewed on both sides of the border, the sample of 167 Peruvian campesinos represented 95 percent of all hacienda employees, while the 167 Bolivians interviewed represented only 25 percent of the total number of campesino family heads on the ex-haciendas. Secondly, while the same number of haciendas and ex-haciendas was included in the sample, the Peruvians had twice the amount of land as the Bolivians. Finally, official governmental statistics and studies of other Peruvian haciendas and Bolivian ex-haciendas were used throughout this study as supplemental sources of data and information. Studies of prereform Bolivian haciendas were also used for the historical comparison of before and after the land reform.

RELATIVE ECONOMIC PERFORMANCE OF PERUVIAN HACIENDAS AND BOLIVIAN EX-HACIENDAS

ECONOMIC RESOURCES

In an attempt to make the analysis of the effect of the Bolivian land reform upon human resource development more readily comprehensible, this section will briefly summarize the economic performance of the sampled Peruvian haciendas and Bolivian ex-haciendas in the Lake Titicaca region.[9] Total population estimates based upon the sample averages obtained in the field study indicate that the Bolivian ex-haciendas supported four times as many people with only half as much land as the Peruvian haciendas. Thus, the population density of the Bolivian ex-haciendas was more than eight times that of the Peruvian haciendas (see table 3).

The greater population density of the Bolivian ex-haciendas was re-

TABLE 3
COMPARISON OF HACIENDA AND EX-HACIENDA POPULATIONS

	Peruvian Haciendas	Bolivian Ex-Haciendas
Total population	998.0	3,847.0
Total "weighted economically active" population [a]	560.0	2,141.0
Population density per square mile	8.3	67.9

Note: In this table and all the following ones, except where indicated, the figures represent projections based on the sample averages obtained in the field study.

a. Computed on the basis of the following weights furnished by the Oficina Nacional de Evaluacion de Recursos Naturales de Puno, Peru: male over seventeen years of age = 1.0; female over seventeen years of age = 0.8; male and female ten to seventeen years of age = 0.5; and all others = 0.0.

flected in the more intensive utilization of the land, as seen in table 4. In the aggregate the Bolivian ex-haciendas cultivated six times as many hectares as the Peruvian haciendas during the agricultural year 1964–1965. Approximately 5 percent of the Bolivian ex-hacienda land was cultivated as compared to less than 0.5 percent of the Peruvian hacienda land.[10]

On the Peruvian estates the lower population density and greater land extension were reflected in the greater specialization in sheep ranching, as seen in table 5. By far the most numerous and important type of capital found on both the hacienda and ex-hacienda was livestock.

Reducing all grazing livestock to the common denominator of a sheep (*"unida animal ovino"* or U.A.O.) enabled the computation of some interesting livestock statistics (table 6). When the livestock is weighted accordingly, data show that the Peruvian haciendas had twice as much livestock as the Bolivian ex-haciendas. Taking population and land into consideration, the livestock density per hectare was nearly equal for both sampled groups, although the Peruvian campesinos shepherded approximately eight times as many animals as their Bolivian counterparts.

Land, labor, and livestock capital were the most important economic resources on these traditional units of production. Of lesser influence upon production and productivity were physical capital and management. It is difficult to say whether haciendas or ex-haciendas possessed the greater quantity of physical capital, since it was virtually impossible to weigh the greater quantity of hand tools and new constructions of the campesinos on the Bolivian ex-haciendas against the old physical plant and more modern machinery and equipment on the Peruvian haciendas.

In addition, the institutional nature of these traditional agrarian units of production suggests that possession of economic resources did not imply their rational or complete utilization in production. For example, although the Peruvian haciendas employed professional managers, owned large tracts of land, and used agricultural equipment such as tractors, the influence of all these upon production was less than one would expect. The Peruvian haciendas were not only absentee owned, but to a degree, absentee managed. This partially explains the observed underutilization of agricultural machinery on the estates.[11] Large extensions of land were also lying idle or underutilized on these estates, since the Peruvian landowners only put about half their total land in production. On the other hand, because a smaller quantity of labor was combined with greater amounts of other resources such as land and livestock, the Peruvian campesino's labor and time were fully utilized on the haciendas.

TABLE 4
UTILIZATION OF LAND
(*In Hectares*)

Type of Land	Cultivated by and for		Pasture and/or Land in Rest of			Total Land Area
	Campesinos	Hacendados	Campesinos	Hacendados	Joint Use	
Peruvian Haciendas						
Level	5.5	53.0	220.0	15,582.0	4,328.5	20,189.0
Hill and/or broken	18.5	41.0	655.0	—	10,219.5	10,934.0
Total	24.0	94.0	875.0	15,582.0	14,548.0	31,123.0
Bolivian Ex-Haciendas						
Level	342.0	10.0	2,678.0	685.0	2,929.0	6,644.0
Hill and/or broken	378.0	2.0	602.0	1,529.0	5,523.0	8,034.0
Total	720.0	12.0	3,280.0	2,214.0	8,452.0	14,678.0

TABLE 5
DISTRIBUTION OF TOTAL LIVESTOCK

	Peru			Bolivia		
	Campesinos	Hacendados	Total	Campesinos	Cooperatives	Total
Sheep	9,592	52,955	62,547	18,156	845	19,001
Cattle	1,334	1,512	2,846	2,348	42	2,390
Horses	385	115	500	16	—	16
Borros [a]	229	7	236	381	—	381
Alpaca	607	236	843	—	—	—
Llama	321	—	321	1,455	—	1,455
Fowl	253	41	295	1,508	—	1,508
Pigs	61	7	68	1,704	38	1,778

Note: Nearly all the sheep and cattle of the Bolivian and Peruvian campesinos were of the degenerate criollo ("domestic") type, while those of the Peruvian hacendados were predominantly crossbreeds between criollos and imported (improved) stock.
   a. Male lambs not yet two years old.

On the Bolivian ex-haciendas the situation was reversed; it was labor which was not completely expended on production, and land which was more fully exploited. Because the Bolivian campesino was not required to render his labor services to any landowner, and because his small holdings and animal herds did not require all his time, he possessed greater leisure and time for work outside the ex-hacienda. Comparing them with the Peruvian haciendas, more labor and an equal amount of livestock were combined with each hectare of land on the Bolivian ex-haciendas. Thus, land was more fully utilized on the Bolivian ex-haciendas.

TABLE 6
COMPARISON OF HACIENDA AND EX-HACIENDA LIVESTOCK

	Peruvian Haciendas	Bolivian Ex-Haciendas
Total livestock (U.A.O.'s)	89,139	44,408
Livestock (U.A.O.'s) per hectare	2.9	3.0
Livestock (U.A.O.'s) per campesino family	512	66

Note: There are various methods used to compute this sheep equivalent unit (U.A.O.) which is the reduction of all grazing animals to the land capacity for an adult sheep. The one used here is that of the Agrarian Reform Office of Puno, Peru: sheep = 1, cattle = 6, horses and burros = 8, alpacas and llamas = 3, and pigs = 2.

TOTAL-VALUE PRODUCTION AND PRODUCTIVITY

The different amounts of economic resources available to the haciendas and ex-haciendas and the diverse utilization of the same manifest themselves most obviously in production and productivity. The Peruvian haciendas raised approximately $170,000 worth of agricultural produce during the 1964–1965 year, which is only slightly larger than the estimated $149,000 produced by the Bolivian ex-haciendas.[12] Four times as many Bolivian campesinos were engaged in producing nearly the same output on only half as much land; in other words the Bolivian ex-haciendas were, on the average, twice as productive with respect to land and one-fourth as productive with respect to labor as the Peruvian haciendas. Productivity statistics and estimates of the average monetary return to each available economic resource are set forth in table 7.

TABLE 7
VALUE PRODUCTIVITY
(*In Dollars*)

Statistics	Peruvian Haciendas	Bolivian Ex-Haciendas
Value output / Hectare	$ 5.47	$10.15
Value output / Man-years of labor [a]	304.00	69.62
Value animal products / Livestock capital [b]	0.38	0.40
Value crops / Hectares cultivated	105.31 [c]	88.45

a. The man-year equivalents of labor figures are the same as the "economically active population" figures computed in table 3, p. 308.
b. This figure of the total value of livestock was computed by multiplying the average prices of animals sold in tables 16 and 17 by the total number of animals on the haciendas and ex-haciendas in table 6 on p. 311.
c. This average-value figure includes only the output of the three haciendas for which data are available, i.e., it excludes that of hacienda IV.

ECONOMIC EFFICIENCY WITH RESPECT TO
SIZE OF FIRM AND LABOR PRODUCTIVITY

Which were more efficient—the Peruvian haciendas or the Bolivian ex-haciendas? Because of the limitations of the data and the lack of a general consensus upon the criteria of efficiency, the reader should be forewarned not to expect a definitive answer to this question. For, although few economists condone the tenure conditions on the large haciendas, many rally to defend the haciendas in the name of economies of scale and labor productivity. Thus, an important consideration is whether size economies resulting from such indivisible inputs as capital equipment and management existed on the Peruvian haciendas. It appears that the underutilization of agricultural machinery, management, and land on the Peruvian estates prevented the realization of any size economies. Also, no evidence of financial economies of scale, such as quantity discounts from marketing, was uncovered. This does not imply that the small campesino holdings on the Bolivian ex-haciendas were either efficient or of optimum size. The implication is, however, that the large landed estates in the sample were not necessarily more efficient than the small campesino holdings by virtue of size alone. In brief, the findings of this study indicate that there probably is no overwhelming advantage to any particular size Altiplano agricultural unit of production under existing institutional and technological conditions.

But what is the economic significance of the difference in labor productivity on the haciendas and ex-haciendas? Was the lower labor productivity of the Bolivian ex-haciendas evidence of a less efficient allocation of resources? What is needed to analyze this allocative efficiency is information on prices of both resources and production at the margin, which, unfortunately, was not available. Even information obtained from production functions would have limited value, since the price of land and labor to the Bolivian campesino were nonmonetary opportunity costs. It appears that the Peruvian haciendas were more efficient in their use of labor. However, when labor is abundant relative to land and capital, as it was in both sectors of the region, the area yielding the higher output per hectare, in this case the Bolivian ex-haciendas, can be considered more efficient.

When technology, incentive, and employment are taken into consideration, neither the Peruvian haciendas nor the Bolivian ex-haciendas could be considered to be more efficient or to perform in a superior economic manner. The evidence suggests that both sampled groups were producing short of their optimum.

PRODUCTION FOR THE MARKET

With more and better breeds of animals, twice as much land, and one-fourth the population of the Bolivian ex-haciendas, one would expect the Peruvian haciendas to produce more for the market. This is precisely what the data reveal, using the total value of products sold as crude approximation of agricultural surplus. In the agricultural year 1964–1965 the sampled Peruvian haciendas sold approximately $142,000 worth of products on the market as compared to about $51,450 sold by the Bolivian ex-haciendas.[13] Not only did the Peruvians sell nearly three times as much in absolute dollar value as the Bolivians, but they sold a greater proportion of their output. The Peruvian haciendas sold 85 percent and the Bolivian ex-haciendas 34 percent of their respective gross outputs. The sale of wool accounts for the greater part of this difference, however. Approximately $65,000 of foreign exchange was earned by the Peruvian hacendados from the sale of wool in international markets.[14] If one subtracts this amount from the Peruvian hacienda sales, the value of products sold in their respective domestic markets by the haciendas and ex-haciendas is more nearly equal. Although the four Peruvian haciendas and the four Bolivian ex-haciendas investigated constituted only a fraction of all those in the Lake Titicaca region, they were quite similar—and in many respects virtually identical—to most other haciendas and ex-haciendas in the region.

THE EFFECTS OF THE BOLIVIAN LAND REFORM

To what extent does this difference in economic performance between the Peruvian haciendas and Bolivian ex-haciendas reflect changes brought about by the Bolivian land reform? In any attempt to answer this question, let us begin by briefly outlining the major characteristics of the prereform Bolivian haciendas, since the Peruvian haciendas investigated, as stated above, served only as imperfect proxies for the prereform Bolivian haciendas.

PREREFORM BOLIVIAN HACIENDAS

The prereform Bolivian haciendas were, to a much greater degree than the Peruvian ones, mere agglomerations of small Indian *sayañas* ("usufructuary tracts of land"). In the Lake Titicaca region, approximately two-thirds of the prereform Bolivian haciendas were cultivated exclusively by and for the Indians, who also owned approximately three-fourths of the livestock.

The Bolivian haciendas did not possess great quantities of productive physical capital or employ production methods other than those traditionally used by their Indian tenants. Nor did they specialize in wool production for the international market, and nearly all their sheep and cattle were of the degenerate criollo type. The prereform Bolivian haciendas also supported larger populations and cultivated a greater portion of their lands than did the Peruvian haciendas.

CHANGES IN RESOURCES

Since the Bolivian land reform, the population of the ex-haciendas in the Lake Titicaca region has doubled as a result of the natural increase in population and migration to these lands from the indigenous communities, vilages, and cities. Perhaps this growth helps to explain why La Paz does not have the extensive *barriadas* ("slums") typical of most large Latin American cities. This population increase, in turn, has given rise to a slightly more intensive use of the land. Although many new campesino sayañas were carved out of the old *hacendado* ("estate owner's") lands to accommodate the larger population, the average sayaña has not changed in size or composition since the land reform.

However, since the land reform, there has been a small reduction in the total number of animals in the sector. This occurred because the landowners were able to sell some of their animals, some perished through neglect, and an additional number were confiscated by the campesinos. Since that time, however, the herds have been gradually built up to nearly their prereform size. But there has been a slight deterioration in the quality of the sheep and cattle, or, at least, there has been no improvement of the herds since 1953. Also, a decrease has occurred in the average size of the campesino herd. These statements are supported in table 8 by data from the field study, the Viacha study, and the 1946 ministry of agriculture study—all major sources of information drawn upon in this comparison.

Finally, since 1953 the old adobe structures of the haciendas have deteriorated, because the campesinos refused to replace their *paja* ("grass") roofs. This destruction, however, has been compensated for by the construction of new campesino homes and schools. In addition, since the Bolivian land reform disinvestment in the form of a decrease in the amount of agricultural machinery has taken place on the ex-haciendas. Rarely does one see a tractor today in the Bolivian sector of the Lake Titicaca region. It is impossible to determine how much of this mobile machinery and equipment was removed by the landowners and how much was destroyed as a result of campesino indifference and neglect. There has been no inflow of agricultural equipment in the area either for re-

TABLE 8
Economic Resources Before and After Land Reform

	Before Land Reform [a]	After Land Reform [b]
Population density per square mile	35.0	68.0
Livestock (U.A.O.) density per hectare	3.3	3.0
U.A.O.'s owned per campesino family	93.0	66.0
Approximate average size of campesino sayaña (in hectares)	6.0–8.0	6.0–8.0 [c]
Total land area cultivated	1.0–6.0%	5.0%

a. *Source: Estudio socio-económica en las provincias de omasuyos, ingavi, y los andes del departament de La Paz* (La Paz, 1946).
b. *Sources:* Author's field study and *Estudio económico estadistico del Canton Viacha* (La Paz, 1965).
c. It is obvious that the average Bolivian campesino did not possess, let alone own, between ten and thirty-five hectares of land as prescribed by article 15 of the Decreto Ley de la Reforma Agraria.

placement or for addition to stock since 1953, because the Bolivian cam-pesinos have neither the funds nor the inclination to purchase this type of capital.

CHANGES IN ECONOMIC PERFORMANCE

It is difficult to compare the economic performance of the prereform Bolivian haciendas with the present-day ex-haciendas, because compari-sons over time may reflect climatic or price changes above all else. Con-sequently, a rigorous historical comparison cannot be made. Nevertheless, the subject will be briefly commented upon because of the controversy surrounding the issue of land redistribution and its economic consequences.

Because there were no verifiable size economies operative on the rela-tively productive Peruvian haciendas, there is even more reason to suspect that no economies of scale were realized by the prereform Bolivian haciendas. Consequently, when the lands used exclusively by the land-owners and portions of their criollo livestock were parceled among the campesinos after the land reform, it is unlikely that any size economies of production were lost.

The evidence accumulated in this study suggests that labor productivity on the Bolivian ex-haciendas has decreased, land productivity has in-creased, and capital productivity has remained unchanged since the land reform. This can be accounted for largely by the increased population, greater use of the more marginal land, and the small decrease in agricul-tural equipment. Also, in part, the decrease in labor productivity reflects the increase in leisure and off-the-farm employment of the Bolivian campesinos.

An increase in the number of people engaged in marginal agriculture and a decrease in agricultural productivity per unit of labor are, however, normally considered by economists to be prima facie evidence of an inefficient allocation of a nation's resources. But Bolivia was not a full employment economy, and the decrease in labor productivity in the agrarian sector must be considered in conjunction with the increased employment in agriculture and the higher land productivity which resulted from the land reform. In short, the increased marginal farming may well be an efficient allocation of the nation's resources in the short run or until such time as alternative employment is available.

For example, agricultural output in the region has increased since the Bolivian land reform. However, because of their greater numbers and greater per capita consumption of food, the Bolivian campesinos have retained a greater share of the region's larger output. At the same time, the agricultural produce sold in the market has equaled prereform levels. At least, this is what most official government statistics indicate.

Bolivian campesinos also have increased their commercial activity since the expropriated landowners no longer supply the markets with food and other agricultural produce. This is seen in the numerous local fairs which have come into existence since the land reform, as well as the increased coming and going of the Altiplano campesinos. The Bolivian campesino, like his Guatemalan counterpart, is a businessman. As Sol Tax observed, "The Indian is perhaps above all else an entrepreneur, a businessman, always looking for a new means of turning a penny." [15]

However, unless technology and human and physical capital are forthcoming, the agricultural output and surplus, at best, will be augmented at a very slow pace within the existing framework of the traditional agrarian sector. As Theodore W. Schultz and others have shown, these apparent traditional optima can only be exceeded by the infusion into the agrarian sector of nontraditional inputs, such as improved seed, equipment, livestock, and modern methods of production.[16] Agricultural credit, extension services, and other forms of assistance are needed for this task.

CAMPESINO INCOME, CONSUMPTION, MOBILITY, AND EDUCATION

The growing emphasis on capital investments in human beings is one encouraging trend in current discussions of the mainsprings of economic growth. This emphasis is of primary importance to agricultural development. Improving the quality of the labor input through new knowledge and new skills offers one rewarding opportunity for agricultural capital investment. For this reason, a major test of the performance of land-tenure structures is to be found in the role they play in advancing capital investment in education.[17]

Labor is one of the most abundant economic resources that underdeveloped nations possess. The labor force is only an asset to economic efficiency and progress when it is healthy, educated, and mobile. Many development economists have theoretically demonstrated the merits of: (1) freeing the agricultural labor force so that its members may migrate to the industrial sector when conditions warrant, (2) providing the laborers with sufficient income to purchase manufactured products as well as to keep body and soul together, and (3) educating and informing these individuals so that they may become more productive economic resources and participating citizens. But how did the two sampled groups of campesinos in the Lake Titicaca region fare under the different land-tenure systems? Did the haciendas of the Peruvian sector or the ex-haciendas of the Bolivian sector afford the campesinos a greater freedom (i.e., mobility and opportunity), income, and education?

To begin with, the sampled populations possessed many similar characteristics. For example, the average size of a household was 5.70 on the Peruvian estates and 5.75 on the Bolivian ex-haciendas. The average ages of the two sampled groups were twenty-four and twenty-three respectively. In both sampled groups roughly 55 percent of the population was under twenty years of age.

CAMPESINO INCOME

An investigation of the income patterns of the campesinos on the sampled Peruvian haciendas and Bolivian ex-haciendas was conducted in the field study. One would expect for a number of reasons the Peruvian campesino to have a higher income and standard of living than his Bolivian counterpart. First of all, the Peruvian campesino owned, on the average, twice as much livestock as the Bolivian campesino and had at his disposal an equal amount of land. Secondly, the Peruvian was more than four times as productive on the hacienda as the Bolivian was on the ex-hacienda. Finally, the Peruvian, unlike the Bolivian campesino, received a money wage for his labor on the hacienda. Table 9 gives an estimate of Peruvian campesino wages for the agricultural year 1964–1965. Table 10 shows the paradox in the data obtained in the field study, indicating that it is the Bolivian campesino, not the Peruvian, who received the greater income.

Part of this apparent paradox can be explained by the higher prices that Bolivian campesinos received in the market for their animals; this higher price is also the one imputed for the animals consumed by the campesinos.[18] However, the Bolivian campesino did, on the average, sell and consume a greater quantity of virtually every agricultural good produced by the haciendas and ex-haciendas in the region. In any case, the Peruvian campesinos did not greatly benefit from their relatively higher labor productivity; nor did the Bolivian campesinos grievously suffer from their lower productivity. There was, in short, little relationship between labor productivity and remuneration, at least in this respect.

TABLE 9
PERUVIAN CAMPESINO WAGES AND SALARIES
(*In Dollars*)

			Haciendas		
	I	II	III	IV	Total
Gross wages	$3,097	$557	$4,060	$13,674	$21,388
State taxes [a]	124	22	162	547	855
Hacienda fees [b]	1,592	—	720	—	2,312
Net wages	$1,381	$535	$3,178	$13,127	$18,221

Note: These wages and salaries do not include the salaries of the administrators. See table 1 on p. 303 for the number of families in each hacienda.
a. A 4 percent social security tax.
b. Compulsory payments made to the landowners for the use of pasture and cultivable hacienda land.

Table 10 gives the impression that the Peruvian campesino, on the average, earned twice as much money income as the Bolivian. But, when one recalls that this table only includes income earned from the production of the haciendas and ex-haciendas, the higher money income of the Peruvian campesino may be no more than an illusion. While interviewing the Bolivian campesinos, it became apparent that they had a source of money income unavailable to the Peruvians—namely, outside employment. The obvious reason for the Peruvian campesinos' inability to work outside the haciendas is that their labor time was fully utilized by the landowners. Each Peruvian campesino had assigned to his care between four hundred and five hundred head of livestock which his family herded, while he devoted most of his working time to the cultivation of the hacendado's land, the shearing of his sheep, and the maintenance of his buildings and other physical plants. He and his family accomplished all this in addition to farming land for their exclusive benefit and caring for their own animals.

Such was not the case on the Bolivian ex-haciendas, where the campesinos often worked part time in the Yungas and elsewhere as agricultural laborers and in La Paz as seasonal construction workers. Unfortunately, due to an oversight in the construction of the questionnaire, no estimate of the money income received by all the surveyed Bolivian campesinos for this outside employment was obtained. Only the campesinos of one

TABLE 10
ESTIMATED CAMPESINO INCOMES FROM HACIENDA AND EX-HACIENDA
PRODUCTION
(*In Dollars*)

	Peruvian Campesinos	Bolivian Campesinos
Money wages	$18,221	$ —
Other money income [a]	7,019	51,451
Total money income	$25,240	$ 51,451
Income-in-kind [b]	10,738	97,604
Total income [c]	$35,978	$149,055
Money income per family	$144.22	$ 77.35
Total income per family	205.59	222.80

a. Earnings from the sale of agricultural products. See table 15, p. 336.
b. Consumption of agricultural products. These figures were obtained by subtracting the value of products sold in table 15 from the value of output in table 14.
c. These figures do not include off-the-farm income.

ex-hacienda were asked to reveal the source and amount of such wages. Approximately one-half of these campesinos were employed at least part time outside the ex-hacienda during the agricultural year 1964–1965 and earned between six and twenty-five dollars a month for their labor. A very rough estimate of the average amount of money income earned per campesino would be between fifty and seventy-five dollars per year. In short, it may very well be that the Bolivian campesino earned not only a greater total income but also a greater money income than the Peruvian campesino.

CAMPESINO CONSUMPTION

Another indication that the Bolivian campesinos had greater money incomes and, therefore, total incomes was their apparent higher standard

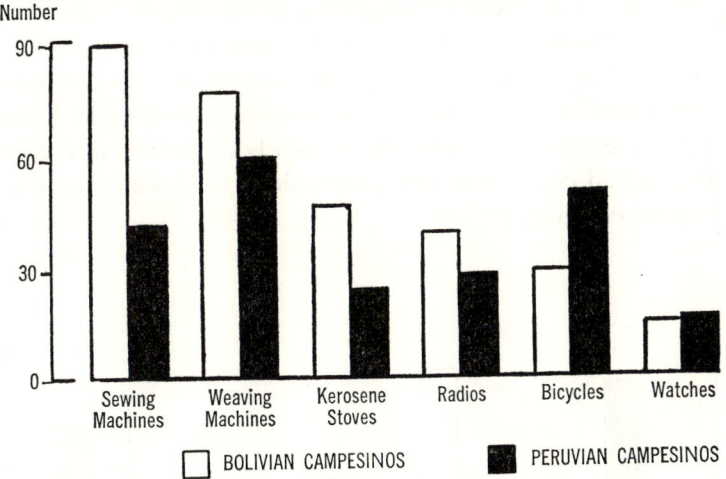

FIG. 2. NUMBER OF DURABLE GOODS OWNED BY SAMPLED CAMPESINOS

of living reflected in a greater consumption of manufactured goods and other purchased products. In figure 2 one sees that the 167 Bolivian campesinos interviewed owned more durable goods of all types than the same number of Peruvian campesinos—with the notable exception of bicycles. Figure 3 shows that the Bolivian campesinos purchased more "store-bought" dry goods. They also claimed to have worn these clothes more

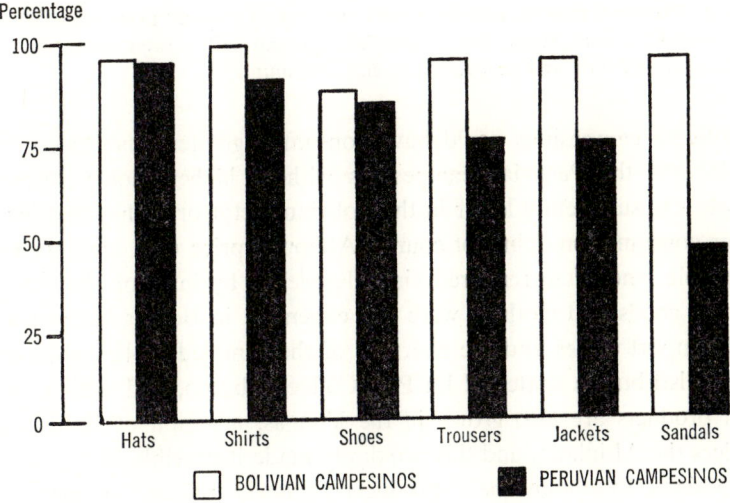

FIG. 3. STORE-BOUGHT DRY GOODS OWNED BY SAMPLED CAMPESINOS

frequently than their Peruvian neighbors. Finally, figure 4 indicates that the Bolivian campesinos purchased and consumed more "luxury" foods and stimulants than the Peruvians.[19] In addition, one out of every two Bolivians interviewed slept on wood or iron beds, as compared with only one out of every ten Peruvians. Finally, nearly 60 percent of the Bolivian campesinos had constructed new homes since 1953 while the Peruvians had built no new ones.

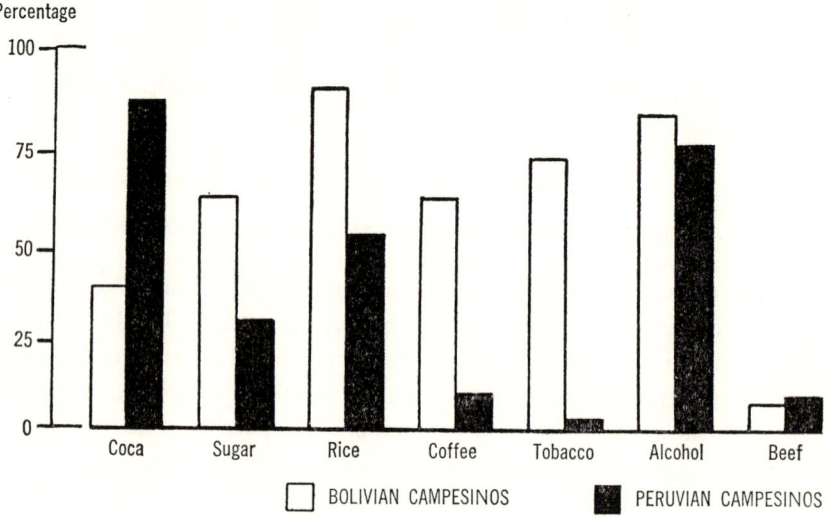

FIG. 4. CONSUMPTION OF LUXURY FOODS AND STIMULANTS BY SAMPLED CAMPESINOS. Percentages for coca, sugar, rice, and coffee represent daily consumption, while those for tobacco, alcohol, and beef reflect weekly consumption.

Bolivian campesinos could have consumed greater quantities of these goods than the Peruvian campesinos without higher money incomes if prices were sufficiently lower in the Bolivian sector or if they had incurred larger consumption debts, of course. Although price data are very scarce, unreliable, and often rendered virtually useless by inflation, it seems that durable goods and clothing were less expensive in Bolivia because of the lower import duties and the nearness of the sampled ex-haciendas to the major distribution center of La Paz. Coffee, tobacco, and similar agricultural products are also grown in the Yungas, a region of Bolivia which borders the Altiplano, and this proximity made it possible for the Bolivian campesinos to obtain these products at lower prices. In short, lower prices in the Bolivian sector probably did account for a small part of the higher consumption of the Bolivian campesinos. None of this difference in consumption can be attributed to indebtedness, however, since campesinos, in general, were not debtors due to their unwillingness and inability to borrow. As seen in table 11, only a fraction of the Bolivian and Peruvian campesinos interviewed were in debt, and the amounts they owed were very small.[20]

In sum, the evidence accumulated in this study indicates that the Bolivian campesino, on the average, had a greater total income, a higher standard of living, and possibly a greater money income than his

TABLE 11
DISTRIBUTION OF INDEBTEDNESS OF CAMPESINOS INTERVIEWED
(*In Dollars*)

	Peruvian Campesinos		Bolivian Campesinos [a]	
Creditor	Number in Debt	Amount of Debt	Number in Debt	Amount of Debt
Hacienda administrators	5	$ 150	—	—
Friends and neighbors	20	480	25	$257
Families	8	280	6	43
Businessmen	5	105	2	24
Agricultural banks	1	225	1	333
Total	39	$1,240	34	$657

a. The Bolivian campesino debt does not include a $15,827 debt of the cooperative of ex-hacienda I which is owed to the Agricultural Bank for the ex-haciendado property.

Peruvian counterpart during the agricultural year 1964–1965. Indeed, because of the lower demand placed upon his labor and time, the Bolivian campesino had greater leisure, which in itself is a form of income. When the more than five hundred campesinos not interviewed—nearly all of them Bolivians—are taken into consideration, the Bolivian ex-haciendas, with half the land extension of the Peruvian haciendas, provided a comparable living for four times as many campesinos. Consequently, the purchase and consumption of manufactured goods typically used by the campesinos were substantially greater on the Bolivian ex-haciendas than on the Peruvian haciendas.

In regard to the disposition of the incomes of the Peruvian hacendados and administrators, a very rough estimate of the economic profit of the four haciendas would be about $80,000. In addition, the administrators drew salaries totaling approximately $5,000. The administrators probably spent the greater part of their salaries in Puno, and this income and consumption of manufactured products should be added to that of the Peruvian campesinos. On the other hand, a portion of the recent investment in the haciendas was debt financed, as evidenced by the $25,000 they owed to local banks. Apparently, most of the hacendado economic profit was consumed or invested outside the Lake Titicaca region and possibly outside the nation.

CAMPESINO MOBILITY

There can be little doubt that the Bolivian campesinos were more free and mobile than their Peruvian counterparts. This enabled them to seek outside employment, engage in political and marketing activity, and

TABLE 12
SCHOOL ATTENDANCE OF THE SAMPLED CAMPESINO POPULATIONS

	Peruvians			Bolivians		
	Male	Female	Combined Average	Male	Female	Combined Average
Percentage of population that has attended school [a] (six years old and over)	54%	24%	39%	63%	30%	47%
Percentage of children attending school (six to seventeen years of age)	75	43	59	75	40	58

a. These figures include all persons who were attending school as well as those who had terminated their education.

most important of all, to educate themselves and their children. Approximately one out of every five Bolivian campesinos questioned had attended some type of adult education course since 1953, as compared with approximately one out of every fifteen Peruvian campesinos interviewed. Of the adult populations—all those over seventeen years of age—38 percent of the Bolivians sampled had attended school as compared with only 23 percent of the Peruvians. Finally, of the entire sampled population over six years of age, 47 percent of the Bolivians and 39 percent of the Peruvians had attended or were attending school. The average level of education of those who attended or were attending school was 2.83 years for the Bolivians and 2.27 years for the Peruvians. Eleven percent of the Bolivians achieved at least a primary education (six years or more) while only 6 percent of the Peruvians did so.

However, in table 12 one notes that approximately 60 percent of both the Bolivian and Peruvian school-age children (six to seventeen years of age) were enrolled in an educational institution. Every Bolivian ex-hacienda sampled had at least one school—nearly all newly constructed —while two of the four Peruvian haciendas investigated had no school. Also, the teachers of the Bolivian ex-hacienda schools were Indians, while the Peruvian teachers were *blancos* ("whites"). In both sectors, females were discriminated against with respect to education. Since the land reform, however, this has been ameliorated in the Bolivian sector of the region. Although the evidence is not overwhelming or conclusive, the data

TABLE 13
ILLITERACY OVER SEVENTEEN YEARS OLD

	Bolivian Campesinos			Peruvian Campesinos		
	Male	Female	Combined Average	Male	Female	Combined Average
Unable to speak Spanish	40%	77%	59%	53%	88%	71%
Unable to read and write Spanish	43	78	61	55	92	74
Unable to read, write, and speak Spanish	39	77	58	50	87	69

accumulated in the field indicate that the Bolivian campesinos were slightly better educated than their Peruvian counterparts (table 13). This increased education has led to a desire for even more. Of the campesinos interviewed 82 percent of the Bolivians professed a desire that their children obtain a primary (six years) or secondary (eleven years) level of education as compared with a similar desire on the part of only 69 percent of the Peruvians. Finally, the Bolivian campesino adults were observed to be more literate than their Peruvian neighbors.

SUPPORTING EVIDENCE

Other studies of Peruvian haciendas and Bolivian ex-haciendas in the Lake Titicaca region provide additional information which confirms most of these findings and thus validates the references to the sampled haciendas and ex-haciendas as representative of those in the region. For example, the Viacha study of eleven ex-haciendas shows that the sixty sampled campesinos possessed an average of seven hectares of land and sixty-six head of livestock (U.A.O.'s) and cultivated approximately one and a half hectares.[21]

Another study found half the campesinos on three Altiplano ex-haciendas with incomes averaging $125 from outside employment.[22] Likewise, a sample study of fifty haciendas in the department of Puno, Peru, provides evidence which indicates that the campesinos on these estates earned approximately the same income as the Peruvian campesinos interviewed in the field. According to this report the average campesino had exclusive use of about six hectares of land, owned between 125 and 220 head of livestock (U.A.O.'s) and shepherded between 300 and 600 U.A.O.'s per family.[23] In short, because they so closely resembled the Peruvian campesinos interviewed by this writer in terms of resources, production, and productivity, it is reasonable to expect their incomes to have been quite similar. In only one respect were the haciendas investigated by this writer different—all four of these haciendas paid their campesinos the minimum wage, while only half of the fifty haciendas investigated by the Agrarian Reform Office fully complied with the decree. But in general, there is every reason to expect the incomes of other campesinos in the region, both Peruvian and Bolivian, to approximate those of the campesinos interviewed by this author. Were it not for compulsory wage payments, the Peruvian campesinos would have had much lower incomes and standards of living than the Bolivians. Since this law has only been in existence since 1964, the Bolivian campesinos in the region, until very recently, probably had a much higher income than the Peruvian campesinos.

There is also additional evidence to support the study's findings that the Bolivian campesinos were more educated and literate than their Peruvian counterparts. In the Bolivian sector the Viacha study found 46 percent of the adult campesinos unable to speak Spanish and 50 percent illiterate. The study of fifty haciendas in the department of Puno, Peru, found one-half to have no schools [24] and the remainder to be "deficient." It has been estimated that 43 percent of the rural children between the ages of five and fourteen in the department of Puno were enrolled in school during 1963. The same report estimated the rural illiteracy rate for adults in the department to be 71 percent.[25] Since these estimates are similar to those arrived at by this author based upon independent samples, they lend support to the contention that the Bolivian campesinos on the ex-haciendas in the region were more literate and more educated than the Peruvian campesinos on the other side of the border.

THE EFFECTS OF THE BOLIVIAN LAND REFORM UPON HUMAN RESOURCES

Once again, the question arises as to what extent these differences in freedom, mobility, income, and education between the Bolivian campesinos and the Peruvian campesinos can be attributed to the Bolivian land reform of 1953. Did the tenancy conditions of the Bolivian latifundio land-tenure system restrict the freedom and mobility of the Indian tenants, and were these arrangements largely responsible for their low standards of living, education, and literacy? And if so, did the Bolivian land reform make it possible for the Bolivian campesinos to achieve higher incomes, standards of living, and education?

INCOME AND CONSUMPTION BEFORE AND AFTER THE LAND REFORM

To reiterate, the Peruvian haciendas investigated in many respects did not resemble the prereform Bolivian haciendas. This is most obvious with respect to the tenancy arrangements. Below is a list of the rights and obligations of the Bolivian hacendado and his Indian tenants under the prereform latifundio land-tenure system.

Obligations of the Hacendado

1. To provide each colono with a tract of cultivable land, called a sayaña, from which he is entitled to all production and upon which he can build his own house out of such materials as are at his disposal. This sayaña includes the piece of land for his house and a composite of fregmanted parcels in various *ainokas*—tracts of land devoted to a particular crop each year and rotated so that one year it is planted in potatoes, the next in barley, etc.
2. To allow the colono certain rights to pasture his livestock on hacienda land which is not being either used for crops or reserved exclusively for grazing the hacendado's livestock.
3. To grant the colono certain rights to irrigation water which is not being used on the lands exclusively reserved for the hacendado.
4. To furnish the colono with coca and occasionally a noonday meal during periods of heavy labor such as seeding, harvesting, etc. It

was often customary to provide the campesino with alcohol for the festivities that usually followed occasions such as a good harvest.

Obligations of the Colonos

1. To devote three days of each week (usually Monday, Tuesday, and Wednesday) to the lands or properties of the hacendado. During the cropping seasons the colono worked as many days as were needed to complete the tasks—which often exceeded the customary three day per week obligation.[26]
2. To furnish his own tools, oxen, burros, etc., as well as family members to prepare, seed, and harvest the crops of the hacendado and carry the produce to market or the town house.
3. To assume certain responsibilities for the care of the hacendado's livestock, land, and buildings.
4. To prepare periodically the products of the hacienda such as *tunta* and *chuño* ("dehydrated potatoes"), etc.
5. To provide certain personal services to the hacendado and administrator at both the estate and town house. These services included kitchen duties, collecting fuel, running errands, etc.[27]

Before the land reform the Bolivian landowners, with few exceptions, did not pay their laborers and tenants a money wage, but they did demand a great deal of the colono's labor-time for their estates. Because the Bolivian campesino had about the same quantity of land and livestock before the land reform as he does today but substantially less labor-time, he probably produced less on his sayaña. In addition, because a great deal of his labor-time was expended in shepherding the landowner's animals, working his lands, and providing him with personal services, the Indian tenant was not free to engage in outside employment. Therefore, one can be reasonably certain that the Bolivian campesinos before the land reform did not earn money income outside the estates as they do today.

There can be little doubt that the Bolivian land reform gave the campesinos the freedom, mobility, and time which has enabled them to obtain greater income. In addition, the Bolivian campesinos not only had higher per capita incomes in 1964–1965 but also supported approximately 50 percent more people on the same estate lands than they did before 1953. Because the Bolivian land reform redistributed most of the land previously used exclusively by the landowners to these new campesinos, it is the redistribution of labor-time which was the most significant benefit received by the ex-colonos. While it cannot be denied that the higher income and standard of living enjoyed by the Bolivian campesinos were achieved largely at the expense of the expropriated landowners, neither can it be denied that a part of the increased campesino income was a result of their increased output on the former estate lands and their outside employment.

This redistribution of income, in turn, created for the first time in Bolivia's history a mass consumption demand in the agrarian sector for manufactured products which could be domestically produced. Unlike the landowners of prerevolutionary days, the campesinos did not consume imported goods. Unfortunately, neither did they purchase investment goods such as fertilizer, tools, etc. Even more regrettable from a developmental point of view was the inability of the domestic manufacturing sector to provide the clothing, bicycles, transistor radios, etc., which the campesinos purchased.

EDUCATION AND LITERACY BEFORE
AND AFTER THE LAND REFORM

The Supreme Decree of August 19, 1936, required all Bolivian haciendas with more than twenty-five colono families to maintain a school for the education of their children. However, as in Puno, Peru, today, many of the Bolivian landowners did not comply with the law. For example, the 1946 ministry of agriculture study reported approximately one-fifth of the sampled haciendas to be without schooling of any type, in violation of the law. Also, where schools were provided, the facilities were reported to be "deficient"; only 11 percent of the school-age children were in attendance, the school buildings were "inadequate," the teachers "underpaid," and the quality of teaching "substandard." The study also pointed out that the Indian tenants themselves were often required to pay the salaries of the teachers. The end result of this latifundio educational system was an illiteracy rate as high as 97 percent on some of the haciendas investigated.[28] To the Bolivian landowners, the cost of educating the Indian children on their estates was very real and current, whereas the benefits to them, if any, were intangible and remote. William H. Nicholls recognized this problem when he wrote:

Increasingly, the principle source for financing social overhead, the socio-politically dominant landlord class will rarely be willing to tax itself in order to support such public services as education and agricultural extension.[29]

In sum, the latifundio land-tenure system was largely responsible for the low educational level and high illiteracy rate of the rural population in the Bolivian sector of the region before the land reform. Undoubtedly, such a low level of investment in human resources contributed to the relatively poor economic performance of these prereform haciendas.

In the Bolivian sector of the Lake Titicaca region, education has greatly increased since the land reform of 1953. Because the Bolivian campesino was no longer required to work for the landowner and because his small sayaña never did require all his family's labor and time, he, and especially his children, experienced enforced leisure. In contrast to the landowners' expenses, the cost of education to him was nominal in both money[30] and foregone opportunity and the potential benefit great. William Carter, who also has found education to be permeating the Bolivian ex-haciendas, has given one of the reasons for it:

> The new roles of the syndicate leaders, particularly those of the secretary general and recording secretary, require these officials to be men with both a speaking and writing knowledge of Spanish. Since schools are a fairly recent innovation in the rural areas of the Altiplano and just about the only bilingual people are those who have attended formal classes, this requirement practically rules out the elder men as candidates for places of authority. Thus, the very basis of qualification for leadership has been altered. Youth has replaced age.[31]

It should be emphasized that this increase in education is in the form of more education, not a better quality of education. In addition, the Bolivian land reform may not have been the sole factor responsible for the postrevolutionary surge in campesino education and literacy. Apparently, however, the new land-tenure system is more conducive to the development of human resources than was the former system.

POSSIBLE EFFECTS OF THE BOLIVIAN LAND REFORM ON THE PERUVIAN SECTOR

Before summarizing, a slight digression is warranted to analyze the effects of the Bolivian land reform upon the economic performance of the haciendas and human resources in the Peruvian sector of the Lake Titicaca region. Since the Bolivian land reform undoubtedly influenced the Peruvian lawmakers in the passage of the 1964 Punonian agrarian reform and minimum wage decrees, it was also partly responsible for a number of changes in the Peruvian sector of the Lake Titicaca region. Since 1964 there has occurred an exodus of Peruvian campesinos from the hacienda to the indigenous communities and towns within the department as well as to the cities of Arequipa and Lima. In addition, the landowners have been investing in a better breed of livestock and improved agricultural machinery. These changes have given rise to a greater specialization in ranching and thus to a more extensive use of the land. As a result, labor productivity has undoubtedly increased. For the hacendado, these changes have probably contributed to a more efficient use of the labor resource and a more inefficient use of land. Production for the market undoubtedly has increased, especially the sale of wool abroad.

From a macroeconomic viewpoint the forced migration from the haciendas intensified the population pressure on the *minifundios* ("small peasant farms") and indigenous communities in the area. This caused an increase in the farming of more marginal and less fertile land than that which was lying idle on the large haciendas. In addition, this forced migration to the overcrowded towns and cities increased the numbers of unemployed and poor urban dwellers.

However, these decrees did reduce the campesino populations on the haciendas and made wage payments to those remaining compulsory, all of which meant a higher income and standard of living for the remaining Peruvian campesinos. The greatest production cost of the sampled haciendas was wage payments. Prior to the 1964 minimum wage decree, this cost was virtually nonexistent. This higher income has indirectly enabled the hacienda campesinos to obtain more freedom, education, and literacy. Unfortunately, there is no way of determining whether these changes would have occurred in Peru had there been no land reform in Bolivia.

SUMMARY AND CONCLUSION

The primary purpose of this chapter was to analyze the socioeconomic effects of the Bolivian land reform upon human resources in the Lake Titicaca region by means of a comparison of Peruvian haciendas and Bolivian ex-haciendas. Most striking was the remarkable similarity in the poor economic performance of those different agricultural units of production operating under dissimilar tenure conditions. Neither the haciendas nor the ex-haciendas were realizing economies or diseconomies of size under existing technological and institutional conditions. Indeed, no definitive value-neutral statement could be made about the relative efficiency of either group. With respect to technology, livestock density per hectare, total production, capital productivity, and production for the domestic market, the haciendas and ex-haciendas in the region were virtually indistinguishable.

The most differentiating feature of these land-tenure systems was their utilization of human resources. On the Bolivian ex-haciendas, the high population density and incomplete use of campesino labor-time largely account for their relatively higher land productivity and employment, as well as their lower labor productivity and agricultural surplus. In spite of the much lower labor productivity on the ex-haciendas, the Bolivian campesinos still earned greater per capita incomes during the agricultural year 1964–1965 and, apparently, enjoyed a higher standard of living. In large part this can be attributed to the lower demand placed on their labor and time by ex-hacienda production, enabling them to seek outside employment and engage in more marketing activity. Finally, the Bolivian campesinos were observed to be better educated, more literate, and better integrated into both the market economy and society than their Peruvian counterparts.

It was also emphasized in this chapter that the Bolivian haciendas in the region were, to a significant degree, mere agglomerations of small Indian sayañas. With the advent of the Bolivian land reform, the Indian tenants obtained possession of their sayañas, and most of the land previously used exclusively by the landowners was redistributed to new campesinos. Population on the ex-haciendas increased and more marginal land was put into production. As a result, total production increased, labor productivity decreased, and capital (livestock) productivity remained virtually unchanged. Total production as well as market production exceeded prereform levels, largely because of the increased inputs of marginal land and labor. Because no size economies were realized by the Bolivian haciendas, none were lost as a consequence of the land reform. Whether any potential size economies were therefore destroyed by the Bolivian land reform is a purely academic question. The creation of small economic units of production does not, however, preclude taking advantage of size economies through cooperative efforts, if capital funds and new technology were made available to the Bolivian campesinos through state agricultural extension and credit services. Finally, because alternative employment in Bolivia is limited, the increase in marginal subsistence farming might be considered an efficient allocation of resources in the short run.

On the one hand, contrary to the expectations of some land-reform proponents, this analysis indicates that the Bolivian land reform was not a panacea for the Lake Titicaca region's agricultural and economic problems. On the other hand, contrary to the dire predictions of land-reform opponents, no evidence was found to indicate that the region's agricultural and general economic efficiency and progress have grievously suffered as a consequence of land reform. These results support those who say that institutional changes such as the Bolivian land reform have little effect upon production, productivity, and efficiency in the short run.

However, in the Lake Titicaca region it was man, not land, capital, production, or productivity, who underwent the greatest transformation with the implementation of the Bolivian land reform. The redistribution of land and, above all, labor and time made it possible for the Bolivian campesinos to earn higher per capita incomes from production on the ex-haciendas, to increase their marketing activity, and to engage in outside employment. Their increased income not only raised the campesinos' standard of living but also created an agrarian demand for manufactured products capable of domestic production.

The Bolivian land reform was not merely a redistribution of land, labor and time, or even income; it was simultaneously a redistribution of opportunity, freedom, and power. The campesinos in the region are gradually becoming more educated, literate, and integrated into the social, political, and economic life of the nation. Where previously the campesino paid a labor tax for the land he used, as of 1969 he pays no tax at all and is the owner of productive private property.[32] If private property is truly the institution which "turns sand into gold," then these new property owners have as their task what the absentee landowners failed to accomplish. If the existence of a socially, occupationally, and geographically mobile labor force is conducive to economic efficiency and development, then the creation of this institution by the Bolivian land reform augurs well for the attainment of these national goals. Bolivian society is no longer divided into Indians and Bolivians as before the MNR revolution and land reform, and the uncertain future of Bolivia will undoubtedly be greatly influenced by the campesino majority who are now free either to succeed or to fail on their own merits. The full impact of these changes will probably not be realized, however, until at least decades, and perhaps generations, have elapsed.

NOTES

1. *Land tenure* is the term used for all rights and relationships that have been created among men to govern their affairs with respect to the land. *Land tenancy* is the system under which land is operated and its product divided between the operator and owner.

2. Erich H. Jacoby et al., *Inter-Relationship between Agrarian Reform and Agricultural Development,* Food and Agricultural Organization of the United Nations (Rome, Italy, September 1953), p. 63.

3. Bolivia, Junta Nacional de Planamiento, *Plan nacional de desarrollo económico y social, 1962–1971* (La Paz, 1961).

4. *Medium properties* and *agricultural enterprises* were defined as those estates which use wage labor, modern technology, capital equipment, and produce for the market.

5. Víctor Paz Estenssoro, *La revolucion boliviana* (La Paz, 1966), p. 19.

6. See map in figure 1 on p. 306 for the location of the sampled haciendas and ex-haciendas.

7. See ONERN y CORPUNO, *Program de inventario y evaluacion de las recursos naturales del departamento de Puno,* vol. 5 (Lima, 1965), chap. 7.

8. In accordance with the provisions of the Peruvian Ley de Reform Agraria no. 15037 of November 25, 1964.

9. Because the material in this and the following section of the study has been published elsewhere, only the salient findings will be summarized in this chapter. For a more detailed presentation of this economic analysis of the haciendas and ex-haciendas, the reader may consult my "Land Reform and Its Effect Upon Production and Productivity in the Lake Titicaca Region," *Economic Development and Cultural Change* (April 1970), pp. 410–50.

10. This difference in land use was not a consequence of soil fertility, irrigation, or surface configuration. Neither the haciendas nor the ex-haciendas irrigated more than a small portion of their pastures. Also, hilly land is often more suitable for cultivation than level land since it affords some protection against frosts.

11. On two of the haciendas investigated, the administrators personally managed the estates only when their organizing abilities were most needed—during planting, harvesting, shearing, etc. Indeed, this was not always the case; this writer arrived at one of the haciendas with the administrator to find the land prepared and the seed planted, all accomplished without the help of the administrator or the new tractor.

12. See table 14 for a breakdown of these total value outputs by product and producer.

13. See table 15 for a breakdown of this production for the market by product and producer.

14. Although the Bolivian and the Peruvian campesinos owned approximately half as many sheep as the Peruvian landowners, they sold almost no wool. According to the agricultural experts of the Utah Team for AID/Bolivia, there is a potential market for this criollo wool and the minimum wool export value to Bolivia is estimated to be about $12 million a year. Kenneth N. Roberts et al., *Bolivian Wool: A Source of National Wealth,* mimeographed (AID, January 1966).

15. Sol Tax, *Penny Capitalism* (Chicago, Ill., 1963), p. 12.

16. Theodore W. Schultz, *Transforming Traditional Agriculture* (New Haven, Conn., 1964), p. 131.

17. Philip M. Raup, "The Contribution of Land Reforms to Agricultural Development: An Analytical Framework" *Economic Development and Cultural Change,* 3 (October 1963), p. 13.

18. See tables 16 and 17 for this difference in market price.

19. It has been suggested that the Indians chew coca to deaden the pain of the hard labor they are required to perform. This study seems to confirm this proposition inasmuch as the Peruvian campesinos did work harder than the Bolivians and chewed more coca.

TABLE 14

VALUE OF AGRICULTURAL PRODUCTS SOLD AND CONSUMED

(*In Dollars*)

Product	Peru			Bolivia		
	Campesinos	Hacendados	Total	Cooperatives	Campesinos	Total
Animal						
Sheep	$ 5,159	$ 46,166	$ 51,325	$1,117	$ 18,258	$ 19,375
Cattle	4,198	14,397	18,595	215	28,665	28,880
Alpaca & Llama	605	65	670	—	3,660	3,660
Pigs	20	—	20	90	3,185	3,275
Wool	200	64,890	65,090	475	1,475	1,950
Milk	—	9,300	9,300	—	—	—
Cheese	3,300	3,185	6,485	525	19,965	20,490
Hides	2,550	3,450	6,000	720	5,955	6,675
Subtotal	$16,032	$141,453	$157,485	$3,142	$ 81,163	$ 84,305
Crop						
Potatoes	$ 675	$ 3,995	$ 4,670	$ 960	$ 26,490	$ 17,450
Quinua	285	535	820	20	1,100	1,120
Cañahua	340	75	415	—	1,100	1,100
Barley	425	1,800	2,225	125	14,265	14,390
Habas	—	—	—	—	4,790	4,790
Oca	—	—	—	—	15,900	15,900
Subtotal	$ 1,725	$ 6,405	$ 8,130	$1,105	$ 63,645	$ 64,750
Total	$17,757	$147,858	$165,615	$4,247	$144,808	$149,055
Plus	—	4,630 [a]	4,630 [a]	—	—	—
Grand Total	$17,757	$152,488	$170,245	$4,247	$144,808	$149,055

a. This figure is an imputed value for crop production on forty hectares of hacienda IV based upon the performance of the other haciendas.

TABLE 15

VALUE OF PRODUCTS SOLD BY THE PERUVIAN HACIENDAS AND BOLIVIAN EX-HACIENDAS
(*In Dollars*)

Product	Peru			Bolivia		
	Campesinos	Hacendados	Total	Cooperatives	Campesinos	Total
Animal						
Sheep	$1,194	$ 40,539	$ 41,733	$ 978	$ 7,587	$ 8,565
Cattle	4,106	14,349	18,455	217	26,861	27,078
Alpaca & Llama	46	—	46	—	3,226	3,226
Pigs	—	—	—	88	2,457	2,545
Wool	—	64,899 a	64,899	475	—	475
Milk	—	9,298	9,298	—	—	—
Cheese	1,650	1,097	2,747	145	7,898	8,043
Hides	23	2,604	2,627	—	185	185
Subtotal	$7,019	$132,786	$139,805	$1,903	$48,214	$50,117
Crop						
Potatoes	$ —	$ 1,250	$ 1,250	$ 120	$ 414	$ 534
Quinua	—	—	—	21	40	61
Cañahua	—	388	388	—	—	—
Barley	—	—	—	125	45	170
Habas	—	—	—	—	266	266
Oca	—	—	—	—	303	303
Subtotal	$ —	$ 1,638	$ 1,638	$ 266	$ 1,068	$ 1,334
Total	$7,019	$134,424	$141,443	$2,169	$49,282	$51,451
Plus	—	1,180 b	1,180 b	—	—	—
Grand Total	$7,019	$135,604	$142,623	$2,169	$49,282	$51,451

a. Of this figure, $1,104 is the value of alpaca wool sold; the remainder is the value of sheep's wool.
b. This figure is an imputed value for crops sold by hacienda IV based upon performance of the other haciendas.

TABLE 16
AMOUNTS AND AVERAGE PRICES OF PRODUCTS SOLD AND CONSUMED ON FOUR BOLIVIAN
EX-HACIENDAS
(*In Dollars*)

Product	Campesino Cooperatives		Campesinos	
	Number	Average Unit Price [a]	Number [b]	Average Unit Price [a]
Sheep				
Rams	36	$ 7.25	2,336	$ 4.65
Ewes	186	4.60	1,692	4.30
Lambs	—	—	56	2.15 [c]
Cattle				
Bulls	1	66.65	376	65.40
Cows	2	75.00	76	43.25
Calves	—	—	20	39.35
Llamas	—	—	436	8.40
Pigs	13	6.75 [d]	472	6.75
Hides	379	1.90	3,220	1.85
	Pounds	Average Unit Price [a]	Pounds	Average Unit Price [a]
Sheep wool	1,900	$ 0.25	5,896	$ 0.25 [d]
Cheese	1,050	0.50	49,912	0.40
Potatoes	16,000	0.03	883,000	0.03
Quinua	700	0.03	43,960	0.025
Cañahua	—	—	44,420	0.025
Barley	5,000	0.025	713,220	0.02
Habas	—	—	136,780	0.035
Oca	—	—	530,048	0.03

a. All prices are those received in the market for products sold except where indicated.
b. Total amounts sold and consumed are based upon the statistical averages of those campesinos interviewed.
c. Estimated price based upon the assumption that a lamb, on the average, is worth half the value of an ewe.
d. Imputed prices based upon the market prices received by the campesinos or cooperatives.

20. However, the larger size of the average campesino animal herd might be viewed as greater savings on their part since livestock is the traditional campesino bank account.
21. *Estudio económico estadistico del Canton Viacha,* mimeographed (La Paz, 1965).
22. Kelso L. Wessel, *Social-Economic Comparison of Eight Agricultural Communities in the Oriente and the Altiplano,* Department of Agricultural Economics of Cornell University, mimeographed (La Paz, June 1966), p. 75.

TABLE 17

AMOUNT AND AVERAGE PRICES OF PRODUCTS SOLD AND CONSUMED ON FOUR PERUVIAN
HACIENDAS
(*In Dollars*)

Product	Campesinos		Hacendados	
	Number [a]	Average Unit Price [b]	Number	Average Unit Price [b]
Sheep				
Rams	9	$ 3.75	3,463	$ 6.05
Ewes	1,825	2.80	4,544	5.40
Lambs	11	1.40 [c]	250	2.70
Cattle				
Bulls	59	45.65	138	50.60
Cows	49	30.70	116	58.15
Calves	—	—	15	44.75
Llamas & Alpacas	119	5.10	13	5.10 [d]
Pigs	3	6.75	—	—
Hides	1,700 [e]	1.50 [d]	2,300	1.50
	Pounds [a]	Average Unit Price [b]	Pounds	Average Unit Price [b]
Alpaca wool	300 [e]	$ 0.26	2,300	$ 0.48
Sheep wool	800 [e]	0.15	155,590 [f]	0.41
Cheese	6,000	0.55 [d]	5,795	0.55
Potatoes	27,063	0.025 [d]	159,846 [g]	0.025
Quinua	9,504	0.03 [d]	17,850 [g]	0.03
Cañahua	11,385	0.03 [d]	2,439 [g]	0.03
Barley	17,000 [e]	0.025 [d]	72,110 [g]	0.025
Milk	—	—	116,221 qts.	0.08

a. Total amounts sold and consumed are based upon the statistical averages of those campesinos interviewed.

b. All prices are those received in the market for products sold except where indicated.

c. Estimated price based upon the assumption that a lamb, on the average, is worth half the value of an ewe.

d. Imputed value based upon the market prices received by the campesinos or hacendados.

e. These figures are estimates based upon the number of animals, hectares cultivated, and average yields.

f. An estimated 95,000 of this figure is an imputed amount for hacienda IV based upon the number of sheep and average yield.

g. Crop production information for one hacendado is not included in these figures.

23. Sample study of haciendas in the department of Puno, Peru.

24. By law, the Peruvian haciendas were required to maintain a primary school only if the number of school-age children on the estate exceeded thirty.

25. ONERN y CORPUNO, *Program de inventario y evaluacion,* pp. 25–26.

26. The rights and obligations varied among colonos within a hacienda. If a colono was a *quarta persona* ("fourth of a person"), he was obliged to render three labor days of service per week to the hacendado in return for the use of a small tract of land. However, if he was a *media persona* ("half of a person"), he was required to provide the landowner with twice as much labor for the use of twice as much land. Finally, if he was a *persona* ("full person"), he and his family gave the hacendado twelve labor days of service each week for the use of four times as much land as a quarta persona.

27. *Estudio socio-económico en las provincias de Omasuyos, Ingavi, y Los Andes del departamento de La Paz* (La Paz, 1946), pp. 24–26, 85–86.

28. Ibid., pp. 27–28.

29. William H. Nicholls, "An Agricultural Surplus as a Factor in Economic Development," *Journal of Political Economy,* 71 (February 1963), p. 17.

30. At the time of this study, the Bolivian government paid the salaries of the rural schoolteachers and provided technical assistance for the construction of these schools. In addition, Bolivia had no income or land tax.

31. William E. Carter, *Aymara Communities and the Bolivian Agrarian Reform,* University of Florida Monograph 24 (Gainesville, Fla., Fall 1964), p. 59.

32. President Barrientos submitted a bill to Congress in 1968 to tax rural land. As of the date of this writing, however, it has not been put into law.

MURDO J. MACLEOD
University of Pittsburgh

The Bolivian Novel, the Chaco War, and the Revolution

Before the third decade of this century, Bolivian literature could be characterized as a frail, almost accidental phenomenon. The few intellectuals who had dedicated themselves to writing were understandably unimpressed by their homeland, and their reaction, with very few exceptions, had been to ignore it by seeking their inspiration and cultural models in Europe.

This scanty, imitative literature was in some ways indicative of the state of the country as a whole. A weak and disorganized state, even in the Latin American context, Bolivia had lost large slices of its national territory to more powerful neighbors, and internally the new state had been chronically misgoverned by a series of barbarous or elitist *caudillos*. As late as 1930, in fact, Bolivia appeared to be as backward as it had been during its colonial days, and few of its intellectuals had shown any awareness of this depressing fact much less a desire to propose remedies.[1]

The few precursors—one thinks mainly of Gabriel René-Moreno, Alcides Arguedas, Franz Tamayo, and Jaime Mendoza—who had "looked around them," had shown rather violent reactions. There was little concern with the identification of specific problems, except in a general sense, and these writers tended to drift toward rather primitive sociological examinations of strong and weak races and race mixtures or to a vague,

The author is grateful to the Social Science Research Council for the grant which facilitated this study. All translations are by the author.

telluric mysticism which debated the effects of the awesome Andean landscape on its inhabitants.[2] So even they, writers of distinction as they were, represented only a small beginning as far as the social literature is concerned.

From 1932 to 1936 Bolivia fought the disastrous Chaco War, losing yet another part of its territory to Paraguay as a consequence of its defeat. The impact of defeat on a nation is a great stimulus for change—the "generation of '98" in Spain and the Nazi movement in Germany are two examples—and the influence of the Chaco War disaster, at least on the urban elites and the middle class, was profound. The various classes and races within the state had never experienced national involvement on such a scale, and the Chaco experience suddenly revealed to those Bolivians conscious of their nationality the true nature of their country.[3] The war served, in fact, as a general awakening for the educated and politically active classes.

After the end of the war a dynamic change came over Bolivian literary life. Since the thirties there has been a flood of writing, particularly novels of social protest, examining the various problems which plague the nation. In them the writers have tried to give form to the passions of their time— the emotions, ideas, and reforms which were shaking their *patria*.

The war itself produced a series of novels. On the burning steppes of the Chaco, young Bolivian intellectuals experienced something so beyond their understanding, so shocking to their sensibilities, that they have continued to write about it ever since.[4]

Many authors began with the romantic image of war, the false patriotism, and the gradual, artificially induced, heady growth of a spurious war fever on the Altiplano before the actual fighting started. It seems that these young intellectuals and workers, like so many innocents before a slaughter, lived in a world of romance and glory, little dreaming of the true nature of modern battle.[5] Even more tragic was the prewar position of the Indians vis-à-vis the incipient conflict. Many were completely confused about the reasons for the war, where it was to be waged, and even, some claim, what the name of their own side was. In novel after novel the Indian flees from the army recruiters, for he has no reason to dislike the distant Paraguayan *pilas* ("common soldiers") but every reason to dread the approach of the white and mestizo recruiters from the city. Those who flee slink back to find their houses burned and their women abused. The fleeing, hiding *emboscados* ("draft-dodging Indians") are characters in many novels. Occasionally the Indians' terror at the thought of having to serve under their white masters was so great that they rose in revolts on the Altiplano.[6] These revolts were put down, the government arguing, logically enough from its point of view, that armed revolt in time of war is treason. But what of the Indians' point of view, the writers ask, when some of them may not even have realized that they were Bolivians?

Another factor which faced the Bolivians in the Chaco region is mentioned repeatedly—the pilas knew the terrain. To combat their own ignorance the Bolivian *andinos* ("Andeans") tried to use their own lowlanders, the *cruceños* and *benianos* (men from Santa Cruz and the Beni), as guides and trackers. But they were few and often unwilling! Here the lack of integration in Bolivia's caste-ridden and regionalistic society is again made plain. The lowlanders and the soldiers from the Altiplano distrusted one another, and the lowland *cambas* ("native lowlanders"), some writers even claim, often felt more racial and cultural affinity with their enemies of the moment, the Guaranís ("Paraguayan Indians").[7]

If the lowlanders did not cooperate fully and the townspeople were dismayed by what the conflict revealed about their nation, then what of the Aymara and the Quechua Indians? Unable to understand their officers, terrorized by modern warfare, dazed by the heat and the lowland terrain, they were little better than cannon fodder. Hundreds deserted or allowed themselves to be taken prisoner. A few resorted to the device of shooting themselves in the left hand or arm, a method, when discovered, punishable by death. Again, the intellectuals discern the hidden absurdities in the situation. How can a subject race be expected to show patriotism or enthusiasm for a national cause? Yet, in spite of the injustice, some writers admire the stoical indifference to death of the Indians, and some express a hope for a post-Chaco future based on them.[8]

The novels about the war do not deal solely with the fighting and the soldiers. A favorite device of these writers is the introduction of campfire conversations and arguments during the oppressive tropical nights. The war, many claim, is merely a battle between the Royal Dutch Shell and the Standard Oil companies, and if Bolivia were a real nation it would not allow itself to be used as a pawn in this fashion.[9] Rancor against the oligarchic government back on the Altiplano grows, especially when some young officers realize that the graft and venality of those in La Paz is affecting the food, fuel, and ammunition supplies.[10] Old themes are reexamined. Bolivia needs a seacoast. What is to be done about the Indian majority? Why, when the tin mines produce riches daily, does the nation remain so backward? As defeat follows defeat and the Bolivian armies retreat farther and farther north and west, the bitterness of these men coming from this painful reeducation sinks deeper.

In every novel written about the Chaco, the problem of the future hangs over all; if the protagonist survives he will presumably have to return to his old life on the Altiplano, resume old habits, and recommence whatever tasks or career the war had interrupted. The problem for these young Chaco veterans is that they have learned too much and, what is more important, have discovered too much about the real nature of their society and its government to be able mentally, or even physically, to resume with satisfaction or self-respect what they had left a few years before. Although they are not yet sure how or what, they have all decided that things must change—and change quickly—if they are to regain pride in themselves or their country. "It is not the man, but rather the system which has been corrupted! What Bolivia demands is a new politics, not new politicians." [11] Toro Ramallo is even more bitter and talks of punishment accompanying the change:

We, the same people who suffered in the war and because of the war, will later be its propagandists. . . . A group of opportunistic and criminal politicians took advantage of the confusion. . . . The army has dragged out a useless calvary across the Chaco. When will the hour of judgment sound for those responsible? It may well be that one day the greatest crime that Bolivia has seen will be punished for the sake of those who remained in the sand and scrub.[12]

Politically the Chaco War started a process which caused the national revolution and which has not yet terminated. The conflict engendered a revolutionary outlook with Marxist and nationalistic overtones, and the young Chaco veterans took the lead in these revolutionary activities. A new spirit was manifest in every aspect of the society's life. While most of this revolutionary effort was directed toward politics, many of the young intellectuals saw it as their task to analyze the new convictions, to convert their fellow countrymen, and to carry their ideas into the cultural as well as the political field. By protest they hoped to publicize the faults of their homeland and to use literature as a propagandistic weapon.

Art, too, can be a weapon! And it is! Through art we can reach sensibilities, and revolutionizing sensibilities to dispose them to favor a new social ideal, that is a beautiful mission! [13]

A truly Bolivian literature had to be created at the same time, for nationalism was one of the intellectuals' banners, and there was no real national literature. Promptly dubbed the "vernacular school" by one of their foremost writers, these young men insisted above all that the nation examine its conscience, indulge in some healthy introspection, and cleanse itself through the knowledge thus strenuously attained. The vernacular school, Diez de Medina says,

seeks the exaltation of *lo propio* ("one's own"), the social theme. Sincere rebellion. These young men want an intrinsically Bolivian literature to be the first step in advancing the nation as a whole, a nation conscious of its own self.[14]

Again, as so often happens in Latin America, the novel was their most frequently used literary medium. Since the end of the war, hundreds of these novels of social protest have been written, and, like many of the novels about the war itself, the general quality of the work is not high. Nevertheless, this fiction as a corpus represents the aspirations, emotions, and propaganda of the young Bolivian revolutionaries and is of some help in understanding the changes which took place in the country. Even more, these novels afford an insight into the collective perception of Bolivian reality which was held by the educated groups whence these writers came.

One of the first tasks which the vernacular school undertook was the discovery and exploration of the country. Bolivians, so disunited in the past, were to be told about their compatriots from other regions of whom they had only vaguely heard, if at all. The war had begun this process; as one of its veterans admits, "The war served the purpose of introducing us to one another, people from all over the country, from the mountains, the valleys, and the Yungas." [15] But even here the author speaks only of Bolivia's heartland. What of the great, empty Bolivian lowlands, now thought of as the nation's land of the future? Cerruto claims that

among us, the man who knows anywhere beyond Potosí or Sucre is rare. We know nothing of the cruceño or beniano, and the beniano or cruceño in turn knows nothing of us. The Beni for us is a land lost in legend! [16]

The result has been a spate of novels about the tropical areas, an attempt through literature to open up this vast unknown to the Altiplano peoples.

One of the most famous novels about the tropical departments of Beni and Pando is *Borrachera verde* by Raúl Botelho Gosálvez. It has been compared to José Eustacio Rivera's famous work *La vorágine,* and there are many similarities in theme and language. The first part of the story is set in the cattle-raising territory of Moxos. A sense of the emptiness of the area is conveyed, and it is a wonder that there are any inhabitants at all since travel is hazardous, uncomfortable, and time-consuming. Formerly, the reader is told, this tropical savannah swarmed with cattle, but, gradually, the numbers diminished as mismanagement, floods, and the tropics took their toll, although the population is still great. Nowadays, the local cambas will slaughter a cow at random just for one steak.[17] Very early in the novel the theme of waste and futility has been set.

Gradually, the tropical environment begins to affect the protagonist. His treatment of his wife becomes extremely cruel, and he is brutal with the *peones* who help him with the cattle. Eventually, completely besotted with drink, loneliness, and the tropics, he drives his wife away to her death. In self-pity, he curses the tropics, "These lonely distances and alcohol are the guilty ones." His degeneration continues and he flees northward to the dense, tropical forests of the Beni. There, among the unfriendly, wild tribes, he tries to hide his shame, but the *selva* ("tropical rain forest") is a brutal teacher—"to say the word *selva* is to say anguish"—and man is merely a puny interloper. He may kill, cut down trees, and burn vast tracts of forest, but the selva will regenerate, teeming with life and death, and will eventually swallow the interloper too.

The novel now becomes one of more open social protest. After wandering for days in the jungle, the disheveled protagonist meets two other victims of the tropics like himself. They are escaped rubber gatherers from the vast feudal estates of Suárez Hermanos, "despotic traffickers in gold, rubber, and human blood, omnipotent lords, masters of immense fortunes amassed through the blood of twenty thousand rubber gatherers." [18]

The three men continue to lead a dissipated, aimless life, too weak to react to the challenge posed by their tropical surroundings. La selva—la *borrachera verde* ("this green madness")—has them in its clutches, and the author becomes lyrical once again about the impersonal, overwhelming nature of the Beni region. The men dream occasionally of the old and better days. Sometimes they are anticlerical, but more often they converse about their native land and feel deeply for its suffering, seeing in their own brutalization the fate of the nation:

We would talk of Bolivia, about our poor country, plaything of the conquests of intellectual and economic imperialism; we would speak of *colla* ["highland"] introversion and of that lack of vision which characterizes the country's landowning and military governments, of the History of Bolivia, which is the absurd story of people who have lost their way, with its pattern of revolutions and idiotic barracks revolts, of our nation's presidents, profiteering and vulgar demagogues who arouse the masses with their trite glibness in order to lead them to the wretchedness of a war or the imbecility of a revolution or coup d'état which switches around the same sorry faces on the same lamentable stage.

We, who didn't know how to weep for ourselves, in that far-off wilderness, then wept for our patria.[19]

Thus, the author manages to combine two purposes at once. In this well-written novel he manages to introduce to his readers a vast and unfamiliar region of Bolivia, and at the same time he introduces his attack on the country's miserable political institutions.

Another novelist Diomedes de Pereyra, who lived and taught for many years in the United States, writing much of his work in English, is rather unique among post-Chaco Bolivian novelists. He is first and foremost a lover of adventure and a teller of tales. His novels have hidden treasures, fantastic exploits, and lost tribes sprinkled liberally throughout. Yet Pereyra knew the far north of Bolivia well, and his descriptions of Acre (now Brazilian) and Pando are highly realistic. His passages on the treatment meted out to the rubber gatherers are even more harrowing than those of Botelho. When an Indian falls ill he is killed, we are told, by a blow on the head like an animal, so as not to waste bullets. Indians caught fleeing have their hands cut off and are tied up in front of the company stores like monkeys, as an example to the others. Naturally the Indian hates all whites. "I hate those of your race." [20] Where Diomedes de Pereyra really excels, however, is in his descriptions of the selva, the life there, and the difficulties of travel down the tropical rivers. This is yet another explorer and pioneer for his fellow countrymen, albeit by means of the written page.

Some of the present writers who come from the tropics feel that it is their duty to record the traditional life of the Beni and Santa Cruz areas. With the new Cochabamba highway now bringing immigrants and technology to the Oriente, it is inevitable that the old ways will vanish. The writers certainly do not regret this but feel a certain nostalgia for the old ways. So we find in their vivid descriptions of the plains much of the quaint and traditional ways of the cambas. Callaú Barbery calls the lowlands "the Bolivian land of promise," yet feels a sneaking regret for the uncomplicated past: "The narratives which make up this book are really written with the soul and with the fervent desire to preserve the traditions and vitality of the beniano life of today and yesterday, before progress— necessary and inevitable—finishes it off." [21]

The MNR revolutionary government openly backed the exploratory novel of the Beni region. Praising the recent work *Guaporé, hombre y río,* former president Víctor Paz Estenssoro wrote, "Its publication will contribute to the formation of a national awareness of the great developmental possibilities which the Beni offers for the future." [22]

The other huge area in the east of Bolivia, lying between the lost territory of the Chaco and the forests of the north, is Santa Cruz, no longer *terra incognita* to Bolivians but before 1952 a remote region. Now the only asphalt highway in the country connects the rapidly growing town of Santa Cruz with Cochabamba in the highlands. Here, too, the fear that the old days will disappear without leaving a record has inspired a writer. The cambas of the area, Enrique Kempff Mercado points out, are morbidly conscious that they are different from the collas of the Altiplano, as, indeed, racially and culturally they are, and this causes an enthusiasm for traditional ways coupled with a hatred for the government on the Altiplano which can only be overcome patiently and slowly. To be heavy handed would be to exacerbate the strong cruceño regionalism into open separation. One story in particular concerns the rejection by the local farmers of a Quechua who settles in the lowlands. Although this stranger is finally driven out the novelist stresses that such intermingling, which will come anyway since the area is so underpopulated, must come on an ever larger scale, for this is the only way to put an end to regional hatreds. [23] But not all the plainsmen are tradition bound. There are many cruceños, the novelists tell us, who wish to participate in any of the advances which the nation will make in the future but who feel that they and the region from which they come are ignored by the national government or, at best, that Altiplano solutions, probably most suitable for situations *allí arriba* ("up there") are imposed on the lowlands where the problems which confront the inhabitants are entirely different. [24]

The romance of their east is drawing more and more Bolivian writers. Many see it as a sunny land of fertile soil, handsome horsemen, beautiful women, and flowing water. [25] Disillusion is bound to come when reality is faced, but at least the people of the mountains are now trying to incorporate this vast *Tierra de Promisión* ("Promised Land") into their lives and culture.

The area to the north and east of La Paz known as the Yungas, although not so distant as the plains, was also practically unknown to many Bolivians, and here, once again, Botelho Gosálvez has led the way for the novelist-explorers. His novel *Coca,* written three years after the more famous *Borrachera verde,* tells a similar story—man trying to come to grips with himself and his life in a strange and difficult environment. It has been estimated that this relatively small area of fertile, semitropical valleys could easily feed the entire population of Bolivia, yet little is grown there besides coca, a narcotic leaf chewed by the Indians. Alvaro Díaz, Botelho's struggling hero, is, of course, a Chaco veteran, but he finds that the loneliness and impossibility of one man defying nature in the Yungas are too much for the single individual, and he dies a miserable death.[26] Many of the other novels about this area are more hopeful, such as Nazario Pardo Valle's *Trópico del norte,* which is staged in the forested province of Caupolicán at the foot of the valleys. Optimistically, many see a great future for the area—once the roads are built and the people can be induced to move to these fertile valleys from the barren Altiplano.

The Altiplano Indian is, as one would suppose, one of the major pre-occupations of the Bolivian postwar novelists of social protest. The Indian, be he Quechua or Aymara, is to some extent the major character in all the novels about the Altiplano, and, in reality, he represents the great majority of the population. The novelists generally recognize that without a radical change in the Indian's status and standard of living, the country as a whole can never advance. One group of novelists has seen it as its duty to examine the daily life of the peón-farmer—a creature tied to his land and, until recently, to his feudal lord, the *hacienda* owner. Two superior novels immediately come to mind, although there is a plethora of mediocre ones from which to choose.

Again, the young novelist Botelho Gosálvez, one of Bolivia's few pro-fessional writers, has provided one of the leading works. His *Altiplano* has been praised by many critics and is his best novel to date. Although a fictional work it has often been acclaimed by sociologists, so well docu-mented and observant is the novel. It is about the Aymaras on the shores of Lake Titicaca, and there the reader is introduced to an Indian *ayllu* ("communal settlement"), where the life is full of work and poverty with the line between sufficiency and starvation so precarious that the least upset can disrupt the whole society. Eventually a drought is enough to drive the Indians off the land, and circumstances disperse them to other parts of the country. Some go to the high Puna as shepherds, where the extreme cold makes their lives even more miserable; some go down to the Yungas to work on coca plantations where, unused to the tropical diseases, many soon die; a few go to find work in the tin mines where they are forced to toil under appallingly dangerous conditions for a daily pittance. The whole book is a plea for those lost children, the Bolivian Indians. It is not strident or revolutionary but gently and pathetically accusing. The novel has been called the Bolivian *Huasipungo.*[27]

In a different style—a style which reminds one of the poetic Cerruto— José Felipe Costas Arguedas has attempted to do for the Quechuas what Botelho Gosálvez has done for the Aymaras. He is a lyrical writer and in his thinking is much of the mysticism of the soil so often found in Bolivian intellectuals. His story tells of the area around Sucre, one of the high valleys on the eastern edge of the Altiplano. *El sol se iba* is an attempt at a Quechua novel or, rather, a novel as a Quechua would write it, with all the actions, thoughts, and emotions linked to the soil and the seasons. The year for these people is a cycle of work and ritual dominated by the soil, *la Pachamama* ("mother earth"), the rain, and the sun. Men and the land which they work are so closely interwoven that the whole land and life of the region achieves a magnificent unity in the novel and are studied by its author as one. There is a sweetness and reasonableness in this book which is refreshing. None of the clergy is a thief, and none of the Indians is whipped to death by evil *latifundistas* ("large landholders"). The criminal, if indeed there has to be one, is the hard, sterile, eroded soil of the high valleys.[28]

It is in another of the high valleys that the agrarian Indian novel has made its home. The Cochabamba valley has long been one of Bolivia's cultural centers, a rich agricultural area, and the scene of some of the greatest rural unrest before 1952. It was and is the great center for the Bolivian land reform which has gone on ever since that date. It has, then, a history of independence, oppression, and violence far greater than the other areas mentioned, and this is reflected in the novels, which often lack the repose found in Costas Arguedas. The most famous writer on the Quechua Indians of the Cochabamba is, without a doubt, Jesús Lara.

It is in Lara's novels that his social ideas are displayed, and, again unlike Costas Arguedas, he certainly believes that he knows where to place the blame for the pathetic, miserable state of the valley's Quechua Indians. In a trilogy of violent, revolutionary novels about the valley and its people, he accuses the white Creoles and *cholos* (town mestizos) of the most depraved, systematic, and varied exploitation of their fellow men. Imbued with harsh, ugly realism, his three novels, *Surumi* (1943), *Yanakuna* (1952), and *Yawarninchij* (1959), are an open call to revolt, and all claim to herald the coming of the Marxist-socialist state to Bolivia.

A very strong anticlerical strain, which at times reminds one of much earlier Latin American literature and seems vaguely old fashioned, runs through all his novels. Many Communist authors have changed to more up-to-date enemies.

Surumi is a novel which relates the events of the early 1930s as seen from an Indian hut in the Cochabamba valley. An Indian boy, who tries to get an education and is to a certain extent successful, finds that both he and his parents are subjected to the most vicious abuses and beatings, partly because of the boy's presumptuousness in trying to go to school. The institution of *pongueaje* ("colono rendering personal service to a land-owner") is especially attacked, and heavy, morbid emphasis is placed on the reduction of the *imillas* ("young Indian girls") to the status of con-cubines in the big house. The youth laments:

I hadn't committed any sin, and I was the victim. My guilt was in my birth, an inherited guilt, a racial guilt, a guilt borne by the Indians since a cross of false stone extended its greedy arms over the gold-filled heart of the Andes. And I was a victim of civilization, of this civilization which classifies by the color of the face or the contents of the purse, of this civilization which tears out the Indian's heart to turn it into bank notes for these hangmen's vaults. And I had been born an Indian and had no right to seek my future welfare beyond my tiny plot of earth.[29]

The Chaco War changes the outlook of Lara's hero completely, as it did so many Indian youths. He meets Bolivians of all kinds and from all regions and hears strange but interesting ideas which accord well with his concealed resentment. He comes back from the war with a revolutionary mission—a plan for the salvation of his enslaved race and the overthrow of the old ways.

Anthorena talks about the veterans' situation with respect to the political situation. He believes that by organizing themselves they would be capable of leading a popular movement which would finish off the traditional oligarchies.[30]

Imprisonment and brutality cannot change his purpose. In an exalted finish to the book Lara forsees the coming of the socialist state as absolutely inevitable.

Yanakuna is a novel in a quieter tone. The anticlericalism and em-phasis on the sexual vices of the local clergy is perhaps more pronounced, but the post-Chaco urge for violence has died down somewhat. The novel describes the period between 1936 and 1952, the period of slow ferment before the national revolution. Militant *indigenismo* ("Indianism") has taken the place of world revolution. Throughout the book, a serious study is made of the relationships between the Indians and the mestizos of the towns. The Indian girl, Wayra, is forced into service in a mestizo household where the family has upper-class pretensions. We gather that Lara has a low opinion of the desire of the Bolivian cholo to become westernized and obtain wealth, thus betraying the Indian part of his makeup. Once again, in this book, the Indians are exploited at every step. This time the emphasis is on lawyers and the unfair administration of justice. But the author still has not lost his confidence. The revolution, he believes, still smolders and will come eventually.[31] *Yanakuna* was the last great cry against oppression of the Indians in the Cochabamba valley before the peasants began to organize themselves into the leagues and unions which hastened and gave foundation to the land reform program of the first MNR government.

The third work in Lara's trilogy is concerned with the peasants' part in the revolution which swept the country during the years immediately after 1952. Unsure of the MNR government, whom Lara considers "bourgeois revolutionaries," some of the peasants seize the land and defend it, encouraged by their "true friends," the Communists of the city who, for the moment, seem to approve of small, private ownership. This is a bitter novel. The Indian's great hope has always been to own his private plot. "Then there remains one refuge for the Indian, the dream, the hope of one day owning a little plot of land." [32] Now Lara sees this great aim for which he has fought so long taken over by a party which he despises. Lara is reduced to applauding the land reform but attacking those who carried it out and the slow speed at which it is going. Again the cholo is presented as a tool of the white exploiters. Once again the church is an evil, scheming force of reaction. And again the law is persistently unjust and on the side of the powerful. Black and white, good and bad, are so clearly different, and the characters such as the latifundista, the lawyer, and the local Communist party workers are so overdrawn that the characterizations deteriorate at times to mere caricature. In spite of the bitter, frustrated note in the book—the work of an idealist whose cause has been adopted by his enemies—Lara remains one of the acutest observers of the Indian's problems in Bolivia. The following analysis of the reasons for Indian misery makes up for much of Lara's crude and obsessive writing:

Ignorance is a useful and sinister tool of oppression. An ignorant man has no idea of human dignity, he has no notion of his rights, he doesn't know if he deserves to live better than he is allowed to live. It is easy to convince him that he was born to the fate of preserving the happiness of the powerful, and that he must content himself with the crumbs that they throw to him, that docility, self-abnegation and resignation should be his cardinal virtues. It is easy to persuade him that he should not demand better living conditions, that it is forbidden to revolt against his fate and his masters.

Another terrible tool of oppression is the wretchedness of poverty. When there is not enough to feed a wife and children, when there is not enough to cover one's nakedness, a man may lose his pride, his honesty, his self-respect, in sum his most cherished human attributes, if by this means he can prevent the death of his family. Then obedience, humiliation, indignity become the regular norms of life. The beggar begins to measure his happiness by his alms. For a man who has nothing to feed his children, any starvation wage is salvation. A man living in misery can be kept in subjection indefinitely. And what is true of one is true of many, even an entire nation.[33]

Lara then proceeds to examine the plight of the Indian on a still higher and more intangible level. A Communist agitator explains to the Indians why they are as they are:

Other forms of ignorance exist, said the Miner, which those in power strive to maintain among the oppressed, such as ensuring that they don't know their own past history, especially if it contains examples and lessons, if it is proud and knows how to defend itself and is not easily taken over by others; for if a man knows of such things, and if he is enslaved by force, he will fight unceasingly for his freedom because there are lessons and ideals there which inspire him and he has a patrimony to regain. On the other hand, it is always possible to hold a people which is ignorant of its own history in subjection indefinitely.[34]

Not all the Cochabamba novelists have concentrated to such an extent on partisan politics. Many have professed to be more objective than Lara in their examination of the land problems of the valley, where pressure on the land is heavier and has caused more strife than anywhere else in Bolivia.

Humberto Guzmán Arce is obviously favorably disposed toward the land-reform program and despises many of the harmful characteristics of the old ruling class, but he also attempts to see the owners' point of view, and, although it is admittedly rare, he praises the occasional latifundista who stays on his land, loves it and the local people, and wishes to improve the lot of both. Writers such as Guzmán Arce and Mario Unzueta generally reflect the MNR's position on land reform in the area at the start of the revolution. They insist that it should be sweeping and thorough but hope that, before other considerations, it will be just.[35]

A new group of writers has taken another tack, however, and while they may all be thought of as pro-MNR, unlike Jesús Lara, they tend, nevertheless, to be critical of the party's land-reform program for doing too much too soon in the valley, the opposite point of view from that held by Lara. They may be thought of as a kind of "loyal opposition."

Augusto Guzmán is one of the leading writers of this more cautious school. His thesis is that land reform was certainly necessary, but that the latifundista was, for all his many undeniable faults, the only cultured element in a totally uneducated rural population. He was the tie, so to speak, between the civilized city and the barbaric countryside. If the latifundista must be driven out at once, then Guzmán suggests that the government's first priority, almost to the exclusion of all else, should be the rural school. If the latifundista could be more gradually displaced, then the Indian could be gradually built up through a more long-term educational program such as the government envisaged. Although the MNR government did build such schools, it did not accomplish this with the speed or in the numbers Guzmán envisioned. What the government did, in fact, by giving in to the impatience of the peasants was to drive out the latifundistas quickly, much to the regret of the moderates, and subsequently to begin a gradual, slower education of the rural masses. Meanwhile, Guzmán believes, this miscalculation produced a power and cultural vacuum in the Cochabamba valley with two dangerous consequences. From time to time there occurs a complete breakdown of authority and law as the formerly repressed Indians, totally lacking in education, go to the other extreme of violent anarchy. The second danger is that in this cultural vacuum demagogues can profit handsomely. Guzmán is obviously thinking of communism, for now that the owner of the big house is gone, there is no cultural bulwark against it.[36]

Typical of Guzmán's attitude is his little-known work, *Pequeño mundo,* published in 1960. In this short novel, the author illustrates all the points mentioned above. His latifundistas, knowing that their days of power in the countryside are numbered, hastily sell all their livestock, including the precious dairy cattle, to profiteering butchers from the towns, since even the low prices which they are forced to accept are better than nothing. Thus, the livestock population in the rural areas goes down catastrophically. The landlords, who are eventually driven off, flee to the towns where they are protected by law and order. Thus, hostility toward the inhabitants of the towns is built up in the countryside. In the rural areas, the peasants not only take over the land but also the roads and villages, interfering with traffic and acting in an irresponsible, often violent manner. All their uneducated prejudices are fostered by local demagogues and the situation inevitably deteriorates still further.

Gradually, as time passes and the first euphoria of land ownership wears off, the Indians begin to have doubts about their actions. Some even wish to reimburse their former landlords for their losses, hoping thus to give their land titles some kind of legality; others wish, at least, to regain some kind of understanding with the town and with the regional representatives of the national government who live there. Some manage to do this, but in many cases, Guzmán writes, Communists have assumed control of the *sindicato campesino* ("rural labor union") and will not hear of such actions, although such conciliatory steps have the hearty approval of the government. Thus many of the Indians feel more insecure than before. Then at least they understood the chain of authority. Now they do not know whom to believe, and their allegiance is demanded from all sides. Guzmán obviously feels that it will take many years before stability returns after such a revolutionary land reform, and while he applauds the reform itself, he fears for it because of the mistakes which he believes have already been made.[37]

Guzmán and the other young writers of more moderate social protest obviously have a deep love for the men and land of the valley which is their home. A series of idyllic works have been written which try to capture some of the spirit and tradition of the area—another part of the attempt to show the whole nation to the Bolivians from the various widely separated regions.[38]

These Indian novels of social protest all aim at destroying the racial and cultural prejudice so common in Bolivian middle- and upper-class thinking. After all, as Carlos Alberto Monjón exclaims: "Are we not all Indians? Where does the Indian start and where does he stop?"[39] The social novel since the war has made education one of its major preoccupations, believing that the Indians cannot play a proper national role and that the country will continue to lack skilled manpower until education becomes universal.

The most outstanding novel about the education of the Indian is *Utama* by the Guilléns, both of whom spent many years as pioneer teachers among the Aymaras. The main character is a new type of hero for Bolivia, the rural schoolteacher carrying out his unnoticed role in the new Bolivia. *Utama,* "your house" in Aymara, is a fictional attempt to make the Indians aware that the school is theirs not a fresh scheme of exploitation from the cities. Progress is slow until the beginning of the Chaco War disrupts the countryside and removes many of the Indian men to the front. As the soldiers trickle back, however, the teachers of *Utama* realize that they do not have to start all over again, that the war, paradoxically, has served their purpose. Many of the Indian men have stopped wearing the traditional *poncho,* have picked up a smattering of Spanish, and have become, in fact, cholos.[40] Soon the rural team decides that the future of the country lies in the hands of this new mestizo and, to become a mestizo, the Indian must be educated.

We do not know what those who direct educational programs are thinking. But if they have their eyes open they will not find any other solution but this one. Bolivia is destined to be an essentially mestizo nation, a synthesis of the values of the native race and of the science and technology of the West.[41]

The local corrupt government officials are a constant threat, for even they are poor and their meager livelihood depends on the maintenance of the *status quo* with regard to the Indian. But the war has also taught many of the Indians some discipline and solidarity so that they are now ready to support their teachers and fight for their education if it is necessary. The authors have two conclusions to make as they finish their novel. To begin with, even in the areas where the rural schools have taken root, education has made only a beginning. "All in all, our long vigils had got us to the point where we could just reach the Indian. Still mere explorers!" But, the authors warn their fellow countrymen, education must not become an end in itself but should be only an integral part of the larger process which will abolish Indian poverty and misery. Land and liberty are just as important as education.

The new novelists are all townsmen, and for this reason the reader is occasionally conscious of a strain of artificiality in many of the rural *indianista* novels. After all, the writers of the novels of social protest are often town intellectuals, and often also they are products of the urban classes. In spite of their social conscience, many have the attributes of the classes from whence they came, including the esoteric, humanistic (with legal overtones) education provided by the Bolivian universities. Thus, these writers feel ill at ease with the rural Indians, who are so different from them in background and culture.

Bolivia's second great revolutionary theme—that of the mining industry—does not present the same problem to the town intellectuals, and, for this reason, the mining novel is one of the most popular means of social protest. The mine presents somewhat of an urban setting, the squalor and related problems are of an urban type, and, although the majority of the miners are Indians, the mine has a westernizing influence with most of the managers and higher officials coming from Spanish-urban rather than Indian-rural backgrounds. It is an often mentioned phenomenon that the mine is one of the fastest methods of turning the Indian into a cholo. He finds himself wearing western clothes, eating western food from the mining commissary (since this is the only available source), learning a smattering of Castillian for his day-to-day social and working dealings with his superiors, and acquiring at least a rudimentary technical proficiency in his handling of a miner's equipment. For all of these reasons, it is obvious that Bolivian novelists have felt more at home when writing about the tin mines than when writing about agriculture. Certainly the number of novels written about the mines is far greater.

In spite of the quantity of Bolivian mining novels, these works are almost invariably extremely bad. They are repetitive to the point of monotony, present squalor of a most unedifying kind, have little in their content of an elevating or inspirational nature (although one presumes that to elevate and inspire is their goal), and they draw their characters so simply and crudely in terms of "good" and "evil" that the protagonists become caricatures with whom the sophisticated reader cannot possibly identify himself. It should be repeated, however, that, good or bad, these novels are being written because there is a compulsion to write them; and, in spite of their inferior quality, they are a reflection of what the problems of the mines actually are, as seen by Bolivians.

In describing one of these novels written about the tin mines, one is hardly exaggerating to say that a description is being provided of them all. There is perpetually an evil *gringo* engineer or manager. Utterly insensitive, treating the Indian as some form of lower animal, and completely devoted to a cold technology rather than the spiritual humanism (which the Latin American intellectuals are wont to claim for themselves, but which they seem to practice no more than elsewhere), these gringos are simply not characters in which the reader can believe.[42]

Roberto Leitón's greatest attack is on the mining superstate. In his book, the management forbids the sale of books and magazines, which it considers dangerous to the peace of the mine. When the Indian miners ask for the rest periods to which they are entitled by law, they are quickly silenced:

Shut up, clod! The company is an independent state. We are not to blame.
Your stupidity and the ignorance of your leaders is responsible for all of it.
You are born to be slaves.

The threat of tuberculosis and silicosis hangs over the miners continually
while the company either provides inadequate medical treatment or re-
fuses it outright. The Indians are *"parias explotados"* ("exploited out-
casts"). *"Presos en medio de su país"* ("They are prisoners in their own
country") yet, Leitón argues, they must do their own fighting for freedom,
for few other Bolivians will help them. The cholo, he claims, who is their
natural ally, is hopelessly turned against them in his desire to become
white.[43]

One of the most deliberately ugly Bolivian novels is *Canchamina* by
Victor Hugo Villegas and Mario Guzmán Aspiazu. The descriptions of
disasters, cold, wind, hunger, depravity, and general gloom are relentless,
and the reader is left at the end under a pall of depression, which surely
defeats the very object of the book. The natural reaction of the reader
to a novel such as this is defeatist pessimism. It is hard to believe that
anyone could draw from such a work emotional or intellectual fuel to
inspire him to seek improvement in the lot of the miners.[44]

Grito de piedra, the book of *cuentos* ("stories"), is almost as depressing
but does leave some hope for the future. The short stories, when taken
together, constitute a kind of history of mining injustice in the Potosí
region of Bolivia. The author, Luis Heredia, is obviously familiar with his
subject and was, himself, a miners' union leader and a left-wing journalist.
His characters are, nevertheless, overdrawn, and the conquistadors presented in the story entitled "Viracoches" are pure barbarians. The book,
which includes stories up through recent times, gives new illustrations of
the human phenomena of the mines. The *cholificacíon* ("becoming cholo-
like") of the Indians; the many superstitions connected with mining,
which the Indians consider in itself a violation of the Pachamama; and
the many mining disasters in Potosí's ancient *Cerro Rico* ("rich hill")
are well described. When he comes to the post–Chaco War revolutionary
struggles, Heredia is obviously most in his element. He vividly describes
the rising of the miners in the abortive pro-MNR revolution of September
4, 1949, and its quick defeat by the army when it marched on
Potosí.[45]

A much better novel is Fernando Ramírez Velarde's *Socavones de
angustia.* This is a beautifully documented novel, often seeming, in fact,
more of an economic and sociological report. Ramírez Velarde brings

out what he has to say by a comparative method. For some time his hero works in a small, private mine where conditions, as was always the case, are appalling. In 1929, in the *Buena Estrella* mine, there was a total of over two thousand workers with their families, all crowded into 250 shacks jammed together in narrow streets of from twenty to thirty houses. The shacks themselves were from thirty-six to forty-five square feet with zinc roofs and walls, six feet high at the back and five feet four inches at the front door. Inside, there was one fairly large room and one small room, originally planned no doubt as the kitchen-living room and the bedroom. In 1929, both rooms were packed in every house, and both were used for all purposes. Between eight and thirteen people lived in each shanty, and the novelist gives us an instance where four new workers arrive at the mine, a house is found with only seven in it, and all four new men are packed in there. The hero, in this case a simple schoolteacher once again, moves on to a bigger mine. There conditions are even worse, for the treatment of the miners is far more cold and impersonal. The miner's reactions to these conditions are drinking bouts and occasional, poorly organized strikes. Over it all hangs the sinister influence of the mining superstate. "Fools!" says the gringo manager Johnson. "Don't you realize that it's the mining companies which manipulate the government of this wretched country?" [46]

One of the gravest problems in the mining industry of Bolivia, indeed in all the Latin American countries where one product dominates the economy, is that vagaries in world prices or economic depression in other countries can cause slack periods in the home industry, thus causing widespread unemployment. Many of Ramírez Velarde's characters are thrown out of work and drift toward the city of Oruro, originally planned as a modern workers' city but now degenerated into a slum. The author cannot understand the paradox of unemployment in a country such as Bolivia. "A nation of nearly two million square kilometers and of only three and a half million inhabitants, full of men without work!" [47] The book ends with a plea from the hero for more education rather than political agitation from those who genuinely want to help the Indian miner.

Augusto Céspedes's *Metal del diablo* is perhaps Bolivia's best-known novel of the postwar period. It is more a work of political propaganda than one about the mines. First published in 1946, its clear aim was to urge the nationalization of the tin mines of the *Rosca* (literally, a padded head ring for carrying weights), a perjorative term for the Big Three tin barons, Patiño, Hochschild, and Aramayo. The protagonist, Zenón Omonte, is obviously Simón Patiño. Some of the scenes in the mines, the description of Omonte-Patiño's youth, and the narration of the growing symptoms of unrest among the masses are telling. In terms of political impact, this novel has been one of the most potent, and it fanned a distinct part of the fever for nationalization which impelled the MNR to do so in 1952.[48] It remains, with *Raza de bronce,* one of Bolivia's most famous novels.

Since the revolution of April 1952 the Bolivian novel of social protest has turned in two main directions. One trend has been toward the glorification of what has been accomplished, a sort of ritual of self-congratulation that the victory has been won and that the evils attacked in so many prerevolutionary writings will now be confronted by revolutionary governments. Some of these novels talk of the revolution itself, of the bitter street fighting which took place in La Paz before the miners seized the heights of El Alto which commanded the city, and of the impact which these events had on the common people of the capital. Many of the Indians and poorer cholos did not know exactly what the fighting was all about but were convinced that whatever changes it brought would be an improvement.[49] There is even a certain nostalgia in some of these novels, a harking back, now that victory is won, to the old, dark days of struggle and despair. Fellmann Velarde's works evoke these days particularly effectively.[50]

The other tendency has been to confront the post-1952 accomplishments of the revolution either critically or in panegyrics. The paens of praise are essentially boring propaganda and of little value. A convenient division among the critical novels is between those of the loyal opposition and those which are basically hostile to the MNR and its governments between 1952 and 1964. We have already seen this division among the agrarian novelists of the Cochabamba valley. Augusto Guzmán and other moderates generally favored the land reform but felt that mistakes had been made in the execution of a basically correct policy. Jesús Lara represents the more severe and essentially hostile kind of criticism.

One of the most penetrating critics of the revolution is Mariano Morales D'Avila. He agrees that a revolution may well be progressive and necessary, and the Bolivian one probably was, but he dissents strongly from the *sequelae* which seem to accompany this and other revolutions. Much of his writing is a warning to the reader to be wary, to watch over advantages already won in the constant battle against tyranny, and such admonitions are those of a conservative critic. He is particularly suspicious of the emotionalism and irrationality of profound revolutions, slogans, uniforms, and deified leaders, especially when the administration of justice becomes a part of the revolution and gets caught up in its enthusiasms and hates. In one of his novels a judge condemns a prisoner as a negative and regressive social entity. The prisoner is being judged not as to whether he has broken a legal code but as to whether he has affected the progress of the revolution and the country, as these terms are defined by the new revolutionary supernationalism. In such a court, Morales asks, what of the rights of the individual against the state? [51]

In the novels since 1952, considered as a body, one detects a certain sterility, perhaps even an exhaustion of the social imagination. Nearly all the post revolutionary novels, as we have seen, have been celebrations of heroic victory or criticisms, friendly and unfriendly, of what the MNR governments have accomplished. But what of the future? Before the revolution Bolivian novelists of social protest apparently felt that one of their main tasks was to lead, to show the country what was wrong in the mines, the schools, and on the land, and to propose solutions. Since 1952 most novelists have been talking about the past. [52]

Various interpretations of this phenomenon are possible. The revolution was a sweeping one and rapidly accomplished many of the changes which the novelists had long been demanding. Perhaps the novel, like the revolution itself in the days of Siles Zuazo, is going through a period of consolidation and self-examination which will eventually give way to another period of proposals for future radical change. Many Bolivian novelists, moreover, are of the Chaco generation, and their grievances were, generally speaking, satisfied in the 1950s. It may take a new generation before demands unrelated to the Chaco experience come forth.

It can also be argued that this postrevolutionary constipation reveals a basic lack of sophistication, subtlety, and imagination in the present generation of novelists. The reforms which they called for before 1952 were, after all, to some extent self-evident to any reformer. Intelligence and imagination of a new and, perhaps, different order are needed to tell Bolivians in which direction the revolution should now drive.

In fact the fate of the Bolivian novel since 1952 may be symptomatic of something basically wrong with the Bolivian Revolution. The failure of the novel to generate new ideas or a new theoretical credo to carry the revolution forward seems to have afflicted the party and its intellectuals also. Several authors have noted the rapidity with which the party lost its revolutionary mystique and descended to *empleomanía* ("mania for public office") and quibbling over details. A similar phenomenon seems to have overtaken the novel of social protest.

Since the Chaco War, then, the writing of fiction has been drastically changed in Bolivia. The number of novels produced year by year has multiplied, and the subject matter has become the problems and the social reality of the nation in which the novelists are living.[53]

Shamed and shocked by the defeat suffered in the Chaco War and the depressing circumstances surrounding it, Bolivia's young intellectuals came home determined to be part of the great revolutionary changes which they hoped were to come, with their role to be that of changing the intellectual climate. Discovery of their own country was the first task posed by novelists, sociologists, historians, and philosophers alike. Having looked long and hard at their native land they became dedicated revolutionaries, and their writing became a propagandistic weapon. A new Indian policy, the problem of the mines, and the filling of the empty lowlands were explained and hopefully resolved again and again in their writings, where previously these questions had been all but ignored. When the revolution did at last come in 1952, the novelists and intellectuals took on new roles. They heralded the glorious past of the revolution and chronicled its struggle for power, and they attempted to watch its reforms with a critical eye. They failed to provide an ideological or philosophical background for the MNR government after it took power and they showed little imagination about the postrevolutionary future, but these failures may be only temporary and seem to have been characteristic of the Bolivian Revolution in general.

Above all, these writings of social protest, especially the novel, are a mirror of national character for the student. We see the irrational nationalism, the new urge for self-knowledge, the emotionalism and mysticism, the hatreds and fanatical attachments, all of which are driving forces in the country today.

NOTES

1. For typical summaries of the state of Bolivian letters before 1930, see Augusto Guzmán, *La novela en Bolivia: Proceso 1847–1954* (La Paz: Librería Editorial "Juventud," 1955), pp. 18–19, and Raúl Botelho Gosálvez, "La novela en Bolivia," *Cuadernos Americanos,* 12 (1960), especially p. 270.

2. See Alcides Arguedas, *Pueblo enfermo* (Santiago de Chile: Ediciones Ercilla, 1937), pp. 36, 57, 61–63, 179; Franz Tamayo, *La creación de la pedagogía nacional* (La Paz: Editoriales de "El Diario," 1944), pp. 138, 151, 172, 194; and Jaime Mendoza, *El macizo boliviano* (La Paz: Ministerio de Educación y Bellas Artes, 1957), pp. 181–93, 218–20. See also the comments of Fernando Diez de Medina in "Twentieth Century Bolivian Letters," *Americas,* 2, no. 10 (1950), p. 46. The author's comments here are not to be construed as a commentary on literary or esthetic quality. *Pueblo enfermo* and the same author's *Raza de bronce* are classics, and their descriptions of the condition of the Indians were new and disturbing.

3. Fernando Diez de Medina, *Literatura boliviana* (La Paz: Alfonso Tijerina, 1953), pp. 326–69; Agustín Barcelli S., *Medio siglo de luchas sindicales revolucionarias en Bolivia* (La Paz: Editorial del Estado, 1956), p. 138; Lilo Linke, *Viaje por una revolución* (Quito: Casa de la Cultura Ecuatoriana, 1956), p. 12.

4. The following sources list most of the novels on the war: W. Knapp Jones, "The Literature of the Chaco War," *Hispania,* 21 (1958), pp. 33–46, and Diez de Medina, *Literatura boliviana,* p. 341.

5. Rafael Ulises Peláez, *Cuando el viento agita las banderas,* 2 vols. (La Paz: Editorial "Universo," 1950). See especially vol. 1.

6. Oscar Cerruto, *Aluvión de fuego* (Santiago de Chile: Ediciones Ercilla, 1935). This novel, written in 1932, describes at length the work of a regiment which devoted its time to hunting Indian emboscados and crushing Indian uprisings. See pp. 72–115.

7. Raúl Leytón Z., *Placer* (La Paz: Ediciones "Canata," 1955), pp. 205–45. See also Augusto Céspedes, *Sangre de mestizos; relatos de la guerra del Chaco* (Santiago de Chile: Editorial Nascimiento, 1936), p. 126, and Luis Toro Ramallo, *Chaco (del cuaderno de un sargento)* (Santiago de Chile: Editorial Nascimiento, 1936), pp. 67–73.

8. Leytón, *Placer,* pp. 100–01, Céspedes, *Sangre de mestizos,* pp. 151–52; Toro Ramallo, *Chaco,* pp. 100–06, 182.

9. Céspedes, *Sangre des mestizos,* pp. 208, 206–65; see also Tristan Maroff, *La tragedia del Altiplano* (Buenos Aires: Colección Claridad, 1935), pp. 159–70. This thesis is also presented in English in Margaret A. Marsh, *The Bankers in Bolivia, Studies in American Imperialism* (New York: Vanguard Press, 1928).

10. Cerruto, *Aluvión de fuego,* pp. 69–70. Céspedes refers to the old governing groups as *la cleptarquía de Bolivia* ("thievocracy of Bolivia").

11. Ibid., p. 70.

12. Toro Ramallo, *Chaco,* pp. 189–91.

13. Cerruto, *Aluvión de fuego,* p. 199.

14. Diez de Medina, *Literatura boliviana,* p. 330.

15. José Fellmann Velarde, *La montaña de los ángeles* (La Paz: Librería Editorial Tijerina, 1958), p. 173.

16. Cerruto, *Aluvión de feugo,* p. 69.

17. Raúl Botelho Gosálvez, *Borrachera verde* (Santiago de Chile: Empresa Editora Zig-Zag, 1938), pp. 18–20.

18. Ibid., p. 55. See also pp. 56–57. The feudal tropical kingdom of the Suárez family, often called the biggest private estate in the world, is attacked in many Bolivian novels. This estate was one of the first to be confiscated after the Bolivian land reform. See also Arthur Karasz, "Experiment in Development: Bolivia Since 1952," in *Freedom and Reform in Latin America,* ed. Frederick B. Pike (Notre Dame, Ind.: University of Notre Dame Press, 1959), p. 269.

19. Ibid., p. 59.

20. Diomedes de Pereyra, *La trama de oro* (Santiago de Chile: Empresa Editora Zig-Zag, 1938), pp. 57–65.

21. Ignacio Callaú Barbery, *Tierra camba* (Buenos Aires: Talleres Gráficos Cadel, S.R.L., 1958), pp. 13–14.

22. Sócrates Chávez Suárez, *Guaporé hombre y río* (La Paz: Ministerio de Educación y Bellas Artes, 1960), foreword.

23. Enrique Kempff Mercado, *Gente de Santa Cruz* (La Paz: Cámara Boliviana del Libro, 1946), p. 176.

24. Genciana, *Jazmín del Oriente: Lágrimas y vientos* (La Paz: Empresa Editora "Universo," 1960), pp. 237, 258.

25. Alfredo Vaca Medrano, *Chendo pedraza* (La Paz: Editorial del Estado, 1959).

26. Raúl Botelho Gosálvez, *Coca* (*motives del yunga paceña*) (Santiago de Chile: Empresa Editora Zig-Zag, 1941).

27. Raúl Botelho Gosálvez, *Altiplano, novela india* (Buenos Aires: Editorial Ayacucho, 1945). The reference is to one of Ecuador's famous Indian novels by Jorge Icaza.

28. José Felipe Costas Arguedas, *El sol se iba* (*o "La siembra"*) *novela quechua,* 2d ed. (Sucre: Editorial "Charcas," 1944).

29. Jesús Lara, *Surumi* (Buenos Aires: Editorial Perlado, 1943), pp. 126–27.

30. Ibid., p. 246. See also p. 252.

31. Jesús Lara, *Yanakuna* (La Paz: Librería y Editorial "Juventud," 1958). The publication of this novel was delayed for several years.

32. Jesús Lara, *Yawarninchij* (Buenos Aires: Editorial Platina, 1959), p. 60.

33. Ibid., pp. 92–93.

34. Ibid., p. 93.

35. Humberto Guzmán Arce, *Borrasca en el valle* (Cochabamba: Editorial Mercurio, 1960). For a somewhat similar, but earlier, point of view, see Mario Unzueta, *Valle* (Cochabamba: Editorial "La Epoca," 1945).

36. Guzmán was no supporter of the *status quo* and was fervently pro-MNR but deplored the expulsion of the latifundista before a substitute for him could be found. He called the latifundista "the only cultural nucleus in the countryside" and further pointed out that he was the only link between town and country, which are now hostile and cut off one from the other. Interview between Augusto Guzmán and the author, Cochabamba, Bolivia, June 12, 1961.

37. Augusto Guzmán, *Pequeño mundo* (Cochabamba: Imprenta Universitaria, 1960). See particularly pp. 13–14, 41, 90–102.

38. Luis Taborga, *Tierra morena* (Cochabamba: Imprenta Universitaria, 1960). See also Augusto Guzmán's historical work, *Gesta valluna* (Cochabamba: Imprenta Tunari, 1953).

39. Carlos Alberto Monjón, *El fugitivo* (La Paz: Editorial Casegural, 1960), p. 226.

40. Alfredo Guillén Pinto and Natty Peñaranda de Guillén Pinto, *Utama; novela vivida en cuatro años* (La Paz: Gisbert y Casanovas, 1945), p. 125.

41. Ibid., p. 84.

42. For example, see Roberto Leitón's highly overrated novel, *Los eternos vagabundos* (Potosí: Editorial "Potosí," 1939), pp. 11, 25, 35, 39, 76. Nearly every mining novel which will be mentioned in this paper has a disagreeable gringo somewhere in it. (The gringo is usually, but not always, a North American.)

43. Ibid., pp. 60–61.

44. Victor Hugo Villegas and Mario Guzmán Aspiazu, *Canchamina* (La Paz: Editorial Canata Ltda., 1956).

45. Luis E. Heredia, *Grito de piedra: Cuentos mineros* (Potosí: Editorial "Potosí," 1954).

46. Fernando Ramírez Velarde, *Socavones de angustia* (La Paz: Editorial "Artística," 1953), p. 161. Another novel which compares the large and small mining enterprises is Hugo Blym, *Títeres de la meseta* (La Paz: Empresa Editora "Universo," 1953). On p. 128 he explains why, in his opinion, the small mines are even more soul destroying than the large. After one has done the day's work, there is absolutely nothing to do in the small mining communities. One can almost feel the lethargy and mental stupefaction in the air.

47. Ibid., p. 167.

48. Augusto Céspedes, *Metal del diablo* (Buenos Aires: Editorial Palestra, 1960).

49. For example, Subsecretaría de Prensa, Informaciones y Cultura, *Antología de cuentos de la revolución* (La Paz: Publicaciones SPIC, 1954), especially p. 64.

50. José Fellmann Velarde, *Una bala en el viento* (La Paz: Editorial Fénix, 1952). See also the same author's *La montaña de los ángeles,* and Jorge E. Mesa, *Cuentos de media noche* (Cochabamba: Editorial Mercurio, 1960).

51. Mariano Morales D'Avila, *Ven, sígueme* (Cochabamba: Editorial Canelas, 1961), p. 51.

52. An exception is Armando Montenegro's *Víctima de los siglos* (Cochabamba: Imprenta Universitaria, 1955). But this is a visionary, almost science-fiction look at the year 6943! It has little to do with the next twenty years.

53. A comparison of the numbers of novels written before and after the war can be found in Guzmán, *La novela en Bolivia,* pp. 106, 179.

APPENDIX TABLES
GLOSSARY
INDEX

Appendix Tables

The appendix tables were compiled by the following contributors to this volume: Professor Thorn, tables 1, 2, 3, 4, 6, and 7; Professor Klein, table 5; Professor Wilkie, tables 8, 10, and 11; and Professor Blasier, table 9.

APPENDIX TABLE 1
Gross Domestic Product, 1951–1968 (*In 1958 Constant Prices*)
(*In Millions of Dollars*)

	1951	1952	1953	1954	1955	1956	1957	19.
I. Gross Domestic Product	$378.6	$387.8	$343.7	$346.2	$371.3	$354.8	$342.9	$35
A. Agriculture	118.1	113.1	105.8	101.7	107.6	104.2	110.7	12
B. Mining	57.4	58.3	59.1	48.3	51.0	46.1	47.4	3
C. Petroleum	2.1	2.1	2.5	6.9	11.1	13.1	14.7	1
D. Manufacturing ª	50.0	49.0	49.0	54.9	55.7	51.4	36.0	3
E. Construction	1.8	3.6	2.5	2.5	3.3	2.6	3.1	
F. Transportation	20.1	23.9	23.6	26.4	29.4	29.7	27.1	3
G. Commerce	44.9	48.5	41.7	42.5	47.2	45.8	47.0	4
H. Government	47.0	55.0	24.9	28.6	30.5	26.0	20.7	2
I. Other services ᵇ	33.3	34.3	34.6	34.4	35.5	35.9	36.2	3
II. Exports of goods & services	84.7	80.3	65.3	65.2	67.3	72.2	61.8	5
III. Imports of goods & services	85.5	92.1	74.3	73.2	88.6	84.9	109.6	9
IV. Total resources available (I − II + III)	382.4	399.6	342.7	354.2	392.6	367.5	390.7	38
V. Memoranda								
A. Per capita GDP (*in dollars*)	123.2	123.7	107.2	105.9	111.3	104.2	98.6	9
B. Total foreign aid	—	0.6	1.4	13.1	25.9	24.7	27.7	2
C. Population (*in millions of people*)	3.1	3.1	3.2	3.3	3.3	3.4	3.5	

Sources: 1951–1961: Secretaria Nacional de Planifacacion, *Plan nacional de desrrollo económico y social, 1962–1* (La Paz, 1961), p. 40; *1961–1968:* Dirección Nacional de Coordinacion y Planeamiento; *Bolivia cuentas naciona 1961–1968,* mimeographed (La Paz, January 1969). *Foreign Aid:* International Monetary Fund, *Balance of P ments Yearbook* (as deflated by U.S. Wholesale Price Index); *Population: International Financial Statistics,* vari issues, 1966, 1969.

1959	1960	1961	1961 c	1962	1963	1964	1965	1966	1967	1968	
361.8	$369.5	$381.9	$300.1	$316.9	$334.3	$353.5	$373.3	$397.0	$419.2	$439.6	I.
128.6	121.9	131.9	95.7	94.7	100.0	102.0	105.2	106.3	99.5	103.0	A.
31.2	33.8	37.7	25.7	27.0	30.3	32.9	33.0	36.0	37.5	38.5	B.
13.3	14.6	13.2	11.0	11.8	12.9	13.7	14.4	34.7	34.7	36.5	C.
41.5	44.6	45.3	38.6	42.3	45.1	47.6	52.5	57.7	61.0	65.1	D.
4.3	5.4	1.9	9.6	12.4	14.5	14.8	18.6	20.6	25.3	29.1	E.
30.8	31.4	33.4	25.1	26.4	28.3	29.8	30.9	32.0	33.7	35.1	F.
46.4	47.3	43.0	38.4	40.4	43.4	45.0	46.7	48.1	49.5	52.1	G.
28.0	31.9	32.5	25.5	29.2	30.2	31.3	34.7	38.1	38.8	39.2	H.
37.7	38.6	43.0	30.6	32.5	32.6	36.4	37.3	38.3	39.3	42.1	I.
61.3	56.5	65.1	57.6	62.2	69.7	70.8	71.2	84.3	106.2	117.8	II.
91.4	90.7	92.2	95.8	113.5	119.2	117.4	147.9	167.8	181.2	181.4	III.
391.9	403.7	409.0	338.3	367.2	387.8	401.1	450.0	480.5	484.2	504.2	IV.
											V.
99.8	99.8	100.9	79.3	81.9	84.5	87.3	90.3	93.8	96.7	99.1	A.
20.9	12.2	24.2	29.1	34.2	49.1	44.3	32.2	34.8	34.1	56.0	B.
3.6	3.7	3.8	3.8	3.9	4.0	4.0	4.1	4.2	4.3	4.4	C.

a. Includes energy.
b. Includes housing.
c. Data for 1961 to 1968 have been revised and are not comparable to prior national income data. Both the un-
revised and revised data are given for 1961.

APPENDIX TABLE 2

PERCENT DISTRIBUTION OF GROSS DOMESTIC PRODUCT BY SECTORS, 1951–1968

	1951	1952	1953	1954	1955	1956	1957
I. Gross Domestic Product							
A. Agriculture	31.2%	29.2%	30.8%	29.4%	29.0%	29.4%	32.3
B. Mining	15.2	15.0	17.2	14.0	13.7	13.0	13.8
C. Petroleum	0.6	0.5	0.7	2.0	3.0	3.7	4.3
D. Manufacturing	13.2	12.6	14.3	15.9	15.0	14.5	10.5
E. Construction	0.7	0.9	0.7	0.7	0.9	0.7	0.9
F. Transportation	5.3	6.2	6.9	7.6	7.9	8.4	7.9
G. Commerce	12.6	12.5	12.1	12.3	12.7	12.9	13.7
H. Government	12.4	14.2	7.2	8.3	8.2	7.3	6.0
I. Other services	8.8	8.8	10.1	9.9	9.6	10.1	10.6
Total	100.0	100.0	100.0	100.0	100.0	100.0	100.0
II. Exports of goods & services	22.4	20.7	19.0	18.8	18.1	20.3	18.0
III. Imports of goods & services	23.4	23.7	21.6	21.1	23.9	23.9	32.0
IV. Total resources available (I − II + III)	101.0	103.0	99.7	102.3	105.7	103.6	113.9
V. Memoranda							
A. Total foreign aid[a]	—	0.05	0.3	3.7	6.6	6.7	8.1

Sources: Sources are the same as those used for appendix table 1.
a. As a percentage of gross domestic product.

958	1959	1960	1961	1962	1963	1964	1965	1966	1967	1968	
1.7%	32.4%	31.0%	31.9%	29.9%	29.7%	28.9%	28.2%	26.8%	23.7%	23.3%	A.
8.3	9.7	8.2	8.6	8.5	9.0 ·	9.3	8.8	9.0	9.0	8.7	B.
2.0	1.9	2.0	3.7	3.7	3.8	3.9	3.9	5.1	8.3	8.3	C.
3.2	13.2	13.7	12.9	13.3	13.4	13.5	14.1	14.5	14.6	14.8	D.
3.6	3.8	4.0	3.2	3.9	4.3	4.2	5.0	5.2	6.0	6.6	E.
8.5	8.4	8.5	8.4	8.3	8.4	8.4	8.3	8.1	8.0	8.0	F.
2.8	13.0	13.0	12.8	12.8	12.8	12.7	12.5	12.1	11.8	11.8	G.
7.7	8.0	7.8	8.5	9.2	9.0	8.9	9.3	9.6	9.3	9.1	H.
7.1	4.8	6.9	10.2	10.3	9.7	10.3	10.0	9.6	9.4	9.6	I.
0.0	100.0	100.0	100.0	100.0	100.0	100.0	100.0	100.0	100.0	100.0	I.
6.0	22.1	19.5	19.2	19.6	20.7	20.0	19.1	21.2	25.3	26.7	II.
25.4	31.5	30.8	31.9	35.8	35.4	33.2	39.6	42.3	43.2	41.1	III.
09.4	109.5	111.3	112.7	116.2	114.7	113.2	120.6	121.0	117.9	114.4	IV.
											V.
7.4	7.4	4.6	9.8	11.0	14.8	11.3	9.1	9.6	8.1	12.3	A.

APPENDIX TABLE 3
BALANCE OF PAYMENTS, 1950–1967
(*In Millions of Dollars*)

	1950	1951	1952	1953	1954	1955	1956	1957
I. Net goods and services	+2.0	+9.7	−10.3	−2.6	−10.3	−13.4	−19.8	−33.2
A. Trade balance	+19.4	+35.6	+14.1	+15.8	+7.2	+4.4	+5.5	−9.0
1. Exports [a]	(75.2)	(121.4)	(106.7)	(83.8)	(70.3)	(76.0)	(81.3)	(73.8)
2. Imports [b]	(−55.8)	(−85.8)	(−92.6)	(−68.0)	(−63.1)	(−71.6)	(−75.8)	(−82.8)
B. Freight and insurance	−8.4	−12.9	−13.9	−10.2	−9.5	−10.8	−14.1	−13.7
C. Investment income	−4.0	−8.0	−5.5	−3.2	−3.0	−2.0	−3.1	−3.0
D. Other services [c]	−5.0	−5.0	−5.0	−5.0	−5.0	−5.0	−8.1	−7.5
II. Capital movements	+1.6	−4.4	+4.7	−2.0	−2.8	+9.0	−0.5	+37.8
A. Net private investment	+1.2	−4.8	+3.7	−4.6	−16.8	−16.9	−19.5	+10.1
1. Direct investment	(n.a.)	(n.a.)	(n.a.)	(n.a.)	(n.a.)	(n.a.)	(5.5)	(5.9)
2. Other [d]	(n.a.)	(n.a.)	(n.a.)	(n.a.)	(n.a.)	(n.a.)	(−25.0)	(4.2)
B. Total official economic aid	0.4	0.4	2.0	2.6	14.0	25.9	19.0	27.7
1. U.S. aid	(0.4)	(0.4)	(0.6)	(1.3)	(12.2)	(24.1)	(23.8)	(25.1)
2. IDB	(—)	(—)	(—)	(—)	(—)	(—)	(—)	(—)
C. Other [e]	(n.a.)	(n.a.)	(1.4)	(1.0)	(1.8) [a]	(1.8) [a]	(−4.8)	(2.6)
III. Deficit (−) or surplus (+) (I + II)	+3.6	+5.3	−5.6	−4.6	−13.1	−4.4	−20.3	+4.6
IV. Memorandum								
A. International reserves of Central Bank	29.6	34.9	29.3	24.7	11.6	7.2	1.2	6.0

Sources: 1950–1955: The data for Exports are from *International Financial Statistics*, 1967/68 Supplement; Imports are from Banco Central de Bolivia, *Boletin estadistico*, no. 181, p. 38, adjusted to f.o.b. basis where necessary. Freight and insurance are 15 percent of imports; Investment income has been estimated from various sources; Other services are assumed constant; Net private investment has been computed as residual. *1956–1957:* International Monetary Fund, *Balance of Payments Yearbook*, various volumes.

Note: n.a. = no data available.
a. Excludes tin-smelting costs.
b. No adjustment for illegal imports before 1956.
c. Includes private donations.
d. Includes errors and omissions.
e. Includes other miscellaneous international transactions of the government.

1958	1959	1960	1961	1962	1963	1964	1965	1966	1967	
−43.9	−25.0	−30.5	−28.0	−49.1	−46.2	−29.9	−38.4	−31.7	−41.0	I.
−22.8	−0.8	−15.8	−10.9	−28.9	−26.2	−6.6	−11.1	−5.7	+3.4	A.
(51.3)	(61.6)	(52.4)	(63.8)	(63.6)	(71.9)	(100.1)	(115.5)	(133.1)	(155.2)	1.
(−74.1)	(−62.4)	(−68.2)	(−74.7)	(−92.5)	(−98.1)	(−106.1)	(−126.6)	(−138.8)	(−151.8)	2.
−11.3	−9.7	−10.2	−10.9	−13.8	−14.7	−14.5	−19.0	−20.4	−22.2	B.
−6.5	−1.9	−3.2	−0.8	−2.9	−2.8	−3.2	−4.4	−4.5	−19.4	C.
−3.3	−16.4	−7.7	−5.4	−3.5	−2.5	−5.6	−3.9	−1.1	−2.8	D.
+41.0	+27.3	+27.8	+30.5	+45.0	+51.6	+46.7	+52.3	+36.5	+35.3	II.
+12.4	+6.4	+14.8	+1.7	+11.4	−0.7	−2.4	+15.9	+1.3	+7.9	A.
(16.6)	(15.5)	(16.5)	(11.4)	(10.1)	(5.8)	(1.5)	(12.5)	(2.0)	(0.5)	1.
(−4.2)	(−9.1)	(−1.7)	(−9.7)	(1.3)	(−6.5)	(−3.9)	(3.4)	(−0.7)	(7.4)	2.
28.6	20.9	13.0	28.8	33.6	52.3	49.1	36.4	35.2	27.4	B.
(22.4)	(22.7)	(13.4)	(23.8)	(26.6)	(41.6)	(34.5)	(26.1)	(14.3)	(14.6)	1.
(—)	(—)	(—)	(2.3)	(4.8)	(5.5)	(5.7)	(3.7)	(3.0)	(2.2)	2.
(6.2)	(−1.8)	(−0.4)	(2.7)	(2.2)	(5.2)	(9.9)	(6.6)	(18.0)	(10.6)	C.
−2.9	+2.3	−2.7	+2.5	−4.1	+5.4	+16.8	+13.9	+4.8	−5.7	III.
										IV.
6.6	6.6	6.7	7.2	3.9	10.4	22.4	36.4	41.2	37.8	A.

APPENDIX TABLE 4
RATES OF EXCHANGE AND CONSUMER PRICE INDEX, 1940–1967

Year	Rates of Exchange (*In Bolivianos per U.S. Dollar*)		Consumer Price Index in La Paz (1950 = 100)
	Official Rate	Free-Market Rate	
1940	40.00	44.56	22
1941	43.36	44.40	29
1942	46.46	45.45	38
1943	42.91	42.28	41
1944	42.42	44.76	44
1945	42.42	48.03	48
1946	42.42	57.45	55
1947	42.42–56.05	59.72	70
1948	42.42–56.05	56.80	67
1949	42.42–56.05	71.41	74
1950	60.60–101.00	123.43	100
1951	60.60–101.00	80.06	127
1952	60.60–101.00	173.30	166
1953	191.90	682.00	334
1954	191.90	1415.00	750
1955	191.90	2979.00	1,351
1956	7760.00	7768.00	3,768
1957	7760.00	—	8,102
1958	8565.00	—	8,355
1959	11935.00	—	9,980
1960–62	11885.00	—	12,279 [b]
1963–67	11.88 [a]	—	16,413 [c]

Sources: 1940–1950: Eduardo Lopez Rivas, *Esquema de la historia economica de Bolivia* (Oruro, 1955); *1951–1960:* René Gómez García and Rubén Darío Flores, *La banca nacional* (La Paz, 1962), p. 226, and Comisión Económica para América Latina, *Análisis y proyecciónes del desarrollo económico IV: El desarrollo económico de Bolivia* (Mexico City, 1958), p. 61; *1967:* Banco Central de Bolivia, *Boletín,* 1968 figures shifted to 1950.

a. Currency unit changed to peso bolivianos which equals 1,000 bolivianos.
b. For 1962 only.
c. For 1967 only.

APPENDIX TABLE 5
BOLIVIAN TIN EXPORTS, 1925–1950

Year	Tin Export (in metric tons)	Value in 1950 Prices (in Thousands of Bolivianos)
1925	32,598	66,114
1926	32,184	64,561
1927	39,972	79,823
1928	42,074	84,346
1929	47,087	94,456
1930	38,772	77,777
1931	31,637	63,464
1932	20,918	41,962
1933	14,957	30,004
1934	23,224	46,587
1935	25,408	50,968
1936	24,438	49,023
1937	25,531	51,215
1938	25,893	51,941
1939	27,648	55,462
1940	38,531	77,293
1941	42,740	85,736
1942	38,899	78,031
1943	40,959	82,164
1944	39,341	78,918
1945	43,168	86,595
1946	38,222	76,673
1947	33,777	67,756
1948	37,829	75,885
1949	34,300	68,806
1950	31,320	62,843

Source: Comisión Económica para América Latina, *El desarrollo económico de Bolivia: Análisis y proyecciónes del desarrollo económico, IV* (Mexico City, 1958), p. 12.

APPENDIX TABLE 6

SELECTED MINERAL PRODUCTION BY COMIBOL AND PRIVATE MINES, 1952–1968
(*In Thousands of Metric Tons*)

	1952	1953	1954	1955	1956	1957	1958	1959
Tin	34.3	35.4	27.9	28.4	27.3	28.2	20.6	24.3
1. COMIBOL	27.3	26.0	25.8	23.5	23.0	21.6	17.4	15.8
2. Private	7.0	9.4	2.1	4.9	4.3	7.6	3.2	8.5
Lead	30.0	24.0	18.2	19.1	21.6	26.3	22.3	22.0
1. COMIBOL	9.8	8.5	7.3	9.6	10.7	8.3	7.5	6.3
2. Private	20.2	14.5	10.9	9.5	10.9	17.0	14.8	14.7
Zinc	30.9	24.0	20.4	21.3	17.1	19.7	9.1	3.4
1. COMIBOL	25.3	21.7	17.9	17.6	21.2	15.0	8.4	2.2
2. Private	5.6	2.3	2.5	3.5	5.9	4.7	0.7	1.2
Copper	4.6	4.5	3.7	3.5	4.4	3.9	3.0	2.4
1. COMIBOL	4.1	8.8	3.3	3.3	4.0	3.0	2.3	1.6
2. Private	0.5	0.7	0.4	0.2	0.4	0.6	0.7	0.8
Antimony	9.7	5.8	5.2	5.4	5.1	6.4	2.1	5.4
1. COMIBOL	0.1	0.1	0.0	0.0	—	—	0.0	0.0
2. Private	9.6	5.7	5.2	5.4	5.1	6.4	2.1	5.4
Wolfram								
1. COMIBOL	1.0	1.2	1.6	1.6	1.5	1.2	0.6	0.6
2. Private	1.5	1.1	0.7	1.6	1.4	1.4	0.8	0.9
Silver	0.2	0.2	0.2	0.2	0.2	0.2	0.2	0.1
1. COMIBOL	0.2	0.2	0.1	0.2	0.2	0.1	0.2	0.1
2. Private	0.0	0.0	0.1	0.0	0.0	0.1	0.0	0.0
Bismuth								
1. COMIBOL	0.0	0.0	0.0	0.0	0.0	0.0	0.1	0.1
2. Private	0.0	0.0	0.0	0.0	0.0	0.0	0.0	0.0
Crude Petroleum [a]	83.6	95.5	269.5	428.1	508.0	568.4	546.2	504.0
1. YPFB	83.6	95.5	269.5	428.1	508.0	568.4	546.2	504.0
2. Private	0.0	0.0	0.0	0.0	0.0	0.0	0.0	0.0

Sources: 1952, 1958, 1960–1968: U.S., Agency for International Development, Bolivia, *Estadísticas económicas* (1969); *1953–1957, 1959:* Banco Central de Bolivia, Sección Estudios Económicos y Estadística, *Boletín estadístico* (December 1969); *1952–1959:* for COMIBOL, see Banco Central de Bolivia, Sección Estudios Económicos y Estadística, and Cabrera (1969), pp. 42–43.

a. In thousands of cubic meters.

1960	1961	1962	1963	1964	1965	1966	1967	1968	
20.5	21.0	22.2	22.6	24.7	24.4	26.5	28.4	29.0	Sn
15.2	14.8	15.3	15.4	17.7	16.5	18.4	18.6	18.4	1.
5.3	6.2	6.9	7.2	7.0	7.9	8.1	9.8	10.6	2.
21.3	19.7	18.6	19.3	16.9	16.4	19.8	20.3	21.7	Pb
7.3	6.8	6.4	7.7	7.3	6.5	8.4	7.5	8.4	1.
14.0	12.9	12.2	11.6	9.6	9.9	11.4	12.8	13.3	2.
4.3	4.9	3.6	4.3	9.6	13.6	16.1	16.8	11.3	Zn
3.5	4.2	3.4	3.4	3.4	4.0	5.8	5.4	3.9	1.
0.8	0.7	0.2	0.9	6.2	9.6	10.3	11.4	7.4	2.
2.4	2.2	2.4	3.0	4.7	4.7	5.8	6.1	7.0	Cu
1.5	1.4	1.5	1.5	1.7	1.8	2.7	2.2	2.6	1.
0.9	0.8	0.9	1.5	3.0	2.9	3.1	3.9	4.4	2.
5.3	6.7	6.6	7.5	9.6	8.7	10.7	11.5	11.1	Sb
0.0	0.0	0.0	0.1	0.1	0.0	0.0	0.0	0.0	1.
5.3	6.7	6.6	7.4	9.5	8.7	10.7	11.5	11.1	2.
1.3	1.7	1.5	1.4	1.2	1.0	1.6	2.0	2.0	W
0.5	0.4	0.3	0.2	0.1	0.1	0.5	0.7	0.5	1.
0.8	1.3	1.2	1.2	1.1	1.0	1.1	1.3	1.5	2.
0.1	0.1	0.1	0.1	0.1	0.1	0.1	0.1	0.1	Ag
0.1	0.1	0.1	0.1	0.1	0.1	0.1	0.1	0.1	1.
0.0	0.0	0.0	0.0	0.0	0.0	0.0	0.0	0.0	2.
0.2	0.2	0.3	0.3	0.3	0.3	0.4	0.5	0.6	Bi
0.2	0.2	0.3	0.3	0.3	0.3	0.4	0.5	0.6	1.
0.0	0.0	0.0	0.0	0.0	0.0	0.0	0.0	0.0	2.
568.3	475.2	463.8	540.7	523.1	536.0	967.4	2,309.5	2,383.6	Pet.
494.5	430.3	413.8	501.6	498.0	528.2	504.5	435.1	660.3	1.
73.8	44.9	50.0	39.1	25.1	7.8	462.9	1,879.4	1,723.3	2.

CONSOLIDATED FINANCES OF THE PUBLIC SECTOR, 1958–1968
(*In Millions of Pesos Bolivianos*)

	1958	1959	1960	1961	1962	1963	1964	1965	1966	1967	1968	
I. Income	1,023	1,022	1,088	1,418	1,413	1,622	2,071	2,335	2,488	2,700	2,873	I.
A. Central government	231	250	277	359	432	428	511	613	724	772	828	A.
B. State mining company a	535	523	525	754	695	565	892	960	942	973	967	B.
C. State petroleum company a	153	152	172	178	212	234	238	266	288	356	411	C.
D. State railways a	69	70	75	75	74	73	72	107	106	119	137	D.
E. Development Corporation a	35	27	39	52	n.a.⎫	321	357	390	430	⎧ 40⎫	530	E.
F. Other ab	n.a.	n.a.	n.a.	n.a.	n.a.⎭					⎩441⎭		F.
II. Expenditures	1,237	1,350	1,404	1,765	1,734	1,967	2,254	2,502	2,588	2,814	3,073	II.
A. Central government	368	403	414	481	515	505	575	764	858	917	1,020	A.
B. State mining company	593	640	652	870	887	744	957	960	918	960	953	B.
C. State petroleum company	140	149	176	205	212	230	225	249	256	313	363	C.
D. State railways	96	94	106	118	120	107	110	123	121	127	151	D.
E. Development Corporation	40	64	56	91	n.a.⎫	382	388	406	434	⎧ 37⎫	586	E.
F. Other b	n.a.	n.a.	n.a.	n.a.	n.a.⎭					⎩459⎭		F.
III. Deficit (−) or surplus (I-II)	−214	−328	−316	−347	−321	−345	−183	−167	−99	−114	−200	III.
A. Central government	−137	−153	−137	−122	−83	−77	−64	−151	−134	−146	−192	A.
B. State mining company	−58	−117	−127	−116	−192	−178	−64	−0	24	13	14	B.
C. State petroleum company	13	3	−4	−27	0	5	13	17	31	43	48	C.
D. State railways	−27	−24	−31	−43	−46	−35	−38	−16	−15	−8	−14	D.
E. Development Corporation	−5	−37	−17	−39	n.a.⎫	−60	⎧−19⎫	27	56	⎧ 3⎫	−56	E.
F. Other b	n.a.	n.a.	n.a.	n.a.	n.a.⎭		⎩−11⎭	−44	−60	⎩−19⎭		F.

Sources: 1958–1967: U.S., Agency for International Development, *Economic and Program Statistics*, nos. 5, 11, supplemented by data supplied by the Bolivian Development Corporation; *1968:* Estimated from data supplied by various agencies.
Note: n.a. = no data available.
   a. Excludes transfers from central government.
   b. Includes National Social Security Fund, state and local governments, and universities.

SUPPLEMENTARY INFORMATION ON
APPENDIX TABLE 8

SOURCE OF CENTRAL GOVERNMENT ACTUAL EXPENDITURES

Projected accounts are published yearly in Bolivia, Ministerio de Hacienda, *Presupuesto General.*

Actual accounts are unpublished since 1934 and may be found in Bolivia's Office of the Contraloría General in the form of yearly Summary Account Books. These summaries are based upon Detailed Account Books of movement of funds by ministry and for State Obligations. The Detailed Account Book for the Ministry of Education, for example, lists all items from the *Presupuesto* and notes all changes while recording amounts actually expended. Detailed Account Books are currently stored in the archival section of the basement in the Ministry of Hacienda. Summary data for 1911–1931 are provided in Jorge Palenque, *Estadística Boliviana, Primera Parte, Análisis Numérico del Presupuesto Nacional, Años 1911–1931* (La Paz: Talleres Gráficos Renacimiento, 1933), 61–67. Palenque includes expenditure outside the budget with his totals on page 67 and these expenditures are classified here as having administrative emphasis. Summary expenditures for 1932 and 1933 are found in Bolivia, Contraloría General de la República, *Informe . . . 1932 a 1933,* (La Paz: Editorial América, n.d.), 157, 273.

Recorded funds expended outside the budget (*fuera del presupuesto*) without authorization are added to total expenditure and appropriately distributed by type of emphasis. Thus the Christmas bonus (*aguinaldo*) to governmental employees, 1940–1954, for example, is integrated into actual accounts (distribution is based upon the percentage ratio given in the *Presupuesto* for 1961: 5.6 economic, 32.5 social, and 61.9 administrative).

Sources for actual expenditure through 1939 exclude Extraordinary Expenditures: *servico de rentas especiales, fondos de custodio, fondo contribución patriótica* (except military).

ACTUAL EXPENDITURE

1932–1933: Bolivia, Contraloría General, *Informe . . . 1932 a 1933,* 157, 273.

1933: Summary Account Book is used in conjunction with the *Informe.*

1933–1935: See note for Projected Accounts.

1937–1938: Revised summaries.

1941: See page 133 in Summary Account Book.

1942: Includes 40.0 million bolivianos in public debt for Standard Oil Co. Aguinaldo is added to expenditures on page 127 in Summary Account Book.

1944: *Aguinaldo* and *anticipos a la defensa* are added to total expenditure given in page 132 of Summary Account Book.

1945: Estimate in Table 6 is on basis of difference in projections and actual outlay for 1944.

1946–1947: Some items are estimated from projections; others are estimated from actual expenditures.

1949: Includes emergency funds (outside of budget) to combat civil war (87.6 million bolivianos for military and 55.9 for Government Ministry).

Adapted from James W. Wilkie, *The Bolivian Revolution and U.S. Aid Since 1952: Financial Background and Context of Political Decisions* (Los Angeles, Calif., 1969), pp. 53–54.

1965–1966: Source is Bolivia, Ministerio de Hacienda, Departamento Estadístico de Presupuestos; preliminary data. Percentages not available for such items in 1965–1966 are included in other categories (for example, Communications is included in Public Works).

1966: Data as of December 28, 1966; some estimation on basis of projected expenditure.

EXPLANATION OF TERMS FOR TABLE 8

ECONOMIC EXPENDITURES

Public Works Formerly Fomento; includes negligible amounts for potable water; includes transportation subsidies

Communications Separated from the Treasury Department prior to 1923

Ministry of Economy Formerly Industry

Agriculture and Livestock Includes irrigation; excludes Colonization and Rural Development

Colonization and Rural Development Separated from Agriculture and Livestock; prior to 1941 funds included government of sparsely populated areas—especially police, defense, and communication

CBF grants Bolivian Development Corporation grants; separated from economic share of State Obligations

Christmas Bonus Economic share, 1940–1954

State Obligations Economic share; includes economic share of expenditure outside the budget, price supports, transfers to industry and commerce, subsidies of decentralized agencies, payments to international agencies operating in Bolivia, buffer stock funds, transport subsidies, civic aeronautics, and contributions to Bolivian-American Cooperatives for Agricultural Development and the Agricultural and Roads Services; excludes grants to Bolivian Development Corporation

SOCIAL EXPENDITURES

State Obligations (*education*) Education share; separated from social share of State Obligations; includes university subventions; excludes seminaries and church schools

Education Ministry Includes negligible amounts for Catholic Education; excludes Fundamental Education for literacy, community development, and agricultural extension (administered by Peasant Affairs)

Peasant Affairs Includes Fundamental Education, administration of cooperatives, and agricultural extension

Labor and Social Security Excludes retirement funds resulting from Chaco War

Public Health Separated from Government, Justice, and Immigration prior to 1929

Social Security transfers Separated from social share of State Obligations

Housing Separated from social share of State Obligations

Christmas Bonus Social share, 1940–1954

State Obligations (*social*) social share; includes social share of expenditure outside the budget as well as contributions to CARE, Catholic Relief Agency, *Restaurant del Niño,* UNICEF, public disaster, U.N. Peasant Rehabilitation Center, and Education and Public Health Services; excludes education share of State Obligations, Social Security transfers, and Housing

ADMINISTRATIVE EXPENDITURES

Judiciary Justice Department transferred to Government, Justice, and Immigration in 1961

Electoral Court   Included in Government, Justice, and Immigration until 1958

Presidency   Included in Government, Justice, and Immigration prior to 1950; includes Press Agency and negligible amounts for Tourism and Social Service to foster career administrators; excludes Planning and Coordination after 1963

Foreign Relations   Excludes Church Affairs

Government, Justice, and Immigration   Justice Department in Judiciary prior to 1961; included Electoral Court until 1958 and Presidency until 1950; prior to 1929 excludes Public Health

Treasury   Includes Controller General's Office and Statistical Agency, as well as old *Compañía Recaudadora Nacional;* excludes Communications prior to 1923 and Public Debt and retirement funds prior to 1929

State Obligations (military)   Military share; separated from administrative share of State Obligations

Public Debt   Separated from Treasury prior to 1929 and from administrative share of State Obligations thereafter; includes interest and amortization; excludes retirement funds

Church Affairs   Separated from Foreign Relations; includes subsidies to seminaries and schools

Planning and Coordination   Included in Presidency until 1963

Christmas Bonus   Administrative share, 1940–1954

Retirement funds   For Chaco War veterans, widows, orphans, and MNR insurrection veterans; separated from Labor and Social Security

Other retirement funds   Separated from Treasury prior to 1929 and separated from administrative share of State Obligations and/or Public Debt thereafter; includes prizes after 1922; distributed by ministry beginning in 1965

State Obligations (administrative)   Includes administrative share of expenditure outside of the budget; includes *subsidios familiares;* includes subsidies of department and municipal government, church construction and affairs (including schools), pension funds, secret funds of the president, and funds for special military and police units; includes contribution to monetary commission and to international organizations; includes *Créditos Reconocidos;* excludes Public Debt, military share of State Obligations, and retirement funds.

APPENDIX TABLE 8

PERCENT DISTRIBUTION OF CENTRAL GOVERNMENT EXPENDITURE, 1930–1966

(*Percent of Total Annual Expenditure*)

Expenditure	1930	1931	1932	1933	1934	1935	1936	1937	1938	1939	1940	1941	1942
Economic													
Agrarian Reform	—	—	—	—	—	—	—	—	—	—	—	—	—
Public Works	1.6%	3.4%	2.4%	1.1%	1.1%	4.9%	1.4%	5.0%	3.9%	8.8%	7.3%	8.8%	8.7%
Communications	3.9	5.6	5.7	2.1	1.5	1.2	3.0	3.1	2.4	3.0	3.4	2.4	2.7
Ministry of Economy	0.6	0.6	0.3	0.1	—	0.1	0.5	0.3	0.2	0.6	0.2	1.2	0.7
Mines and Petroleum Ministry	—	—	—	—	—	—	0.3	0.3	0.5	1.2	0.7	—	—
Agriculture & Livestock	0.2	0.3	0.3	—	0.1	0.1	0.2	0.9	0.3	0.8	0.9	—	4.0
Colonization & Rural Development	1.2	1.5	1.5	0.4	0.3	0.2	0.6	0.5	0.8	0.9	0.7	0.4	0.5
CBF grants	—	—	—	—	—	—	—	—	—	—	—	—	10.2
Christmas Bonus	—	—	—	—	—	—	—	—	—	—	0.1	0.1	0.1
State Obligations	—	—	—	—	—	—	0.1	2.4	1.6	0.2	1.5	0.9	1.0
Social													
State Obligations (education)	—	—	—	—	—	—	—	0.5	—	—	1.5	0.9	0.4
Education Ministry	7.3	10.5	9.8	2.8	2.4	2.7	6.4	6.6	6.7	9.4	13.4	8.5	12.4
Peasant Affairs	—	—	—	—	—	—	—	—	—	—	—	—	—
Labor & Social Security	—	—	—	—	—	—	0.1	0.3	1.0	2.0	1.6	1.0	1.4
Public Health	0.2	0.6	0.3	0.2	0.1	0.1	2.0	4.3	3.8	4.4	4.7	4.4	5.4

Social Security transfers	—	—	—	—	—	—	—	—	—	—	—	—	—
Housing	—	—	—	—	—	—	—	—	—	—	0.8	0.5	0.7
Christmas Bonus	—	—	—	—	—	—	—	1.1	0.9	7.8	—	—	—
State Obligations (social)	—	—	—	—	—	—	—						
Administrative													
Legislature & Vice-Presidency	1.0	3.7	2.7	0.6	0.4	0.3	0.2	—	1.3	0.7	1.7	1.5	1.5
Judiciary	3.3	4.6	4.2	1.5	1.1	0.8	1.7	1.7	1.4	1.9	2.3	1.6	2.2
Electoral Court	—	—	—	—	—	—	—	—	—	—	—	—	—
Presidency	—	—	—	—	—	—	—	—	—	—	—	—	—
Foreign Relations	2.6	2.5	2.7	1.0	0.9	0.9	1.4	2.8	2.2	2.5	3.8	2.1	2.4
Govt., Justice & Immigration	6.1	6.5	6.0	2.2	1.7	1.5	4.5	6.2	5.0	5.8	5.3	5.7	7.6
Treasury	6.7	7.7	6.0	2.0	1.6	1.3	4.9	4.0	3.4	5.5	4.8	3.2	3.6
Military	23.6	31.3	32.2	78.5	80.4	78.9	50.5	36.0	36.0	30.9	28.3	21.7	19.9
State Obligations (military)	—	—	—	—	—	—	—	—	—	—	—	—	—
Public debt	34.6	17.6	23.5	6.9	7.8	6.5	11.3	15.6	6.0	8.4	8.0	0.9	4.7
Church Affairs	0.2	0.3	0.3	0.1	0.1	0.1	0.1	—	0.1	0.1	0.1	0.1	0.2
Planning & Coordination	—	—	—	—	—	—	—	—	—	1.5	1.1	1.4	
Christmas Bonus	—	—	—	—	—	—	—	—	—	—	—	4.0	
Retirement funds	—	—	—	—	—	—	—	—	—	—	—	—	
Other retirement funds	1.0	1.8	1.8	0.5	0.5	0.4	1.0	0.9	1.0	1.7	1.2	0.6	0.7
State Obligations (administrative)	5.9	1.5	0.3	—	—	—	9.8	7.5	21.5	3.4	6.2	32.4	3.6

Source: James W. Wilkie, *The Bolivian Revolution and U.S. Aid Since 1952: Financial Background and Context of Political Decisions* (Los Angeles, Calif., 1969), pp. 54, 65–73.
Note: See preceding supplementary information on table 8 for Bolivian sources and definitions.

Appendix Table 8 (*continued*)

Expenditure	1943	1944	1945	1946	1947	1948	1949	1950	1951	1952	1953	1954	1955
Economic													
Agrarian Reform	—	—	—	—	—	—	—	—	—	—	—	0.8%	1.5%
Public Works	8.6%	7.1%	—	4.2%	2.4%	2.2%	1.3%	1.5%	2.0%	1.4%	1.2%	0.7	0.8
Communications	2.9	3.0	—	3.2	3.3	4.1	3.8	3.6	3.7	3.6	3.6	3.5	3.5
Ministry of Economy	0.7	1.1	—	0.7	0.6	0.5	0.5	0.6	0.4	0.3	0.2	0.2	0.2
Mines & Petroleum Ministry	—	—	—	—	—	—	—	—	0.2	0.4	0.3	0.4
Agriculture & Livestock	2.4	2.3	—	1.6	1.4	1.3	1.0	0.9	1.0	1.5	1.0	0.9	1.1
Colonization & Rural Development	0.4	0.3	—	0.2	0.2	0.2	0.1	0.1	0.2	—	0.2	0.2	0.1
CBF grants	10.5	10.8	—	—	1.5	—	—	0.2	—	—	—	5.4	7.7
Christmas Bonus	0.1	0.1	—	0.1	0.1	0.2	0.2	0.2	0.2	0.2	0.2	0.2	—
State Obligations	1.0	1.3	—	1.6	1.7	1.2	1.2	1.4	2.0	1.3	2.1	1.5	2.1
Social													
State Obligations (education)	0.5	0.5	—	2.5	0.3	—	0.3	0.5	0.3	0.2	0.2	0.1	—
Education Ministry	13.8	13.9	—	15.3	18.7	22.5	19.9	21.5	20.3	23.5	18.6	16.8	16.0
Peasant Affairs	—	—	—	—	—	—	—	—	—	—	6.4	6.6	6.4
Labor & Social Security	1.5	1.6	—	3.0	0.7	1.7	1.7	3.3	1.4	2.2	2.9	1.7	2.2
Public Health	4.5	4.3	—	5.5	5.1	4.8	5.0	4.6	3.6	4.0	3.8	3.6	4.3
Social Security transfers	—	—	—	—	—	—	—	—	—	—	—	—	—
Housing	—	—	—	—	—	—	—	—	—	—	—	—	—
Christmas Bonus	0.8	0.5	—	0.5	0.8	0.8	1.1	1.3	1.3	1.3	1.0	1.3	—
State Obligations (social)	0.1	—	—	—	1.1	0.9	—	—	1.5	1.0	1.2	3.4	3.2

Administrative

Legislature & Vice-Presidency	1.4	1.0	—	0.9	1.7	2.0	1.8	1.6	0.5	—	0.1	0.2	0.2
Judiciary	2.6	3.3	—	2.8	2.8	2.6	2.7	2.5	2.5	2.4	2.0	2.1	1.8
Electoral Court	—	—	—	—	—	—	—	—	—	—	—	—	—
Presidency	—	—	—	—	—	—	—	0.5	0.7	0.9	1.3	1.1	1.0
Foreign Relations	2.6	2.6	—	2.7	2.9	2.8	2.2	2.2	2.0	1.9	1.1	1.5	1.2
Govt., Justice & Immigration	8.0	7.7	—	7.6	11.5	11.4	13.1	11.6	12.4	12.3	11.8	10.7	10.8
Treasury	4.5	5.4	—	5.5	4.5	4.4	4.1	4.0	3.6	4.0	3.2	3.1	3.0
Military	20.5	22.2	—	23.5	17.5	22.9	26.2	23.5	24.7	23.0	13.7	11.4	12.8
State Obligations (military)	—	0.3	—	—	3.9	—	—	2.3	—	—	—	—	—
Public debt	1.6	2.3	—	1.2	3.6	3.4	0.8	4.7	2.9	1.6	0.9	0.9	2.3
Church Affairs	0.3	0.4	—	0.2	0.3	0.2	0.2	0.3	0.3	0.3	0.2	0.2	0.2
Planning & Coordination	—	—	—	—	—	—	—	—	—	—	—	0.1	—
Christmas Bonus	1.5	1.1	—	1.1	1.6	1.6	2.1	2.4	2.4	2.5	1.8	2.4	—
Retirement funds	3.5	3.5	—	5.6	4.8	5.1	4.9	3.6	4.9	4.3	3.0	3.2	4.2
Other retirement funds	0.4	0.6	—	0.5	1.7	1.0	1.1	0.8	0.6	0.5	0.9	0.2	0.1
State Obligations (administrative)	5.3	2.8	—	10.0	5.3	2.2	4.7	0.3	4.6	5.6	17.0	15.7	12.9

Appendix Table 8 (continued)

Expenditure	1956	1957	1958	1959	1960	1961	1962	1963	1964	1965	1966
Economic											
Agrarian Reform	0.9%	0.4%	0.4%	0.4%	0.5%	0.4%	0.5%	0.5%	0.4%	—	—
Public Works	0.6	1.0	1.3	2.0	2.5	2.7	2.0	2.1	2.0	4.7%	6.3%
Communications	3.8	1.6	1.8	2.1	2.5	2.3	2.6	2.6	2.4	2.5	—
Ministry of Economy	0.2	0.2	0.3	0.2	0.1	0.2	0.3	0.3	0.3	2.0	0.5
Mines & Petroleum Ministry	0.2	0.1	0.1	0.1	0.2	0.3	0.3	0.3	0.2	0.3	0.3
Agriculture & Livestock	0.7	0.9	0.4	0.5	0.7	0.7	0.8	1.1	1.1	2.1	1.8
Colonization & Rural Development	—	—	—	—	—	—	0.1	0.1	0.1	—	—
CBF grants	—	11.4	4.4	6.8	2.6	2.6	3.1	0.3	2.4	—	—
Christmas Bonus	—	—	—	—	—	—	—	—	—	—	—
State Obligations	6.1	11.7	4.6	7.2	6.6	7.4	5.9	5.7	4.7	—	3.1
Social											
State Obligations (education)	—	1.1	1.0	0.5	1.5	1.2	1.3	1.7	1.1	—	—
Education Ministry	22.0	8.6	11.3	13.1	14.2	13.2	14.5	15.4	14.7	21.0	24.4
Peasant Affairs	8.5	3.6	4.5	5.6	6.4	6.3	7.1	7.6	7.3	8.6	10.1
Labor & Social Security	1.4	1.2	1.3	1.3	1.0	1.5	1.1	1.2	1.2	1.1	1.4
Public Health	3.1	2.7	2.6	3.5	3.6	3.5	3.3	3.2	3.0	3.1	3.4
Social Security transfers	0.8	7.6	5.2	9.5	8.5	6.6	6.1	5.7	4.9	—	—
Housing	—	—	—	—	—	0.5	0.4	0.4	0.3	—	—
Christmas Bonus	—	—	—	—	—	—	—	—	—	—	—
State Obligations (social)	15.0	0.8	3.9	2.2	2.0	0.7	1.4	1.1	0.8	0.3	1.5

Administrative

Legislature & Vice-Presidency	0.5	0.4	0.4	0.6	1.2	1.4	1.5	1.4	1.3	0.1	0.6
Judiciary	1.4	0.7	0.9	1.0	1.0	0.7	0.9	0.9	0.8	1.6	1.6
Electoral Court	—	—	0.1	—	0.5	—	0.4	—	0.5	0.1	0.6
Presidency	0.6	0.5	0.5	0.6	0.6	0.5	0.6	0.7	0.7	1.2	1.3
Foreign Relations	5.0	2.6	2.8	2.8	3.2	2.8	3.1	3.0	2.6	2.3	2.2
Govt., Justice & Immigration	9.4	5.0	5.4	6.0	6.8	7.0	6.9	8.0	7.3	8.7	7.9
Treasury	2.1	1.3	1.4	2.0	2.0	1.8	1.8	1.9	1.7	16.6	7.7
Military	8.7	6.7	8.6	10.6	10.9	12.2	12.6	12.4	12.0	18.3	18.0
State Obligations (military)	—	—	—	—	—	0.1	0.9	1.1	1.9	—	—
Public debt	1.5	2.6	4.1	5.0	4.0	2.5	4.6	4.3	5.0	3.1	5.0
Church Affairs	0.1	0.1	0.1	0.2	0.2	0.2	0.2	0.2	0.2	0.1	0.1
Planning & Coordination	0.1	0.1	0.1	0.1	0.2	0.4	0.4	0.4	0.4	0.4	0.4
Christmas Bonus	—	—	—	—	—	—	—	—	—	—	—
Retirement funds	2.8	1.2	2.0	3.6	3.1	2.4	2.5	2.4	1.7	1.8	1.8
Other retirement funds	0.1	0.3	0.5	0.6	0.8	1.1	0.7	0.7	0.6	—	—
State Obligations (administrative)	4.4	25.6	30.0	11.9	12.6	16.8	12.1	13.3	16.4	—	—

APPENDIX TABLE 9
U.S. ECONOMIC AND MILITARY AID TO BOLIVIA, 1946–1968
(*In Millions of Dollars*)

	1946	1947	1948	1949	1950	1951	1952	1953	1954	1955	1956
I. Economic and military	$0.4	$3.4	$0.4	$0.7	$16.5	$0.5	$1.5	$1.3	$18.2	$33.5	$28.0
A. Loans	—	3.0	—	0.3	16.0	—	—	—	2.4	4.7	—
B. Grants	0.4	0.4	0.4	0.4	0.5	0.5	1.5	1.3	15.8	28.8	28.0
II. Economic	0.4	3.4	0.4	0.7	16.5	0.5	1.5	1.3	18.2	33.5	28.0
A. Loans	—	3.0	—	0.3	16.0	—	—	—	2.4	4.7	—
B. Grants	0.4	0.4	0.4	0.4	0.5	0.5	1.5	1.3	15.8	28.8	28.0
III. Military	—	—	—	—	—	—	—	—	—	—	—
A. Loans	—	—	—	—	—	—	—	—	—	—	—
B. Grants	—	—	—	—	—	—	—	—	—	—	—
IV. Economic aid by program											
A. AID	—	—	—	—	—	—	1.5	1.3	7.5	12.8	25.3
1. Loans	—	—	—	—	—	—	—	—	—	—	—
2. Grants	—	—	—	—	—	—	1.5	1.3	7.5	12.8	25.3
B. Social Progress Trust Fund	—	—	—	—	—	—	—	—	—	—	—
C. Food for Freedom	—	—	—	—	—	—	a	—	0.3	16.0	2.7
1. Repayable in Bolivian currency	—	—	—	—	—	—	—	—	—	—	—
a. Less U.S. uses	(—)	(—)	(—)	(—)	(—)	(—)	(—)	(—)	(—)	(—)	(—)
2. Available for country use	—	—	—	—	—	—	—	—	—	—	—
a. Economic development loans	—	—	—	—	—	—	—	—	—	—	—
b. Cooley loans	—	—	—	—	—	—	—	—	—	—	—
3. Repayable in dollars	—	—	—	—	—	—	—	—	—	—	—
4. Emergency relief and economic development	—	—	—	—	—	—	—	—	—	14.6	—
5. Voluntary agencies	—	—	—	—	—	—	a	—	0.3	1.4	2.7
D. Export-Import Bank loans	—	3.0	—	0.3	16.0	—	—	—	2.4	4.7	—
E. Other	0.4	0.4	0.4	0.4	0.5	0.5	—	—	8.0	—	—
F. Grants	0.4	0.4	0.4	0.4	0.5	0.5	—	—	8.0	—	—
G. Technical assistance and IIAA [b]	0.4	0.4	0.4	0.4	0.5	0.5	—	—	—	—	—
H. Public Law 216	—	—	—	—	—	—	—	—	8.0	—	—
I. Peace Corps	—	—	—	—	—	—	—	—	—	—	—

Source: U.S., Agency for International Development, Bureau for Program and Policy Coordination, Office of Statistics and Reports, *U.S. Overseas Loans and Grants and Assistance from International Organizations* (Washington, D.C., 1968).
  a. Less than $50,000.
  b. IIAA = Institute of Inter-American Affairs.

1957	1958	1959	1960	1961	1962	1963	1964	1965	1966	1967	1968	Total	
$26.8	$22.1	$24.6	$13.8	$29.9	$38.6	$65.4	$79.0	$13.8	$38.8	$31.0	$23.6	$513.2	I.
—	—	4.0	—	9.7	10.4	41.3	51.1	0.2	27.3	21.6	14.1	205.8	A.
26.8	22.1	20.6	13.8	20.2	28.8	24.2	28.0	13.6	11.5	9.4	9.5	307.3	B.
26.8	22.0	24.3	13.8	29.5	36.4	63.0	75.8	11.9	36.4	28.1	20.1	492.8	II.
—	—	4.0	—	9.7	10.4	41.3	51.1	0.2	27.3	21.6	14.1	205.8	A.
26.8	22.0	20.3	13.8	19.8	26.0	21.8	24.8	11.7	9.1	6.5	6.0	286.5	B.
—	0.1	0.3	ª	0.4	2.2	2.4	3.2	1.9	2.4	2.9	3.5	20.8	III.
—	—	—	—	—	—	—	—	—	—	—	—	—	A.
—	0.1	0.3	ª	0.4	2.2	2.4	3.2	1.9	2.4	2.9	3.5	20.8	B.
													IV.
22.8	22.0	23.9	13.6	26.7	32.1	35.7	58.5	14.4	27.5	14.3	7.8	335.5	A.
—	—	4.0	—	7.3	7.9	18.5	42.7	6.0	21.8	10.9	4.5	111.5	1.
22.8	22.0	19.9	13.6	19.4	24.2	17.2	15.8	8.4	5.7	3.4	3.3	224.0	2.
—	—	—	—	—.	—	10.5	0.8	3.3	—	—	—	14.6	B.
4.0	—	0.4	0.2	2.8	3.4	16.1	14.0	4.0	6.3	1.5	10.6	82.4	C.
—	—	—	—	2.4	2.5	9.6	6.2	2.9	4.9	—	—	28.6	1.
(—)	(—)	(—)	(—)	(0.8)	(0.7)	(2.9)	(1.6)	(1.0)	(1.6)	(—)	(—)	(8.5)	a.
—	—	—	—	2.4	2.5	9.6	6.2	2.9	4.9	—	—	28.6	2.
—	—	—	—	2.4	2.3	8.8	5.5	2.7	4.6	—	—	26.1	a.
—	—	—	—	—	0.2	0.9	0.8	0.2	0.3	—	—	2.4	b.
—	—	—	—	—	—	2.6	1.3	—	0.6	0.6	9.6	14.7	3.
2.8	—	—	—	—	0.1	0.2	1.4	0.6	ª	—	0.4	20.1	4.
1.2	—	0.4	0.2	0.4	0.8	3.7	5.1	0.5	0.8	0.9	0.6	19.0	5.
—	—	—	—	—	—	—	—	—	—	10.1	—	36.5	D.
—	—	—	—	—	0.9	0.7	2.5	2.2	2.6	2.2	1.7	23.4	E.
—	—	—	—	—	0.9	0.7	2.5	2.2	2.6	2.2	1.7	23.4	F.
—	—	—	—	—	—	—	—	—	—	—	—	2.6	G.
—	—	—	—	—	—	—	—	—	—	—	—	8.0	H.
—	—	—	—	—	0.9	0.7	2.5	2.2	2.6	2.2	1.7	12.8	I.

APPENDIX TABLE 10
BOLIVIAN PRESIDENTS SINCE 1926

Assumption of Office		Name
1926	January 10	Hernando Siles Reyes
1930	June 28	Carlos Blanco Galindo (acting)
1931	March 5	Daniel Salamanca
1934	November 28	José Luis Tejada Sorzano (acting)
1936	May 16	Germán Busch (acting)
	May 22	David Toro (acting)
1937	July 13	Germán Busch (acting)
	May 28	Germán Busch
1939	August 23	Carlos Quintanilla (acting)
1940	April 15	Enrique Peñaranda
1943	December 20	Gualberto Villarroel (acting)
1944	August 6	Gualberto Villarroel
1946	July 21	Néstor Guillén (acting)
	August 16	Tomás Monje Gutiérrez (acting)
1947	March 10	Enrique Hertzog
1949	May 7	Mamerto Urriolagoitia (acting)
1951	May 16	Hugo R. Bavillián (acting)
1952	April 9	Hernán Siles Zuazo (acting)
	April 15	Víctor Paz Estenssoro
1956	August 6	Hernán Siles Zuazo
1960	August 6	Víctor Paz Estenssoro
1964	August 6	Víctor Paz Estenssoro
	November 4	Alfredo Ovando Candia (acting)
	November 5	René Barrientos Ortuño (acting)
1965	May 26	René Barrientos Ortuño and Alfredo Ovando Candia (acting)
1966	January 3	Alfredo Ovando Candia (acting)
	August 6	René Barrientos Ortuño
1969	April 27	Luis Adolfo Siles Salinas (acting)
1969	September 26	Alfredo Ovando Candia (acting)
1970	October 8	Juan José Torres (acting)

Sources: 1926–1956: Andrés de Santa-Cruz Schuhkrafft, *Cuadros sinópticos de los gobernantes de la república de Bolivia, 1825 a 1956 y de la del Perú, 1820 a 1956* (La Paz, 1956), pp. 40–52; *1960–1969: New York Times*, various issues.

APPENDIX TABLE 11
U.S. AMBASSADOR TO BOLIVIA SINCE 1928

Assumption of Office	Name
May 1928	David E. Kaufman
November 1930	Edward Francis Feely
August 19, 1933	Fay A. Des Portes
April 25, 1936	R. Henry Norweb
May 4, 1937	Robert G. Caldwell
June 22, 1939	Douglas Jenkins
March 5, 1942	Pierre De L. Boal
September 21, 1944	Walter Thurston
April 27, 1946	Joseph Flack
November 19, 1949	Irving Florman
December 14, 1951	Edward J. Sparks
October 11, 1954	Gerald A. Drew
March 28, 1957	Philip W. Bonsal
April 8, 1959	Carl W. Strom
June 24, 1961	Ben S. Stephansky
December 3, 1963	Douglas Henderson
September 3, 1968	Raul Hector Castro

Source: U.S. Embassy in La Paz.

Glossary

alcalde Mayor of a community

Altiplano The high plateau formed by the eastern and western ranges, or *cordilleras*, of the Andean mountains in Bolivia and Peru

ayllu A self-governing and landowning peasant community in the Andean region

caciques Regional bosses of strong men who controlled rural *sindicato* organizations after 1952

campesinos Countrymen—official term for Indian peasants adopted by the government after 1952

campo Countryside

candidatura única Phrase used to designate a multiparty slate which supports a common list of candidates for an election

carabineros The national police force

caudillismo System of rule by *caudillos*

caudillo Chief or leader who rules through a combination of armed might and personalized control

chicha Corn alcohol usually produced by mastication. It is the primary intoxicating beverage consumed by Bolivian Indians.

cholo A person of mixed Indian-white descent, often known as a *mestizo* in other parts of Latin America

chuño Dehydrated potato flour

co-gobierno Co-government—a concept through which the COB was recognized as holding co-governmental status with the MNR after 1952

colono A landless peasant who supplies free agricultural labor on a *latifundia* in return for the use of usufruct land for his own crops. The system of colono labor is known as *colonato*. See also *pongo*.

Portions of this section are adapted from the glossaries in *Parties and Political Change in Bolivia, 1880–1952* by Herbert Klein (Cambridge, 1969) and *Bolivia: The Uncompleted Revolution* by James M. Malloy (Pittsburgh, 1970).

comunidad A self-governing and landowning Indian peasant community. The comunidad contains three types of *comunarios,* or members of the community: *originarios,* original settlers of the community; *agregados,* postsettlement arrivals who possess land; and *forasters sin tierra,* late arrivals who do not possess land. The latter usually sell their labor to the community.

corregidor The official in republican Bolivia charged with administering local Indian affairs. He is almost invariable a white or cholo.

emboscados A derogatory term appled to those in the Chaco War who deliberately sought safe rearguard positions

empleados White-collar workers paid on a weekly or monthly basis, as opposed to *obreros* who are blue-collar workers and, therefore, paid on a daily or piece basis

entrismo Infiltration—used in reference to the infiltration of leftists in the MNR in order to radicalize the party from within

fabriles Factory workers

ferroviarios Railway workers

finca The most common Bolivian term for a large landed estate; used synonymously with *latifundia* or *hacienda*

Fuero Sindical A pro-labor decree affording labor special legal status

gobierno obrero-campesino Government of workers and peasants—concept of labor left wing of the MNR projecting a state socialist society dominated by a mixed elite based on the working class

golpe de estado Coup d'état; sometimes shortened to *golpe*

hacienda See *finca.*

hispanicismo An ideological position which is prowhite and prohispanic culture

indígena Indian

indigenismo An ideological position which is pro-Indian and antihispanic culture. A person supporting these views is an *indigenista.*

latifundia See *finca.*

mayordomo A manager of a *finca;* also the patron of a religious festival

mestizo See *cholo.*

minifundia Very small landholdings

Oriente The eastern lowland region of Bolivia

patria Homeland

patrón The owner of a *finca*

pensadores Intellectuals who theorize about social problems

político Professional politician

pongo A landless Indian peasant required to perform nonagricultural work obligations for the *patrón* and his family. The labor system is known as *pongueaje* and is associated with colonato.

programa A political plan, scheme, program, or platform

proyecto A proposed law, project, or plan; and/or a set of political proposals

pulperiás Originally, company stores; later, state-subsidized stores selling goods at stable prices to miners and other labor groups

Rosca A derogatory term used to designate the oligarchy in general; in particular, the supportive group of lawyers and others who acted as administrators for the ruling elite

sayañas   The plots of land used by either the *colono* or *comunario* to produce his own crops

sexenio   Period of six years—refers to the period from 1946 to 1952 when the MNR leaders were persecuted and driven into exile

sindicalismo diregido   Directed or controlled unionism—state-controlled labor organizations

sindicato   Labor union

sociedad democrática burguesa   Democratic bourgeois society—concept of center and right wing of MNR projecting a state capitalist society dominated by a progressive middle-class elite

super-estado   Superstate, referring to the mining companies who were above the law

universidades populares   Institutions of free adult education

Index